MEASURING CORRUPTION

Measuring Corruption

Edited by
CHARLES SAMPFORD, ARTHUR SHACKLOCK
and CARMEL CONNORS
Key Centre for Ethics, Law, Justice and Governance,
Griffith University, Australia
and
FREDRIK GALTUNG
TIRI and Central European University, Budapost, Hungary

ASHGATE

Published by
Ashgate Publishing Limited
Gower House
Croft Road
Aldershot
Hampshire GU11 3HR
England

Ashgate Publishing Company
Suite 420
101 Cherry Street
Burlington, VT 05401-4405
USA

Ashgate website: http://www.ashgate.com

British Library Cataloguing in Publication Data
Measuring corruption. - (Law, ethics and governance)
   1.Corruption 2.Social sciences - Methodology 3.Corruption -
   Case studies 4.Social sciences - Methodology - Case studies
   I.Sampford, C. J. G. (Charles J. G.)
   353.4'6

Library of Congress Cataloging-in-Publication Data
Measuring corruption / edited by Charles Sampford ... [et al.].
      p. cm. -- (Law, ethics and governance)
   Includes index.
   ISBN 0-7546-2405-6
   1. Corruption. 2. Social indicators. I. Sampford, C.J.G. (Charles
J.G.) II. Series.
HV6768.M43 2006
363.25'9323--dc22

2005031673

ISBN 0 7546 2405 6

Printed and bound in Great Britain by Athenaeum Press, Ltd, Gateshead, Tyne & Wear.

Contents

PART II: THE CASE STUDIES

List of Figures

List of Tables

Notes on Contributors and Editors

A.J. Brown BA LLB PhD is a Senior Lecturer and Senior Research Fellow in Law, Griffith University. A constitutional lawyer and political scientist, he has worked in Commonwealth and State governments and the judicial system, he also teaches and researches in constitutional theory, public accountability and environmental policy.

Carmel Connors BAdmin, GradCert Arts (Writing, Editing and Publishing), MPubAd is a Senior Research Assistant and Publications Manager with the Key Centre for Ethics, Law, Justice and Governance, Griffith University. She was a contributing author to *Encouraging Ethics and Challenging Corruption* (Noel Preston and Charles Sampford, Federation Press, 2002) and co-editor of *Management, Organisation, and Ethics in the Public Sector* (Patrick Bishop and Charles Sampford, Ashgate, 2003).

Nick Duncan Research Fellow, School of Development Studies, University of East Anglia, MA Development Economics is the founding co-director of the University of East Anglia Centre for Corruption Research. His research interests include analytical and measurement issues in corruption. Nick is co-editor (with Indranil Dutta) of the forthcoming *World Development*, Special Issue on Analytical and Measurement Issues in corruption. Prior to academic research, he had a career in international business. He was an organiser of the 2002 international conference 'Re/Constructing Corruption'.

Fredrik Galtung began his career as the founding staff member and Head of Research of Transparency International (TI). Since October 2003, Fredrik has been co-director, with Jeremy Pope, of TIRI (the governance-access-learning network). Over the past ten years, Fredrik has consulted on strategic corruption control with numerous governments, international organisations (Council of Europe, World Bank, UN secretariat, UNDP, UNESCO, UNICEF, UN Office of Drugs and Crime, etc.), several companies (especially in the pharmaceutical and defence sectors), foundations and governments and development agencies. He is the director of the Public Integrity Education Network organised jointly by TIRI and the Central European University.

Angela Gorta PhD is the Research Manager of the NSW Police Integrity Commission, based in Sydney. After teaching psychology and statistics at Macquarie University, she conducted criminological research for more than ten years and has spent the past eleven years focusing on better informing efforts to reduce corruption in the public sector through her work with the New South Wales Independent Commission Against Corruption (ICAC) and the New South Wales Police Integriy Commission (PIC).

Leo Huberts is Professor of Public Administration and Integrity of Governance at the Department of Public Administration and Organization Science of the Free University of Amsterdam, The Netherlands.

Johann Graf Lambsdorff holds a Chair Position in economic theory at the University of Passau, Germany and is Senior Research Consultant for Transparency International. He has published on corruption, institutional economics and monetary economics.

Petter Langseth PhD is Programme Manager, Global Programme against Corruption, Centre for International Crime Prevention, Office of Drug Control and Crime Prevention, United Nations Office at Vienna and former Senior Public Sector Management Specialist at the World Bank.

Karin Lasthuizen works as a researcher within the research group, Intengrity of Governance, Free University of Amsterdam, The Netherlands.

Ambrose Lee is a former Commissioner of the Independent Commission Against Corruption of the Hong Kong Special Administrative Region. Mr Lee is the Secretary for Security of the Hong Kong Special Administrative Region and became a member of the Executive Council (the highest policy-making body in Hong Kong) in August 2003. He graduated with a Bachelor of Science degree from the University of Hong Kong. He also received professional training from Tsinghua University, China, Oxford University in the United Kingdom, as well as Harvard University in the USA.

William L. Miller MA (Edinburgh) PhD (Newcastle) FBA FRSE is the Edward Caird Professor of Politics, *University of Glasgow.* His research interests are political behaviour and public opinion in Eastern and Western Europe (including Britain) and East Asia – with particular reference to voting, elections and the media; democratic values, civil rights and corruption; immigration, ethnicity and identity; globalisation and contrasts between the general public, state officials and elected representatives.

Elena A. Panifilova is General Director of the Center for Anti-Corruption Research and Initiative, Transparency International-Russia. Elena Panifilova graduated from Moscow State University's Department of Political Science and the Diplomatic Academy's political science department with a specialisation in international development. She began her career as a freelance political columnist before taking a position with the OECD.

Carel Peeters bworks as a researcher within the research group, Intengrity of Governance, Free University of Amsterdam, The Netherlands.

Mark Philp MA MPhil DPhil is Head of Department and CUF Lecturer in Politics and Tutorial Fellow, Oriel College, Oxford. His research interests include Political Theory, Corruption and Standards in Public Life and History of Political Thought.

Charles Sampford became the Foundation Dean and Professor of Law at Griffith University in 1991. He later became Director of the Key Centre for Ethics, Law, Justice and Governance and the Director of the Institute for Ethics, Governance and Law (a joint initiative of the United Nations University and Griffith University). Charles has written 80 articles and chapters in Australian and foreign journals and collections ranging through law, legal education and applied ethics and has completed 19 books and edited collections. He has also won more than $12 million in grants, consultancies and awards. Foreign fellowships include the Visiting Senior Research Fellow at St John's College, Oxford (1997) and a Fulbright Senior Fellowship to Harvard University (2000). Business, government and parliamentary committees in England and Australia have consulted Professor Sampford. In September 1998, he went to Indonesia on a special mission for the World Bank to advise the Indonesian government on governance reforms to deal with corruption. Since early 2002, he has been a member of a task force on responding to threats to democracy chaired by Madeleine Albright. In September 2004, Charles became Convenor of the new ARC Governance Research Network (GovNet).

Arthur Shacklock PhD is a Senior Research Fellow and Program Director for Integrity and Anti-Corruption, Key Centre for Ethics, Law, Justice and Governance, Griffith University. He has extensive experience in human resource management within the Australian and West Australian Public Services both as a manager and policy advisor. Arthur researches and teaches in the areas of organisational ethics, leadership and human resource management.

Gopakumar K. Thampi PhD is Chief of Programmes of the Public Affairs Foundation, India and former Executive Director for Asia at Transparency International. *Sita Sekhar* PhD (Economics) is Chief Research Officer of the Public Affairs Centre, Bangalore.

Anne Waiguru MA Econ. Policy is a member of the Kenyan local chapter of Transparency International. Principal Assistant to TI Research Advisor Dr David Ndii, for the 'Kenya Urban Bribery Index'. Anne is also Programme Consultant, Kenya Leadership Institute. The Kenya Leadership Institute is a pioneering initiative to establish an African centre of excellence in leadership development.

Preface

More than a decade of activism in the field of anti-corruption has made clear that the measurement of corruption is necessary to achieve progress towards greater integrity, transparency and accountability in governance. Only by understanding the baseline of corruption – how much corruption, in what areas, with what consequences – can we begin to formulate the necessary policy responses to it. Yet the 'need to measure', which is growing, has not always been met by the 'means to measure', whether due to lack of funding, or vision, or both.

In that sense, the contributors to this volume represent a small but burgeoning group of researchers who have taken on the corruption measurement challenge. We at Transparency International support this effort wholeheartedly. Our worldwide movement of anti-corruption activists, some of whom contribute to these pages, have themselves been at the forefront of corruption measurement research – finding new ways and means to identify the corruption threat and to evaluate the efforts to eradicate it.

One major challenge in the measurement of corruption that runs throughout the volume is how to define this phenomenon, in order to delimit its measurement. While there is no consensus on an ideal definition, Transparency International's use of the formulation 'the misuse of entrusted power for private gain' provides a broad framework for purposes of assessment – a framework that can be adapted to focus on a number of non-ethical behaviour and practices, from bribery to nepotism to conflict of interest. At the same time, other relevant phenomena, such as lack of trust, can be measured to help us understand corruption. As a number of authors argue, however, the norms embedded in many ready-made definitions of corruption force us to consider carefully not only what it is we are measuring, but where we are measuring it, as the two go hand in hand.

Methods to assess corruption vary, with survey work still providing the core tool for evaluation. Given the difficulties that remain in the measurement of corruption, however, from lack of data to the high cost of carrying out certain methodologies, there is a need for both pragmatism and proxies in this field. Perception indices are valuable and powerful, particularly as a global and comparative corruption measurement tool, but they are not sufficient for certain purposes, such as diagnostics. As many authors point out, it is necessary to triangulate measurements of corruption – instruments both top-down and bottom-up, reflecting subjective and objective data – to provide as holistic a view of the problem as is possible. At the same time, the ends must justify the means – all measurement tools need to take account of what they can achieve, and how they can contribute both to better understanding and to necessary reform.

In our own work, Transparency International has introduced the concept of the measurement chain to help us embed our corruption research tools in a policy and advocacy framework. Following the measurement chain means includes (i) identifying the right measurement tool for the right purpose, (ii) adapting it to the local conditions, (iii) implementing it, (iv) processing and communicating its results and, finally, (v) evaluating the tool's impact. This model of measurement tool development and implementation has enabled a wide variety of tools to emerge from the TI movement, enabling innovation and complementarity of tools. At the same time, it recognises the need to assess the impact of measurement, which can be substantial, as TI's own Corruption Perceptions Index has shown over the past decade.

There is no question that corruption measurement must continue, and must continue to make great strides, if we are to meet the challenges posed by this most 'hidden' phenomenon. This volume, which emerged from a project funded by Transparency International and the Key Centre at Griffith University, is a testament to the keen interest of scholars and activists alike in this pursuit. Clarity and accuracy are of the essence in refining our measurement tools, but much more is at stake than academic debate. For the sake of those suffering the effects of corruption around the world, we have an obligation to find the resources to do more, and to do better.

Robin Hodess
Director of Policy and Research
Transparency International

Acknowledgements

This edited collection is the result of a partnership between Transparency International (TI) and the Key Centre for Ethics, Law, Justice and Governance (KCELJAG), Griffith University.

Transparency International (TI) has established a formidable reputation for the development of anti-corruption strategies. Transparency International, the only international non-governmental organisation devoted to combating corruption, brings civil society, business, and governments together in a powerful global coalition. Through its International Secretariat and more than 85 independent national chapters around the world, TI works, at the national and international level, to curb both the supply and demand of corruption. In the international arena, TI raises awareness about the damaging effects of corruption, advocates policy reform, works towards the implementation of multilateral conventions and subsequently monitors compliance by governments, corporations and banks. In an effort to make long-term gains against corruption, TI focuses on prevention and reforming systems.

The Key Centre for Ethics, Law, Justice and Governance aims to provide a distinctive and significant response to the challenges facing the values and institutions of liberal democracy, through the application of the insights of academics and practitioners in the fields of law, ethics, politics and criminology. It pursues these aims through a range of research programs, consultancies, teaching and support programs.

Funding for the project, Development and utilisation of indices to measure corruption: calculating and combating bribery, was provided through a grant from the Australian Research Council's Strategic Partnerships with Industry – Research and Training (SPIRT) and Transparency International.

Chapter 1

Introduction

Arthur Shacklock, Charles Sampford and Carmel Connors

Why Measure Corruption?

Corruption undermines the fairness, stability and efficiency of a society and its ability to deliver sustainable development to its members. Levels of individual bribes and the incidence of corruption are merely symptoms of the deeper distortions introduced by corruption. Bribery that moves public resources into private pockets is serious enough. However, even more importantly, corrupt payments influence policy choices made by public officials.

Corruption distorts the procurement process and has resulted in the selection of uneconomic 'white elephant' projects which have saddled many developing countries with debts which they cannot repay. The viability of democratic institutions and of market economies is threatened if corruption cannot be brought under control. Moreover, a widespread expectation of corruption can breed a cycle in which its incidence increases inexorably. The unscrupulous are rewarded and the honest become demoralised. As a consequence, the legitimacy of the state in the eyes of ordinary people is compromised.

Corruption should be pursued, not merely because it is a moral issue (which it is), and not just because it is bad for business (which again, it is), but because people everywhere pay the cost of corruption one way or another, and none more so than the people of the developing world and countries in transition. This is not to say that developed countries can afford the luxury of corruption, as various scandals in the UK, the USA and Australia have indicated.

With the advance of an increasingly globalised market, the opportunities for, and scale of corruption, are growing. The size of corporations and their wealth, relative to nations, provides the resources for corrupt practices. The liberalisation of international financial markets make transferring and hiding the proceeds of corruption easier. Moves towards privatisation in the East and West are providing once-only incentives for corruption on an unprecedented scale, as officials not only deal with the income of the state but with its assets as well.

This edited collection arises out of a collaborative project involving the Key Centre for Ethics, Law, Justice and Governance (KCELJAG) and Transparency International (TI). TI was the industry partner and was funded for this project by the Macarthur Foundation and the Open Society Institute (OSI). The generous support provided by the ARC, Macarthur, OSI and TI is gratefully acknowledged. This project allowed TI to develop its measures of corruption – refining its famous corruption perception index (CPI) and supplementing the CPI with two new measures, the bribery perception index (BPI, from 2000) and Global Corruption Index (from 2003).

Overview

This book will examine various attempts to measure corruption and consider the extent to which these various studies are reliable measures of corruption. The latter chapters present case studies from nations that have made particular efforts to measure corruption.

Petter Langseth, in Chapter 2, sets-up the framework for the book by asking the fundamental question – why measure? He argues that corruption represents a 'leakage' of resources from institutions that are supposed to be using them for social objectives. Whether it is large-scale leakage, such as contract rigging, or small-scale grease payments, leakage creates a fertile breeding ground for grand corruption and diverts already scarce public service resources. Another reason to measure corruption is that resources may not be maximised and public service users have a right to know what services their money should be buying. Langseth discusses data requirements, data gathering methods and appropriate assessment instruments that he then applies to a case study of Nigeria.

One of the difficulties of studying corruption lies in determining a precise definition. While it may appear to be a semantic issue, how corruption is defined actually ends up determining what gets modelled and measured. Mark Philp, in Chapter 3, offers a brief discussion of the conceptual issues associated with arriving at a definition of corruption and the difficulties of developing appropriate measurements for assessing the incidence and seriousness of political corruption.

In Chapter 4, A.J. Brown discusses various definitional approaches and typologies covered in the literature. In the first part of the chapter, he highlights the commonalities and differences in current corruption concepts and traces existing shifts in definitional approaches. He suggests a new primary and secondary taxonomy based on a relational/behavioural approach. Brown argues that, while the basic fundamentals of this approach are not new, it seeks to capture an evolution already underway to reformulate basic principles from which to work.

Difficulties are encountered once a definition had been determined. These include: how to measure the phenomenon? and, more importantly, can corruption be measured? Johann Lambsdorff, in Chapter 5, discusses Transparency International's Corruption Perception Index (CPI) and provides an in-depth explanation of the methodology behind the 2002 index. The CPI is an annual index that has been complied since 1995. Its global impact has been considerable and publication of the index by mainstream media has given prominence to corruption issues.

In Chapter 6, Frederick Galtung presents an alternative view. He outlines what he considers to be the failings of the Corruption Perception Index (CPI). He concludes by arguing that 'the seven failings of the CPI call for a complete reassessment and an overhaul of this influential social indicator' and that '… it should no longer be published in its present form as it actually undermines the efforts of reformers'.

Nick Duncan, in Chapter 7, points out the extensive use of perception-based measures and discusses the consequent problems associated with their use. Duncan suggests a 'transactions network structure' as a benchmark against which to interpret both the suitability of certain techniques and the comprehensiveness of the meaning of measures that result.

In Chapter 8, William Miller concludes that 'a debate over "*the*" definition of corruption is best avoided'. He suggests a focus on less all-embracing and more concrete and specific concepts than 'corruption' itself. Further, he argues the value of 'separating the empirical research from the moral condemnation' (p. 000). He concludes that images or perceptions of corruption, while interesting, are not an accurate measure of corrupt behaviour. Accurate survey-based measures, however, require a clear and specific definition of the behaviour as well as clear and explicit questions and a sceptical approach to responses. He exhorts that, whatever the shortcomings, we should not abandon attempts to measure corrupt behaviour.

Within the field of corruption research, much attention has been paid to variations of corruption across localities. The following chapters discuss aspects of research and methods adopted across a range of countries and regions. Elena Panifilova, in Chapter 9, discusses the results of a public opinion survey conducted by the Center for Anti-corruption Research and Initiative (Transparency International). The main objective of this survey was to create a multi-dimensional picture of corruption in the Russian Federation and its regions. This survey was a pilot study but surveys on a regular basis are planned to monitor changes in the scope and structure of corruption.

In Chapter 10, Angela Gorta provides an example of an empirical approach taken by the New South Wales Independent Commission Against Corruption. The purpose of the study was to identify corruption risks in order to measure 'corruption resistance'.

In Chapter 11, Ambrose Lee outlines the work of Independent Commission Against Corruption (Hong Kong ICAC). The Commission reinforces the importance of community engagement in fighting corruption and specifically highlights the importance of a vigilant press in spreading Hong Kong ICAC's anti-corruption message.

Gopakumar Thampi and Sita Sekhar, in Chapter 12, discuss the development and use of 'citizen report cards' in Bangalore. They argue that the 'citizen report cards' methodology offers a simple, and widely replicable, tool for improving transparency and public accountability. The technique presents a simple but highly flexible approach for organising public feedback and, in more practical terms, permits benchmarking public service delivery as well as providing other strategic uses.

In Chapter 13, Anne Waiguru examines '*Harambee*' in Kenya and its tendency to encourage political corruption. Waiguru reports on the pilot study that was undertaken to compile definitive data on *harambee* activity and effects.

Finally, Leo Huberts, Karin Lasthuizen and Carel Peeters present information about corruption research in the Netherlands. The first part of the chapter outlines conceptual and methodological aspects of their research. This is followed by a discussion of a number of research projects on corruption. The final section offers a summary of results and a reflection on the usefulness of the methods adopted. The authors conclude that 'corruption research should involve the collection and comparison of information from different sources and methods, at different levels and in different sectors as well as at different points in time' (p. 316).

PART I
THE PROBLEM AND ITS
IDENTIFICATION

Chapter 2

Measuring Corruption

Petter Langseth[1]

Why Measure?

From the perspective of public service users, inefficiencies and inequities in public services are a misuse of public power. They 'leak' resources from the system that should serve the public. Petty corruption and system leakage may not be as newsworthy as grand corruption but they do create a favourable environment for it.

If, on the other hand, managers and/or project staff in the development agencies such as the World Bank had been asked to identify the levels of leakage due to corruption across their projects and/or client countries, you would probably have a newsworthy story. The problem is that accountable managers in international aid institutions have not been asked to identify the levels of leakage due to corruption across their projects, and if they had been asked to do so, they probably would not have any idea how to specify such leakages.

Corruption represents a 'leakage' of resources from institutions that are supposed to be using them for social objectives. It is not only the large-scale larceny of contract rigging, kickbacks and misuse or simply misappropriation of public funds that represent leakage. Leakage can be in the form of unofficial user fees, grease payments or even free time from services not performed. Under-the-table user charge, absenteeism, the sale of drugs or fertilisers that should be dispensed free of charge, or the sale of examination papers all represent the misuse of public funds for private profit.

Leakage results in the creation of a fertile breeding ground for grand corruption, diverting already scarce public service resources. Moreover, it 'double taxes' the public. Validation that corruption reduces service effectiveness is shown by corruption surveys carried out in Uganda and Tanzania. In Uganda, farmers who are subjected to corrupt agricultural extension agents had to pay more for fertilisers and pesticides than those in other areas. In addition, they also experienced lower levels of production. In Tanzania, households who had to pay bribes for police assistance and for land transfers often found their problems were not resolved by such payment; and, to make matters worse, the police and land officials frequently accepted bribes from people on the other side of the conflict – often leaving the issue inappropriately unresolved (or resolved in favour of whoever paid the most money). Such facts are frequently uncovered by surveys.

Another reason to measure corruption is that resources may not be maximised because of information asymmetries and constraints. A major reason for asymmetry is the introspective nature of institutional information system. Public service requires that virtually all countries have recourse to data generated by routine information systems. Even in the best of environments, however, the data tends to be introspective, concerned with the viewpoint of the institution (school, clinic or police station) rather than the users of the services (the public). Many 'users' are not in contact with the services and their opinions cannot be registered in a service-based information system. Furthermore, conventional planning of public services, since it begins with institutions rather than the public, often does not consider key concerns such as coverage or impact of services, let alone the question of system leakage.

The second asymmetry concerns the lack of information on which people base their expectations. Frequently, public service users have little idea of precisely what services their money should be buying and are consequently subjected to local market dynamics. In any case, as they cannot tell whether a particular shortfall in services is due to the service workers, under-investment in public services, or any number of reasons linked to system leakage, the formation of expectation becomes rather difficult.

Reform can further aggravate the information constraints that they attempt to correct. It is true that managers often have an accurate 'big picture' of the reforms necessary to improve equity, effectiveness, efficiency and deal with system leakage. Streamlining, downsizing and refocusing service objectives are some examples of such reforms. Yet, the promise of increased responsiveness and improvement in quality often does not materialise because the streamlining often reduces the institutional ability to measure the coverage and impact of services (as well as system leakage).

In public service provision, there are a number of questions to which managers of public services need the answers if they are to overcome information constraints.

The first set of questions addresses the issue of what requires reform. What can be changed? What should be changed first? How much is gained from each of the actions taken? How is progress measured? What is the confidence level of the answers?

The second set of questions focuses on the actions. Some of the questions include the following. Should we focus on particular service providers? Are there any special groups of service users (ethnic, generational and gender divisions are typical stratifications) especially harmed by system leakage? Are there any multiplier effects or combinations of actions that produce more than the sum of their individual effects?

A third set of questions concerns the financial and political costs of reducing system leakage. How much will the stakeholder information system cost to implement? How long do we have to wait for the returns? What evidence exists of community or constituency acceptance or a public mandate for change? What is the level of institutional acceptance from the service delivery agencies?

The solution that such information asymmetries and constraints require is a measurement interface between services and users: a process whereby the community voice can be developed into planning. Service delivery surveys have been designed and implemented in a number of countries with the goal of providing such a measurement interface.

Defining Corruption[2]

There is no single, comprehensive, universally accepted definition of corruption. Attempts to develop such a definition invariably encounter legal, criminological and, in many countries, political problems.

When the negotiations of the United Nations Convention against Corruption began in early 2002, one option under consideration was not to define corruption at all but to list specific types or acts of corruption. Moreover, proposals to require countries to criminalise corruption mainly covered specific offences or groups of offences that depended on what type of conduct was involved, whether those implicated were public officials, whether cross-border conduct or foreign officials were involved and if the cases related to unlawful or improper enrichment.[3]

Many specific forms of corruption are clearly defined and understood, and are the subject of numerous legal or academic definitions. Many are also criminal offences, although in some cases Governments consider that specific forms of corruption are better dealt with by regulatory or civil law controls. Some of the more commonly encountered forms of corruption are considered below.

'Grand' and 'Petty' Corruption

Grand corruption is corruption that pervades the highest levels of a national government, leading to a broad erosion of confidence in good governance, the rule of law and economic stability (Rose-Ackerman, 2000, pp. 321–36). Petty corruption can involve the exchange of very small amounts of money, the granting of minor favours by those seeking preferential treatment or the employment of friends and relatives in minor positions.

The most critical difference between grand corruption and petty corruption is that the former involves the distortion or corruption of the central functions of government, while the latter develops and exists within the context of established governance and social frameworks.

'Active' and 'Passive' Corruption

In discussions of transactional offences such as bribery, 'active bribery' usually refers to the offering or paying of the bribe, while 'passive bribery' refers to the receiving of the bribe.[4] In criminal law terminology, the terms may be used to distinguish between a particular corrupt action and an attempted or incomplete offence. For example, 'active' corruption would include all cases where payment and/or acceptance of a bribe had taken place. It would not include cases where a bribe was offered but not accepted, or solicited but not paid. In the formulation of comprehensive national anti-corruption strategies that combine criminal justice with other elements, such distinctions are less critical. Nevertheless, care should be taken to avoid confusion between the two concepts.

Bribery

Bribery is the bestowing of a benefit in order to unduly influence an action or decision. It can be initiated by a person who seeks or solicits bribes or by a person who offers and then pays bribes. Bribery is probably the most common form of corruption known. Definitions or descriptions appear in several international instruments, in the domestic laws of most countries and in academic publications.[5]

The 'benefit' in bribery can be virtually any inducement – money and valuables, company shares, inside information, sexual or other favours, entertainment, employment or, indeed, the mere promise of incentives. The benefit may be passed directly or indirectly to the person bribed, or to a third party, such as a friend, relative, associate, favourite charity, private business, political party or election campaign. The conduct for which the bribe is paid can be active: the exertion of administrative or political influence, or it can be passive: the overlooking of some offence or obligation. Bribes can be paid individually on a case-by-case basis or as part of a continuing relationship in which officials receive regular benefits in exchange for regular favours.

Once bribery has occurred, it can lead to other forms of corruption. By accepting a bribe, an official becomes much more susceptible to blackmail. Most international and national legal definitions seek to criminalise bribery. Some definitions seek to limit criminalisation to situations where the recipient is a public official or where the public interest is affected, leaving other cases of bribery to be resolved by non-criminal or non-judicial means.

In jurisdictions where criminal bribery necessarily involves a public official, the offence is often defined broadly to extend to private individuals offered bribes to influence their conduct in a public function, such as exercising electoral functions or carrying out jury duty. Public sector bribery can target any individual who has the power to make a decision or take an action affecting others and is willing to resort to bribery to influence the outcome. Politicians, regulators, law enforcement officials, judges, prosecutors and inspectors are all potential targets for public sector bribery. Specific types of bribery include:

1. *Influence-peddling*: public officials or political or government insiders peddle privileges acquired exclusively through their public status that are usually unavailable to outsiders, for example access to or influence on government decision-making. Influence-peddling is distinct from legitimate political advocacy or lobbying.
2. *Offering or receiving improper gifts, gratuities, favours or commissions*: in some countries, public officials commonly accept tips or gratuities in exchange for their services. As links always develop between payments and results, such payments become difficult to distinguish from bribery or extortion.
3. *Bribery to avoid liability for taxes or other costs*: officials of revenue collecting agencies, such as tax authorities or customs, are susceptible to bribery. They may be asked to reduce or eliminate amounts of tax or other revenues due; to conceal

or overlook evidence of wrongdoing, including tax infractions or other crimes. They may be called upon to ignore illegal imports or exports or to conceal, ignore or facilitate illicit transactions for purposes such as money laundering.

4. *Bribery in support of fraud*: payroll officials may be bribed to participate in abuses such as listing and paying non-existent employees ('ghost workers').

5. *Bribery to avoid criminal liability*: law enforcement officers, prosecutors, judges or other officials may be bribed to ensure that criminal activities are not investigated or prosecuted or, if they are prosecuted, to ensure a favourable outcome.

6. *Bribery in support of unfair competition for benefits or resources*: public or private sector employees responsible for making contracts for goods or services may be bribed to ensure that contracts are made with the party that is paying the bribe and on favourable terms. In some cases, where the bribe is paid out of the contract proceeds themselves, this may also be described as a 'kickback' or secret commission.

7. *Private sector bribery*: corrupt banking and finance officials are bribed to approve loans that do not meet basic security criteria and cannot later be collected, causing widespread economic damage to individuals, institutions and economies.

8. *Bribery to obtain confidential or 'inside' information*: employees in the public and private sectors are often bribed to disclose valuable confidential information, undermining national security and disclosing industrial secrets. Inside information is used to trade unfairly in stocks or securities, in trade secrets and other commercially valuable information.

Embezzlement, Theft and Fraud

In the context of corruption, embezzlement, theft and fraud all involve the taking or conversion of money, property or valuable items by an individual who is not entitled to them but, by virtue of his or her position or employment, has access to them.[6] In the case of embezzlement and theft, someone to whom it was entrusted takes the property. Fraud, however, consists of the use of false or misleading information to induce the owner of the property to relinquish it voluntarily. For example, an official who takes and sells part of a relief donation or a shipment of food or medical supplies would be committing theft or embezzlement; an official who induces an aid agency to oversupply aid by misrepresenting the number of people in need of it is committing fraud.

As with bribery and other forms of corruption, many domestic and international legal definitions are intended to form the basis of criminal offences. Thus, they include only those situations involving a public official or where the public interest is crucially affected. 'Theft', *per se*, goes far beyond the scope of corruption, including the taking of any property by a person with no right to it. Using the same example of the relief donation, an ordinary bystander who steals aid packages from a truck is committing theft but not corruption. That is why the term 'embezzlement', which is essentially the theft of property by someone to whom it was entrusted, is commonly used in corruption cases. In some legal definitions, 'theft' is limited to the taking of tangible items, such as property or cash, but non-legal definitions tend to include the taking of anything of value, including intangibles such as valuable information.

Examples of corrupt theft, fraud and embezzlement abound. Virtually anyone responsible for storing or handling cash, valuables or other tangible property is in a position to steal it or to assist others in stealing it, particularly if auditing or monitoring safeguards are inadequate or non-existent. Employees or officials with access to company or government operating accounts can make unauthorised withdrawals or pass to others the information required to do so. Elements of fraud are more complex. Officials may create artificial expenses; 'ghost workers' may be added to payrolls or false bills submitted for goods, services, or travel expenses. The purchase or improvement of private real estate may be billed against public funds. Employment-related equipment, such as motor vehicles, may be used for private purposes. In one case, World Bank-funded vehicles were used for taking the children of officials to school, consuming about 25 per cent of their total use.

Extortion

Whereas bribery involves the use of payments or other positive incentives, extortion relies on coercion, such as the use or threat of violence or the exposure of damaging information, to induce cooperation. As with other forms of corruption, the 'victim' can be the public interest or individuals adversely affected by a corrupt act or decision. In extortion cases, however, a further 'victim' is created, namely the person who is coerced into cooperation.

While government officials or insiders can commit extortion, such officials can also be victims of it. For example, an official can extort corrupt payments in exchange for a favour or a person seeking a favour can extort it from the official by making threats.

In some cases, extortion may differ from bribery only in the degree of coercion involved. A doctor may solicit a bribe for seeing a patient quickly but if an appointment is a matter of medical necessity, the 'bribe' is more properly characterised as 'extortion'. In extreme cases, poor patients can suffer illness or even death if medical services are allocated through extortionate methods rather than legitimate medical prioritising.

Officials in a position to initiate or conduct criminal prosecution or punishment often use the threat of prosecution or punishment as a basis for extortion. In many countries, people involved in minor incidents, such as traffic accidents, may be threatened with more serious charges unless they 'pay up'. Alternatively, officials who have committed acts of corruption or other wrongdoings may be threatened with exposure unless they themselves pay up. Low-level extortion, such as the payment of 'speed money' to ensure timely consideration and decision-making of minor matters by officials, is widespread in many countries.

Abuse of Discretion

In some cases, corruption can involve the abuse of discretion, vested in an individual, for personal gain. For example, an official responsible for government contracting may exercise the discretion to purchase goods or services from a company in which he or she holds a personal interest or propose real estate developments that will increase the value of personal property. Such abuse is often associated with bureaucracies where there is broad individual discretion and few oversight or accountability structures, or where the decision-making rules are so complex that they neutralise the effectiveness of any accountability structures that do exist.

Favouritism and Nepotism

Generally, favouritism and nepotism involves abuse of discretion. Such abuses, however, are governed not by the self-interest of an official but the interests of someone linked to him or her through membership of a family, political party, tribe, religious or other group. If an individual bribes an official to hire him or her, the official acts in self-interest. If a corrupt official hires a relative, he or she acts in exchange for the less tangible benefit of advancing the interests of family or the specific relative involved (nepotism). The favouring of, or discriminating against, individuals can be based on a wide range of group characteristics: race, religion, geographical factors, political or other affiliation, as well as personal or organisational relationships, such as friendship or membership of clubs or associations.

Conduct Creating or Exploiting Conflicting Interests

As noted in the *United Nations Manual on Anti-corruption Policy*, most forms of corruption involve the creation or exploitation of some conflict between the professional responsibilities of a corrupt individual and his or her private interests. The acceptance of a bribe creates such a conflict of interest. Most cases of embezzlement, theft or fraud involve an individual yielding to temptation and taking undue advantage of a conflict of interest that already exists. In both the public and private sector, employees and officials are routinely confronted with circumstances in which their personal interests conflict with those of their responsibility to act in the best interests of the State or their employer.

Improper Political Contributions

One of the most difficult challenges in developing anti-corruption measures is to make the distinction between legitimate contributions to political organisations and payments made in an attempt to unduly influence present or future activities by a party or its members once they are in power. A donation made because the donor supports the party and wishes to increase its chances of being elected is not corrupt; it may be an important part of the political system and, in some countries, is a basic right of expression or political activity protected by the constitution. A donation made with the intention or expectation that the party will, once in office, favour the interests of the donor over the interests of the public is tantamount to the payment of a bribe.

Regulating political contributions has proved difficult in practice. Donations may take the form of direct cash payments, low-interest loans, the giving of goods or services or intangible contributions that favour the interests of the political party involved. One common approach to combating the problem is to introduce measures that seek to ensure transparency by requiring disclosure of contributions, thus ensuring that both the donor and recipient are politically accountable. Another is to limit the size of contributions to prevent any one donor from having too much influence.

Assessment of the Nature and Extent of Corruption

Introduction

Assessment of the nature and extent of corruption is used to provide quantitative measurements of the extent of corruption in a country or within specific sectors of a country. It also provides qualitative assessments of the types of corruption that are prevalent, how corruption occurs and what may be causing or contributing to it.

Such assessments will generally be used prior to the development of the national anti-corruption strategy:

1. *In the preliminary phase*, to assist with the development of the national anti-corruption strategy, to help set priorities, to make a preliminary estimate of how long the strategy will last and to determine the resources required implementing it. The preliminary assessment should cover all sectors of the public administration and, if necessary, the private sector, to ensure no detail is overlooked. The data gathered at this stage will be the baseline against which future progress will be assessed.
2. *In the follow-up phase*, to help assess progress against the baseline data gathered at the preliminary stage, to provide periodic information about the implementation of strategic elements and their effects on corruption, and to help decide how strategic elements/priorities can be adapted in the face of strategic successes and failures.
3. *To help in setting clear and reasonable objectives for the strategy* and each of its elements, and set measurable performance indicators for those objectives.
4. *To raise the awareness of key stakeholders and the public* of the true nature, extent and impact of corruption. Awareness raising will help foster understanding of the anti-corruption strategy, mobilise support for anti-corruption measures and encourage and empower populations to expect and insist on high standards of public service integrity and performance.
5. *To provide the basis of assistance to other countries* in their efforts against corruption.

Types of Data Sought

Occurrence of corruption Such information may include the identification of particular public or private sector activities, institutions or relationships. Data are often gathered about particular government agencies, for example, or about relationships or processes, such as public service employment or the making of contracts for goods or services.

Types of corruption While an overall assessment of what types of corruption are prevalent may be undertaken, a more detailed focus will be usually involved on what types of corruption tend to occur in each specific agency, relationship or process for which corruption has been identified as a problem. Research may show that bribery is a major problem in government contracting, for example, while public service appointments may be more affected by nepotism.

Costs and effects of corruption Understanding the relative effects of corruption is critical to setting priorities and mobilising support for anti-corruption efforts. Where possible, information should include the direct, economic costs plus an assessment of indirect and intangible human consequences.

Factors that contribute to or are associated with corruption There is seldom a single, identifiable cause of a particular occurrence of corruption but a number of contributing factors will usually be identifiable. They often include factors such as poverty or the low social and economic status of public officials that makes them more susceptible to bribery; the presence of specific corrupting influences, such as organised crime; or structural factors, such as overly broad discretionary powers and a general lack of monitoring and accountability. Information about such factors is critical to understanding the nature of the corruption itself and to formulating countermeasures. The presence of known contributing factors may also lead researchers or investigators to identify previously unknown or unsuspected occurrences of corruption.

The perception of corruption by those involved or affected by it All assessments of corruption should include objective measurements (of what is actually occurring) and subjective assessments (of how those involved perceive or understand what is occurring). The information is needed because the reactions of people to anti-corruption efforts will be governed by their own perceptions. The following specific areas should be researched:

1. Impressions of those involved (offenders, victims and others) about the types of corruption occurring.
2. Impressions of those involved about relevant rules and standards of conduct, and whether corruption is in breach of those standards.
3. Impressions of those involved about the actual impact or effects of the corruption.

4. Views of those involved as to what should be done about corruption and which
   of the available remedies may prove effective or ineffective in their particular
   circumstances.

Methods of Gathering Data

Corruption is, by its nature, a covert activity. It makes accurate information hard to
obtain and gives many of those involved a motive for distorting or falsifying any
information they do provide. To obtain an accurate assessment, therefore, it is essential
to obtain information from as many sources as possible and to ensure diversity in the
sources and methods used. That enables biases or errors due to falsification, sampling
or other problems to be identified and either taken into account or eliminated. The
major techniques for gathering information include:

Desk review An early step is usually to gather as much data as possible from pre-
existing sources: previous research or assessments by academics, interest groups,
public officials, auditors-general or ombudsmen, as well as information from media
reports.

Surveys Surveys are an important means of assessment. Surveys gather information
from responses to written questionnaires or verbal interviews. They may be directed
at general populations or be samples specifically chosen for comparison with other
samples. They may gather objective data (for example, the nature or frequency of
occurrences of corruption known to the respondent) or subjective data (the views,
perceptions or opinions of the respondent).

A wide range of data can be obtained about the types, nature, extent and locations
of corruption, the effectiveness of efforts against it and the public perceptions of
all of those. Considerable expertise is needed, however, to gather valid data and to
interpret it correctly.

When conducting a survey, it is important to choose representative samples of
the population, as the nature of the sample is a major factor in assessing the survey
results. A general public survey may show that only a small part of the population has
experienced public sector corruption; a sample selected from among those who have
had some contact with the government or a particular governmental area or process,
such as employment or contracting, may produce a different result. Results of samples
from government insiders may also differ from samples based on outsiders.

The comparison of data taken from different samples is one valuable element of
such research but comparisons can be valid only if the samples were correctly selected
and identified in the first place. For general public surveys, care must be taken to
sample all sectors of the population. A common error is to over-sample urban areas,
where people are more accessible at a lower cost, and to under-sample rural or remote
populations. Valid results will not be yielded if the reality or perception of corruption
is different in urban and rural areas. Samples selected more narrowly, for example, by
asking the users to comment on a particular service, must also ensure that a full range of

service-users is approached. Anonymity and confidentiality are also important; corrupt officials will not provide information if they fear disciplinary or criminal sanctions, and many victims may also fear retaliation if they provide information.

The formulation of survey instruments is critical. Questions must be drafted in a way that can be understood by all those to be surveyed, regardless of background or educational level. All survey respondents must understand the question in the same way. In cases where many respondents are illiterate or deemed unlikely to respond to a written questionnaire, telephone or personal interviews are often used. In such cases, it is essential to train interviewers to ensure that they all ask the same questions using the same terminology.

Focus groups Another diagnostic technique used in country assessments is focus groups, whereby targeted interest groups in government and society hold in-depth discussion sessions. The technique usually produces qualitative rather than quantitative assessments, including detailed information concerning views on corruption, precipitating causes of corruption and valuable ideas on how the government can combat it. Specific agendas for focus groups can be set in advance, or developed individually, either as the group starts its work or by advance consultations with the participants. Focus groups can also be used to generate preliminary assessments as the basis of further research, but should not be the only method used for such assessments. A focus group of judges may well be useful in developing research into corruption in the legal or criminal justice system, for example, but others, such as law enforcement personnel, prosecutors or court officials, may yield different results.

Case studies Following basic quantitative and qualitative assessments that identify the extent of corruption and where it is occurring, case studies can be used to provide more detailed qualitative information. Specific occurrences of corruption are identified and examined in detail to identify the type of corruption involved, exactly how it occurred, who was involved and in what manner, what impact the occurrence had, what was done as a result, and the impact of any action taken. Information is usually gathered by interviewing those involved, although other sources, such as court documents or reports, may also be used if reliable. Case studies are particularly useful in assessing the process of corruption and the relationships that exist between participants, observers and others, as well as between causal or contributing factors. They are also useful in educating officials and members of the public about corruption. As with other areas of research, care in the selection or sampling of cases is important. Cases may be chosen as 'typical' examples of a particular problem, for example, or attempts may be made to identify a series of cases that exemplify the full range of a particular problem or of corruption in general.

Field observation Observers can be sent to monitor specific activities directly. If they are well trained, they can obtain very detailed information. Field observation, however, is too expensive and time-consuming to permit its widespread use; it is usually limited to the follow-up of other, more general, methods and to detailed examinations of particular problem areas.

Field observers can be directed to gather and report information about any aspect of the activity being observed, and this can generate data not available using the majority of other methods, for example the speed, efficiency or courtesy with which public servants interact with the public. In one recent example, as part of a comprehensive assessment of judicial integrity and capacity in Nigeria, field observers attended courts and reported on whether they were adjourning on time and how many hours a day they were actually sitting.

In many cases, it can be difficult to distinguish between the use of observers, whose function is simply to gather data for research purposes, and investigative operations, the function of which is to identify wrongdoers and gather the evidence needed for prosecution or discipline. That is particularly true where observers are working under cover or anonymously, which will often be the case so as to ensure that their presence does not influence the conduct they are observing. Officials, working in countries where constitutional or legal constraints apply to criminal investigations, should bear in mind that constraints may apply to covert or anonymous observation or may operate to prevent the use of information thus obtained against offenders in any subsequent prosecution. Observers should also be given appropriate rules or guidelines governing whether or when to notify law enforcement agencies if serious wrongdoing is observed.

Professional assessment of legal and other provisions and practices In most countries, criminal and administrative law provisions intended to prevent, deter or control corruption already exist and range from criminal offences to breaches of professional codes of conduct or standards of practice. The most important of these usually include: criminal offences, such as bribery; public service rules, such as those governing disclosure and conflict of interest; and the regulations and practices of key professionals, such as lawyers and accountants. Other sectors, such as the medical or engineering professions and the insurance industry, may also have codes or standards containing elements relevant to efforts against corruption. An assessment of those instruments, conducted and compiled by researchers who are professionally qualified but independent of the sectors or bodies under review, can be conducted. Where it is appropriate, professional bodies can also be requested to review and report.

Reviews should be compiled to generate a complete inventory of anti-corruption measures that can then be used for the following purposes:

1. Comparison of each individual sector with the inventory to determine whether elements present in other sectors are absent and, if so, whether they should be added.
2. Comparison of parallel or similar rules adopted by different sectors to determine which is the most effective and to advise improvements to others.
3. Survey of members of the profession and their clients, once the measures have been identified, to assess their views as to whether each measure was effective, and if not, why not.

4. Identification of gaps and inconsistencies and their closure or reconciliation.

The entire legislative anti-corruption framework should be assessed which will require some initial consideration of which laws could or might be used against corruption and how. Such an assessment will include:

1. Criminal laws including the relevant offences; elements of criminal procedure; laws governing the liability of public officials as well as laws governing the tracing and seizure of the proceeds of corruption and, where applicable, other property used to commit or in connection with such offences.
2. Elements treated as regulatory or administrative law by most countries, including relevant public service standards and practices and regulations governing key functions, such as the operation of the financial services sector (for example, banking and the public trading of stocks, securities and commodities), the employment of public servants and the making of government contracts for goods and services.
3. Other areas of law, including legislation governing court procedures and the substantive and procedural rules governing the use of civil litigation as a means of seeking redress for malfeasance or negligence attributable to corruption.
4. Any area of professional practice governed by established rules, whether enacted by the State or adopted by the profession itself, may also be open to internal or external review. Critical areas include the legal and accounting professions and subgroups, such as judges and prosecutors; but other self-governing professional or quasi-professional bodies may also be worth examining. It should be noted that the primary purpose of such examination is not necessarily to identify corruption but to assess what measures have been developed against it, so that they can be used as the basis of reforms for other professions, or to identify and deal with inconsistencies or gaps.

Assessment of institutions and institutional relationships Most of the assessment of institutions and institutional relationships will involve consideration of their capacity or potential capacity to fight corruption. They should also be assessed to determine the nature and extent of corruption within each, as well as in the context of the relationships between them. The assessment should include public agencies and institutions as well as relevant elements of civil society, including the media, academe, professional bodies and relevant interest groups.

Pre-conditions and Risks

The major risks associated with assessment are that data obtained will be inaccurate, or that they will be misinterpreted, leading to the development of inappropriate anti-corruption strategies or to incorrect conclusions about progress against corruption, both of which represent a serious threat. If initial strategies are too conservative, a country can fall short of its potential in dealing with corruption and, if they are too ambitious, the strategies are likely to fail. If populations are convinced that the national strategy is not working, either because it was too ambitious or because the data used to assess progress are not valid, compliance with anti-corruption measures will decline, leading to further erosion of the strategy.

The methods for gathering, analysing and reporting data and conclusions must therefore be rigorous and transparent. Not only must the assessments be valid, but they must also be perceived to be valid by independent experts and by the population as a whole.

Assessment of Institutional Capabilities and Responses to Corruption

Assessment of institutional capabilities and responses to corruption deals with the assessment of institutions. Its aims are:

1. To determine the potential of each institution to participate, at the outset, in the anti-corruption strategy.
2. To measure the degree of success achieved at each stage to determine the role each institution could or should be called upon to play in subsequent stages.

Institutional assessment is also important for the development of strategies and the setting of priorities. In many areas, it will overlap with the assessment described in the assessment of levels of corruption. For example, an assessment of judges or courts showing high levels of institutional corruption would also, in most cases, indicate that the potential of judges to fight corruption was relatively low. That could, in turn, lead to giving the reform of the judiciary a high priority in the early stages of the strategy. Elements of the strategy depending heavily on the rule of law and impartial judges and courts would have to be deferred until a further assessment showed the judiciary had developed sufficient capacity against corruption.

Determining which Institutions Require Assessment, and Setting Priorities

The broad and pervasive nature of corruption may require that virtually every public institution, as well as many elements of civil society and the private sector, should be assessed at some point. To conserve resources, however, and maintain a relatively focused national strategy, priorities must be set.

In many cases, determining which institutions should be given priority in the assessment process will depend on factors individual to the country involved. Those factors may vary over time, particularly if the strategy is relatively successful. Indeed, periodic reassessment may show that institutions have progressed from being part of the problem of corruption to becoming part of the solution. Alternatively, the assessments may raise warnings that previously corruption-free institutions are coming under pressure from corrupt influences displaced from areas where anti-corruption efforts have been successful. In assessing the roles to be played by various institutions, therefore, it is important to consider their existing or potential roles in the major areas (social, political, economic, legal and others), in which anti-corruption efforts are generally required. In most countries, that will include the following areas.

Assessment Reliable assessment will be needed at the beginning of, and at various points during, the anti-corruption process. Those public and private sector institutions that gather statistical and other information from original sources will need to be involved, as well as those that compile and analyse information obtained from other sources. Where the assessment suggests that such institutions are unreliable, the establishment of specific, dedicated agencies may be necessary.

Prevention Many institutions can be called upon to play a role in corruption prevention. Some elements of the criminal justice system can be classified as preventive, for example, those handling prosecutions and those charged with imprisoning, or removing from office, individuals convicted of corruption. More generally, institutions such as schools, universities and religious institutions can play a role in awareness raising and mobilising moral and utilitarian arguments against corruption. Social and economic institutions can play a similar role, as well as developing and implementing institutional, structural and cultural measures to combat corruption in their own dealings.

Reaction Reactive roles are generally those assigned to the criminal justice system and to institutions with parallel or analogous civil functions, in other words any institution charged with detecting, investigating, prosecuting and punishing corruption and recovering the corrupt proceeds. In many countries, non-criminal justice institutions deal with matters such as the setting of integrity and other relevant standards, the discharge or discipline of those who fail to meet them and the recovery of proceeds or damages through civil litigation.

In general, assessment and reforms will, as a matter of priority, focus on public sector institutions and their functions. The nature of corruption, however, and the reluctance of populations to fully trust public officials and institutions in environments where corruption is a serious problem will provide elements of civil society with an important role in monitoring public affairs and anti-corruption efforts and in providing accurate and credible information to validate (or invalidate) those efforts.

A similar process of assessment in respect of the relevant civil society elements or institutions should therefore be undertaken with particular focus on the media, academia, professional bodies and other relevant interest groups. The assessment of each element will usually include consideration of what roles it is already playing or could be playing in efforts against corruption, its capacity to fulfil that role and the relationship between each element and other elements of government and civil society.

Consideration of the media, for example, may include an assessment of the types of media present (computer networks video, radio, print media) and their availability to various segments of the society (literacy rates, access to radios, televisions and computers); the role being played by each medium in identifying corruption; the capacity of each to expand that role; as well as other relevant factors, such as the ability of the media to gain access to the information needed to review and assess government activities.

The institutions or agencies that perform one or more of these functions will usually include the following:

- *Political institutions*, such as political parties (whether in power or not) and the partisan political elements of government;
- *Legislative institutions*, including elements of the legislature and public service that develop, adopt or enact and implement constitutional, statutory, regulatory and other rules or standards of a legislative nature;
- *Judicial institutions*, including judges at all levels, quasi-judicial officials and those who provide input or support to judicial proceedings, such as prosecutors and other lawyers, court officers, witnesses, law enforcement and other investigative personnel;
- *Criminal justice institutions*, including those responsible for investigation, prosecution, punishment and assessment of crime;
- Other *institutions with specific anti-corruption responsibilities*, such as auditors, inspectors and ombudsmen;
- *Civil society institutions*, in particular those involved in transparency, such as the media; in the setting of standards, such as professional bodies; and in assessment or analysis, such as academic institutions;
- *Private sector institutions*, in particular those identified as susceptible to corruption, such as government contractors, and those who provide oversight, such as private auditors.

Institutional Assessment

Once specific institutions have been identified, they should be assessed both individually and in the context of their relationships with other institutions and relevant extrinsic factors. The overall assessment of the potential role of judges, for example, may be affected not only by their degree of professional competence and freedom from corruption but also by the competence and integrity of prosecutors and court personnel. The nature of the legislation judges will have to apply in corruption cases will also affect the role they play.

The primary purpose of assessment using the assessment tool for anti corruption institutions is to determine the potential capacity of each institution to act against corruption. Inevitably, however, that will be linked to the assessment tool identified in cost, levels and types of corruption, of the nature and extent of corruption within the institution and linked entities. Judges cannot be relied upon to combat corruption if they themselves, or those they depend upon, such as court officials or prosecutors, are corrupt. In such cases, a finding using the first assessment that corruption is present in an institution would normally suggest that reform of that institution should be a priority. Until reforms are in place, the potential of the institution to combat corruption elsewhere will be relatively limited. The major objectives of institutional assessment include the following:

1. The drawing up, within each institution, of an analysis of strengths and weaknesses to form the basis of a strategy and action plan for anti-corruption efforts within the institution. The individual plans, thus elaborated, can be compared and harmonised across the full range of institutions;
2. Within each institution, identification of specific areas of corruption and/or areas at risk of corruption;
3. Development of a complete inventory of institutions and agencies. The inventory would include a brief outline of the establishment and mandate of each institution and the responsibilities each has in corruption-related efforts. It would be used to make institutions aware of their mutual existence and roles, which, in turn, would facilitate cooperation and coordination of mandates and activities;
4. An assessment of the mandates and activities of each institution to identify and to address gaps or inconsistencies. Consideration could then be given to enhancing mandates or resources in areas identified as weak or under-resourced.

Methods of Gathering Data or Information for Use in Assessing Institutions

The data-collection methodology for assessing the potential roles of institutions is essentially the same as that used for assessing the extent of corruption and many of the same caveats apply.

As institutions rather than individuals are being assessed, there may be a greater reliance on subjective assessments of whether an institution is functioning effectively or not, for example, the opinions of those served by the institution, those who work in it or other interested parties. The required procedural mechanisms, for example, that statistics or other records be kept or specific incidents or occurrences reported can be incorporated into institutional rules. In many cases, such a requirement amounts to asking the institution to compile and assess data about itself. Thus, safeguards against manipulation or falsification may be required in some cases.

There should be a review of specific laws against corruption, as well as of institutions and anti-corruption measures taken by them, so that a complete institutional inventory can be compiled. The inventory can be used as follows:

1. To comprehensively review legislation in order to identify provisions that can be used effectively as part of the initial anti-corruption strategy, as well as areas of deficiency requiring amendment or the addition of new measures. International legal instruments and the model laws and practices of other countries may provide assistance in identifying deficiencies and suggesting areas and methods of law reform;
2. To assess each institution or sector individually against the inventory. If the institution lacks anti-corruption elements that are present in other sectors, a decision can be taken as to whether those 'new' elements should be taken on board;

3. To allow parallel or similar rules adopted by different institutions to be compared and the most effective identified. That will assist in advising improvements to other institutions;

4. Once the anti-corruption measures of an institution have been identified, surveys of their 'clients' can take place to ascertain if the measures have been effective and, if not, why not;

5. Gaps and inconsistencies in anti-corruption measures can be identified and reconciled or closed.

Different Assessment Instruments

Service Delivery Surveys (SDS)

The service delivery survey (SDS) is useful in a number of ways; it gives service providers the information necessary to implement reform and it gives service users information to help them promote reform. SDS are valuable for a number of reasons:

1. They give consumers a 'voice' and allow them to exert pressure on service providers to deliver higher quality services;
2. They provide concrete data about perceptions in a relatively unambiguous way;
3. They provide greater participation among service users in the service delivery process.

The SDS is especially useful as a management tool. Ultimately, it could be used internally by managers at all levels of the government and externally by governmental oversight agencies, politicians, the public and international donors. The SDS would establish a baseline for service delivery to the public that could be used to improve the design of a reform programme. The indicators could be measured periodically to ascertain the progress of the reform. A service delivery survey would also build capacity within the country to design and implement surveys, as well as to implement results-oriented management.

Description Service delivery surveys originate from a community-based action-research process developed in Latin America in the mid-1980s, known as Sentinel Community Surveillance. Since then, such stakeholder information systems have been implemented with World Bank support in Bosnia and Herzegovina, Mali, Nicaragua, Tanzania and Uganda. With the help of UNICEF and UNDP, they have been established in Bolivia, Burkina Faso, Colombia, Costa Rica, Hungary, Nepal, Nigeria and Pakistan.

The scheme was originally conceived to build capacities while producing accurate, detailed and 'actionable' data rapidly and at low cost. Ordinarily, SDS focus on the generation and communication of evidence for planning purposes at the level of a municipality, city, state, province or an entire country. In each of the settings, a representative sample of communities is selected to represent the full spread of conditions. The approach permits community-based, fact-finding through a reiterative process, addressing one set of issues at a time.

The SDS process starts with a baseline of service coverage, impact and costs in a representative panel of communities. That involves a household survey, where local interviewers are trained to knock on doors and ask a limited number of well-focused questions about use of services, levels of satisfaction, bribes paid and suggestions for change. Such data, and the institutional review from the same communities, are discussed in each community with the service workers and community leaders. The quantitative aspects are used to benchmark progress with subsequent reiterations of the survey. The logistics of the SDS focus on repeated measurement at the same sites, reducing sampling error and making impact estimation straightforward. The qualitative dimensions reveal what should be done about the problem.

Central to SDS is interaction with the research partners – the communities. The product is therefore the aggregation of data from the epidemiological analysis distilled through interaction with communities. By feeding information back to the communities, dialogue for action is stimulated within households, in communities and between communities and local authorities. The resulting mobilisation to resolve specific problems also serves as a basis for empowerment. That involves initiation of cycles following a fairly constant rhythm, independent of the subject matter involved. Experience over more than a decade of implementation in 40 countries has shown that ownership and commitment on the part of the client is vital to successful development projects. The greater the intensity of participation is (in terms of information sharing, consultation, decision making and initiating action) the greater the sustainability.

The method has been used to measure impact, coverage and cost of land mines, economic sanctions, environmental interventions, urban transport, agricultural extension, health services, judiciary and institutional restructuring. It has also proved useful in generating community-designed strategies to combat corruption in the public services in several countries. Actionable results are provided in a short time and at low cost. Typically, the duration of a whole cycle, from the design stage to the report writing, is six to eight weeks.

Some results of the Service Delivery Survey (SDS) Corruption (almost by definition) represents a separation between leaders and their constituencies and between public servants and the public. The first contribution of a SDS in overcoming that separation is that all segments of the public are reflected in the collected data. The data give a voice to the urban and rural, male and female, rich and poor, young and old and even those who do not have access to certain public services for physical or social reasons. Stratified focus groups are assembled to identify potential solutions so that each group is enabled to voice its opinions and solutions.

Simply to be included in the sample as people who give opinions on the services is, however, a fragile representation of the community voice. The second way in which SDS reduce the separation is by involving stakeholders actively in the social audit process. Feedback of the data to the communities (as in Tanzania and Uganda) and systematic use of data to build solutions adds another dimension to the community voice in planning. In the examples given, the participants of the focus groups were invited to meetings with the local community leaders to discuss the feasibility and implications of the solutions.

The third way, in which SDS close the gap, is by providing feedback in a positive way, using results to reveal options for the achievement of goals rather than underscoring deficiencies. Communities or districts with the poorest indicators are shown how certain reforms can improve their situation. Further, having a voice in the interpretation and analysis of the resulting data helps to build confidence among the stakeholders and provides a favourable climate for community mobilisation.

The fourth way SDS can help to bring the governed and governing together is by using the results to manage a change process. The process starts with a necessary commitment by the government to communicate the results. The results of each cycle are then communicated to public service providers through a series of 'change management' workshops. In Tanzania, the results were discussed in a cabinet retreat, where a national policy against corruption was formulated. In Uganda, the results were presented at a retreat of parliamentarians. Media workshops in both countries familiarised journalists with the data and the correct management of positive examples. In that way, the change-management workshops help to build a sense of accountability, transparency and open government.

SDS also provides data necessary for results-oriented development planning. It is a fact that most local governments in developing countries are characterised by poor fiscal outcomes. A results-oriented approach can help improve the outcomes. Results-oriented management, however, needs detailed 'actionable' quantitative data. For a government or municipal authority to act on behalf of a vulnerable subgroup, hard data are required to identify the subgroup concerned and for it to act as a benchmark to measure progress. Complementary qualitative data are also needed to indicate the cultural and gender constraints and opportunities as well as to confirm the analysis given to the quantitative data.

Different types of monitoring at the international level At least, three types of monitoring mechanisms are currently in use as part of anti-corruption programmes:

1. those based on international instruments;
2. those based on national instruments;
3. those of a more general nature.

The advantage of instrument-based mechanisms is that the legal framework is clear: the monitoring focuses on the implementation and impact of the various provisions of the instruments. Examples of such monitoring are the mechanisms relating to the *Convention on Combating Bribery of Officials in International Business Transactions of the Organisation of Co-operation and Development (OECD)*, the *GRECO Programme of the Council of Europe* and the various monitoring exercises within the European Union.[7]

Even without such a formal framework, however, monitoring the effectiveness of national strategies has been accomplished *via* the use of surveys. An example is the recently established monitoring mechanism used in Lithuania, Poland and Romania. Instead of being based on a legal instrument, monitoring takes place on the basis of questionnaires, listing relevant questions on national policies and legislation. Two other examples include the perception indices developed by Transparency International as well as the annual independent survey conducted by Independent Commission Against Corruption (ICAC) in the Hong Kong Special Administrative Region (SAR) that measures, *inter alia*, the trust level between ICAC and the public, the prosecution rate, as well as levels, types, location and causes of corruption. The United Nations is currently testing a method in two pilot countries using a so-called country assessment based on both facts and perceptions using hard facts, surveys focus groups and case studies.

Challenges of measuring the impact of anti-corruption strategies There are certainly many challenges in accurately measuring the impact of anti-corruption strategies, policies and measures.

First, collected data must be analysed by a competent and independent institution capable of extracting its true essence. Analysis highlighting differences and identifying so-called 'best practices' can then be carried out. Availability of resources will always be a factor influencing credibility. That holds true, even for monitoring mechanisms based on international instruments, for it is not always evident that the secretariats of the organisations concerned have the necessary resources to ensure effective support and analysis of such mechanisms.

Second, current international monitoring mechanisms are unevenly distributed throughout the world. In some regions, countries tend to participate in more than one monitoring exercise, while in other parts of the world there are no operational monitoring mechanisms at all, as, for example, in most parts of Asia. Of course, the other extreme involves instances where there are multiple mechanisms applicable to the same region, and the challenge arises as to how to avoid duplication of effort.

Third, monitoring can never be an end in itself. Rather, it should be an effective tool to bring about changes in international and national policies and improve the quality of decision-making. If the monitoring exercise is linked to an international instrument, the primary objective should be to ensure proper implementation of the technical aspects of the instrument and then the practical impact of its implementation. Monitoring can thus serve two immediate purposes. It helps to reveal any differences in interpretation of the instruments concerned and it can stimulate swift and effective translation of the provisions of those instruments into national policies and legislation. If it is determined that incomplete or ineffective implementation has occurred, sanctions can be imposed to motivate stronger efforts to achieve success. Accurate monitoring is therefore critical with respect to launching any successful anti-corruption initiative.

In the case of the OECD Convention, a built-in sanction requires that reports of the discussions on implementation be made available to the public. Such publicity can be an important mechanism in helping promote more effective measures. Reference can be made in that regard to the publicity surrounding the perception indices of Transparency International (TI). Even though the indices simply register the level of corruption as perceived primarily by the international private sector, they gain wide publicity. While the TI indexes are useful, however, a distinct disadvantage is that they:

- do not always reflect the real situation;
- do not involve the victims of corruption in the countries surveyed;
- offer little or no guidance of what could be done to address the problem;
- can discourage countries from taking serious measures when their anti-corruption programme efforts are not seen as being successful by an improved score against the TI Index.

Fourth, monitoring exercises cannot be separated from the issue of technical assistance. It is critical that monitoring not only addresses levels of corruption, but also its location, cost, cause and the potential impact of different remedies. Furthermore, since the trust level between the public and anti-corruption agencies is critical for the success of anti-corruption efforts, public trust levels should also be monitored.

It may be that participating countries agree on the need for implementing the measures identified as 'best practices' but lack financial, human or technical resources to implement them. Under those circumstances, monitoring exercises would be much more effective if they were accompanied by targeted assistance programmes. It should be added, however, that not all measures require major resources, especially in the context of preventive measures where much can be done at relatively low cost.

Most of the data collection by the traditional development institutions is based on an approach that can be described as 'data collection by outsiders for outside use'. International surveys help spark debate about countries that fare badly. They help to place issues on the national agenda and keep them at the forefront of public debate. International surveys are, however, comparative and fraught with statistical difficulties.

They have, however, been important in highlighting the need for national surveys, which are now being undertaken with increasing thoroughness. With public awareness of levels, types, causes and remedies of corruption having dramatically improved over the last five years, collecting data about corruption is useful because it increases the accountability of the State towards its public by establishing measurable performance indicators that are transparently and independently monitored over time.

United Nations Country Assessment

United Nations country assessments aim to produce a clear and coherent picture of the current condition of a given country with respect to the:

- levels, locations, types and cost of corruption;
- causes of corruption;
- remedies for corruption.

Only about 20 per cent of the resources and efforts, however, are spent on the assessment as such. The main objective is to use and disseminate collected data in order to:

- raise awareness among key stakeholders and the public;
- empower civil society to oversee the state;
- provide a foundation for evidence-based action plans;
- establish measurable performance indicators;
- monitor the implementation of the anti-corruption action plan.

Description Country assessments resulting in a corruption monitoring protocol could be issued regularly (once every two to four years) to document levels and locations of corruption as well as progress by a Member State in fighting it. The United Nations Office on Drugs and Crime (UNODC) can conduct such country assessments in collaboration with the United Nations International Criminal Justice Research Institute (UNICRI) and various other research institutes, for instance, Gallup.

Types, levels and locations of corruption The assessments monitor trends regarding the three main types of corruption:

1. Corruption in public administration and 'street-level' corruption.
2. Business corruption (especially in medium-sized businesses).
3. High-level corruption in finance and politics.

In order to assess the types, levels and locations of corruption, various techniques as previously mentioned include, *inter alia*, desk review, surveys, focus groups, case studies, field observation, legal assessment and institutional assessment. These techniques should be combined into an integrated and comprehensive approach.

Preconditions and risks While international surveys tend to be conducted by outsiders for use outside the country, national or sub national surveys are ideally performed by local people (in some cases with the assistance of outsiders) and for local use.

International surveys help trigger public debate in the countries with the most problems. They also help to place the issue on national agendas and to keep them at the forefront of public debate. Public awareness regarding the levels, types, causes of and remedies for corruption have improved dramatically over the last five years, and collecting data about corruption will increase the accountability of the State towards its public by establishing measurable performance indicators that can be transparently monitored over time.

Case Study from Nigeria

In the following, I would like to share with the reader a case study from Nigeria, where the approach described in this chapter was applied.

The project invokes and employs 'Action Learning' principles to pass ownership for the development and implementation of activities, and responsibility for outcomes, to the host country. Sometimes reduced to the acronym CDAR (Connect/Decide/Act/ Reflect), the concept is simple and uncomplicated. Applied to the case study in Nigeria, the elements were: bring stakeholders together (Integrity Meetings); identify the nature and extent of the underlying problem (the Assessments); use what had been learned from the assessments to develop an intervention (Action Plans), implement three pilots, measure the impact (Evaluation), and finally, full circle – bring stakeholders back together, learn from what worked and what did not during the implementation and from the impacts, and then refine the Action Plans accordingly. Action Learning principles were also employed in the construction and activities of the Implementation and sub committees. The principle role of UNODC was that of facilitator.

The project described in this case study, was launched in 2001 and was recently evaluated by an independent consultant – Mr Williams.

Understanding a problem in its proper context is an important step in finding a solution to it. Whereas, in the past, a few empirical studies have been carried out on the problem of corruption generally, there is a dearth of concrete data on the specific nature, extent and locations of corruption that would guide meaningful policy formulation and enforcement.[8] One of the main objectives of the Judicial Integrity and Capacity Project was to bridge this gap by conducting a survey to determine the nature, pattern, extent, location and impact of corruption in the criminal justice system in three pilot states. Subsequently, in order to facilitate this evidence-based planning action, the UNODC subcontracted the task of conducting a comprehensive assessment of judicial integrity and capacity in the above-mentioned pilot states to the Nigerian Institute of Advance Legal Studies (NIALS).

Objectives

The main thrusts and objectives of this assessment were to have a full understanding of the country's problem of corruption in the Judiciary and, specifically, in respect to (1) the levels, locations, types and costs of corruption in the justice system; (2) the institutional structures and weaknesses that facilitate corrupt practices; and (3) possible remedies to corruption within the justice system. In short, the assessment would provide the baseline for monitoring the judicial reform programme. Therefore the objectives of the study included:

- determine the types, manifestations, and patterns of corruption in the judicial system;
- examine practices which encourage corruption and their specific locations within the criminal justice process;

- determine the extent and impact of corruption on the criminal justice system;
- conduct a desk review the laws pertaining to corruption and other related offences; and
- make appropriate recommendations.

Information Items and Variables

Since the assessment was aimed at strengthening the integrity and capacity of the justice systems in the three pilot states, comparative information items identified included the attitudes and perceptions towards the efficiency and effectiveness of the criminal justice system. Therefore, the variables and targets of this survey were the judges, lawyers, prosecutors, court users and business people (both men and women).[9]

Methodology

Quantifying corruption, in whatever form, represents a major challenge for this assessment and the overall effort to ameliorate the menace. That is not entirely impossible however, provided we accept the probabilistic assumptions and results of our findings occasioned by field limitations and constraints. The methodology for the research includes:

1. A desk review of existing literature on the Justice system, including rules of procedure, laws, reports and journals in the pilot states in comparison with other Jurisdictions both (local and foreign).
2. Desk review of laws relating to corruption as well as case analysis of judgments/ rulings on bail applications for Drug related Cases and Land matters in Lagos.
3. Armed robbery and land cases in Delta.
4. Theft and land cases in Borno state.

The Research was based on the guidelines approved at the First Federal Integrity Meeting held from 26–27 October 2001 at Abuja, where it was resolved that the following impact indictors be measured in the pilot states in order to assess the level of judicial integrity and capacity of the pilot states. These are:

1. access to justice;
2. quality of justice;
3. timeliness;
4. public confidence: fairness and political neutrality;
5. corruption.

Sampling Techniques/Procedures

The research team, through the field workers, adopted a one-on-one interview process using prepared surveys/questionnaires on the following segment/groups:

1. judges;
2. lawyers/prosecutors/defenders;
3. court users;
4. business people;
5. serving court staff;
6. retired court staff;
7. persons awaiting trial.

Although the initial target was the pilot courts, to ensure that the sampling technique adopted was robust and representative enough of the various groups that made up the universe of the research, sampling was extended to other courts and cities within the various pilot states.

The sampling also took account the diverse characteristics of the pilot states, the peculiarities of the legal environment, variety and density of courts, lawyers and court users in the pilot states.

A combination of multi-stage stratification and simple random sampling was used to ensure that equal chance/opportunity is given to every segment of the sample frame and that each category or social group was represented in proportion to the size of the group in the universe as a whole.

To ensure that the sample technique is representative of the different judicial divisions and magisterial districts in the three pilot states, a given number of places/courts in each State were chosen for the purpose of sampling. To achieve maximum results, semi-structured, open-ended and closed-ended questionnaires were administered.[10]

Organisation of Analysis

The data gathered from the field was examined by NIALS for completeness, consistency and accuracy of responses. It revealed some instances of poor appreciation of the questions by the respondents. However, these were clearly negligible in number.

The data was entered on Microsoft Excel files as the first stage of analysis. The second stage was carried out by a team of specialists from the Crime Reduction and Analysis Branch of the Global Programme against Corruption within the UNODC. This phase consisted of the categorisation of the data in three main parts as follows.

A descriptive part This collates the evidence of interviewees: the data were aggregated to have a general view on the phenomena and then answers have been separated according to the above-mentioned indicators. A further comparison across states and across categories of respondents has been subsequently developed.

Data analysis This involves the development of assumptions/hypotheses for linkages concerning the findings of the descriptive part, by the usage of 'experience' data and 'perception' data. Through the creation of indexes[11] of corruption, accessibility, timeliness, quality, public trust, independence, fairness and impartiality of the courts, it was possible to measure the extent of these issues. Through the use of statistical parametric and non-parametric techniques, it was possible to identify the existence and the magnitude of the relations between those variables. Specific relevance has been given to such links that possibly could be, or are already being addressed through targeted measures. Based on results found, hypotheses[12] have then be compared and verified by applying mainstream statistical and criminological theories.

Policy recommendations First, measures identified by judges and lawyers as the most important measures to enhance integrity and capacity of the justice system have been investigated, according to the main problems and deficiencies that court users and business persons also identified. Secondly, more recommendations have been suggested. The analysis revealed the causes for certain deficiencies of the judicial system relating to access to justice, corruption, timeliness, quality of justice delivery and public trust. New measures have been proposed, taking into account, in particular, those objective factors e.g. computerisation, procedures, disciplinary mechanisms, etc., which could be, or are already being addressed through targeted measures within the framework of ongoing judicial reform in Nigeria

Limitations

It should be noted that although Nigeria is considered as a Common Law country, strictly speaking, it operates a structural mix of Common Law, Sharia Law and Customary Law. This diversity was clearly understood at the outset during the selection of the pilot states, with Borno state as the only state where Sharia is fully operational among the three states. It is, therefore, not unusual that such a study would encounter some constraints and relative differences. The report of the experiences of field workers in the course of the research revealed the following:

1. Judges and lawyers were particularly difficult to interview individually on account of their busy schedules. They generally preferred the survey instruments to be left for them to attend to at their own time.
2. Court users were not easily accessible to fieldworkers as some demanded money before answering questions, others were screened away by their lawyers while others expressed apathy in the research, contending that previous efforts were yet to bring about the expected benefits.
3. The survey instruments contained many questions some of which needed explanations for rational answers to be given to them. Thus, those who could not be interviewed in person could not benefit from the explanations of fieldworkers and consequently a few of the respondents misunderstood the purport of the questions.

4. Persons awaiting trial were generally apprehensive in answering questions relating to corruption in the justice system especially with respect to the police, prison officials and judges for fear of repercussions. The problem was compounded as most of them had to be interviewed in the presence of prison officials. There was a general feeling that they had been instructed not to make disparaging remarks about the system.
5. Serving court staff were also not generally forthcoming on the issue of corruption and discipline within the judiciary for fear of repercussions.
6. Retired court staff who would have been able to throw light on the state of the Judiciary during their service were generally difficult to access as many had left for their respective villages soon after retirement. It was, therefore, not surprising that the fieldworkers could not interview anyone in this category in Lagos State.
7. On the issue of corruption within the judiciary, lawyers and business people were more forthcoming on their experiences of corrupt practices within the judicial system and who should be blamed for the corruption.

While there was public outcry about the incidences of corruption in the country in general, and the judiciary in particular, only few respondents were willing to discuss it frankly, let alone put their views and experiences on paper. The above limitations notwithstanding, a reasonable number of respondents – 5,766 – were interviewed, thereby making it one of the largest judicial integrity surveys ever conducted in Africa.

Key Findings from the Assessment

Public Trust Index

The level of public trust in the criminal justice system is a crucial element and in Nigeria it needed to be analysed carefully. An attempt was made to create two indexes, one based on experiences and the other based on perceptions. However, the nature and scale of the variables could only allow one index of both types of variables. Eventually, the study developed a statistically reliable single index showing the perception of trust in the different institutions in the criminal justice system.

The variables used for the index are related to the ability of the country's justice system to uphold civil rights, to guarantee the safety of lives and property and to support the economy. Citizen's rights and accessibility to justice, i.e. to litigate the government in the courts was also used as variable to test the level of trust in the system. The index was constructed by compiling these variables in one scale from 0 (high level of trust) to 10 (low level of trust). Across the states, analysis of the data shows that the Delta State Judiciary scored the highest in rating with 4.7 while Borno and Lagos State, both scored 5.12.

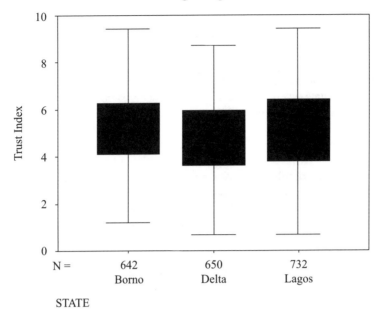

Figure 2.1 Public trust index

Corruption Indexes

Perception and experience related data are important variables for the purpose of gaining a more profound insight into the levels as well as the causes and consequences of corruption within the criminal justice system. Perception of 'corruption' could be influenced by various factors, many not related to the actual prevalence of corrupt practices, but other factors such as delays or incompetence. On the other hand, actual experiences may not always be truthfully reported. Often, respondents may not feel comfortable admitting openly, that they have bribed a judge or a court staff or they may be reluctant to criticise their own institution or profession by indicating corruption among colleagues. For these reasons, it seemed advisable to consider both 'experiences' and 'perceptions'.

More specifically, the *Corruption Experience Index* is composed of indicators relating to the experiences of unofficial payments to court officials, court staff and the police, as well as to payments made with the purpose of obtaining a favourable judgment, accelerating the procedure, or more generally, for a positive outcome of the dispute. In addition, the number of payments made during the lifetime of a case was taken into account.

The *Corruption Perception Index* includes the responses of the various stakeholders of the justice system to questions on their opinions concerning the levels of corruption in the courts. Furthermore, the Index includes the findings from various questions that asked the respondents whether they considered corruption as a major hindrance to efficient and effective justice delivery, and how they rated corruption *vis-à-vis* two other important factors affecting the system.

Both indicators were compiled in a scale of 0 (low corruption) to 10 (high corruption), and from a cross-state comparison of the two indices, Lagos with 5.6 rating emerged as the state where corruption in the justice system seemed more prevalent than in Delta (4.7) and Borno (4.17).

Timeliness Indexes

The perception of timeliness varies among different people, especially in the assessment of the criminal justice system. On the one hand, a 'long' trial could be justified for diligence and fair result/judgement; on the other hand, the length of trial could be a deliberate way of seeking rent. How long would a businessman or a court user be willing to wait for the solution of a dispute before they will ask to accelerate the procedure by bribing an officer? In the case of timeliness of justice, a 'perceptional' variable is used to show the difference between what might be considered 'too long' and what is the 'appropriate' duration of a trial.

The *Timeliness Perceptional Index* was analysed as an indicator of the speed of the country's justice system. The perception of timeliness was also compared to other factors to determine the extent to which it affects judicial service delivery.

The *Timeliness Experience Index* considered the actual time it took to dispose of the case and the experiences of delays in the various stages of the proceeding.

Both indexes were compiled in order to define a scale (this is not clear) from 0 (few delays) to 10 (high delays). A cross-state comparison revealed that the CJS in Borno is by far the fastest, both in terms of experiences (4.29) and perceptions (4.37) compared to Delta (6.32; 5.20) and Lagos (4.68; 5.16).

Independence, Fairness and Impartiality

The study sought to determine the fairness and impartiality of the justice system by evaluating whether exogenous factors, such as political relations and influences, wealth, gender and ethnicity did influence or affect the disposition of the case in any way. These variables were cross-rated with the correct and predictable interpretation of the law and the ultimate judgment passed.

Other variables, such as the political pressure on the judiciary, the extent to which the executive could control the judiciary (particularly in regard to funding and appointment of judges), and social status were also applied to determine the level of independence, fairness, and impartiality of the judiciary. The Index was based on a scale of 0 (more independence) to 10 (less independence). And, a cross-state analysis shows that Lagos (5.53) appeared to be the state where the judiciary is more biased, or less independent and less impartial, compared to Borno (5.07) and Delta (4.78).

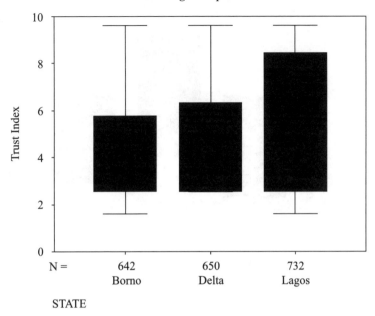

Figure 2.2   Corruption experience index

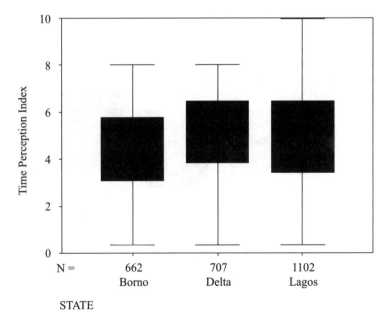

Figure 2.3   Timeliness perceptional index

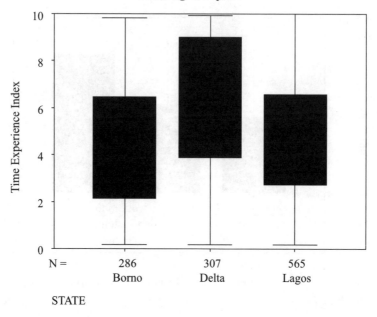

Figure 2.4   Timeliness experience index

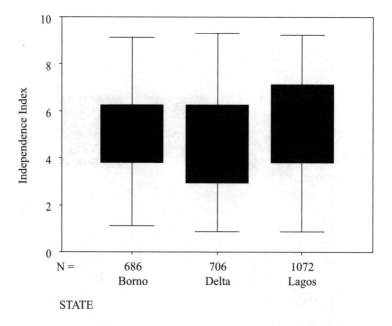

Figure 2.5   Independence index

Lessons Learned from the Action Learning Project in Nigeria[13]

General Lessons

1. Curbing systemic corruption is a challenge that will require stronger measures, more resources and a longer time horizon than most politicians and 'corruption fighters' will admit to or can afford.
2. Left unchecked, corruption will only increase and make the poorest and least educated poorer. Where personal risk and punishment are minimal, the risk of grand, administrative and petty corruption naturally increases.
3. Raising awareness without adequate and visible enforcement will lead to cynicism among citizenry and possibly increase the incidence of corruption.
4. A country's national institutions do not work in isolation. Where they do, they will fail in their totality. A transparent and integrated system of checks and balances, designed to achieve accountability among the various arms and agencies of government, disperses power and limits opportunities for conflicts of interest.
5. Public trust in government, anti-corruption agencies and anti-corruption policies and measures is key when a country invites the public to take an active role in monitoring the performance of its government.

More Specific Lessons

Because this is a pilot Project, it should be expected that there would be results that are less than desired. Part of the action learning and process is the testing of the United Nations Office on Drugs and Crime (UNODC) approach. Similarly, there will be positive results, which were unexpected. Perhaps, the most valuable outcome is in lessons learned.

There is no substitute for 'on-the-ground' vigilance The Project was impeded by the relative lateness of appointment of the National Project Coordinator (NPC) and many of the duties/functions attached to the position preceded the appointment. To carry out functions remotely from Vienna, rather than involve the local field office, was not an optimal solution. As a result, monitoring and evaluation during the first 12 months was impeded, and an opportunity to embed a routine, standardised reporting format/data collection process was lost.

Raising expectations Despite apparent consistent messages that funding was limited, unrealistic expectations still built up, affecting the perception of the sincerity of UNODC. Management of expectations is key.

'Loose lips sink ships' Seemingly innocuous comments can have widespread consequences. The comment that UNODC 'might be able to do something' in relation to the complaints and registry software was seized upon and used as justification for

stalling development in those areas. Failure to provide was used as further evidence of UNODC promising without delivering.

Acceptance of personal recommendations, even from the highest authority can be problematic The failure to let the assessment research out to tender had far-reaching consequences. Similarly, the selection of Delta State, on the imminent retirement of the Chief Judge and the Chief Registrar, as a state that possessed the willingness and readiness, the 'strength of vigour' necessary to carry the project, appears to have been unwise.

Similarly, verbal assurances are worthless The judiciary does not exist in a vacuum. Outside of the wider social and political environment, it is more closely aligned with other organs of the justice system (e.g. legislature, executive). The closest of the relationships is with the police, and specifically concerning corruption, independently appointed 'watchdogs', in Nigeria's case, the Independent Corrupt Practices Commission (ICPC). Both these agencies promised much but, for a variety of reasons, commitments did not eventuate.

Cooperation can lead to competition and/or duplication The Project envisaged close cooperation between UNODC and other donor agencies. In particular, United States Agency for International Development (USAID) and the Department of Interior and Local Government (DILG) were identified. USAID was 'concerned and annoyed' that Lagos, a state in which its own governance Project was being run, was selected by UNODC. Despite the best attempts, UNODC was unable to bring DILG 'to the table' on the Project (or on other matters of mutual interest).

Courtesy comfort infrastructure contributions can lead to wider dissatisfaction The small (in $ value) improvements made to various courts in the Pilot states, and in particular the information technology/voice equipment contributions led to an expectation that ongoing maintenance would be met by UNODC (despite consistent advice to the contrary). The subsequent 'failure' of the UNODC to provide same, again led to a perception that UNODC promised more than it delivered.

Action learning works Courtesy, respect, tolerance and willingness to accept locally developed solutions, rather than attempting to impose external solutions, engenders far greater enthusiasm and sense of ownership, and appears to promote higher likelihood of success.

It takes integrity to fight corruption Any successful anti-corruption effort must be based on integrity and credibility. Where there is no integrity in the very system designed to detect and combat corruption, the risk of detection and punishment to a corrupt regime will not be meaningfully increased. Complainants will not come forward if they perceive that reporting corrupt activity exposes them to personal risk.

Building integrity and credibility takes time and consistency In the eyes of the public, most international agencies have not demonstrated sufficient integrity to fight corruption. These agencies have not accepted that integrity and credibility must be earned based upon 'walk rather than talk'. The true judges of whether or not an agency has integrity and credibility are not the international agencies themselves but rather the public in the recipient country.

It is important to involve the victims of corruption Most donor-supported anti-corruption initiatives primarily involve only the people who are paid to fight corruption. Very few initiatives involve the people suffering from the effects of corruption. It is therefore critical to do more of what Independent Commission Against Corruption (ICAC) in Hong Kong has done over the past 25 years. For example, the ICAC interfaces directly in awareness raising workshops with almost 1 per cent of the population every year. Most donor agencies cannot interface with the public without increased partnerships with credible local non-government organisations.

Notes

1   Global Programme Against Corruption, United Nations Office on Drugs and Crime (UNODC). The views expressed herein are those of the author and not necessarily of the United Nations.
2   See Langseth, P. (2003), *United Nations Anti Corruption Toolkit*, Vienna.
3   Initial proposals for the Convention were gathered at an informal preparatory meeting held in Buenos Aires from 4–7 December 2001 and compiled in documents A/AC/261/3, Parts I–IV. Proposals to define 'corruption' are in Part I, and proposals to criminalise acts of corruption are found in Part II.
4   See, for example Articles 2 and 3 of the *European Criminal Law Convention on Corruption*, ETS #173.
5   Provisions that define or criminalise bribery include: article 8 of the *UN Convention Against Transnational Organized Crime*, GA/Res/55/25, Annex and article VI of the *Inter-American Convention against Corruption* of 29 March 1996 (OAS Convention), which require Parties to criminalise offering of, or acceptance by a public official of, an undue advantage in exchange for any act or omission in the performance of the official's public functions. Article 1 of the *OECD Convention on Combating Bribery of Foreign Public Officials in International Business Transactions* and Article VIII of the OAS Convention require Parties to criminalise the offering of bribes by nationals of one State to a government official of another in conjunction with a business transaction. Articles 2 and 3 of the *European Union Convention on the Fight Against Corruption Involving Officials of the European Communities or officials of Member States of the European Union*, Journal C 195, 25/06/1997, pp. 2–11 (1997), requires Parties to criminalise the request or receipt by a public official of any advantage or benefit in exchange for the official's action or omission in the exercise of his functions ('passive bribery'), as well as the promise or giving of any such advantage or benefit to a public official ('active bribery'). *The Council of Europe's Criminal Law Convention on Corruption*, ETS No. 173 (1998), goes further by criminalising 'active' and 'passive' bribery of, *inter alia*, domestic public officials, foreign public officials, domestic and foreign public assemblies, as well as private sector bribery,

trading in influence and account offences. See also *UN Declaration against Corruption and Bribery in International Commercial Transactions*, GA/Res/51/191, Annex (1996), calling for the criminalisation of corruption in international commercial transactions and the bribery of foreign public officials; and *Global Forum on Fighting Corruption, Washington*, 24–26 February 1999, *Guiding Principles for Fighting Corruption* and *Safeguarding Integrity among Justice and Security Officials* document E/CN.15/1999/CRP.12, Principle #4. The working definition used in this Tool Kit and by the CICP's *Global Programme against Corruption (GPAC)* is 'the misuse of (public) power for private gain'. The *United Nations Manual on Anti-Corruption Policy* discusses models based on the idea that all forms of corruption involve either the creation of conflicting interests or the exploitation of such interests that already exist.

6   A number of recent international legal instruments have sought to ensure that Parties have offences addressing this type of conduct with varying degrees of specificity. These include the Organization of American States' Inter-American Convention Against Corruption (1996) and the European Union's Convention drawn up on the basis of Article K.3 of the Treaty on European Union, on the protection of the European Communities' financial interests (1995). Article XI(1)(b) and (d) of the Inter-American Convention call upon Parties to consider criminalising a government official's improper use or diversion of government property, including money and securities, regardless of the person or entity to whom the property is diverted, while Article XI(1)(a) calls upon Parties to consider criminalising the improper use of classified information by a government official. Article IX requires, subject to a Party's Constitution and the fundamental principles of its legal system, criminalisation of 'illicit enrichment', meaning 'a significant increase in the assets of a government official that he cannot reasonably explain in relation to his lawful earnings during the performance of his functions'. Addressing the narrow area of protection of the financial interests of the European Community from fraud and corruption, Article 1 of the European Union's Convention requires Parties to criminalise the use or presentation of false or incorrect representations or non-disclosure of information the effect of which is the misappropriation or wrongful retention of funds from the budget of the European Communities. For a more detailed analysis of these instruments, see UN document E/CN.15/2001/3 (Report of the Secretary General on Existing International Legal Instruments Addressing Corruption).

7   It is expected that the future *United Nations Convention against Corruption* will also contain a provision on monitoring.

8   Previous studies on corruption in Nigeria include Odekunle, Femi (1982) (ed.), *Nigeria: Corruption in Development*, University of Ibadan Press; Lame, et al. (2001) (eds), *Corruption and Organized Crime: The Challenges in the New Millennium*, Spectrum Books, Abuja. On law and order, the most empirical study till date is the *Report of A Special Study Group on Law and Order* (1985), The Presidency, Federal Government Printers, Lagos. Mention should also be made that the NIALS had earlier published a *Technical Report on the Nigerian Court Procedures Project* (2001) containing proposals for the *Reform of the High Court of Lagos State Civil Procedure Rules*.

9   Unfortunately, by design or omission law enforcement, particularly the police were not included among interviewees.

10   In some cases, trained research assistants administered the questionnaires.

11   The Indexes were compiled as an average of selected variables, each converted in a scale from 1 to 10 (as a consequence the indexes are in a scale from one to ten). It was decided to give a negative to the score in the indexes. Hence, the higher the score is in the Corruption

Experience Index, the higher the level of corruption that is experienced by that person. The higher the score in the Accessibility Perception Index, the lower is the court accessibility according to that respondent perception, and so forth.

12 What is referred to here as critical readers could fault hypothesis. Perhaps, 'assumptions' might be a better term.

13 See Gordon, Paul Williams (2003), *Independent Evaluation Report of the Judicial Integrity and Capacity Project in Nigeria*, December 2003.

References

Anderson, Neil (1996), *Implementing your strategic plan: a Workbook for Public and Nonprofit Organisations*, Jossey-Bass Publishers, San Francisco.

Chong, Alberto and Calderón, César (1998), *Institutional Efficiency and Income Inequality: Cross Country Empirical Evidence*, Mimeograph, World Bank, Washington, DC.

Gray, C. and Kaufman, D. (1998), 'Corruption and Development', *Finance and Development*, vol. 35, no. 1, pp. 7–11.

Grindle, Merilee S. (1996), *Challenging the State: Crisis and Innovation in Latin America and Africa*, Cambridge University Press, UK.

Klitgaard, R. (1988), *Controlling Corruption*, University of California Press, Berkeley, CA.

Lai, A. (1999), 'Corruption Prevention: A Hong Kong Perspective', *Proceedings from the 9th SPAC Conference in Milan*, 19–20 November 1999.

Lai, A. (2001), 'Building Public Confidence; The Hong Kong Approach', *Forum on Crime and Society* (forthcoming 2002).

Langseth. P. (ed.) (2003), *United Nations Anti Corruption Toolkit*, Vienna, Austria.

Langseth. P. (ed.) (2003), *United Nations Guide on Anti Corruption Policy*, Vienna Austria.

Langseth, P. (2002), 'Global Dynamics of Corruption, the Role of United Nations', *Strengthen Judicial Integrity and Capacity in Nigeria*, State Integrity Meeting in Lagos, May 2002.

Langseth, P. and Abba, Mohammad (eds) (2002), *Strengthening Judicial Integrity and Capacity in Nigeria*, Abuja, Nigeria.

Langseth, P. and Stolpe, O. (2001), 'Strengthen the Judiciary against Corruption', *International Yearbook for Judges*, Australia.

Langseth, P., Stapenhurst, Rick and Pope, Jeremy (1997), *The Role of a National Integrity System in Fighting Corruption*, EDI Working Papers Series, World Bank, Washington, DC.

Mauro, P. (1997), *Why Worry about Corruption?*, International Monetary Fund, Washington, DC.

National Performance Review Office/Office of the Vice President of the United States (1994), *Putting Customers First: Standards for Serving the American People*, Report of the National Performance Review, Washington, DC.

Pope, J. (2000), *The TI Sourcebook*, Transparency International, Berlin.

Rose-Ackerman, S. (1997), 'Corruption and Development', Paper prepared for the *Annual World Bank Conference on Development Economics*, Washington, DC, 30 April and 1 May.

Rose-Ackerman, S. (2000), 'Democracy and grand corruption', reprinted in R. Williams (ed.), *Explaining Corruption*, Elgar Reference Collection, UK, pp. 321–36.

Ruzindana, A., Langseth, P. and Gakwadi, A. (1998), *Building Integrity to Fight Corruption in Uganda*, Fountain Publishing House, Kampala, Uganda.

Selener, D. (1997), *Participatory Action Research and Social Change*, Cornell Participatory Action Research Network, Cornell University, Ithaca, New York.

Smith, S., Williams, D. and Johnson, N. (1997), *Nurtured by Knowledge: Learning to Do Participatory Action-Research*, The Apex Press, New York.

Stevens, Robert (1993), *The Independence of the Judiciary: The View from the Lord Chancellor's Office*, Oxford University Press, Oxford.

Chapter 3

Corruption Definition and Measurement

Mark Philp

Introduction

This chapter offers a brief discussion of the conceptual issues associated with the definition of corruption and the associated difficulties in the development of appropriate measurements for the incidence and seriousness of political corruption. This chapter is divided into two major sections – the first on corruption and its definition, the second on the difficulties raised by definition for measurement. A brief final section suggests ways forward.

Defining Corruption

There is some consensus in the literature that we have a case of corruption when: A public official (A), acting for personal gain, violates the norms of public office and harms the interests of the public (B) to benefit a third party (C) who rewards A for access to goods or services which C would not otherwise obtain. The key components of this definition are as follows.

1. A conception of public office with rules and norms for the conduct of that office – which entails the view that the office is defined in terms of the public interest it serves, and that this may run against the personal interests of the office-holder.
2. A view that corruption involves the distortion of the exercise of public office so that it meets private rather than public interests – so that some gain who should not and some lose who should not.
3. The idea that three actors are normally involved or affected by corrupt activity: the occupant of the public office (A), the intended beneficiary of that office (B), and the actual beneficiary of the particular exercise of that office (C).[1]

Activities that satisfy this definition are corrupt. However, there are many cases where activities fall short of the definition but are nonetheless viewed as corrupt.

The implicit assumption of a triadic relationship (even if it is not always present) is significant in marking the difference between cases of fraud and embezzlement (where A simply steals from the state), and cases of corruption are more properly understood, where the exercise of power (i.e., A's power or authority over B) is perverted. Nonetheless, there are cases in which the triad of actors collapses into a dyad: in a kleptocracy, there may be no independent agent C benefiting (since A is identical with the beneficiary C), yet few doubt that such a regime is corrupt. On the other hand, stealing supplies from one's office is not usually thought of as a case of corruption. Corrupt dyads as distinct from cases of theft, etc, seem to be marked by three conditions – they involve high public office; the expropriation of benefits for A tends to be substantial and systematic; and, there is a correspondingly significant degree of damage to the public interest. My guess is that most people intuitively regard the first as the most important of these, and see the other elements as complementary to, and entailed by this, rather than as properly independent conditions. (We must also recognise, however, that there are many ways in which someone may act in dereliction of their public office while falling short of corruption: a civil servant who is lazy or incompetent is not usually thought of as corrupt; to rule tyrannically is also not necessarily corrupt.)

We also have cases where the benefit to C is something to which C has a right (so that (B) = (C)), but where the public official levels a tax on access.

To further complicate matters, there are cases in which an official (A) is bribed to induce him to act in a way that is in B's interests, even though the formal role A occupies denies that B has such an interest. For example, where A (a policeman) is bribed by C (a businessman) to overlook the presence of Jews in C's factory although A is under a legal obligation to report them for deportation, he acts on the basis of a corrupt incentive, and acts against his formal responsibilities, but does so in ways which can be regarded as being of broader public benefit. Here, we want to say that the policeman acts corruptly, but we might also want to say that the public interest is served – so corrupt activity does not always go against the public interest. (Note that someone who acts in the same way but does so for ideological reasons and without financial incentive would not be described as corrupt, because there is no private gain.)

However, the private gain aspect is complicated by cases where the pay-off is not private but political – campaign contributions, traded political support, electoral or 'log-rolling' deals. Equally, a public official may act to avoid certain costs rather than to incur certain benefits (so that the claim about gain rests on a counter-factual).

Finally, there may also be a hierarchy in the goods that the official trades that may lead to certain actions being classified as something other than corrupt. For example, while an official who trades tax exemptions is corrupt; one who trades state secrets to another country is engaged in treason. We can make sense of this by seeing it as a case in which the more serious offence (treason) descriptively crowds out the lesser (corruption). However, we may still want to distinguish between those who commit treason corruptly (for personal gain), and those who do so because of ideological commitments. In the latter case, the second component for corruption is not met (since the agent does not act for private gain), and the claim that A acts contrary to the public interest is disputed (essentially the same case as the policeman who fails to betray a fugitive on ideological or humanitarian grounds).

Not all disputed claims are necessarily acceptable – those who claim that their actions are in the public interest (as T. Dan Smith and John Poulson claimed) need to show that they acted to serve the public interest, rather than their own, even where a predictable consequence of their action was that the public interest was served in some way. That they sought illicit (i.e. excluded by the rules of their office) private gain from the exercise of their office trumps facts of the matter about who else benefited.

The proposed definition does not assume that A's behaviour must break the law to be corrupt. It recognises that there are cases where A and C can conspire to subvert the political process so as to introduce laws which entrench A and/or C's corrupt gains. This is one reason why legal definitions of corruption fail to capture some of the worst cases of corrupt activity – where corrupt transactions become institutionalised in the state and economy, as recognised by recent work on 'state capture' and regulatory capture.[2] Nonetheless, any definition of corruption must retain as a core component that the agent's action be, in some way, 'illicit' – where the grounds for identifying it as illicit is that it violates the rules, norms, or public expectations of the office s/he occupies. There is an abiding problem as to what grounds our judgments about these norms, but the idea that they can be grounded in a manner wholly external to a given political culture and society is implausible. To classify as corrupt, behaviour that conforms to public office norms that are widely approved and endorsed does not make sense. Where official behaviour follows widely held local norms that other cultures regard as corrupt, it may be that, rather than public office being corrupt, it is poorly defined (by Western standards), or defined in patrimonial, familial, or other than legal-rational terms. But just as there are problems using the law, there are equally problems in using norms, not least because these can vary both in their content and in the intensity with which they are held depending on the reference group one uses. When one talks of the norms for public office, politicians, civil servants, members of the public and so on might construe these differently.

The difficulties arising in the definition of political corruption nonetheless revolve around a core concerning the character of public office. *Political* corruption involves the exercise of public, political office for private gain. What remains central to political corruption is the implied construction of public office which identifies the character, extent of, and responsibilities associated with, the relationships between A, B and C. The distinction between A-led and C-led types of corruption, with A-led involving the public official imposing the terms on C (from extortion to informal 'taxation'), while in C-led the relationship is reversed (from bribery to systematic subversion of the political domain), underlines the centrality of public office for political corruption: A-led corruption does not always require a C, but C-led does require an A. There has to be someone exercising a public office whose conduct falls short of the appropriate standards for political corruption to occur. Someone who threatens or provides cash incentives to someone who does not hold public office to get something that they want is not engaged in political corruption. For example, someone who intimidates a private citizen into selling his or her house below market value, or who (as in a recent film) pays another person to let him sleep with that person's spouse, is not engaged in political corruption, because in neither case is there a public office involved.

Of course, this raises the problem of 'adjectival corruption': economic corruption, moral corruption, personal corruption and so on. Are we to regard these as part of a broader concept of corruption and as sub-sets of corruption that should be captured by the same definitional core? *Economic* corruption looks like a possible candidate for having a similar structure to political corruption, except that we cannot always identify a sharp disjunction between a 'positional' requirement to act in keeping with a formally identified role within a company and the legitimate incentive for agents to act as private interest-maximisers. Indeed, we can make most sense of the idea of economic corruption in the context of publicly registered companies, which have a structure, formal requirements for the occupants of certain roles and potential conflicts between the interests of the actor and those that his or her role is intended to serve.

It is also possible to stress market rules and standards – such as fair practices, etc, from which people may fall short. But someone who cheats me by selling me shoddy goods is not usually thought of as 'corrupt'. In addition, there is no triadic relationship – although, in contrast to political office where we can see extortion by a public official as corrupt, there is less sense that it is anything other than extortion in the context of the market. However, these concerns do help us to see that corruption itself might be predicated of any role that involves a public dimension that is potentially in conflict with private interests. Political corruption focuses predominantly on political office, but it is not a huge step to think of corruption as linked more generally to public office – which is a much broader category than strictly political office.

One way to make sense of 'adjectival corruption' is simply to say that the root meaning of the term corruption is a decay in the basic nature or character of a thing, so that *x-corruption* is just the corruption of the basic nature or character of *x*. This is plausible enough, but it leaves open the question of whether something has a basic nature or character and what that basic nature or character might be.

The basic nature, or character, of politics is rather contested, but there is some sense that it involves the use of public office to pursue a range of collective ends, of which order and security are only the most basic. Economic corruption is more contested still, since on some models the natural order is one in which interest maximising is the sole end and in which self-interest maximising behaviour is collectively optimal! Moral corruption similarly depends on a 'thick' conception of personal morality for us to flesh out an account of the corruption of the individual, rather than thinking of him or her as simply weak-willed, or ethically slimy! Clearly, in each case, the higher the standards we ascribe to the essential character of the *x*-term, and the more essentialist or naturalistic we make those standards, the easier it is to have a sense that derogation from that standard involves some kind of corruption. But this promptly faces us with two difficulties: how do we ground those standards in a way which is widely intelligible and acceptable; and should not the exact account of those standards be highly culturally conditioned, so that they are recognisably standards for those who work in, and are ruled by, a particular system.

Recent work on 'state capture' by the World Bank raises a series of other relevant distinctions between types of corruption and different measures of seriousness. It distinguishes between the types of institutions that are captured (the executive, legislature, judiciary, or independent regulatory agencies), who are doing the capturing (private firms, interest groups, political leaders), and the type of benefits provided to public officials (bribes, equity stakes, informal control rights). The last two of these categories can be further expanded: as Hellman's work has shown, capture can occur across state boundaries, by foreign firms and investors, or by the activities of foreign governments.[3] We should also recognise the extent to which corrupt transactions and capture can be effected or sustained through the use of the use or threat of violence and the marketing of 'protection'. Also, 'throffers' – a combination of threat and offer ('do x and you'll get y, fail to and we'll impose sanction z'), are a powerful and often highly efficient incentive for groups working in areas where they either control the law or its enforcement, or where this is in disarray. Two further distinctions concern the depth of the penetration of the institutional structure of the state and its duration. Buying a Member of Parliament's vote on a single issue is less corrosive than being able to design and have passed a law (depth). Always being able to buy a vote, or have a law passed, is more corrosive than if one can only do so exceptionally (duration). These distinctions might be characterised as between deep and shallow, entrenched and occasional capture. These distinctions will be associated with the others we have drawn. For example, where capture is deep and entrenched – so that an office and its regulatory or law-making powers become wholly subordinate to the private interests of some individual, group or organisation – it is less likely to rely on substantial direct payments to officials, and more likely that it will be a part of a network of relationships and exchanges, in which monetary exchange plays a lesser role.

Such distinctions can help deepen our understanding of the 'reach' of corrupt practices within a state. But acknowledging these different dimensions of corruption and recognising that it is essential in understanding corruption to capture issues of depth, entrenchment, symmetry vs. asymmetry and identify the various currencies of corrupt transactions – monetary, favours, violence and protection – will inevitably make us wary of indices of corruption that rely on a single dimension or scale and focus wholly on people's perceptions. It may not be wary to identify the facts of the matter, but there are facts of the matter that are germane to assessing the seriousness of corruption in a state.

Measurement

There are four[4] commonly recognised methodological problems posed by existing corruption measures:

1. There is a problem of scaling. The Corruption Perception Index (CPI) employs a ten-point scale to one decimal place, across a range of different indicators. This has already been the subject of serious reservations in the academic community, reservations which Transparency International (TI) itself shares to some degree. The scale, as currently devised, seems spuriously precise, given that it depends on the largely ordinal and relatively imprecise judgments of its respondents. One way forward might be to look at techniques associated with other multiple-component perception surveys used in political and commercial research (such as competitiveness, or levels of education indices).

2. There is an issue of the appropriateness of the choice of respondents: whose perceptions matter? There is serious concern about the tendency of the CPI survey to capture the views of Western businessmen involved in business with firms overseas. Given that bias, it is perhaps not wholly surprising that countries in the South and East tend to do less well than countries in the North and West. Again, comparison with the sampling procedures used in other multiple-component perception surveys could make an important contribution to a more reliable index.

3. Existing corruption indices almost wholly avoid the challenge of integrating 'harder' sources of data into the 'softer', perception-driven sources. Such data includes, for example, figures for prosecutions for corrupt activity. There are problems of comparability, because of differences in legal instruments – and difficulties in knowing whether high levels of prosecutions should be weighed as evidence of high corruption, or as evidence of low tolerance for corruption. Nevertheless, such data has relevance, and there is a good deal of it available to provide more subtle and complex accounts of the problem of corruption within individual states. Council of Europe GRECO reports, the reports to be produced under the OECD Working Group on the Anti-Bribery Convention, and the in-depth country specific reports of organisations like the World Bank, Transparency International and OSI, provide a substantial amount of material in which judgments about corruption, its seriousness and its incidence are made.

4. There is a problem concerning the reliability of the CPI. There are concerns that it may show too much reliability over time and that its reliability might be a function of the dominance in the Index of a small number of surveys (nine components of the 1999 index were essentially the results of three years worth of each of three surveys).

In my view, however, the most fundamental difficulty for corruption measurement arises from the problems I have indicated concerning the definition of corruption and the variability of governmental and business practices in different parts of the world. The definitional problems associated with corruption are not simply a conceptual irritant; they raise questions about the feasibility of the measurement project itself. There might be a slightly higher consensus with respect to political corruption than in relation to other forms of corruption (it is difficult to see that corruption has any intelligible place in classical economics), but even with political corruption there is likely to be variation in the way that public office is conceived, variation in the types of activities which are seen as acceptable or unacceptable on the part of public officials (paying members of the legislature was once seen as risking their corruption – that position in most states has been reversed) and variation in the way that the line is drawn between corruption and activities such as theft, fraud, extortion and malpractice.

While measurement depends on variation, it also depends on that variation being measured against a constant and the difficulty in the measurement of corruption is that the constant is elusive because of the variability in the way in which corruption is conceived. Because there is no consensus on the 'nature' that is corrupted by a certain activity and because there seems to be widely varied cultural expectations concerning the nature and norms of public office, there is no clear 'natural kind' to political corruption that is sufficiently similar across all contexts to provide the basis for a measurement and comparison (or indeed for the development of explanatory frameworks). On this account, whatever corruption measurement measures, it is not going to measure it against a natural standard (in the way one might measure malnutrition, or the incidence of illness, against a standard of health or normal human functioning). That may seem obvious, but there is an increasing tendency to talk of democracy as offering one such natural standard. It is not difficult to see the attractions of this – especially if one believes that there is at least a convergence in standards of what modern democracy entails. But there is a considerable danger that the assumption of convergence leads to the development of norms for democracy that are essentially local to certain Western states and fail to capture the differences and complexities of the local political cultures to which they are exported.

This is not an academic nicety. For example, US assumptions about the nature of political parties, party competition and the electoral process in general are widely divergent from the assumptions that operate in most European states, which have a history of mass-based, solidaristic political parties sharply divided on ideological grounds, in which political contributions are in general made to party funds rather than to individual candidates. That parties are different means that the regulation of party funding has to be tailored to the particular context. Similarly, the US does not have a tradition of Parliamentary or legislative sovereignty (given the existence of the Supreme Court), and recommendations about disclosure and the protection of the rights of those in office which assume a more fundamental set of protections for individuals in the constitution are inappropriate in contexts where the institutional structure and underlying democratic principles are very different. Moreover, what counts as corruption does simply vary. Recent work on the 'embeddedness' of economic and political institutions in the Far East suggest forms of industrial and financial organisation in which the boundaries between political and economic spheres are extremely porous.[5] In one view, this is corrupt – it shuts out foreign competitors, provides privileged access and protection for domestic firms, and leads to a symbiotic relationship between the state, parties and major corporations. Yet, it can equally be seen as an alternative form of economic (and political) organisation with substantial benefits for the domestic economy. Doing business differently is not the same as doing it corruptly and the assumption that there will be a growing convergence on liberal-democratic, constitutional regimes with free-market capitalist economies, is essentially to impose a conception on states whose political and economic organisation is different. Finally, it is crucial that hegemonic states recognise that their own practices might not withstand scrutiny in other societies. Consider the Senate procedures for confirmation of presidential appointees to Federal regulatory boards – procedures that have their legitimacy because they ensure executive accountability.[6] In 1949, Lyndon Johnson chaired the confirmation hearings concerning Leland Olds, the re-nominated Chair of the Federal Power Commission whom Truman sought to confirm for a third term. Seeking to secure the political and financial support of Southern oil and energy interests, Johnson led a devastating attack on the re-nomination hearings (by wielding anti-communist rhetoric) to deny reappointment to Olds. The result was formally and procedurally sound, it was democratic, it was directed against someone with considerable discretionary power and it put energy policy at the mercy of oil, gas and electricity interests for the best part of a decade. Moreover, it did so as part of a concerted effort by Johnson to protect and advance his political interests. This is not an isolated case: the US political system allows certain types of interests, it endorses a degree of political opportunism on the part of its legislators and it takes the satisfying of certain formal procedures as a sufficient condition for the outcome of those procedures to be acceptable and legitimate. Interests are a party to policy making (and to policy blocking) in the US to a huge extent. That other countries manage those relationships differently should not automatically be taken as indicative of their corruption – nor *vice-versa*.

In the face of cultural variability in the norms and expectations governing public office and the variability they introduce into the concept of political corruption, one solution for those wishing to measure corruption is to stipulate a class of events as corrupt and to attempt to identify the relative incidence of those events within the society. (There is an additional, related problem here concerning how one weights information about different societies – for example, size of GDP or per capita GDP – in calculating the significance of corruption. It seems odd to think that such factors have no relevance.)

The attempt to measure the incidence of bribe giving is one such stipulative move. Corruption is identified as the giving of bribes and a comparative rate of bribe paying is then constructed. But it is clear that a society in which decisions are coerced can be more corrupt than one in which decision is accompanied by *ex post* gift giving. Bribe paying indexes will miss that.

The difficulties in finding a baseline for the identification of corruption that has genuinely cross-cultural relevance have led some researchers to look instead for proxies for corruption. Some definitions of corruption certainly encourage such an approach. Klitgaard's formula, for example,[7] that 'corruption = monopoly + discretion – accountability', encourages us to assess the incidence of corruption through an assessment of the amount of monopoly, discretion and lack of accountability in a system. The opacity index works essentially on these lines. Moreover, there is a strong component of this in TI's National Integrity System, and to some extent also in the GRECO reports, the search for functional equivalence in the OECD working party on the International Convention Against Bribery and in some components of the OSI assessment reports on corruption in candidate states for EU accession.[8] These different assessments are not exclusively concerned with proxies but the proxy element enters in as soon as we attempt to use evidence of the presence or absence of formal instruments or particular institutional arrangements for public office as evidence, in and of itself, of corruption. The objections to this way of proceeding are, I think, pretty clear.

1. That I have the opportunity to bribe or to take bribes does not mean that I will bribe or take bribes. The model assumes that public officials and politicians have

no integrity and cannot be trusted to exercise power. Of course, there is something attractive in that characterisation (especially for neoclassical economists who find it difficult to see that markets require structures, institutions and rules which cannot themselves be a function of bargaining between players). But there is also a basic paradox in calling on politics to end politics by using power to eliminate monopoly and discretion – it is basically a version of Juvenal's 'Who guards the guardians' problem. Proxies are, at best, judgments about the causal conditions for corruption; they are not judgments about corruption itself. And, judgments about causal conditions imply a substantially more robust and successful science of politics than currently exists. Moreover, announcing proxies as corruption measurements is misleading; it can be damaging to anti-corruption efforts in states, and it can unfairly impose substantial reputational costs on a state that is institutionally weak, but relatively clean.

2. Klitgaard's model suggests an implicit counter-factual of perfect accountability for all monopoly and discretion. Yet, that is simply to say that we should never trust any political system or public officeholder with any discretion or monopoly. It also suggests that accountability is not itself capable of being used corruptly. Neither proposal is helpful. And, it is especially true that accountability can have detrimental effects – it can be politicised, it can impose stultifying levels of red tape and it can exploit volatile and ill-informed public opinion (consider Johnson's holding of Olds to account).

3. There is an implicit view at work of convergence in modern democratic states – that there is a right way (or a number of right ways) of ordering their political systems so that the potential for corruption is eliminated. That is the principle behind the idea of a National Integrity System.[9] But that view is very naïve about the potential degree of convergence even among Western states (see the earlier comments about party systems).

Alternatives

The definition of corruption is complex and contested. That makes measurement of relative levels of corruption extremely difficult. One conclusion that might be drawn, as a result, is that we should abandon the search for comparative indices of corruption and should stick to country-based studies.

These would allow us to say what corruption related problems exist in a given country, and could also allow an assessment of some of the issues such as its depth, its degree of entrenchment, the extent to which exchanges are largely monetary as opposed to involving fundamental threats to people's lives and sense of security and so on. We could say, if we had a number of such country studies, that on some dimensions country X has a more serious problem than Y, that on others Y has a more serious problem than X and that on still others Z has only minor problems in the areas which affect X and Y, but has a particularly spectacular set of problems in, for example, the area of corporate financial corruption, which X and Y simply do not have.

Constructing this kind of comparative account would start from a rather different position than many existing measures. It begins with the construction of a number of crosscutting dimensions: on the one hand, we need to identify potentially discrete domains of activity in which corrupt practices may develop (police, law-making, administrative action, the judicial process, the political process, relations between the state and the market, market institutions, customs and taxation and so on). On the other hand, we need a set of variables by which we assess the depth of penetration of certain practices, their robustness, the character of the exchanges involved and so on. What cannot be delivered by such an account is a single linear scale for corruption. Nor are we looking at a number of scales – one for corruption, one for the level of violence, one for the degree of political oligarchy, one for economic oligarchy etc. While that route sounds tempting, it fails to acknowledge that these are just different dimensions of corruption within a state, and the assessment of corruption within a state is an assessment that must take account of those various dimensions.

That said, an essential component of such a program would be additional comparative work. One of the concerns which the Bank's BEEPS survey raises is the issue of how far we really are dealing with a transitional situation and how far the kind of data which can be collected in relation to CEE and CIS states could also be collected elsewhere. It may be that there are strong regional patterns of corruption associated with regional path-dependencies; but there may also be important cross-regional patterns which attempt to measure corruption and which we must attempt to assess.

Two forms of corruption assessment, which deserve further attention within the corruption measurement industry, are the GRECO country evaluations and the Working Party on the OECD Anti-Bribery Convention (and their criteria of functional equivalence). In both cases, there is an attempt to produce a country-specific analysis of problems relating to corruption and bribery, while operating with a broader template concerning the conditions under which corruption and bribery occur. Although there is a certain amount of emphasis on legal instruments, some attempt is also made to assess their implementation. Although in both cases, the opportunity for in-depth country analysis is quite sharply limited. OSI's monitoring of CEE candidate states provides a still deeper account of a range of dimensions of corruption, but is regionally restricted (unlike GRECO or OECD). Similarly, country-based reports are also produced by the World Bank and TI (and other regional reports are also attempting to tackle corruption – for example, the State of the Region report for Central America).

The advantage of country-based in-depth reports is that they are able to identify issues which may be particular to states, and (in principle) can undertake further research to assess the character of the political culture and the extent to which there is wide endorsement or condemnation of certain practices and to identify the issues which are central to different participants in the political process.

The importance of placing such work in a more comparative frame is to help identify which aspects of that society and culture are distinctive and which are more widely shared with other societies with different paths.

Any attempt to provide relatively robust claims about the relationship between economic and demographic features of a state and levels of corruption (of which there has been a considerable amount) faces two central problems. One is the problem of small ns[10] (which limit the validity of many statistical instruments). But, the second problem, which arises from the kind of multi-dimensional analysis for corruption for which I have been arguing, is that we have to reject the assumption that it cannot assign constant weights to the different dimensions across different countries. Moving towards the more sensitive and differentiated country-based study, coupled with the development of a range of different corruption dimensions which we should not expect to see consistently weighted or correlated across states and regions, will inevitably reduce the prospect for serious statistical analysis of cross country data and its relation to corruption. That is a loss. The fact that we would have a much better understanding of the nature of corruption within states, and a more sophisticated understanding of the types and dimensions of corruption in the world is, I would suggest, a more than compensatory gain.

Notes

1   On definition see Heidenheimer, A.J. (ed.) (1970), *Political Corruption*, Transaction, New Brunswick; Heidenheimer, Johnston and Levine (eds) (1989), *Political Corruption*, New Brunswick; Heidenheimer and Johnston (eds) (2002), *Political Corruption*, New Brunswick.
2   See World Bank Report (2002), *Anti-Corruption in Transition*, Washington.
3   See Hellman, J. et al. (2000), 'Seize the State, Seize the Day: An Empirical Analysis of State Capture and Corruption in Transition', *World Bank Working Paper*.
4   See Johnston, M. (2002), 'Measuring the New Corruption Rankings: Implications for Analysis and Reform', in Heidenheimer et al., pp. 865–84.
5   Evans, P. (1995), *Embedded Autonomy: States and Industrial Transformation*, Princeton.
6   See Caro, R. (2003), *Master of the Senate*, Knopf, NY.
7   See Klitgaard, R. (1988), *Controlling Corruption*, University of California Press, Berkeley.
8   See for example, www.Greco.coe.int; and Open Society Institute 2002, *Monitoring the EU Accession Process: Corruption and Anti-Corruption Policy*, OSI, Budapest.
9   Pope, J. (2000), *Confronting Corruption: The Elements of a National Integrity System*, Transparency International, Berlin.
10 The validity of statistical instruments improves the larger the set of cases and the numbers in the cells being compared but country-based analysis produces relatively small sets with still smaller cell values that resist testing for significance.

References

Caro, R. (2002), *Master of the Senate*, Alfred Knopf, NY.
Evans, P. (1995), *Embedded Autonomy: States and Industrial Transformation*, Princeton.
Heidenheimer, A.J. et al. (ed.) (1970), *Political Corruption*, Transaction, New Brunswick.
Hellman, J., Jones, G. and Kaufmann, D. (2000), 'Seize the State, Seize the Day: An Empirical Analysis of State Capture and Corruption in Transition', *World Bank Working Paper*.

Johnston, M. (2002), 'Measuring the New Corruption Rankings: Implications for Analysis and Reform', in A.J. Heidenheimer et al., *Political Corruption*, Transaction, New Brunswick.

Klitgaard, R. (1988), *Controlling Corruption*, University of California Press, Berkeley.

Open Society Institute (2002), *Monitoring the EU Accession Process: Corruption and Anti-corruption Policy*, OSI.

Pope, J. (2000), *Confronting Corruption: The Elements of a National Integrity System*, Transparency International.

World Bank (2002), *Anti-Corruption in Transition*, Washington.

Chapter 4

What are We Trying to Measure? Reviewing the Basics of Corruption Definition

A.J. Brown

Introduction

The measurement of corruption, whether directly or indirectly, based on perception or actual incidence, relies on an agreed understanding of 'corruption' itself. However corruption is a word with many meanings, each dependent upon the specific social and political context in which it is used. Over the last 30 years, there has been unprecedented demand for a single, universal understanding of the idea of corruption, capable of spanning international, cultural and religious borders. This demand has come from many quarters. In the 1960s–1980s, many developing countries accepted high levels of official bribery, embezzlement and insider trading almost as if these were conditions of their transition to greater political and economic independence. Western economics and political science recognised these forms of corruption as international phenomena and usually as negative, but also tended to accept them as an inevitable cost of doing economic and political business in a modernising world.

In the 1990s, three triggers arose for a new international debate more directly attacking corruption as a public policy problem. In a period of rapid globalisation, international business became less tolerant of the costs and uncertainties associated with foreign bribery, as reflected in the OECDs recommendations for international anti-bribery efforts in 1994 (Glynn et al., 1997, pp. 16–24). Civil society organisations including Transparency International, founded in 1993, spread a new global message that bribery, embezzlement and insider trading were common problems, in some places worsened by the transition to democratic and economic liberalisation. Thirdly, international financial institutions admitted that corruption was an endemic, pervasive problem in the implementation of aid programs and began identifying anti-corruption reform as a necessary condition of aid and then as an aid objective in its own right. These three trends have been interrelated, sometimes in very obvious ways.

What definition of 'corruption' has this new global discussion been working with? Is it the 'right' definition, and if not, what are the ingredients of a more useful one? This chapter takes as its starting point the familiar 'three-pronged typology' of corruption definitions repeated recently by Heidenheimer and Johnston (2002, pp. 3–14):

- public office-centred definitions;
- market-centred definitions;
- public interest definitions.

In summarising the state of English-language definitions, Heidenheimer and Johnston note the pressure for expansion of this threefold classification to also recognise definitions based on 'public opinion'; and to better deal with emerging priorities such as political party finance abuses. While somewhat ambivalent about the necessity of definitional adjustment, they set out the nature of the continuing typological challenge:

> Analysts of political corruption over the past decades might tend to agree that 'corruption' is a contested concept. Whether it is a *basically* contested concept is less evident. ... The question ... is whether acceptance of additional types of corruption definitions would contribute to solutions, rather than adding further complexity to the analytical problem. In retrospect it seems that the case for a distinct public opnion-based definition has not been irrevocably established.
>
> The presumption that 25 years of varied corruption research could call for a reformulation of the three-pronged typology is reasonable. On the other hand, not much research has been conceptually self-conscious and oriented toward coping with broader cross-language challenges. Most optimal in the new millennium might be an attempt to resynthesise the typology. Conceivably the typology might be reformulated while not expanding the numbers. Although there is no inherent virtue in small numbers, in this case the advocates of conceptual multiplication might be asked to shoulder the burden proving 'need'. (Heidenheimer and Johnston, 2002, p. 13)

Accepting these challenges, this chapter offers a reformulated taxonomy[1] of corruption definitions that might be both conceptually more rigorous and potentially of greater utility in the world of public policy. The motivation is not merely theoretical, since as discussed in the first part of the chapter, the limitations of the existing three-pronged taxonomy seem to be increasingly recognised, to the point of threatening to become a practical barrier to sensible or sustainable reform. The need for more sound, reflexive and relatively clear conceptual frameworks in integrity and corruption research is being highlighted from a variety of quarters and is a challenge some of us are also trying to meet through the current Australian National Integrity System Assessment project (see Brown and Uhr, 2004; more generally, www.griffith.edu. au/centre/kceljag/nisa).

In the first part, I review some of this discussion, highlighting commonalities and differences in current corruption concepts and tracing existing shifts in definitional approach. The fundamental problem, it seems, is that the base 'public office-centred' definition of corruption (abuse of public power for private gain) from which most Western definitions continue to take their starting point, has been interpreted as a wide definition capturing a broad gamut of corrupt behaviour, when it actually captures only a specific cross-section of concerns. The additional categories so far suggested do not help relieve this problem. 'Market-centred' definitions are usually interpreted as no more than economic restatements of 'public office-centred' ones, and 'public interest' and 'public opinion'-based definitions only tend to emphasise the contestability of standards by which behaviour is judged corrupt.

The second part of the paper seeks a way out of this impasse by separating out these two different issues, the breadth (or specificity) of current definitions, and the various sources of standards and values that inform their interpretation and application. The issue of breadth emerges clearly from existing shifts, because in important quarters the recent policy preference has *not* been to extend definitions by adding new, specific categories, but rather to strip the definition of corruption back to more general, holistic fundamentals, on which legislators, law reformers or social change agents might then construct their own, more specific but still consistent variations. Transparency International has moved in this direction; and the analysis here was catalysed by a governance dialogue between Indonesian and Australian scholars, in Bogor in October 2003, which concluded in favour of yet greater generality again. The common theme seems to be a shift away from specific types of office, or organisation, or behaviour, or even standards as the defining characteristic of corrupt behaviour, towards a 'relationship-centred' approach in which corruption can be defined simply as *the abuse of entrusted power*.

How can such excessive generality assist in the 'real-world' fight against specific forms of corruption? The answer suggested here, is that it provides a new anchor for the classification of corruption definitions according to a taxonomy that remains threefold (satisfying Heidenheimer and Johnston's desire for continued simplicity), but makes it easier to place past definitions in context (see Table 4.1).

Table 4.1   Primary taxonomies of corruption definition

New Primary Taxonomy (Relational, Gambetta 2002)	Old Primary Taxonomy
Broad definitions Corruption is the abuse of entrusted power	
Intermediate definitions Corruption is the abuse of entrusted power for private gain	*Market-centred* version of the 'public office'-centred definition
Specific definitions E.g. corruption is the abuse of public/private power for private/personal/unlawful/financial//pecuniary profit/benefit/gain	*Public office-centred* definition (in effect, bribery)
	Public interest-centred
	Public opinion-based etc.

The argument is that by forcing us to focus on the trust relationships that we suspect or know to have been abused, the new taxonomy enables us to more accurately identify the nature of the abuse, the nature and seriousness of damage, the causes and contributing factors, the immediate remedies for stemming such abuse and longer-term systemic responses. This can be considered preferable to an automatic assumption that behaviour deemed damaging or sanctionable in one political setting will necessarily represent a similar problem in others, thus driving institutional reforms in one direction, when more reflexive analysis might identify other more major problems or different root causes.

What of the public interest-centred prong of the old taxonomy? Or its subsequent contenders? The analysis here suggests that a valid reason for halting development of the previous typology was the confusion caused by mixing two different things. Past definitions have come under attack not only because they are failing to capture all behaviour perceived to be corrupt, but because the standards – and sources of standards – underpinning such judgements have also been shifting. Exacting delineation of each and every standard by which any corrupt behaviour might be identified as such, around the world, is a task beyond this chapter – but recent debates do show the importance of a more sophisticated grasp of the range of *sources* for such standards in any given setting. Thus the second part of the chapter concludes that a simple primary taxonomy can usefully be supported by a secondary (and not final) classification based on recognition of these sources. The chapter concludes with the hope that this taxonomic approach may provide a more reflexive framework for understanding and comparing definitions within the 'real' work of legal and institutional reform.

Table 4.2   A secondary taxonomy of corruption definition

Old Primary Taxonomy	New Secondary Taxonomy (Sources of standards/values) (Behavioural, Gambetta 2002)
Public office-centred definitions	Secular legal
	Religious legal
	Moral and/or ethical (including religious but not legal)
Market-centred definitions	Economic
	Institutional
Public interest-centred definitions	Public interest
Public opinion-based definitions	Public opinion
Etc.	Etc.

Defining 'Corruption'

'Corruption' is a word with many meanings, each dependent upon the specific social and political context in which it is used. The fact that this is so, even within the world's many variants of the English language, should provide a salient warning against assumptions that corruption is a universally common concept across all societies and cultures. Introducing modern Western political science definitions, Heidenheimer and Johnston (2002, pp. 6–9) note that the Oxford English Dictionary recognises no less than nine common definitions of corruption, grouped quite differently from the three public policy concepts already reviewed above:

1. Physical – for example, 'the destruction or spoiling of anything, especially by disintegration or by decomposition ...; putrefaction'.
2. Moral – for example, 'perversion or destruction of integrity in the discharge of public duties by bribery or favour; the use or existence of corrupt practices, especially in a state, public corporation etc.'; 'moral deterioration or decay'.
3. The perversion of anything from an original state of purity – for example, 'the perversion of an institution, custom and so forth from its primitive purity'.

This diversity of definitions comes as a salient reminder that everyday language often holds keys to concepts readily forgotten by technical policy disciplines. While prominent, the familiar association between corruption and bribery of public officials is categorised as an issue of moral decay... whereas modern public policy tends to accept bribery as economically rational behaviour, disapproved of more because its costs outweigh its benefits. Similarly, policy concepts of corruption often look to the law to provide guidance as to impermissible behaviour, rather than looking to first or 'primitive' principles to identify when social institutions have been perverted, whether already recognised criminal behaviour or not. By taking each of the primary categories of policy definition identified in the introduction, we can see more clearly why contemporary definitions leave something to be desired, having drifted away from the basic essence of the concept and replaced them with three fragments of the original picture.

Public Office-centred Definitions

Since at least 1931, corruption has often been defined as 'the misuse of public power for private profit' (J.J. Senturia's definition of 'Corruption, Political' in the Encyclopaedia of the Social Sciences, see Theobald, 1990, p. 2). This definition continues to be widely used today (e.g. Lapalombara, 1994; Kaufmann and Siegelbaum, 1997; Vittal, 2001; Collier, 2002). It dominates the World Bank's *Combating Corruption* literature of 1997 and 2000 (see e.g. McCoy, 2001, p. 68, n.16; Sajo, 2003, p. 175) and is the base definition used in the well-known work of Susan Rose-Ackerman, to the extent that this now effectively takes the definition for granted (Rose-Ackerman, 1999, p. 91). Indeed her definition is so specific, that it defines corruption by illegality, 'an illegal payment to a public agent to obtain a benefit that may or may not be deserved in the absence of payoffs' (Rose-Ackerman, 1997/2002, p. 353; 1999, p. 9). This means that in a country that has not criminalised side payments or self-authorised fee collection by public officials, such payments would not constitute corruption, no matter how damaging to society. Is this an adequate general definition of corruption?

In fact, the 'public office definition' does not define corruption, but rather one specific, albeit critically important example of corruption, that is, bribery of public officials, or like offences. This example has dominated public policy for perhaps two reasons, it remains one of the most persistent, pervasive and widespread examples of corruption across many societies over many centuries; and its focus on pecuniary transactions has made it a special focus for recent economic analysis. However the reduction of all understandings of corruption to official bribery has three major problems. First, there are many other known and potential abuses of public office that are also often regarded as corrupt or corrupting, including nepotism and public graft – i.e. direct theft or embezzlement by public officers – which are not captured by the definition (see e.g. Elliott, 1997, p. 178) and are thus proclaimed to 'not constitute corruption' (Jain, 2001, p. 73). Second, by focusing on public office, the definition suggests that no such abuses occur in private business or other areas of social interaction (or if they do, that they are not abuses), identifying corruption as primarily a 'disease' of government. Third, a focus on bribery encourages the somewhat hopeful idea that it might be possible to 'entirely' eliminate corruption, were it not for cost and unacceptable infringements on human rights and freedoms (possibly true of bribery as a contemporary financial crime, but seemingly unlikely for corruption as an entire phenomenon, Pope, 1999, p. 97).

The solutions are not simple. The common answer to a narrow definition based on official bribery, is to extend the same basic definition with long lists of the various behaviours that might constitute abuses of public power (see e.g. Lancaster, 2001). Usually the starting point is to extend from personal financial payments as a corrupt benefit, to recognition that corrupt benefits can also be political advantages or social privileges (e.g. Sung, 2002). Certainly, unless the lists are lengthened, there is real concern that support for anti-corruption efforts will disappear once present anti-bribery campaigns are regarded as complete or passé, leaving unresolved a host of other public corruption issues including 'ethics violations, illegal asset accumulation, violations of procurement regulations, political nepotism, cronyism, campaign finance violations, money laundering, illegal drug transactions, black market activity, freedom of information and many other issues' (McCoy, 2001, pp. 68, 84, 86; Williams and Beare, 1999, p. 116). However as the list grows, it becomes more and more difficult to recall why specific types of behaviour, and specific types of gain are corrupt, and others not; why some are corrupt in some countries, and in others regarded as acceptable.

Even so, the second problem remains. Even if we unbundle public office definitions of corruption, we make no allowance for corruption that lies wholly within the private sector and involve no public office or public property, for example, the sale of client information to organised criminals by corrupt bank officials for a share in burglary profits, or insider trading (Braguinsky, 1996). Rarely do adherents of public office definitions explain why, conceptually, they are confining their discussion to 'the "public sphere"' i.e. wholly within the public sector or at the interface between public and private sectors (e.g. Heywood, 1997, p. 421). More often the fact that corruption is also a feature of private sector activity, and that corruption in both spheres is interconnected, are issues that simply go unstated. One Western author maintains the narrow approach simply because it *is* narrow, 'the topic is already complex, and need not be made even more unwieldy' (Elliott, 1997, p. 178).

The problem of a public-private separation may be familiar enough in Western contexts to be fairly unproblematic, but when linked to modern 'good' governance reform based on certain ideas about the size and value of 'public' and 'private' domains, this definition of corruption becomes fraught with danger. We tend to forget that we focus on *public* power and/or *public* office because the rise of the modern Western administrative state from the late nineteenth and early twentieth centuries made it both possible and necessary to articulate corruption in this way. The 'integrity' of the new administrative regimes relied on a conceptual separation of the personal and official interests of individual office-holders, with *public* office the site of new benchmarks for this integrity as against the *private*, unregulated or 'wild' spheres of social activity where such standards did not necessarily apply. Indeed in the century preceding the Great Depression, the very venality of the private sphere was often presumed in the West to be a necessary/positive good for the generation of 'progress' and its 'corruptness' epitomised why the new administrative state was needed to ensure social balance. As Dobel (1999, p. 130) points out, this notion of corruption as a 'pollution' of the public by the private is no longer necessarily apposite, since 'there is nothing inherently wrong with pursuing personal goals or even self-interest while in office ... the moral problems with sleazy actions lie in the person's failure to limit personal goals to the right context'.

Even when extended, the traditional public office definition thus omits to explain why, or when, the combination of private interests and official duties becomes corrupt. The main effect of the implicit desire for separation is the reinforcement of an ideal of honest, impartial public administration which, according to Theobald, gives Western corruption definitions a 'spurious precision', 'informed too closely by Weber's ideal type of rational-legal bureaucracy' based on a universalism and impersonalism that is, in reality, 'unfamiliar, not to say alien, to many if not most of the societies in the world today' (Theobald, 1990, pp. 3, 8, 11, 73). Little wonder, perhaps, that Western policymakers reverting to this ideal should have continued difficulty with the allowable limits of 'patrimonialism' and/or 'clientelism' as longstanding bases for political rule in many societies (see respectively Lancaster, 1997, pp. 189–90; and Sajo, 2002).

Also naturally problematic is the Western European tendency to presume that the relevant concepts, organisational forms and institutional options for managing the public-private divide begin with European industrial-era bureaucratisation, rather than India in the fourth century BC (Bardhan, 1997), China in the eighteenth century (Park, 1997) or a variety of Islamic settings (Alatas, 1990, pp. 40ff, 118). Reinforcing Theobald's concerns, there is now also basis for revisiting the assumption of individual moral choice that underpins the traditional Western definition, given that while the human factor remains crucial (Alatas, 1990), the assumption that corruption is always a question of choice is quite mythical (Arora, 1993, p. 6). Even in wealthy countries this is increasingly clear; for example, attempts to clean up British public life, in the 1990s, have been criticised as sociologically weak because they remain 'premised on the idea that *individuals* have a choice between acting correctly or incorrectly in situations in which the rules are increasingly "grey"' (Hodgkinson, 1997, p. 34).

What have been the responses to the perceived inadequacy of the public-office definition of corruption? An important recent trend, accompanying the multiplication of the types of private, political or other benefits most likely to clash with public duties, has been effort to broaden out the original definition in a bid to reconnect with the 'essence' of what makes corrupt behaviour corrupt. Michael Johnston once suggested a broader one-line definition operating across public and private sectors, tailored to the growing importance of non-bribery issues, the 'abuse of public roles or resources or the use of illegitimate forms of political influence by public or private parties' (Johnston, 1997, p. 62; see also Ghazanfar, 2000). But what is our agreed reference point for knowing when a particular type of behaviour is abusive or illegitimate? Some of those interested in national integrity systems take a step closer, when they identify corruption as, 'in its simplest terms, the abuse of power, most often for personal gain or for the benefit of a group to which one owes allegiance' (Stapenhurst and Sedigh, 1999). Thus not merely 'public roles or resources' provide the key reference point, but the abuse of 'power' itself. The problem, naturally, is that to identify *any* alleged abuse of power as corruption is to open up the boundaries of the concept to a uselessly subjective extreme. What some may allege to be abusive, others may validly regard as heroic. Between the unhelpfully specific and the hopelessly wide, some key reference points wait to be re-established.

Market-centred Definitions

The survival of the 'three-pronged' taxonomy may owe something to an illusion of balance, the idea that the second prong, at some stage christened 'market-centred', might provide some account of corrupt abuses of private sector and/or market power, as opposed simply to public or government power. Unfortunately, market-centred definitions tend to do no such thing, typically representing an economic description of the same behaviour identified in the above, public office definition. The critical feature of that behaviour – again with official bribery as the overwhelming focus – is the 'income-maximising' behaviour of corrupt public officials (see Heidenheimer and Johnston, 2002, p. 8). As Mark Philp has readily pointed out, while it may be important to *note* market-centred understandings of corruption, the idea that they 'offer an alternative definition is itself conceptually muddled' (Philp, 1997, p. 444; Philp, 2002, p. 50). Rather, they demonstrate the intensity of interest shown by Western economists, particularly since the 1960s, in a concept that had previously been treated in the social sciences as primarily a problem of ethics, morals, law and political science rather than political economy.

Are economists any more content with the public office definition than many contemporary political scientists? The answer is, not necessarily – for example, in 1998 the Director of the International Monetary Fund's Fiscal Affairs Department, Vito Tanzi, endorsed the World Bank's continued use of a definition based on 'abuse of public power for private benefit' as still the 'the most popular and simplest', but went on to point out that indeed, it ignored corruption within the private sector and any corruption not revolving around direct personal benefits (Tanzi, 1998; see also Bardhan, 1997). However economic analyses have had little immediate need to go beyond official bribery as an already sufficiently complex and important problem for theoretical and empirical study. Economic analyses naturally find the pecuniary transactions at the heart of official bribery relatively straightforward to conceptualise, and thus to investigate and measure. All the more so when the payment is already clearly identifiable as 'illegal', as per Rose-Ackerman's approach earlier, saving economists much of the problem of why particular behaviour has been defined as odious because that task has been performed by others. There are also those for whom the specific focus provided by official bribery as the be-all of corruption, or surrogate for other forms, provides clarity for the practical task of attacking at least one major manifestation (see e.g. Sun, 2001, p. 247).

Nevertheless, particularly when translated internationally, all the problems identified above tend to be exacerbated by economic perspectives. The focus on abuses of public power has taken on an additional problem, above and beyond a presumption in favour of particular styles of bureaucratisation – somewhat inconsistently, the suggestion that public bureaucracy is *itself* central to the problem. The market solution to bribery remains wealth creation, explaining the close 1990s association between transnational anti-corruption efforts, the reduction of local barriers to transnational business activity (bribery being one such barrier), and economic reform based on market liberalisation and deregulation (Heywood, 1997, pp. 428–30; see e.g. Elliott, 1997, p. 176; or Rose-Ackerman, 1999 as quoted by Sung, 2002, p. 143, 'a more impersonal society with strong market and public sector institutions'). Once again there are cultural assumptions buried in this approach, since modernising emphases 'on rationality, small family size, [Christian/protestant] achievement, social mobility and universalism' are all given clear priority over traditionalist values of familism, feudal-type stratification or any social systems 'which run counter to those functional for a market economy' (Lipset and Lenz, 2000, p. 123). On these arguments, 'the only effective way' of getting rid of corruption is to 'get rid of the controls and regulations that give rise to corruption opportunities', primarily through conversion of public and communal property into the private property of individuals (Cheung, 1996; cf Rose-Ackerman, 1997/2002, p. 355). Economic reform agents such as the World Bank have defended themselves against such allegations of a 'one size fits all' approach, emphasising their concepts as 'a framework for *self-assessment* of corruption within each country rather than as a device for providing a fixed reform blueprint' (Anticorruption in Transition 2000, p. 54, quoted Sajo, 2003, p. 175); but the reality has been a 'fairly unitary and cohesive discourse' with a focus on the 'effects of corruption on foreign investment, and only a secondary focus on its impact *within* developing countries' (Williams and Beare, 1999, p. 116).

This market-centred interpretation of the problem leaves two further definitional difficulties, apart from neglect of any corruption not directly related to government. First, it again has low sensitivity to problems of official corruption other than bribery, as demonstrated by for example as in Huntington's infamous 1968 predictions:

> Corruption is … a product of modernisation and particularly of the expansion of political consciousness and political participation. The reduction of corruption in the long run requires the organisation and structuring of that participation. Political parties are the principal institution of modern politics which can perform this function …. (Huntington, 1968/2002, p. 262)

The idea that corruption represents a 'transitional phenomenon' on the road to full market liberalisation is now more contested (Whitehead, 2002; Kotkin and Sajo, 2002). However the notion that corruption would somehow be resolved by all countries' liberal democratic 'modernisation' is made particularly quaint by reference to political parties as a corruption solution, when they are today identifiable as one of the greatest causes of public concern (Alatas, 1990, pp. 104–5, 114–15, 154ff; Lapalombara, 1994; Doig and McIvor, 1999). Second, the often unwitting assumption is that corruption problems run deeper in certain (i.e. non-Western and transitional) economies. This assumption stands to perpetuate political and cultural divisions in ways that can only make genuine reform dialogue more difficult. Contrary to the economic theory, there is plausible evidence that leading Western democracies have experienced *increased* corruption challenges in the age of market-based economic reform (Theobald 1990, pp. 164–69; Hodgkinson, 1997; Neild, 2002, pp. 165–206). Consequently destructive cultural stereotypes about endemic tendencies toward corruption, typical of the colonial-era, are not disappearing but rather perhaps being reversed:

> Confidence in 'westernisation' being emblematic of 'modernisation' has (at last) been eroded, but in its place has emerged a vision in which western civilisation is facing a challenge from the morally integral alternatives of Islamic and Asian-capitalist states. In such a scenario, growing corruption and decadence are symptomatic of western civilisation in decline. (Heywood, 1997, p. 435)

While economic versions of the public office definition tend to exacerbate its problems, they do throw a particular light on elements of that definition. Rather than focusing on the abuse of power implicit in official bribery, they focus on the exchange itself and the relationship between the parties involved – including the principal-agent relationship for which a corrupt exchange represents a major 'agency cost'. In this relationship, public officials are meant to act only (or primarily) as agents for a principal; either a superior official or the general taxpaying public, depending on one's view of democracy. As we will see, this quite different focus on relational rather than behavioural elements of corruption is an important step towards an improved taxonomy.

Public Interest Centred Definitions

The third prong of the established taxonomy is usually traced to Carl Friedrich, who argued that corruption was best identified not through technical conflict between official duty and private interest, nor economic explanation of the relationships involved, but when 'damage to the public and its interests' is caused by a responsible office-holder or functionary being induced by monetary or other rewards to take illegitimate actions (Friedrich quoted Heidenheimer and Johnston, 2002, p. 9; Philp, 2002, p. 45). While consistent with bribery, this definition is clearly much broader, since 'all kinds of practices' may potentially contribute to 'a decomposition of the body politic' in this way (Friedrich, 1972/2002, pp. 15–16). This approach builds on the original definition by identifying the clash between private interests and public duty as problematic wherever 'partisanship … challenges statesmanship' by virtue of its concrete effect (Werlin, 1994; see also Hodgkinson, 1997; Werlin, 2002).

As with the characterisation of corruption as a simple abuse of power, however, it becomes an open question as to when the 'public interest' is to be judged as having been damaged, as opposed to furthered. Consequently most attempts to make the definition more tangible have foundered on the different benchmarks for judging matters that may be politically very subjective. For example Meny advances a concept of 'the general interest' as a standard, but ultimately falls back on the 'clandestine' or covert nature of corrupt behaviour as the only sure indicator that 'the public rules of law and ethics' have been violated (Meny, 1996, p. 313). Such an approach to defining the public interest scarcely accounts for corruption that everyone knows is occurring, but is powerless to stop. Similarly, Deflem looks to sidestepping of 'the legally prescribed procedure to regulate the action' as a reference point for establishing that the public interest has been breached, which does not account for situations where officeholders are bribed to make certain that which was only possible (Deflem, 1995, p. 248). Obviously, it is not enough to use the law as a guide (Lui, 1996), given all we know about the gaps between social, political and legal mores, and what communities consider 'wrong' as opposed to 'unlawful' (Gorta and Forell, 1995). Moreover it can be difficult to establish clearly that 'damage' to the public has occurred, such as in the case of 'institutional corruption' where power is abused simply for official or political gain (see Dennis Thomson, as reviewed by Johnston, 1996, pp. 331–33; Philp, 2002, pp. 42–44); or 'noble cause corruption' where the result is ostensibly in the public interest, but the methods depart from proper process (e.g. police fabricating evidence to ensure the conviction of someone accurately believed to have committed an offence).

As noted in the introduction, another suggested method of crystalling the public interest is by reference to 'public opinion' – suggested as a fourth definitional approach by some, but resisted by others (Heidenheimer and Johnston, 2002, p. 10; Gardiner, 1993/2002, pp. 10–36). Public interest and public opinion may indeed be argued to be quite different things, but for present purposes they have the same problem of providing an unhelpfully subjective, shifting and culturally variable platform for assessing when power has been harmfully abused, as opposed to used positively.

In any case, a 'public interest' or 'public opinion' test still shares similar problems with the approaches above, if used as the basis for transferring a template of governance norms from one society to another. It makes little difference which way the norms are being transferred – norms derived from 'western views of politics' may simply not fit mass concepts of the public interest in other settings (Philp, 2002, pp. 45, 47–48), while standards of public life in some non-Western contexts may be too high for Western institutions to easily accept (for example, Chinese traditions suggesting that mere bureaucratic negligence occasioning harm to the general interests of society should receive equivalent moral censure to deliberate bribery, see Park, 1997; Sun, 2001, p. 248). Even when public norms and standards of conduct have a superficial universality, the fact remains that in *any* society, the only truly reliable means of identifying the standards that define corruption is through detailed ethnographic description, of which comparatively little has been done (Gupta, 1995, p. 388, n.44). Some time ago, while adhering to the basic public-office definition, Johnston concluded that corruption was necessarily 'a politically contested or unresolved concept', which could only be defined in context, according to 'the legal *or* social standards constituting a society's system of public order' (Johnston, 1996, pp. 331, 333; 1997, p. 62; also Doig and McIvor, 1999). In many respects, therefore, public interest approaches ultimately tend to mitigate against any universal definition, suggesting that appearances of international consensus on the nature of corruption as a policy problem may be more illusory than much of the Western literature suggests.

More Definitions Needed ... or Less?

For some, the inadequacy of the existing English-language definitional framework indeed provides an excuse to abandon the exercise altogether. Some argue that in 'the real world, when corruption reaches endemic proportions, it seems to matter less that an agreement be reached on what it is, than that there is radical, innovative thinking about how it can be stopped' (Bull, 1997, p. 182). Beyond the well-described area of official bribery, however, how can we stop a problem that we have not been able to collectively identify? How do we even know when we have been successful?

The conceptual problem at the heart of the difficulty, according to Barry Hindess, is that although corruption prevents, undermines or reroutes conduct as it is meant to have happened, we lack a universally satisfying concept of the latter against which suspicions or intuitions of corruption can be applied (Hindess, 1997). To be clear about what is wrong, we need a clearer idea of what would have been right. Philp agrees, but concludes there is no reason to expect any such universal approach to ever be found:

> the term corruption is not in itself problematic... the problem arises in the application of this to politics. Definitional problems are legion because there is a hardly a general consensus on the 'naturally sound condition of politics'. ... One line definitions of political corruption are inherently misleading because they generally obscure the extent to which the concept and its components are rooted in ways of thinking about the distinctive

character of public office [to say nothing of private office], and the distinctive ends to which political activity is directed. (Philp, 1997, pp. 445–46; 2002, pp. 51–52; also Heywood, 1997, p. 422)

Accordingly Williams (1999) suggests that the search for an 'all-purpose definition ... is futile' for comparative purposes, reminding us that while it is important to be clear about what we mean, it is not compulsory, and may not be desirable, to adhere rigidly to only one meaning. And Moran concludes that there is no realistic alternative to studying corruption using a '"moving target" approach ... in order to situate it in context ... and to avoid the tortuous attempt to develop a single definition of corruption, a task that, like the attempt to define class, is unrealisable' (Moran, 2001, p. 380).

On these analyses, we should simply stop talking about corruption and instead refer with greater specificity to the particular problems, behaviours or offences with which we are concerned in a given context. Unfortunately this does not seem to deal with the very real problem of explaining the inadequacy of the existing generic concept, with reference to one that would have been better; nor address the continuing imprecise state of the *realpolitik* – or *realgeopolitik* – of international standard-setting on issues of corruption and governance reform. Given the pervasiveness and ubiquity of the term, it would seem extremely disappointing if there was no prospect of a more satisfying, overall definitional approach. This is where existing shifts in Western definitions, and a step outside Western definitions into other contexts, may yield some hope.

Corruption as the Abuse of Entrusted Power: Lessons from Bogor

The Essence of the Concept

This chapter takes its hope for a more satisfying definitional approach from four sources, all of which point to the reestablishment of some clarity around the 'essence' of corruption as a social science and public policy concept. What is important is not whether any of what is suggested here is particularly 'new', but rather the clarificatory trends that already seem to be emerging from an obviously inadequate state of affairs. Whether the taxonomy that best flows from these trends is that suggested at the outset, is a secondary question hopefully to be further debated.

The first source of hope is pressure among policy communities for a broader definition than the original 'public office' one, as opposed to its simple reformulation by different disciplines. The recognition that corruption is fundamentally about the abuse of power provides the leaping-off point. But to return to an earlier question, what types of power? A highly symbolic answer has now been presented by Transparency International, the global non-government anti-corruption coalition founded in 1993, which, within its first decade, recast its one-line definition of corruption from the original official bribery definition, to something much broader, *the abuse of entrusted power for private gain* (see Pope, 2000). The adjustment of 'public' to 'entrusted' has a complex history, related to the fact that TI has attracted more than its share of criticism for some of its approaches. Not least among these was the impression caused by the Corruption Perception Index that only governments were to blame for corruption, not the businesses seeking to bribe them. TI is sometimes even inaccurately blamed for inventing the public office definition in the first place (Werlin, 2002) and critical analysis of the implications of TI's approaches remains wise (Hindess, 2004). Nevertheless, by meeting head-on the need for expansion of the public office definition of corruption to cover related and equivalent non-public-office behaviour, TI has reopened the door to a base concept at the root of corruption definition. Not all power (public or private), when abused, causes us to cry, 'corrupt!'. The aspect central to the identification of corruption is the fact that the power was not the officeholder's to abuse at will, but rather a power held and wielded 'on trust'.

The second source of hope, underpinning this chapter, is the positive results of a governance dialogue held on this very issue between Australian and Indonesian social scientists, in Bogor (West Java) in October 2003. Funded by the Open Society Institute, the dialogue was one of a series between the author's institution and Indonesia's national Islamic university (UIN) with collaborators from elsewhere in Australia and Indonesia.[2] Faced with the option of throwing out the term 'corruption' as sociologically and empirically useless for cross-cultural purposes, the dialogue group searched for the essence of its shared meaning and found it in a definition even broader than TI's revised definition (which was noted as a definite improvement). The Bogor definition of corruption was simply, *the abuse of entrusted power*. The continuing deficiency of the improved TI definition, it was felt, was that by maintaining an equal focus on 'private gain' as a defining characteristic of the problem, one again confronted the issue that individualistic notions of pecuniary or similar benefit are not necessarily at the core of some major corruption problems. 'Political gain' must also immediately be added and then other types of behaviour, possibly ad infinitum, in a manner that continues to subjectivise and muddy the root concept. The Bogor definition consciously emphasises that the essence of the idea lies simply in our ability to identify that power has been entrusted, in socially recognisable ways (for example, in ways that a Western lawyer would identify *ex post facto* as a 'constructive trust') – but then abused. The character of the abuse is a secondary issue, given that its types and forms clearly change, and given that this change is guaranteed ever to continue.

The third source of hope is that this focus on 'entrusted power' as the essence of the concept is also supported by the more useful fundamental insights of the economic interpretations of the public office definition, reviewed above. By focusing on the principal-agent relationship ruptured by corruption such as bribery, economic interpretations provide a reminder that it is not so much the substantive behaviour that concerns us as its inconsistency with the relationship between the original source of power and those to whom they have entrusted it (Johnston 1996; see also Lancaster and Montinola, 1997, p. 190, n.23). The advantage of this focus is that it restores a more universal and less contestable notion of 'public interest', extrapolated from these relationships rather than presented as a fixable standard of substantive behaviour:

> the PAC [principal-agent-client] approach makes room for a notion of the public interest in the form of the principal's interests. Even if it is … 'an unreasonable assumption' to

equate the two, the PAC approach does focus more directly on the public interest and mechanisms of accountability as elements of the political and institutional setting, rather than attempting (as did Freidrich) to load those issues onto our assessment of individual actions themselves. (Johnston, 1996, pp. 325–26, quoting R.E. Klitgaard)

Of course, the principal-agent-client relationships of keenest interest to economists may also be construed very narrowly, based on presumptions that no agent will ever behave entirely altruistically but will *always* be motivated towards maximising private gain. This precept continues to support arguments that because it is natural self-maximising behaviour, corruption can theoretically be positive (e.g. Lui's 1996 argument that corruption can be 'an optimal response to market distortions and may improve allocative efficiency'). Perhaps more importantly, the factors noticed by economics as likely to influence principal-agent relationships tend to be somewhat oversimplified – for example Szanto (1999) calculates that an agent will become corrupt whenever his or her 'net benefit' from corruption exceeds the net benefit of being 'honest', defined entirely in terms of two elements, salary and 'the moral satisfaction resulting from remaining honest'. This disregards a vast array of other positive and negative social, political and institutional factors that bear upon the likely outcome. Nevertheless, the focus remains usefully on the relationship that stands to be corrupted.

Finally, while the presence of, and offence against, a relationship of political trust has long been associated with concepts of corruption (see Theobald, 1990, p. 44), its centrality to the concept has recently begun to re-emerge with greater clarity in sociology and political science. A focus on trust is not without its difficulties, as noted by Philp (2002, p. 42) who has at times identified the 'violation of the trust placed in [a public official] by the public' as a defining characteristic of official bribery, but sees a basic problem in the fact that 'the materials from which such trust is manufactured are often the very things which [formal] accountability mechanisms regard as corrupt – local networks, clientelism, and personal loyalties and friendships' (Philp, 2001, p. 357; see similarly Sung, 2002, p. 142). However, lifted away from presumptions about the automatic incompatibility of private interests and public duties, or preferences for an impersonal universalism over the ongoing reality of particularised human contact, the problem ostensibly created by the basic personalism inherent in concepts of trust tends to recede. Indeed somewhere between entirely personal-subjective and formal-institutionalised concepts of trust lie the political and sociological concepts of trust as the 'glue' of effective social functioning:

> To see trust as a modality of action as central to the understanding of politics is certainly not to commend a strategically inept credulity or a sentimental misconstruction of the intelligence, ability, or benignity of the great… Over considerable areas of the world, however, it is now reasonable to believe that establishing or sustaining a social frame that facilitates human flourishing does depend upon establishing and sustaining structures of government and responsibility which in some measure merit and earn trust. (Dunn, 1988/2000, pp. 75–80; see also Bouckaert and Van de Walle, 2003, p. 340)

Without necessarily presupposing a particular type of political regime (e.g. democratic, contractarian, communitarian, religious), this concept begins to fill the need identified earlier by Hindess – the need for a better sense of how we want the conduct of the powerful to be discharged, in order to be able to identify when that conduct has instead been corrupted. It is perhaps no surprise that Diego Gambetta, being such a close student of trust (Gambetta, 1988/2000), would approach corruption in these terms, but the logic of his approach is as powerful as it is helpful in explaining why corruption remains such a pervasive, regenerating problem in modern democratic societies:

> Corruption is parasitic on the existence of trusting relations; corruption corrupts first and foremost the trust between [a Truster, T] and [a Fiduciary], and, by implication, between T and whoever else trusts T's rules of allocation. It follows that *the greater the number of trusting relations, the greater is the potential for corruption.* A society that is more corrupt in absolute terms is not, therefore, necessarily worse than a society that is less corrupt, in that lower levels of corruption may result from fewer opportunities and greater lack of trust than from good behaviour. (Gambetta, 2002, p. 54; see also Sajo, 2003, p. 176)

Over an even longer period, one of the world's leading sociologists of corruption has consistently maintained the concept of entrusted power at the heart of his working definition of corruption, in similar terms to those later adopted by Transparency International, *the abuse of trust in the interest of private gain* (Alatas, 1990; see also Heywood, 1997, pp. 425–26). While corruption can have various characteristics, according to Syed Hussein Alatas it is a critical feature that 'any form of corruption is a betrayal of trust' (Alatas, 1999, pp. 7–9). While agreeing that 'the nucleus of the corruption phenomenon' has always been bribery or similar behaviour, he reinforces the validity of a broader and more thorough definitional exercise since 'failure to make the distinction between the different types of corruption and to place them in their proper evaluative context only leads to confusion and time-wasting' (Alatas, 1990, p. 3). While retaining the criterion of private gain in his definition, Alatas emphasises this betrayal of a trust as the 'essence of corruption', and as generalisable internationally because the betrayal of trust is 'rejected by the universal morality of [hu]mankind in its daily life' (Alatas, 1990, p. 10):

> Every society has a concept of the personal and collective. As long as this distinction is made corruption can take place. In a society without private ownership, with no cash economy and without division of labour, there can still be corruption but this will not involve the exchange of wealth or property. Corruption is similar to the concept of authority. The concept of a significant social phenomenon always has universal meaning, the core of which persists through the ages. It is the related, situational manifestations, peripheral to the core, that change with time and condition. (Alatas, 1990, p. 109)

It seems somewhat fitting, if not inevitable, that such clear definitional guidance should have been available all along, since the late 1960s when Alatas wrote his first edition; that it should be a definition based not in politics, law or economics, but sociology; and that it should come from outside the West.

Differentiating between Relationships, Behaviours and Standards

How does the rediscovered 'essence' of the concept of corruption help us with a new definitional taxonomy? Clearly such a taxonomy is still required, because even if essential, the definition of corruption as *the abuse of entrusted power* (to use the Bogor approach) is still very general. Its advantage lies in being a better first anchor for any taxonomy from which further explication can then swing. By contrast with public office-centred, market-centred, or public interest-centred approaches, this general definition is fundamentally *relationship-centred definition*. It requires the analyst to conceptualise a given problem with reference to the express, implied or constructive terms of the trust which *should* dictate how power is exercised, in order to then identify whether and how that trust has been breached. The notion of trust alludes directly to relationships and some kind of agreement about the terms of engagement or relating. Judgments as to breach then rest on a second tier of considerations, relating specific types of behaviour to specific social, political or legal standards.

The second key step in arriving at an improved approach, therefore, may not just be to identify a more 'essential' definition, but to separate out the mix of definitional issues lumped together in the old three-pronged taxonomy. As Tables 4.1 and 4.2 suggest, above, this separation may be consistent with Gambetta's (2002) diagnosis of the properties of corruption as being both 'behavioural' and 'relational' – the latter in terms of the trust relationship, and the former in terms of specific behaviours identified as breaching it.

Table 4.1, therefore, both boils down and extends the existing taxonomy, recasting it around a simple continuum from general to specific representations of the relational properties at the heart of the corruption concept. The old 'public interest' category of definition drops off, however, because it is not primarily a relational concept, but something different – referring directly to the standards by which we might judge behaviour to have breached the trust relationship. While specific behaviours are, and ever will be, an ever expanding, contracting and shifting list, what remains important from this is more explicit acknowledgement of the range of standards, or sources of standards, that we use in different settings to make that judgment. Greater clarity about when we are shifting and mixing these standards may ease the path to more 'objective' (or at least agreed) understandings of when and why specific behaviours are being judged as corrupt. Australian experience suggests this would have some benefit, as an alternative to a lawyerly delineation of the many types of behaviour that do (in practice) or might (conceivably) represent sufficient abuses of entrusted power to be considered actionable or morally reprehensible, which officeholders will then happily use to explain why their particular act of corruption action falls outside those technically delineated offences.

Contrary to assumptions that only clear pre-existing legal standards are relevant to identifying corruption, it is clear that any or all of existing legal, ethical, moral, normative or religious standards might be used to interpret when the integrity of entrusted power had been breached. It is also not necessarily illegitimate for this to be an *ex post facto* process rather than an interpretation of behaviour against pre-existing rules, in a classic instrumental legal-rational fashion. Arguably, significant advances in the standard of public behaviour can only ever occur when a new standard is articulated, rather than existing legal standards fully enforced (by definition usually impossible). In Australia, this was the lesson of the 1992 Greiner-Metherell affair and remains an abiding lesson of the demise of Queensland's Bjelke-Petersen era in 1989 – in both cases, the dominant political leaderships felt themselves to have been judged not 'fairly' against the standards of their own time, but 'unfairly' against new ones (see Philp, 1997; 2002, pp. 53–54. This is consistent with international evidence that technical economic, legal or institutional responses in themselves are never likely to be enough to drive anti-corruption reform, but rather that standards will only ever truly shift when the impetus for doing so has a deeper popular or cultural base (Arora, 1993, p. 19).

The eight types of standard already commonly in use, delineated in Table 4.2, are not final and are reasonably self-explanatory. The list runs somewhat arbitrarily from the more 'objective' or explicit sources of standards, to those that might be regarded as increasingly likely to be contested notwithstanding their obvious validity (indeed, inevitability). The differentiation between *secular-legal* and *religious-legal* standards is informed by the Bogor discussion and arises wherever a discernable system of enforceable religious law exists alongside or in relationship with the secular legal systems that now dominate most states. *Economic* standards of corruption are worth differentiating, because their primary point of reference may well be the 'integrity' of markets and economic activity judged by economic rules that, while clearly valid within themselves, may or may not have a close relationship to other standards or concepts. *Institutional* concepts of corruption recognise that the integrity of legally or morally prescribed processes may be being damaged, even if the damaging behaviour is itself not illegal, not normally regarded as immoral, or is even well motivated.

Finally, *public interest* and *public opinion* standards are worth differentiating because in political and sociological terms they have quite different sources – claims to public interest usually being defined through processes of debate driven or controlled by particular elites, sectional interests or institutions such as the media, while public opinion is usually recognised as mass phenomena measured in particular ways (from elections to polling to rigorous social science research). Moreover 'public opinion' standards for the identification and rejection of corruption need not be merely a reference to democratic institutions on the dominant secular, liberal representative, universalist model. In Bogor, Professor Fadhil Lubis argued that, in moderate Indonesian Islam, the primary trust relationship that must be honoured by the powerful is with God rather than with the people, but that the people's well-being is of such paramount priority to God that the people's will constitutes a legitimate surrogate on such issues – it being better for the powerful to respond to the anger of the *ulama* (religious officers), or failing them the *ummah* itself (Muslim nation or polity), than for the *ummah* to have wait for the powerful to experience the direct anger of God. Lubis entreats Muslims concerned about corruption to remember 'God's warning in the Qur'an':

Verily, God will not change the condition of a nation, until they have changed themselves. (quoted Lubis, 2003, p. 13)

If there is a single advantage to the new definitional approach, it is to force the enquirer/reformer to more clearly articulate *within social and political context* why unwanted behaviour is undesirable – what fundamental social values and processes it breaches or undermines – before effort can be made to measure it or any significant reform effort made to change it. Of course, the approach has its own limitations, mainly the difficulty of categorising which types of entrusted power are or are not regarded as sufficiently important to be brought within the broad definition. For example, there is no question in Australia that sexual exploitation of a consent-age student by a teacher, when not criminal, represents a breach of a relationship based on entrusted power which is sufficiently recognised to fall within the broad definition – a bigger corruption risk than, for example, that of parents or students bribing teachers for improved marks. However, although we usually regard *parental* sexual exploitation of the trust of a consent age child as even more socially and morally anathematic, we would rarely categorise it as a 'corruption' problem. Similarly, in the commercial world we recognise practices such as insider trading, fraud and undisclosed financial dealings between shareholders, directors and managers to be corrupt. However misleading and deceptive conduct towards *consumers* is unlikely to be considered 'corrupt' even when it represents a breach of a socially recognised form of trust (for example when legally actionable both civilly and criminally), because the social expectation is more that companies should face the consequences when caught 'lying' than that they should never be permitted to push the boundaries of 'truth'. Perhaps, however, the new definition provides some new departure points for considering these dilemmas.

Conclusion: A Reformulated Taxonomy?

The attempted reformulation of the definitional taxonomy in Tables 4.1 and 4.2 may perhaps be regarded as overly simplistic, obvious, vague and, certainly, its fundamental principles are not new. Rather, it seeks to capture an evolution already underway, in which a range of debates spanning political science, law, economics and ethical perspectives are seeking a new reformulation of fundamental principles from which to work. Prominent among the demands for this reformulation is the realisation that today, any attempt to define corruption across cultural, social and political borders, whether for research or reform purposes, has to deal more actively with the complex problem of achieving sufficient generality and specificity at one and the same time. Perhaps the most practical utility of the proposed approach, over the old 'three-pronged typology' reproduced by Heidenheimer and Johnston, is that it forces close study of the attitudes and practices surrounding concepts of corruption within their own context, based around identification of the relevant trust relationships and the practices are perceived as abusing them. This necessarily increases the likelihood that responses to perceived corruption problems will be custom-designed to those problems, rather than imported as templates developed for corruption problems that may appear comparable, but are not actually necessarily the same, or of the same order, in other contexts. The hope underpinning the new primary taxonomy is that it may prove beneficial to generalise where we can generalise at the right level, finding and striking a genuinely common theme. The hope behind the secondary taxonomy is that it can provide a flexible matching path to the specificity needed to drive concrete political, legal and institutional action. A major problem underpinning lack of practical progress in lifting the quality of public life in many countries is the prevalence of 'reform proposals that emphasise the same factors everywhere, and thus do not readily fight anywhere' (Johnston in Quah, 2003, p. 244). The intention here has been to show the potential feasibility of constructing a definitional approach to corruption that can be *recognised* everywhere, but forces researchers and reform proponents to bed their analysis deeply in the specific social context with which they are concerned before they actually try to *do* anything about it.

Notes

1   'Taxonomy' is used rather than typology because the former is the conventional scientific term for a classification system, whereas strictly speaking, 'typology' means the study of such systems and their method of construction.
2   The Open Society Institute-funded governance dialogue on Accountability, Transparency and Corruption was held in October 2003, at Bogor, West Java, between the Indonesian Centre for the Study of Islam and Society (Pusat Pengkajian Islam dan Masyarakat – PPIM), a centre of the State Islamic University (Universitas Islam Negeri – UIN), Syarif Hidayatullah, Jakarta, Indonesia; and the Key Centre for Ethics Law Justice and Governance (KCELJAG), Griffith University, Nathan, Brisbane, Australia. I am indebted to the participants for the discussion there, particularly Tunku Abdul Aziz, Jamhari Mukraf, Fadhil Lubis, Fuad Jabali, Ismat Ropi, Azyumardi Azra, Tim Lindsey, Barry Hindess, Manu Barcham, Robyn Lui and Theresa Chataway. I am also deeply indebted to Carmel Connors for subsequent research assistance and of course to Charles Sampford. Somewhat dangerously, however, the interpretation of the dialogue given here is my own.

References

Alatas, S.H. (1990), *Corruption, Its Nature, Causes and Functions*, Avebury, Aldershot.
Alatas, S.H. (1999), *Corruption and The Destiny of Asia. Malaysia*, Prentice Hall and Simon and Schuster.
Arora, D. (1993), 'Conceptualising the Context and Contextualising the Concept: Corruption Reconsidered', *Indian Journal of Public Administration*, vol. 39, pp. 1–19.
Bardhan, P. (1997), 'Corruption and Development: A Review of Issues', *Journal of Economic Literature*, vol. 35, no. 3, pp. 1320–46.
Bouckaert, G. and Van de Walle, S. (2003), 'Comparing measures of citizen trust and user satisfaction as indicators of "good governance": difficulties in linking trust and satisfaction indicators', *International Review of Administrative Sciences*, vol. 69, no. 3, pp. 329–43.

Braguinsky, S. (1996), 'Corruption and Schumpterian Growth in Different Economic Environments', *Contemporary Economic Policy*, vol. 14, no. 3, pp. 14–25.

Brown, A.J. and Uhr, J. (2004), *Integrity Systems, Conceiving, Describing, Assessing*, Australasian Political Studies Association (paper accepted for programme and submitted for refereeing), Adelaide.

Bull, M.J. and Newell, James L. (1997), 'New Avenues in the Study of Political Corruption', *Crime, Law and Social Change*, vol. 27, pp. 169–83.

Cheung, S.N.S. (1996), 'A Simplistic General Equilibrium Theory of Corruption', *Contemporary Economic Policy*, vol. 14, no. 3, pp. 1–6.

Collier, M.W. (2002), 'Explaining Corruption: An Institutional Choice Approach', *Crime, Law and Social Change*, vol. 38, pp. 1–32.

Deflem, M. (1995), 'Corruption, Law, and Justice: A Conceptual Clarification', *Journal of Criminal Justice*, vol. 23, no. 3, pp. 243–58.

Dobel, J.P. (1999), *Public Integrity*, Johns Hopkins University Press, Baltimore.

Doig, A. and McIvor, S. (1999), 'Corruption and its Control in the Developmental Context: An Analysis and Selective Review of the Literature', *Third World Quarterly*, vol. 20, no. 3, pp. 657–76.

Dunn, J. (1988/2000), 'Trust and Political Agency', in D. Gambetta (ed.), *Trust: Making and Breaking Cooperative Relations*, Basil Blackwell 1988; electronic edition 2000, Department of Sociology, University of Oxford, <http://www.sociology.ox.ac.uk/papers>, pp. 73–93.

Elliott, K.A. (1997), 'Corruption as an International Policy Problem: Overview and Recommendations', in K.A. Elliott (ed.), *Corruption and the Global Economy*, Institute for International Economics, Washington DC, pp. 175–233.

Friedrich, C. (1972/2002), 'Corruption Concepts in Historical Perspective', in A.J. Heidenheimer and M. Johnston (eds), *Political Corruption: Concepts and Contexts*, Transaction Publishers, New Jersey, pp. 15–23.

Gambetta, D. (ed.) (1988/2000), *Trust: Making and Breaking Cooperative Relations*, Basil Blackwell, Oxford 1988; electronic edition 2000 Department of Sociology, University of Oxford, <http://www.sociology.ox.ac.uk/papers>.

Gambetta, D. (2002), 'Corruption: An Analytical Map', in S. Kotkin and A. Sajo (eds), *Political Corruption in Transition: A Skeptic's Handbook*, Central European University Press, Budapest, pp. 33–56.

Gardiner, J. (1993/2002), 'Defining Corruption', in A.J. Heidenheimer and M. Johnston (eds), *Political Corruption: Concepts and Contexts*, New Jersey, Transaction Publishers, pp. 25–40.

Ghazanfar, S.M. and May, Karen S. (2000), 'Third World Corruption: A Brief Survey of the Issues', *The Journal of Social, Political, and Economic Studies*, vol. 25, no. 3, pp. 351–69.

Glynn, P. and Kobrin, S.J. et al. (1997), 'The Globalization of Corruption', in K.A. Elliott (ed.), *Corruption and the Global Economy*, Institute for International Economics, Washington DC, pp. 7–27.

Gorta, A. and Forell, S. (1995), 'Layers of Decision: Linking Social Definitions of Corruption and Willingness to Take Action', *Crime, Law and Social Change*, vol. 23, pp. 315–43.

Gupta, A. (1995), 'Blurred Boundaries: The Discourse of Corruption, the Culture of Politics, and the Imagined State', *American Ethnologist*, vol. 22, no. 2, pp. 375–402.

Heidenheimer, A.J. and Johnston, M. (eds) (2002), *Political Corruption: Concepts and Contexts*, Transaction Publishers, New Jersey.

Heywood, P. (1997), 'Political Corruption: Problems and Perspectives', *Political Studies*, vol. 45, no. XLV, pp. 417–35.

Hindess, B. (1997), 'Democracy and Disenchantment', *Australian Journal of Political Science*, vol. 32, no. 1, pp. 79–93.

Hindess, B. (2004), *International Anti-Corruption as a Program of Normalisation*, Occasional Paper to Political Science Program, Research School of Social Sciences, Australian National University, Canberra, 9 June 2004.

Hodgkinson, P. (1997), 'The Sociology of Corruption, Some Themes and Issues', *Sociology*, vol. 31, no. 1, pp. 17–36.

Huntington, S.P. (1968/2002), 'Modernisation and Corruption', in A.J. Heidenheimer and M. Johnston (eds), *Political Corruption: Concepts and Contexts*, New Jersey, Transaction Publishers, pp. 253–63.

Jain, A.K. (2001), 'Corruption: A Review', *Journal of Economic Surveys*, vol. 15, no. 1, pp. 71–121.

Johnston, M. (1996), 'The Search for Definitions: The Vitality of Politics and the Issues of Corruption', *International Social Science Journal*, vol. 48, no. 3, pp. 321–35.

Johnston, M. (1997), 'Public Officials, Private Interests, and Sustainable Democracy: When Politics and Corruption Meet', in K.A. Elliott (ed.), *Corruption and the Global Economy*, Institute for International Economics, Washington DC, pp. 61–82.

Kaufmann, D. and Siegelbaum, P. (1997), 'Privatization and Corruption in Transition Economies', *Journal of International Affairs*, vol. 50, no. 2, pp. 419–59.

Kotkin, S. and Sajo, A. (eds) (2002), *Political Corruption in Transition: A Skeptic's Handbook*, Central European University Press.

Lancaster, T.D. and Montinola, Gabriella R. (1997), 'Towards a Methodology for the Comparative Study of Political Corruption', *Crime, Law and Social Change*, vol. 27, pp. 185–206.

Lancaster, T.D. and Montinola, Gabriella R. (2001), 'Comparative Political Corruption: Issues of Operationalization and Measurement', *Studies in Comparative International Development*, vol. 36, no. 3, pp. 3–28.

Lapalombara, J. (1994), 'Structural and Institutional Aspects of Corruption', *Social Research*, vol. 61, no. 2, pp. 325–51.

Lipset, S.M. and Lenz, G.S. (2000), 'Corruption, Culture and Markets', in L.E. Harrison and S.P. Huntington (eds), *Culture Matters: How Values Shape Human Progress*, Perseus/Basic Books.

Lubis, N.A.F. (2003), *Muslim Fight Against Corruption: some Bases in Islamic Criminal Law*, Islamic-Western Dialogue on Transparency, Accountability and Corruption, Bogor.

Lui, F.T. (1996), 'Three Aspects of Corruption', *Contemporary Economic Policy*, vol. 14, no. 3, pp. 26–29.

McCoy, J.L. and Heckel, Heather (2001), 'The Emergence of a Global Anti-Corruption Norm', *International Politics*, vol. 38, pp. 65–90.

Meny, Y. (1996), '"Fin de siecle" Corruption: Change, Crisis and Shifting Values', *International Social Science Journal*, vol. 48, no. 3, pp. 309–20.

Moran, J. (2001), 'Democratic transitions and forms of corruption', *Crime, Law and Social Change*, vol. 36, pp. 379-393.

Neild, R. (2002), *Public Corruption: The Dark Side of Social Evolution*, Anthem Press, London.

Park, N.E. (1997), 'Corruption in Eighteenth-century China', *The Journal of Asian Studies*, vol. 56, no. 4, pp. 967ff.

Philp, M. (1997), 'Defining Political Corruption', *Political Studies*, vol. 45, pp. 436–62.

Philp, M. (2001), 'Access, Accountability and Authority: Corruption and the Democratic Process', *Crime, Law and Social Change*, vol. 36, pp. 357–77.

Philp, M. (2002), 'Conceptualizing Political Corruption', in A.J. Heidenheimer and M. Johnston (eds), *Political Corruption: Concepts and Contexts*, Transaction Publishers, New Jersey, pp. 41–57.

Pope, J. (1999), 'Elements of a Successful Anticorruption Strategy', in R. Stapenhurst and S.J. Kpundeh (eds), *Curbing Corruption: Toward a Model for Building National Integrity*, Economic Development Institute, World Bank, Washington DC, pp. 97–104.

Pope, J. (2000), *Confronting Corruption: The Elements of a National Integrity System (The TI Source Book)*, Transparency International, Berlin and London.

Preston, N., Sampford, C. and Connors, C. (2002), *Encouraging Ethics and Challenging Corruption: Reforming Governance in Public Institutions*, Federation Press, Sydney.

Quah, J.S.T. (2003), *Curbing Corruption in Asia: A Comparative Study of Six Countries*, Eastern Universities Press, Singapore.

Rose-Ackerman, S. (1997/2002), 'When is Corruption Harmful?', in A.J. Heidenheimer and M. Johnston (eds), *Political Corruption: Concepts and Contexts*, Transaction Publishers, New Jersey, pp. 353–71.

Rose-Ackerman, S. (1999), *Corruption and Government: Causes, Consequences and Reform*, Cambridge University Press, Cambridge.

Sajo, A. (2002), 'Clientelism and Extortion: Corruption in Transition', in S. Kotkin and A. Sajo (eds), *Political Corruption in Transition: A Skeptic's Handbook*, Central European University Press, Budapest.

Sajo, A. (2003), 'From Corruption to Extortion: Conceptualization of Post-commmunist Corruption', *Crime, Law and Social Change*, vol. 40, pp. 171–94.

Stapenhurst, R. and Sedigh, S. (1999), 'Introduction: An Overview of the Costs of Corruption and Strategies to Deal With It', in R. Stapenhurst and S.J. Kpundeh (eds), *Curbing Corruption: Toward a Model for Building National Integrity*, Economic Development Institute, World Bank, Washington DC, pp. 1–9.

Sun, Y. (2001), 'The Politics of Conceptualizing Corruption in Reform China', *Crime, Law and Social Change*, vol. 35, no. 3, pp. 245–70.

Sung, H.-E. (2002), 'A Convergence Approach to the Analysis of Political Corruption: A Cross-national Study', *Crime, Law and Social Change*, vol. 38, p. 137–60.

Szanto, Z. (1999), 'Principals, Agents, and Clients: Review of the Modern Concept Of Corruption', *Innovation*, vol. 12, no. 4, pp. 629–34.

Tanzi, V. (1998), 'Corruption Around the World: Causes, Consequences, Scope, and Cures', *International Monetary Fund Staff Papers*, vol. 45, no. 4, pp. 559–94.

Theobald, R. (1990), *Corruption, Development and Underdevelopment*, Duke University Press, Durham.

Vittal, N. (2001), 'Corruption and the State', *Harvard International Review*, vol. 23, no. 3, pp. 20–25.

Werlin, H.H. (1994), 'Revisiting Corruption with a New Definition', *International Review of Administrative Sciences*, vol. 60, pp. 547–58.

Werlin, H.H. (2002), 'Secondary Corruption: The Concept of Political Illness', *The Journal of Social, Political, and Economic Studies*, vol. 27, no. 3, pp. 341–62.

Whitehead, L. (2002), 'High Level Political Corruption in Latin America: "Transitional" Phenomenon?', in A.J. Heidenheimer and M. Johnston (eds), *Political Corruption: Concepts and Contexts*, Transaction Publishers, New Jersey, pp. 801–17.

Williams, J.W. and Beare, M.E. (1999), 'The Business of Bribery: Globalization, Economic Liberalization and the "Problem" of Corruption', *Crime, Law and Social Change*, vol. 32, pp. 115–46.

Chapter 5

Measuring Corruption – The Validity and Precision of Subjective Indicators (CPI)

Johann Graf Lambsdorff[1]

Introduction

The Transparency International Corruption Perceptions Index (CPI) is an annual index, compiled since 1995. I started the operational work behind the index many years ago at the University of Goettingen; this work is done now at the University of Passau under my leadership. The index has assumed a central place in research on the causes and consequences of corruption, based on regressions for a cross-section of countries. A review of contributions is provided in Lambsdorff (1999). This document provides an in-depth explanation of the methodology behind the index.

The goal of the CPI is to provide data on extensive perceptions of corruption within countries. This is a means of enhancing the understanding of levels of corruption from one country to another. In an area as complex and controversial as corruption, no single source or polling method has yet been developed that combines a perfect sampling frame, a satisfactory country coverage and a fully convincing methodology to produce comparative assessments. This is why the CPI has adopted the approach of a composite index.

Objective Versus Subjective Data

Unbiased, hard data is difficult to obtain and usually raises questions with respect to validity. One such set of data has been assembled by the United Nations (1999). This is a survey of national agencies and collects data on the incidence of reported crime. All national data are derived from the official national criminal statistics. However, the precise legal definition of bribery and corruption can be different in each national context. The differences drawn between bribery, embezzlement and fraud may be troublesome and the statistical methodology of counting and aggregating the data used in each national agency can differ considerably from that used elsewhere. Countries such as Singapore and Hong Kong have extremely high per capita conviction rates for bribery. This lends itself to the conclusion that the data are to a large extent determined by the effectiveness and capacity of a country's judiciary in prosecuting corruption. High levels, in this case, indicate the success of anti-corruption initiatives rather than high levels of actual corruption. As such problems commonly arise with objective data, international surveys on perceptions serve as a superior means of compiling a ranking of nations.

Sources in 2002

Prior to selecting sources, guidelines have been set up which organise the underlying decision making process. These include the actual criteria that a source needs to meet in order to qualify for inclusion as well as organisational guidelines on how the final decision is reached with the help of the Transparency International Steering Committee. This process aims at making the final decision as transparent and robust as possible. As a result of this, it was decided that the 2002 CPI includes data from the following sources:

*   The World Economic Forum (WEF)
*   The Institute for Management Development, Lausanne (IMD)
*   PricewaterhouseCoopers (PwC)
*   World Bank's World Business Environment Survey (WBES)
*   The Economist Intelligence Unit (EIU)
*   Freedom House, Nations in Transit (FH)
*   Political and Economic Risk Consultancy, Hong Kong (PERC)
*   Gallup International on behalf of Transparency International (TI/GI)
*   State Capacity Survey by Columbia University (CU).

An essential condition for inclusion is that a source must provide a ranking of nations. This condition is not met if a source conducts surveys in a variety of countries but with varying methodologies. This is can be true, for example, for the multitude of National Integrity Surveys that are carried out currently. Comparisons from one country to another are not feasible in this case and a ranking cannot be produced. Another condition is that sources must measure the overall level of corruption. This is violated if aspects of corruption are mixed with issues other than corruption such as political instability, or nationalism, or if changes are measured instead of levels of corruption.

For example, the index 'Corruption in Government' from the International Country Risk Guide (ICRG), conducted by the Political Risk Services (PRS), do not meet these requirements, albeit being widely used in research as a measure of levels of corruption. This index does not determine a country's level of corruption but the political risk involved in corruption. As pointed out to us by Tom Sealy, the ICRG-editor, these two issues can differ considerably, depending on whether there exists a high or low tolerance towards corruption. In a personal correspondence, he explained that the:

> Corruption Index is an attempt to provide a comparable measure of corruption (under the standard international definition), while our Corruption Risk is an attempt to provide a comparable measure of the political risk involved in corruption ... this produces some apparently odd assessments with countries with reportedly high levels of corruption being

assessed by us as having a lower corruption risk than countries with reportedly low levels of corruption. The reason for this is that, in general terms, countries with low measurable corruption often have a high degree of democratic accountability and a low tolerance of corruption. Because of this, an instance of corruption that would hardly raise an eyebrow in some countries could contribute to a government's fall ... So, although the measurable corruption in such countries is low, the political risk might be high. On the other hand, countries with reportedly widespread corruption often have low levels of democratic accountability and a high tolerance of corruption. Such a country could end up with a lower Corruption Risk rating under our system than would be the case if we were taking account of measurable corruption.

Corruption only leads to political instability if it is not tolerated. Due to this, the data by PRS-ICRG does not depict levels of corruption, contrary to widespread belief.

The 2002 CPI combines assessments from the past three years to reduce abrupt variations in scoring that might arise due to random effects. Some sources, such as TI/GI, WBES and PwC, provided only one recent survey. Others such as PERC, WEF and IMD conducted various surveys between 2000 and 2002, which are all included. In addition to its Global Competitiveness Report (GCR), the WEF also published the Africa Competitiveness Reports (ACR) in 2000, which is also included.

While this averaging is valuable for the inclusion of surveys, it is inappropriate for application to the data compiled by country experts. Such assessments as compiled by FH, CU and EIU are conducted by a small number of country experts who regularly analyse a country's performance, counterchecking their conclusions with peer discussions. Following this systematic evaluation, they then consider a potential upgrading or downgrading. As a result, a country's score changes rather seldom and the data shows little year-to-year variation. Changing scores, in this case, are the result of a considered judgment by the organisation in question. To then go back and average the assessments over a period of time would be inappropriate.

Year-to-Year Comparisons

Comparisons to the results from previous years should be based on a country's score, not its rank. A country's rank can change simply because new countries enter the index and others drop out. A higher score is an indicator that respondents provided better ratings, while a lower score suggests that respondents revised their perception downwards. However, year-to-year comparisons of a country's score do not only result from a changing perception of a country's performance but also from a changing sample and methodology. With differing respondents and slightly differing methodologies, a change in a country's score may also relate to the fact that different viewpoints have been collected and different questions asked. The index primarily provides an annual snapshot of the views of businesspeople, with less of a focus on year-to-year trends.

However, to the extent that changes can be traced back to a change in the results from individual sources, trends can cautiously be identified. Noteworthy examples of a recent downward trend between 2001 and 2002 are Argentina, Ireland and Moldova.

The considerable decline in their scores does not result from technical factors – actual changes in perceptions are therefore likely. With the same caveats applied, on the basis of data from sources that have been consistently used for the index, improvements can be observed for the Dominican Republic, Hong Kong, Russia, Slovenia and South Korea.

Validity

All sources generally apply a definition of corruption such as the misuse of public power for private benefit, for example bribing of public officials, kickbacks in public procurement, or embezzlement of public funds. Each of the sources also assesses the 'extent' of corruption among public officials and politicians in the countries in question:

- In 2002, the IMD asks respondents to assess whether 'bribing and corruption prevail or do not prevail in the economy'. Previously the question related to whether corruption prevails in the public sphere. This slight change seemed to have a negligible impact on the results.
- The WEF asks in its 2002 Global Competitiveness Report: 5.11 – In your industry, how commonly would you estimate that firms make undocumented extra payments or bribes connected with the following:

  A – Import and export permits Common |1|2|3|4|5|6|7| Never occur
  B – Connection to public utilities (e.g. telephone or electricity) Common |1|2|3|4|5|6|7| Never occur
  C – Annual tax payments Common |1|2|3|4|5|6|7| Never occur
  D – Loan applications Common |1|2|3|4|5|6|7| Never occur
  E – Awarding of public contracts (investment projects) Common |1|2|3|4|5|6|7| Never occur
  F – Influencing of laws and policies, regulations or decrees to favour selected business interests Common |1|2|3|4|5|6|7| Never occur
  G – Getting favourable judicial decisions Common |1|2|3|4|5|6|7| Never occur.

From these questions, the simple average has been determined. Slightly different questions had been posed in 2000 and 2001. In the Africa Competitiveness Report, it was additionally asked how 'problematic the following areas are for doing business: … corruption' and 'when firms in your industry do business with the government, how much of the contract value must they offer in additional or unofficial payments to secure the contract?'. For details, see Lambsdorff and Cornelius (2000).

1. The PERC asks in 2001, 'How do you rate corruption in terms of its quality or contribution to the overall living/working environment?' A slightly different question had been asked previously.

2. The EIU defines corruption as the misuse of public office for personal (or party political) financial gain and aims at measuring the pervasiveness of corruption. Corruption is one of over 60 indicators used to measure 'country risk' and 'forecasting'.

3. PwC asks for the frequency of corruption in various contexts (e.g. obtaining import/export permits or subsidies, avoiding taxes).

4. FH determines the 'level of corruption' without providing further defining statements.

5. The WBES asks two questions with respect to corruption, one determining the 'frequency of bribing' and another one relating to 'corruption as a constraint to business'.

6. Columbia University asks for the severity of corruption within the state.

7. Gallup International, on behalf of Transparency International, asks:

> 13. Which are the countries, besides this one, with which you have had the most business experience in the last 3–5 years? Please name up to five countries. 13a. In [country 1], how common are payments (e.g. bribes) to obtain or retain business or other improper advantages to senior public officials, like politicians, senior civil servants, and judges? From 'Very Common [01] to 'Very Uncommon/Never' [04]. Don't know [88]. In [country 1], how significant of an obstacle are the costs associated with such payments for doing business? From 'Very significant [1] to 'Insignificant' [4]. Don't know [88]. The questions continue for countries 2-5.

The terms 'prevalence', 'commonness', 'frequency', 'constraint', 'contribution to working environment' and 'severity' are closely related. They all refer to some kind of 'degree' of corruption, which is also aim of the CPI. This common feature of the various sources is particularly important in view of the fact that corruption comes in different forms. It has been suggested in numerous publications that distinctions should be made between these forms of corruption, e.g. between nepotism and corruption in the form of monetary transfers. Yet, none of the data included in the CPI emphasise one form of corruption at the expense of other forms. The sources can be said to aim at measuring the same phenomenon. It is also important to note that most of the sources do not distinguish between administrative and political corruption and that both types of corruption are addressed equally by the various questions posed. The IMD asks about corruption in the economy. This inevitably includes corruption in administration and corruption in politics, as they both interact with the economy. The WEF addresses particular areas where corruption can occur and in each of these, either politicians or administrators can be the relevant actors. Similarly, the broad definition used by FH includes both types of corruption. The EIU explicitly notes that its assessments include corruption among public servants and politicians alike. This largely justifies a blending of political and administrative corruption, since there is no strong evidence that countries differ in the prevalence of one type of corruption over another. Future research is needed to find out whether it is possible to disentangle political and administrative corruption and to assess them separately.

The term 'degree of corruption' may imply different things (Rose-Ackerman, 1999, p. 4). In particular, it may either relate to the frequency of bribes or the size of bribes. The questions posed may relate more to frequency or more to the costs imposed on business. But we know from the results of our sources that frequency and the size of bribes tend to correlate highly. For a more elaborate treatment of this issue see Lambsdorff (2001). In countries where corruption is frequent, it also amounts to a high fraction of firms' revenues. In sum, the term 'degree of corruption' seems to equally reflect the two aspects, frequency of corruption and the total value of bribes paid. Also here, future research is required to find out whether frequency and costs can be assessed separately.

Perceptions and Reality

While the sources all aim at measuring the degree of corruption, the sample design differs considerably. The data by IMD, WBES, PwC and WEF largely sample residents (sometimes also from multinational companies). In contrast, the data by PERC, FH, TI/GI, CU and EIU largely relate to expatriates. Whether this difference between samples may lead to different outcomes, still requires scientific study. For the purposes of the CPI, it added to the robustness of the resulting figures, since the data correlate well, irrespective of whether expatriates or residents had been polled. This correlation suggests that there being different samples makes no great difference to the results.

Interpreting Perceptions

As the data collected relates to perceptions rather than to real phenomena, it has to be considered whether such perceptions improve our understanding of what real levels of corruption may be. Since actual levels of corruption cannot be determined directly, perceptions may be all we have to guide us. However, this approach is undermined, at least to some extent, if the perceptions gathered are biased. Such a potential bias might originate from the particular cultural background of respondents, depending on whether the sample consists of locals or expatriates; this suggests two potential biases to be relevant.

Imagine that being asked to assess the level of corruption, a local estimates a high level of corruption in the country of residence. Such an assessment would be a valid contribution to the CPI only if the respondent makes the assessment as a result of comparisons with the levels of corruption perceived in other countries. But this is not necessarily the viewpoint taken by the respondent. A respondent may also assign high levels by comparing corruption to other (potentially less pressing) problems facing the country, or by evaluating it according to a high ethical standard (e.g. which assumes any kind of gift-giving to a public official to be corrupt and not culturally acceptable). In the case of such an outlook, a high degree of observed corruption may reflect a high standard of ethics rather than a high degree of real misbehaviour. Perceptions would be a misleading indicator for real levels of corruption. This bias can occur particularly if only locals are surveyed, each assessing only the level of perceived corruption in their own countries.[2] If respondents are asked to assess foreign countries or to make comparisons between a variety of countries, this bias should not occur.[3] Respondents will, in this case, compare a foreign country with their home country or with an even larger set of countries. They will be forced to apply the same definition of corruption and make use of the same ethical standard for all countries, which produces valid comparative assessments.

However, in this context, a second type of bias might arise, originating from the potential dominance of a particular cultural heritage in the sample questioned or because expatriates lack a proper understanding of a country's culture. The results would be meaningless to locals who have a different understanding and definition of corruption. While samples of expatriates are susceptible to this kind of bias, surveys which question local residents clearly avoid it.

The strength of the CPI rests with the idea that we include surveys which are not susceptible to the first type of bias. Particularly these are EIU, TI/GI, CU, FH and PERC. Since the data provided by these sources refers to assessments by expatriates, they are subject to a homogeneous definition of corruption and a consistent ethical standard. In case of TI/GI, respondents have been asked to compare between different countries. This ensures that a consistent ethical standard is applied.

The CPI also incorporates the data from the IMD, WEF, PwC and WBES. Since these refer to assessments made largely by local residents, they are less likely to represent the perception of a certain cultural heritage. The second type of bias can clearly be rejected for these sources.

Since the data from the EIU, TI/GI, CU, FH and PERC correlate well with the other data, there seems to be no support for the suggestion that the second type of bias might influence them. Similarly, since the data by the IMD, WEF, PwC and WBES correlate well with data from the other five institutions; the notion that the first type of bias might be present is clearly not supported. The validity of the sources is mutually confirmed and no hint is found for the existence of a bias in our data.

Another criticism of the CPI was that expatriates surveyed are often western businesspeople. The viewpoint of less developed countries seemed underrepresented. TI/GI now surveys respondents from less developed countries, asking them to assess the performance of industrial countries. This balances the sample; yet, as shown in the correlations, it does not bring about significantly different results. Thus, the comparative assessments gathered in the CPI do not disproportionately reflect the perceptions of western businesspeople.

In sum, it seems that residents tend to have a consistent ethical standard with regard to assessments of corruption, while expatriates do not tend to impose an inappropriate ethical standard or to lack cultural insights. Our approach clearly suggests that the perceptions gathered are a helpful contribution to the understanding of real levels of corruption. They can also be shown to relate to actual experience made and less to hearsay, see Lambsdorff (2001) for further discussion of this point.

The Index

Standardising

Since each of the sources uses its own scaling system, aggregation requires a standardisation of the data before each country's mean value can be determined. This standardisation is carried out in two steps.

Until 2001, a simple means and standard deviation approach was adopted for step 1. The aim was to ensure that inclusion of a source consisting of a certain subset of countries should not change the mean and standard deviation of this subset of countries in the CPI. In 2001, the 2000 CPI was the starting point for standardisation, except for older sources that were already standardised previously (where the standardised values determined in previous years were utilised). Standardisation meant that the mean and standard deviation of a new source must take the same value as the respective subset in the 2000 CPI. With S'(j, k) being the original value provided by source k to country j, the standardised value, S(j, k), was determined by:

$$S'(j, k) = [S'(j, k) - \text{Mean}(S'(k))]\,\frac{\text{SD}(2000\ \text{CPI})}{\text{SD}(S'(k))} + \text{Mean}(2000\ \text{CPI})$$

where the means and standard deviations (SD) for the source k and the 2000 CPI have been determined for the joint subset of countries. After standardising each source, the simple average was taken for each country.

Step 2 is a final standardisation of the average values determined previously. Taking the average implies that the resulting index has a standard deviation across countries which is smaller than that of the CPI of previous years. In order to avoid a year-to-year trend towards a continuously smaller diversity of assessments, the scores had to be stretched. This ensured that the standard deviation of countries in the index[4] remained constant over time.

This approach was subject to intense debate last year. It was decided that a modified approach should be used for step 1: matching percentiles. Instead of equalising means and standard deviations, the *ranks* (and not the scores) of countries is the only information processed from our sources. For this technique, again the common sub samples of a new source and the previous year's CPI are determined. Then, the largest value in the CPI is taken as the standardised value for the country ranked best by the new source. The second largest value is given to the country ranked second best, etc.[5] Imagine that a new sources ranks UK best, Singapore second, Venezuela third and Argentina fourth. In the 2001 CPI, these countries obtained the scores 9.2, 8.3, 3.5 and 2.8. Matching percentiles would now assign UK the best score of 9.2, Singapore 8.3, Venezuela 3.5 and Argentina 2.8.

Matching percentiles is superior in combining indices that have different distributions. But, as it makes use of the ranks, and not the scores of sources, this method loses some of the information inherent in the sources. What tipped the balance in favour of this technique is its capacity to keep all reported values within the bounds from 0 to 10 – all countries in the CPI obtain scores between 0 (very corrupt) and 10 (highly clean). While we report these absolute bounds, the previous standardisation provided no guarantee that all values remained within these bounds. In effect, equalising means and standard deviations can bring about standardised values above 10 or below 0. This has indeed happened in the past with e.g. Finland obtaining standardised scores above 10. In 2001, standardised values for Bangladesh of –1.7 have led to confusion among observants. Matching percentiles, on the other hand, guarantees that all standardised values are within these bounds. This results because any standardised value is taken from the previous year's CPI, which by definition is restricted to the aforementioned range.

In sum, matching percentiles has the disadvantage of wasting some information by processing only the ranks reported by sources. Yet, this disadvantage seems to be offset because the approach is free of assumptions regarding the distribution of sources, and all standardised values remain within the range from 0 to 10.

Step 2

Having obtained standardised values that are all within the reported range, a simple average from these standardised values can be determined. As already argued before, the resulting index has a standard deviation that is smaller than that of the CPI of previous years. Without a second adjustment there would be a trend towards a continuously smaller diversity of scores. If, for example, Finland were to repeat its score from the previous year, it would have to score best in all sources listing this country. If it scores second to best in any source, the standardised value it obtains after using matching percentiles and aggregation would be lower than its current score. Thus, given some heterogeneity among sources, it seems inevitable that Finland's score would deteriorate. The opposite would be true of Bangladesh, which would obtain a better score if it were not consistently rated worst by all its sources. A second standardisation is required in order to avoid a continuous trend to less diversity among scores.

However, applying a simple mean and standard deviation technique might again bring about values that are beyond our range from 0 to 10. The proposal would, therefore, be to apply a more complicated standardisation for this second step – a beta-transformation. The idea behind this monotonous transformation is to increase the standard deviation to its desired value, but to keep all values within the range from 0 to 10. Each value (X) is therefore transformed according to the following function:

$$10 * \int_0^1 (X/10)^{\alpha-1} (1 - X/10)^{\beta-1} dX.$$

This beta-transformation is available in standard statistics programmes. The crucial task is to find the parameters α and β so that the resulting mean and standard deviation of the index have the desired values. An algorithm has been determined that carries out this task. Applying this approach to the 2002 CPI, the change in the scores is depicted by figure 5.1. The parameters were $\alpha=1.1756$ and $\beta=1.1812$. As shown in the figure, scores between 5 and 10 are increased slightly, while those between 0 and 5 are lowered. This effect makes sure that the previous standard deviation is preserved. Yet, once a score of 10 has been reached, the score is not further increased. Equally, a score of 0 is not further decreased. This guarantees that all values remain within the range. The beta transformation is first applied to all values that were standardised in step 1. Afterwards, the average of these are computed to determine a country's score.[6] While the methodological adjustments were considerable, their impact on the outcome was rather small. Had the 2002 CPI been determined with the previous methodology, the result would correlate 0.996 with our current one. In spite of the methodological modifications, there exists a high numerical continuity of the CPI across years.[7]

Reliability and Precision

A ranking of countries may easily be misunderstood as measuring the performance of a country with absolute precision. This is certainly not true. Since its start in 1995, TI has provided data on the standard deviation and the amount of sources contributing to the index. This data already serves to illustrate the inherent imprecision. Also, the high-low range is provided in the main table accompanying our data. This depicts the highest and the lowest values provided by our sources, so as to portray the whole range of assessments. However, no quick conclusions should be derived from this range to the underlying precision with which countries are measured. Countries which were

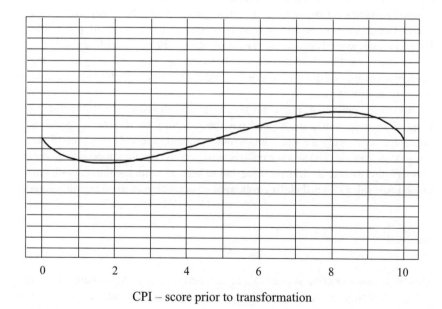

CPI – score prior to transformation

Figure 5.1   Beta transformation

assessed by 3 or 12 sources can have the same minimum and maximum values, but in the latter case we can feel much more confident about the country's score. In order to arrive at such measures of precision, other statistical methods are required.

The strength of the CPI is based on the concept that a combination of data sources combined into a single index increases the reliability of each individual figure. As in previous years, the 2002 CPI includes all countries for which at least three sources had been available. The idea of combining data is that the non-performance of one source can be balanced out by the inclusion of at least two other sources. This way, the probability of misrepresenting a country is seriously lowered. This is valid even in case the sources are not totally independent of each other. Such partial dependency may arise if some respondents are aware of other people's perception of the level of corruption, or of other sources contributing to the CPI.

An indicator for the overall reliability of the 2000 CPI can be drawn from the high correlation between the sources. Since the standardisation approach makes use only of the ranks (and not the scores) provided by the sources, we report Kendall's rank correlation. Referring only to countries included in the CPI, this data is in Table 5.1.[8] As the correlations on average are 0.7, the sources do not differ considerably in their assessment of levels of corruption. It should be noted that the rank correlation is lower than the more commonly used Pearson-correlation, which is 0.84 on average for the various sources.

In addition to these correlations, the reliability of each individual country score can be determined. The larger the number of sources and the lower the standard deviation between the sources, the more reliable is the value for a country. The relatively large standard deviation for Poland of 1.1 signifies that 95 per cent of the sources ranged between a value of 1.8 and 6.2. In contrast, the low standard deviation for Canada of 0.2 means that 95 per cent of the scores range between 8.6 and 9.4.

Confidence Range

We have been providing readers with the additional information on the confidence range for some years now. These were based on the determination of the standard error for a country's average score and a resulting parametric assessment of a 95-confidence range. This approach required the assumption that there is no imprecision associated with the source's values and that these values are independent of each other. Another strong assumption required is that errors are normally distributed. While it is statistically difficult to relax the first two assumptions, one can relax the assumption of a normal distribution and apply tests that are valid throughout any type of distribution. Another drawback of the older confidence ranges was, again, that they sometimes violated the given range from 0 to 10. For example, while in 2001 Bangladesh had a score of 0.4, its 95 per cent confidence range was between –3.6 and 4.4. For Finland, on the other hand, the range went as high as 10.4. This type of a range is confusing even to an expert. Since it is in contradiction to the official range reported, the public is equally disoriented.

In 2002 in order to restrict the confidence range to our pre-specified limits, we introduced a different approach – a non-parametric approach applying the bootstrap

Table 5.1   Kendall's Rank Correlation

	IMD 2000	IMD 2001	IMD 2002	PERC 2000	PERC 2001	GCR 2002	GCR 2000	GCR 2001	ACR 2000	WBES 2001	EUI 2002	PwC 2001	FH 2002	TVGI 2002	CU 2001
IMD 2000	1	0.84	0.88	0.77	0.97	0.86	0.81	0.85	/	0.71	0.78	0.68	/	0.68	0.74
IMD 2001		1	0.88	0.64	0.79	0.85	0.78	0.79	/	0.66	0.79	0.67	0.43	0.60	0.70
IMD 2002			1	0.77	0.92	0.86	0.78	0.79	/	0.66	0.77	0.66	0.24	0.69	0.70
PERC 2000				1	0.75	0.71	0.80	0.73	/	0.62	0.74	0.89	/	0.61	0.80
PERC 2001					1	0.80	0.83	0.92	/	0.62	0.68	0.89	0.28	0.76	0.84
GCR 2002						1	0.79	0.79	0.57	0.64	0.72	0.70	0.59	0.68	0.64
GCR 2000							1	0.78	/	0.63	0.76	0.72	0.36	0.57	0.75
GCR 2001								1	/	0.61	0.73	0.74	/	0.65	0.69
ACR 2000									1	0.81	0.45	/	0.46	/	0.48
WBES 2001										1	0.60	0.39	0.84	0.53	0.55
EIU 2002											1	0.63		0.70	0.70
PwC 2001												1		0.67	0.65
FH 2002													1		0.67
TVGI 2002														1	0.52
CU2001															1

Note: Only correlations which relate to at least six countries are reported.

methodology. The principal idea of such a bootstrap confidence range is to resample the sources of a country with replacement. If five source values (3, 5, 4, 4.5, 4.2) had been given, an example of such a sample would be (5, 5, 4.2, 3, 3). A sufficiently large number of such samples (in our case 10,000) are drawn from the available vector of sources and the sample mean is determined in each case. Based on the distribution of the resulting means, inferences on the underlying precision can been drawn. The lower (upper) bound of a 90 per cent confidence range is then determined as the value where 5 per cent of the sample's means are below (above) this critical value. In addition to the 'percentile' method just described, more complicated approaches exist. First, the confidence levels can be adjusted if (on average) the mean of a bootstrap sample is smaller than the observed mean. The relevant parameter is called z_0. Another adjustment is to assume the standard deviation also to be dependent on the mean of the bootstrap sample. The relevant parameter is a. If both these adjustments are considered, the resulting approach is called a bootstrap-BC_a-method (bias-corrected-accelerated). A precise description of this approach can be obtained from Efron and Tibshirani (1993, chap. 14.3, 22.4 and 22.5). One concern with the BC_a approach is that it throws a lot of machinery at very few observations. Due to statistical considerations, a simple method might prove superior. Brad Efron had, therefore, suggested the use of a BC-approach for our purpose. In this case, z_0 is determined endogenously from the bootstrap sample but a is set equal to zero. There are two interesting characteristics of the resulting confidence range.

1. When requiring a 90 per cent confidence range (which allows with 5 per cent probability that the true value is below and with 5 per cent probability that the value is above the determined confidence range) the upper (lower) bound will not be higher (lower) than the highest (lowest) value provided by a source. This implies that our range from 0 to 10 will never be violated.
2. The confidence range remains valid even if the data (i.e. the standardised values for a given country) are not normally distributed. The range is even free of assumptions with regard to the distribution of these data.

It should not be ignored that confidence ranges cannot be very solid when only very few sources are available. This is true for any methodology applied. Regardless of whether a normal distribution is assumed or a bootstrap approach is taken, the confidence range must not be overrated when only three sources exist; it serves only as a rough guide in this case. Above that, there can arise boundary effects when only three or four sources exist. Since only 10 different combinations are possible in the case of three sources, a 5 per cent confidence point can 'hit' one resulting boundary. If this is the case, the BC-approach could produce, at random, two different values for the upper (or the lower) confidence point. These boundary effects have been identified and, if existent, the more conservative range is reported in the Table 5.2. The resulting confidence range is graphically illustrated in Figure 5.2.

Table 5.2   Survey sources for the TI Corruption Perceptions Index (CPI) 2002

	1	2	3
Number	1	2	3
Source	Columbia University (CU)	Political and Economic Risk Consultancy	
Name	State Capacity Survey	Asian Intelligence Issue	
Year	2001	2000	2001
Internet address		http://www.asiarisk.com/	
Who was surveyed?	US-resident country experts (policy analysts, academics and journalists)	Expatriate business executives	
Subject asked	Severity of corruption within the state	Extent of corruption in a way that detracts from the business environment for foreign companies	How do you rate corruption in terms of its quality or contribution to the overall living/working environment?
Number of replies	251	1,027	ca. 1,000
Coverage	121 countries	14 countries	

	4	5	6
Number	4	5	6
Source	Institute for Management Development, IMD, Switzerland		
Name	World Competitiveness Yearbook		
Year	2000	2001	2002
Internet address	www02.imd.ch/wcy		
Who was surveyed?	Executives in top and middle management; domestic and international companies		
Subject asked	Bribing and corruption exist in the public sphere		Bribing and corruption exist in the economy
Number of replies	4,160	3,678	3,532
Coverage	47 countries	49 countries	

	7	8
Number	7	8
Source	World Bank	PricewaterhouseCoopers
Name	World Business Environment Survey	Opacity Index
Year	2001	2001
Internet address	info.worldbank.org/governance/wbes/index1.html	www.opacityindex.com/
Who was surveyed?	Senior managers	CFOs, equity analysts, bankers and PwC staff
Subject asked	'Frequency of bribing' and 'corruption as a constraint to business'	Frequency of corruption in various contexts (e.g. obtaining import/export permits or subsidies, avoiding taxes)
Number of replies	10,090	1,357
Coverage	79 countries[9]	34 countries

Number	9	10	11
Source	Economist Intelligence Unit	Freedom House	World Economic Forum
Name	Country Risk Service and Country Forecast	Nations in Transit	Africa Competitiveness Report
Year	2002	2002	2000
Internet address	www.eiu.com	www.freedomhouse.org	www.weforum.org
Who was surveyed?	Expert staff assessment (expatriate)	Assessment by US academic experts and FH staff	Senior business leaders;domestic and international companies
Subject asked	Assessment of the pervasiveness of corruption (the misuse of public office for private or political party gain) among public officials (politicians and civil servants)	Levels of corruption	How problematic is corruption? Are irregular, additional payments required? In large amounts?
Number of replies	Not applicable	Not applicable	1,800
Coverage	115 countries	27 transition economies	26 countries

Number	12	13	14
Source	World Economic Forum		
Name	Global Competitiveness Report		
Year	2000	2001	2002
Internet address	www.weforum.org		
Who was surveyed?	Senior business leaders; domestic and international companies		
Subject asked	Undocumented extra payments connected with import and export permits, public utilities and contracts, business licenses, tax payments or loan applications are common/not common		In addition: payments connected to favourable regulations and judicial decisions
Number of replies	4,022	ca. 4,600	ca. 4700
Coverage	59 countries	76 countries	80 countries

Number	15
Source	Gallup International on behalf of Transparency International
Name	Corruption Survey
Year	2002
Internet address	http://www.transparency.org/surveys/index.html#bpi
Who was surveyed?	Senior businesspeople from 15 emerging market economies
Subject asked	How common are bribes to politicians, senior civil servants, and judges and how significant of an obstacle are the costs associated with such payments for doing business?
Number of replies	835
Coverage	21 countries

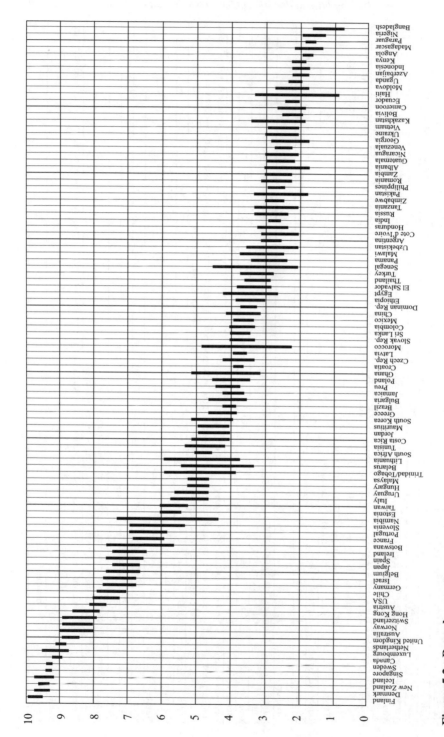

Figure 5.2 Boundary ranges

Weighting

With the various sources having some differences with respect to sample and date, a number of ideas can be considered for weighting the sources before aggregating them. It was decided to adopt the simple approach of assigning equal weights to those sources which have been found to meet the criteria of reliability and professionalism. Other procedures may have their merits, but this averaging system is simple and transparent.

It was suggested in this context that data from various years provided by the same source should not obtain the same weight as other data. One may adhere to the viewpoint that the data provided by an institution is independent to that from another institution, but the same independence may not prevail for surveys originating from the same institution. But this argument may push too far an issue which is, in fact, difficult to assess, since an institution may lean on the data produced by others in reaching a conclusion. Since the matter of independence is therefore difficult to quantify, there was no clear argument in changing the methodology used so far. As a result of giving each survey an equal weight, some institutions obtain a larger weight than others. While other approaches can certainly be justified, there is also some rationality in this. It reflects previous recommendations by the Transparency International Steering Committee that continuous annual surveys are superior for our purposes than one-off surveys: they may have gathered more expertise in providing their service and their inclusion helps to avoid abrupt year-to-year changes in the CPI. In addition to that, continuous annual surveys may be seen to be superior to expert assessments because the methodology of producing data is more transparent and subject to a clear procedure.

Another approach to weighting sources was adopted by Kaufmann, Kraay and Zoido-Lobaton (1999). They assume that each source is a noisy indicator for actual levels of corruption, which is the 'unobservable component' they seek to determine. Since the error term varies with the sources, an approach must be presented which determines for each source how precisely it measures corruption, that is the quality of the source. Included in their approach is the assumption that those sources which better correlate with the resulting aggregate index are of higher quality (and receive a higher weight), while those which correlate less well are considered to be of lower quality. The quality of sources is, therefore, determined endogenously and is not an expert's opinion on a source's validity and reliability. There might be some truth behind this idea, but it can also be misleading. If an assessment is based on hearsay or prejudice, it may correlate well with other sources. To the contrary, if a source engages in discovering original insights, it may end up with results differing from those of others. The first source would obtain a higher weight because it tends to say what all the others say, while the second one would be punished for its original research. The weighting system would then be in contrast to experts' viewpoints regarding the quality of sources. While it may certainly be that sources exhibit differences in quality, there does not appear to be a feasible approach to endogenously determine these differences.

Notes

1   The author is senior research consultant for Transparency International and holds a chair position in economic theory, Department of Economics, University of Passau, Innstrasse 27, 94030 Passau, Germany, Tel: 49-851-5092550, jlambsd@gwdg.de. The author is grateful to B. Efron, F. Galtung, J. Pope, S. Rose-Ackerman and particularly to W. Zucchini. Thanks to M. Schinke and C. Schinke for collecting data.

2   The distinction between locals and expatriates becomes blurred when executives from multinationals are polled. While these are locals, they will have a higher tendency to compare their country of residence with other countries, particularly with their home country (Levinson, 1999, p. 83).

3   Indeed, IMD asks its respondents explicitly to compare their country to other countries.

4   More precisely, we should talk about the standard deviation of a common sub-sample of countries in the index.

5   In case two countries share the same rank, their standardised value is the simple mean of the two respective scores in the CPI. The scores for countries where no CPI value was available are determined by referring to neighbour countries in the source's ranking. Linear interpolation is applied to their scores, suggesting that if a source assigns such a country a score close to the upper neighbour, also its standardised value is closer to that of this neighbour. If such a country is ranked best (or worst) by a source it would have only one neighbour, not two. The second neighbour is constructed by using the highest (or lowest) attainable score by the source and the CPI value 10 (or 0). This approach guarantees that all values remain within the range between 10 and 0.

6   In our publication we also report the high-low range. This refers to all standardised values after carrying out the beta-transformation. This procedure ensured that the high-low range is consistently related to a country's mean value. All these values remain within the range from 0 to 10.

7   Matching percentiles as compared to a linear transformation provided a particularly unfavourable score for Tunisia, bringing about a deterioration of about 0.5 in its final score.

8   Abbreviations relate to the sources used, Africa Competitiveness Report (ACR) of the World Economic Forum, Economist Intelligence Unit (EIU), Freedom House (FH), Global Competitiveness Report (GCR) of the World Economic Forum, Institute for Management Development (IMD), Political and Economic Risk Consultancy (PERC), PricewaterhouseCoopers (PwC), World Business Environment Survey of the World Bank (WBES), Gallup International on behalf of Transparency International (TI/GI) and Columbia University (CU).

9   The survey was carried out in 81 countries, but data for two countries was insufficient.

References

Efron, B. and Tibshirani, R. (1993), *An Introduction to the Bootstrap*, Chapman and Hall: New York and London.

Kaufmann, D., Kraay, A. and Zoido-Lobaton, P. (1999), 'Aggregating Governance Indicators', *World Bank Policy Research Working Paper No. 2195*, The World Bank, Washington DC.

Lambsdorff, J. Graf, and Cornelius, P. (2000), 'Corruption, Foreign Investment and Growth', *The Africa Competitiveness Report 2000/2001*, World Economic Forum, Oxford University Press, New York, Oxford, pp. 70–78.

Lambsdorff, J. Graf (2001), 'Framework Document', *Background Paper 2001 Corruption Perceptions Index*, www.gwdg.de/~uwvw/2001_CPI_FD.pdf.

Lambsdorff, J. Graf (2001), 'Corruption in Empirical Research – A Review', *Transparency International Working Paper, November 1999*, http://www.transparency.org/working_papers /lambsdorff/lambsdorff_eresearch.html.

Lancaster, T.D. and Montinola, G.R. (1997), 'Toward a Methodology for the Comparative Study of Political Corruption', *Crime, Law and Social Change*, vol. 27, pp. 185–206.

Levinson, M. (1999), 'Competitiveness and Globality', *The Global Competitiveness Report 1999*, World Economic Forum, Oxford University Press, New York, Oxford, pp. 82–85.

Rose-Ackerman, S. (1999), *Corruption and Government. Causes, Consequences and Reform*, Cambridge: Cambridge University Press.

United Nations (1999), 'Global Report on Crime and Justice', *Report by the United Nations Office for Drug Control and Crime Prevention*, New York: Oxford University Press. A full description of the methodology and the complete data can be obtained *via* the internet at: http://www.ifs.univie.ac.at/~uncjin/.

Chapter 6

Measuring the Immeasurable: Boundaries and Functions of (Macro) Corruption Indices

Fredrik Galtung

Introduction

Intuitively, corruption does not lend itself to measurement. Significant corruption transactions are hidden from public view and the parties to a successful agreement seldom have an incentive to be open about their dealings. Until the mid-1990s, most of the empirical findings on corruption in the academic literature were of an incidental or anecdotal nature. The evidence was based on particular, well-defined events or settings. Sometimes this was drawn from fieldwork and interviews, occasionally on legal and other primary sources and quite often on items and scandals reported in the media. The general problem in writing about corruption was that 'the facts cannot be discovered, or that if they can, they cannot be proved' (Leys, 1965, p. 215).

Aggregated analyses, whether across time, for a given business sector, or in cross-country comparisons, tended to be speculative or unsubstantiated, sometimes citing 'impressionistic evidence' as their basis (Huntington, 1968, p. 59). Corruption was held by some to be both 'immeasurable and imponderable' (Wraith and Simpkins, 1963, p. 4). Furthermore, comparisons between nations and between time periods were viewed as 'all but impossible' or 'meaningless' (Scott, 1969, p. 317). A 1,000 page introductory textbook with 56 chapters on political corruption published in 1989, widely cited in the subsequent literature, did not contain any statistics on the incidence of corruption (Heidenheimer, Johnston and Le Vine, 1989).

The difficulties of developing indicators for phenomena that may be legally or morally condemned are not entirely unknown in the social sciences. This becomes more difficult when one attempts to objectify the findings and produce information that has validity across administrative and legal systems as well as diachronically. A 'hard data' survey of conviction rates for embezzlement, extortion and bribery – although fascinating in itself – would, after all, reveal more about the independence and effectiveness of the judiciary than it would about the actual incidence of corruption or the size of bribes in any given country.[1] It would hardly serve as an indicator in countries where corruption was reasonably under control, such as Finland. The absence of many cases would probably mean that the preventive aspects of the countries' integrity systems were functioning well. Moreover, Hong Kong and

Singapore have some of the world's highest *per capita* conviction rates. Similarly, the number of articles or column inches devoted to the issue in the press says more about the investigative zeal and freedom of the media, and the interest of the public in such matters, than it would about actual corruption levels.[2] An effort to estimate the size of bribes or the percentage of illicit commissions for a given sector may also seem implausible when one considers the lengths that prosecutors and the police go to when investigating major embezzlement and bribery cases. In a methodological essay on 'What cannot be analysed in statistical terms', corruption is cited as the prime example of an observable social phenomenon that is not quantifiable since 'there cannot be statistics on a phenomenon which by its very nature is concealed' (Dogan and Kazacigil, 1994).

This widely held assumption is one possible explanation for the relegation of the study of corruption to the periphery of the social sciences. Development economists, with few exceptions, were not particularly interested in the issue until the mid to late 1990s, whereupon it emerged as one of the primary explanations for maldevelopment. The World Bank's Research Department, perhaps the most influential and certainly the largest think tank of development economics, produced its first empirical study on corruption in the late 1990s, a couple of years after the IMF. The epiphenomenon of corruption – political scandals – has interested some political scientists and sociologists, but the scale and nature of the underlying systems have only been explored with caution. Numerous major works on the political systems of advanced industrialised democracies that purport to explain their inner workings have, until recently, also successfully avoided addressing the role of corruption and the attendant phenomena of nepotism, clientelism and patronage politics. Nor has corruption been incorporated into the mainstream analysis of transitions to democracy in spite of a widely held view that it may play an important role in undermining nascent and embryonic democracies, that it is almost invariably used to legitimise military coups[3] or, in its modern, more benign manifestation, to underpin the democratic reinstatement of former military leaders.[4]

The interesting question is not whether it is possible to assign statistics to a phenomenon that is hidden – after all, few social phenomena are wholly observable across space and time.[5] The more interesting questions are twofold: Firstly, how credible are the emerging measures of corruption? Secondly, what is the utility and limitations of such measurements?[6] This chapter will demonstrate that what was long held to be immeasurable is indeed measurable and that a number of increasingly sophisticated techniques have been developed to do just that. The chapter will also analyse the impact and uses that have been made of such measurements. The primary case study will be Transparency International's Corruption Perceptions Index.[7] The chapter will conclude with a note on the limitations and constraints of these measurements and some possible ways forward.

Methodological Quandaries: A Brief Review of (Macro) Corruption Indices

Opinion surveys are the most commonly used diagnostic tools to assess corruption levels. Part of the explanation for this approach has been alluded to in the introduction. A standardised comparable objective indicator of corruption levels has yet to be credibly established. Opinion surveys have therefore been used by government agencies, the World Bank, UN agencies, NGOs, corporations, newspapers, etc. in dozens of countries. The samples range from randomised general population samples to surveys of the private sector and segments of the public administration. The size and nature of the samples has varied considerably.

Business people are frequently surveyed since they are thought to be knowledgeable in this field. PricewaterhouseCoopers, the accountancy firm, has undertaken a private sector survey to measure the effects of opacity in the public administration on the cost and availability of capital.[8] Their sample consists of chief financial officers of major companies, equity analysts, bankers and PricewaterhouseCoopers employees. The index covers over 70 countries, with an average sample of *circa* 50 respondents per country. Although the sample is relatively small, the Opacity Index is a reasonably credible exercise from a survey standpoint. A company with a worldwide reputation in the field of government regulations and foreign investment the Index was commissioned, with the support of some prominent academics in finance, economics and management. It draws on a targeted sample with a high-level of firsthand expertise in the field. And since it is a composite indicator of five different factors that may affect international capital markets (corruption; the legal system: government economic and fiscal policies; accounting standards and practices; and the regulatory regime), it does not rely on a single indicator or question.

Another major effort is the *World Business Environment Survey*, a joint project of the World Bank, the European Bank for Reconstruction and Development, the Inter-American Development Bank and Harvard that has surveyed over 10,000 enterprises in 90 countries.[9] The aim of the survey was to move away from a qualitative, attitudinal approach to the measurement to a quantitative measures of actual bribe payments, their size, frequency, etc. Questions were 'based on the direct experience of firms rather than subjective comparisons across countries' (WBES, 2001, p. 2). In truth, most questions remain attitudinal, but the survey does contain numerous compelling questions on the scale, frequency and utility of bribe payment. These 'quantitative' findings are all derived from self-assessments. Wisely, they are generally phrased in a non-confrontational manner. For example: 'On average, what per cent of revenues do firms *like yours* typically pay *per annum* in unofficial payments to public officials?' (WBES, 2001, p. 37).

The authors acknowledged that there are potential sources of bias in cross-country comparisons. Individual respondent biases are inevitable and would be incorporated in the standard error of the survey estimates. The risk of country aggregated biases, however, are another matter. Using Yiddish, they point to the risk of a country perception bias if there is a 'national tendency' by respondents to 'kvetch' (i.e. to 'complain, gripe, grunt or sigh') or to 'kvell' (i.e. to 'beam with immense pride and pleasure')' (WBES, 2001, p. 6). To control for these potential biases, the questionnaire included two external objective measures: exchange rate variability with the US dollar, and the telephone infrastructure, defined as the number of telephone lines *per capita*. Corresponding questions were included in the questionnaire, asking respondents to assess how problematic the exchange rate is for conducting business and to rate the overall quality and efficiency of the telephone service. The results were satisfactory and contained few outliers.

Such tests are crucial but they do not, evidently, exclude the possibility of other biases or widespread dishonesty by the respondents. In Albania, for example, the thirty-fifth biggest taxpayer in 1999 in the country was found to be a lone pizza parlour in Tirana (*The Independent*, 27 March 1999). If this is the case, what does it mean to survey one hundred companies in Albania and a similar number in Russia? Are pizza parlours being compared with major utility companies? That is unlikely as the survey had rigorous sampling criteria to ensure that a wide selection of enterprises were included in the sample. What is more difficult to gauge is the honesty of the respondents when one can safely assume that there are more than 35 enterprises and individuals with a larger taxable revenue base than a pizza parlour in Albania.

The difficulties involved in obtaining honest responses in opinion surveys are well established. This is particularly difficult when addressing a social or cultural taboo or an issue in which the respondent has a high degree of complicity. The *International Crime Victims Survey* of the UN investigates household experiences with 'crime, policing, crime preventions and feelings of unsafety'.[10] In addition to asking about the incidence of car vandalism, assault and burglary, the questionnaire also addresses the experience of corruption 'by a government official'. The results show wide variations in the firsthand experience of what is largely going to be petty forms of corruption, ranging from more than 60 per cent in Tirana, Albania, to 8 per cent in Prague and insignificant numbers in most Western European countries. The general findings were that 16.6 per cent of respondents in the developing world were asked or expected to pay a bribe to a public official. The rate in the 'transition countries' was 12.3 per cent and 1.1 per cent in the industrialised world (Zvekic, 1998).

The difficulty with this survey design, as with the *World Business Environment Survey*, is that it positions the respondent as a victim of corrupt practices. And yet oftentimes, whether in cases of petty or grand corruption, the initiative can be taken by the respondent to the survey (whether entrepreneur, manager, hospital patient or parent), and not necessarily by the public official (whether a tax official, doctor or headmaster). People who have taken the initiative to pay a bribe are unlikely to be entirely forthcoming when logging the incidence and scale of such occurrences on an anonymous questionnaire. And yet this is precisely what the World Bank has sought to measure, for example by asking companies in Eastern Europe and the former Soviet Union about the level of bribery as a percentage of a firm's revenues. The average for the region appears to be 3 per cent (Hellman, Jones and Kaufman, 2000).

While randomised nationwide samples of adult populations are particularly useful to assess attitudes, they do confirm – on a broad level – wide variations in the incidence of corruption. The Transparency International *Afrobarometer* of seven Southern African countries, for example, shows a range from 20 per cent of respondents in Namibia to 69 per cent of respondents in Zimbabwe who consider officials in government to be 'involved in corruption'. In Eastern Europe and the former Soviet Union, the Transparency International *New Europe Barometer* also showed that the readiness to pay bribes varies between countries. An in-depth study of four post-Communist countries that combines surveys with focus groups and interviews confirms this view (Miller, Grødeland and Koshechkina, 2001). Their research focuses on bribery to low-level public officials. Across the sampled countries, large numbers of respondents admit to paying bribes or offering other favours for public services. A majority of public officials also confess to having accepted presents from clients.

Meaningful comparative samples of public officials are particularly difficult to establish. A United Nations University study on bureaucracies and corruption in Africa draws on assessments by an average of five senior bureaucrats in each of the 20 countries surveyed (Galtung, 2001). Of the 20 countries polled, they report that there are eight in which firms 'mostly' or 'frequently' need to pay bribes in order to operate. In five, it is 'seldom' and in one, bribes are 'never' needed. Furthermore, the senior bureaucrats say that corruption adds on average less than approximately 2.5 per cent to the salaries of bureaucrats, up from around 2 per cent 20 years ago. These low figures are somewhat at odds with the widely held notion that corruption has had a significantly detrimental impact on governance in Africa. A poll of this size, in particular one with a sample of respondents who have little apparent incentive to be entirely forthcoming, does not lend itself to statistical analysis.

Three main corruption datasets use expert panels, mostly academics and journalists: DRI/Standard and Poor's *Global Outlook Risk Scores*, the Economist Intelligence Unit's *Country Risk Service* and *Country Forecasts*, and the Political Risk Consultancy's *International Country Risk Guide*. The DRI data, much like PRS, is a forecasted risk analysis that does not purport to measure the overall level of corruption. EIU's scores use corruption as one of 60 variables and it does measure the incidence of corruption. Since 1997, EIU staff also use a pared down TI Corruption Perceptions Index that excludes the EIU contribution from the standardised data as a benchmark for their country assessments.

The ideal Greenfield survey would combine an omniscient and honest sample with a minimal margin of error in each country estimation and minimal variance between the respondents; a combination of questions covering the whole typology of the phenomenon for cross-country comparative purposes; and an extensive coverage of at least 120 countries. The World Business Environment Survey probably comes closest to this description and yet there is no *a priori* rationale for favouring this survey design above all others covered in this review, including others that will be outlined in the subsequent section. A prudent approach would call for an attempt at producing a credible aggregate indicator. Only if this approach is shown to be invalid or less reliable than a single valid indicator, might it be more sensible to make use of the best available single source of data?

A review of the most prominent corruption indicators supports the case for an aggregate index as the most prudent means of capturing information on corruption levels at the macro level. No single technique can be held to be inherently superior to all others and important information in the divergences of findings would otherwise be lost. The best-known indicator of this kind is the Corruption Perceptions Index (CPI). Johann Graf Lambsdorff's chapter in this book describes in some detail the methodology and rationale behind the CPI.[11]

The CPI's Impact

The first CPI appeared in the German newsmagazine *Der Spiegel* on 10 July 1995. The ranking was naively provided as background information to the journalist, with the proviso that it not be published since it had not been cleared by the Transparency International Board for publication. Once the index was published, the management of the organisation, facing a *fait accompli*, had a choice of distancing itself from the results or embracing them.[12] The formal press release asserting ownership of the index followed five days after the first article appeared, in the wake of several inquiries by national and foreign media. In the next two weeks several newswires and newspapers in Australia, Brazil, Chile, Finland, Indonesia, Italy, Norway, Philippines, Spain, Switzerland and Taiwan carried the story, with leading papers in the USA, UK, France and Germany ignoring it. In mid-August, the *New York Times* published two versions of the same article on the CPI in both the Monday and Sunday editions of the paper. After this account, *The Financial Times, Guardian, International Herald Tribune, BBC* and newswires followed suit in the subsequent week, as did numerous other radio stations and papers.

The impact of the CPI has been considerable. It has been credited as a factor that gave the issue of corruption 'greater international prominence' (Florini, 1998). Most regular readers of mainstream newspapers will have come across the CPI at some time in the past few years. The CPI has facilitated a qualitative shift in the journalistic writing and public discourse on corruption. Before 1995, according to one of Germany's leading dailies, 'it was nearly impossible to write a serious [newspaper] article about corruption' (*Frankfurter Allgemeine Zeitung*, 16 May 2002). In recent years, corruption ratings have entered the mainstream lexicon of descriptors for the general state of a country, frequently used in conjunction with GDP growth rates and foreign direct investment rates. This interest and awareness of the CPI extends well beyond the business and financial press. A journalist quotes his driver in an article on corruption in Pakistan:

> 'You know', asked Ahmad, swerving around a crater that could have swallowed his little taxi, 'how Pakistan was No. 2 in the world in corruption?'.
> I said that I'd heard something about it. Pakistan had been ranked second only to Nigeria in a 1996 'global corruption index' by an outfit called Transparency International.
> 'Actually', Ahmad went on, 'we were No. 1. But we bribed the Nigerians to take first place'. (Stein, 1997, p. 15)

Similar jokes are told in other countries.

In its second year, 1996, the CPI contributed to a political upset. Pakistan was ranked second to last that year, after Nigeria. This finding was reported extensively in the domestic media. When Prime Minister Benazir Bhutto was confronted with the results in parliament, she retorted that hers was 'the most honest administration in Pakistan's history'.[13] Public demonstrations calling for her dismissal followed. The president of Pakistan removed her from office a few days later. She lost her re-election bid later that year, tarnished by corruption charges against both her and her convicted husband, who was, by then, already serving a prison sentence.

In the Bolivian presidential election in 1997, the former dictator Hugo Banzer won the presidency that year on an anti-corruption platform bolstered by the release of the CPI shortly before the election (O'Brien, 1999). The threat by the incumbent president to sue TI for defamation lends some credibility to this claim.[14]

Defensive responses by senior politicians abound. Carlos Corach, the Argentine minister of the interior qualified it:

> de manifiesta irresponsable. Es injusto, absurdo y arbitrario hablar de la Argentina en estos terminos.[15]

Two years later, still minister of the interior, Corach remained incredulous:

> Es un misterio, aún para los entendidos, de qué manera hacen las clasificaciones.[16]

President Carlos Meném suggested in a press statement that the country's low rating was politically motivated:

> This is a subjective and partial study which is aimed at feeding the political opposition's campaign against the government and renew their attacks on the integrity and credibility of the country. (Webb, 1998)

According to Guatemalan president Alvaro Arzú:

> Cualquiera que venga a decir que este es un Gobierno corrupto, no solo es un imbécil – pónganlo así por favor – sino que, además, es un sinvergüenza.[17]

Cameroon's prime minister, Peter Mafany Musonge, expressed surprise and frustration at the report. He said on radio in his country that TI appeared to have ignored efforts by his government to uphold accountability:

> 'I must say it has come as a great surprise', Musonge said. 'Ours is one of the rare governments in Africa to have launched an anti-corruption campaign which was heavily carried by the media. We have a feeling that our quest for transparency has been misunderstood.' (Musa, 1999)[18]

The official government statement in 1998 was stronger:

> The Cameroon government condemns strongly the arrogance of certain bodies that are in the pay of neo-colonial clusters of people at work to impede the progress of our countries

instead of supporting efforts and sacrifices made by our peoples. (*Reuters*, 25 September 1998)

In Honduras, which came close to the lowest position in the ranking and was the lowest of all Latin American countries, presidential chief of staff Gustavo Alfore stated: 'This really surprised us a lot because it's precisely during the government of President [Carlos] Flores that we have made great efforts to combat corruption. There's a culture of suspicion in Honduras which is a legacy from the sort of impunity there has been in this country' (*Reuters*, 26 October 1999).

One of the few overtly positive statements came from Nigeria. An official statement by the recently elected Government declared:

> President [Olusegun] Obasanjo has no objections to the results shown in the poll. In his view, the poll shows the magnitude of the challenge the present administration is facing and addressing energetically. It should also draw further attention to the need for Nigerians to collectively support the Federal Government's efforts to stem corruption and redeem Nigeria's image with the international community. (*Agence France-Presse*, 27 October 1999)

In spite of multi-pronged and lauded efforts by the Obasanjo administration to bring corruption under control, well into its second term, Nigeria's CPI score and ranking would decline – not improve.

The CPI has been cited in thousands of newspaper articles. It is cited almost on a daily basis. In some contexts, as illustrated above, it can be credited with influencing a country's political trajectory. The CPI was a watershed in the mid-1990s. It contributed towards the formation of a global movement and widespread consensus against corruption. The CPI was a formidable instrument in raising awareness about the international scope and shared burden of corruption and driving corruption onto the front pages of newspapers throughout the developing world. The CPI levelled the playing field by comparing, for the first time, disparate and distinct countries on the same scale. The international shaming that ensued, encouraged a race to the top, that is, to lower levels of corruption. The race was on the international stage for some (e.g. a senior advisor to South Korea's prime minister sharing his stated goal for Korea to be among the top-15 countries within five years);[19] frequently the race was regional (e.g. between Hong Kong and Singapore; between Kenya and Uganda; Hungary and the Czech Republic, etc.); and for some selected countries at the bottom of the league table (e.g. Bangladesh, Nigeria and Paraguay) it has spurred a determination to shed the label of being 'one of the world's most corrupt countries'.

With the advent of the UN Anti-Corruption Convention in 2003, international efforts to curb corruption entered the phase of implementation and enforcement. International efforts moved on from the short-term goals of setting international standards and general awareness raising. The value of the CPI as an awareness raising tool is not called into question.[20] This new international context, however, has called for a reassessment of the functions and limitations of the CPI. The failings of the CPI can be grouped under seven headings. They are referred to as the CPI's seven failings:

1. Only Punishing the Takers, not the Givers or Abetters
2. Irregular and Uncontrolled Country Coverage
3. Biased Sample: More Than 90 per cent of the World is Missing
4. Imprecise and Sometimes Ignorant Sources
5. Far Too Narrow and Imprecise a Definition of Corruption
6. Does not Measure Trends: Cannot Reward Genuine Reformers
7. Guilty by Association – Aid Conditionality

The first five failings are significant. Yet a nuanced and reflected understanding of the CPI recognises that no single indicator can fulfil all expectations or counter every criticism. The most effective response to these 'failings' is to recognise the inherent limitations of any given instrument and to balance it, where possible, with other indicators. The last two failings, however, are far more problematic. As the following pages will outline, they contribute to undermining the very rationale for the CPI, which is to be a tool 'to *create change* towards a world free of corruption'.[21]

CPI Failing Nr 1: Only Punishing the Takers, not the Givers and Abetters

The first criticism of the CPI is that it is one-sided. Mahathir Mohamed, then prime minister of Malaysia, responded critically when informed of the CPI at a press conference: 'Who are they to determine how our people should live? This is our country, so we are the ones to decide' (*The Straits Times* (Malaysia), 5 June 1996). Mahathir suggested that 'a movement to monitor the index of European nations on racial discrimination, corruption and morality be set up in Malaysia', a 'Europe Watch' (Abdullah and Ang, 1996).

The major omission is not that the CPI ignores Europe. Many European countries score poorly on the CPI, ranking worse than a number of poorer, less developed countries in Asia, Africa and Latin America. The blind spot is that while CPI casts a spotlight on the major bribe takers of the world, it lets the major bribe givers and safe havens of looted funds off the hook. To correct this imbalance, I was responsible for an effort to develop a brand new index for TI in 1999 to track international bribery. The result was the Bribe Payers Index of leading exporting countries. The imbalanced message of the CPI was, to some extent, corrected through the commission of this (relatively expensive) new instrument. Yet TI has only produced two BPIs in the ten years between the first launch of the CPI in 1995 and 2004. The BPI remains virtually unknown in the wider public and is generally ignored in the world press.

Furthermore, no instrument has been developed that measures or ranks the willingness by major industrialised and 'clean' countries, like Switzerland, the United Kingdom, USA, but also Singapore, Botswana and Chile, to provide banking and investment safe havens for looted public funds and corruptly obtained fortunes. Numerous reformers in Southeast Asia complain that while Singapore undoubtedly deserves the moniker as Asia's 'cleanest country', it has also become a safe haven for corrupt politicians and dealmakers in the region to deposit or invest their looted fortunes. Similar complaints are made in Africa about Botswana and South Africa; and about Chile and the United States in Latin America.

TI was initially formed as the 'coalition to curb corruption in international business transactions'. But has TI done enough to highlight the mechanisms and extent of the involvement by major corporations and banks in industrialised countries in facilitating the infrastructure of international bribery? By producing only two BPIs in the ten years, may TI have unwittingly contributed to a biased assessment that places the overwhelming burden for reform on developing countries (with their comparatively weaker institutions and governance structures) and with far less pressure being exerted on the industrialised world?

There is a more general sense in which the CPI and its attendant sources may be seen as unfairly biased against poor countries. While corruption has been shown to contribute to perpetuate maladministration and underdevelopment there is also ample evidence to support the notion that poverty itself contributes to corruption. If this is the case, is it fair to compare countries with widely differing levels of industrialisation and GDP *per capita* on the same scale, almost inevitably reinforcing the notion that all good things go together at the upper end of the scale and all bad things come together at the bottom? One solution, inspired by an experiment in British paper, *The Observer*, in collaboration with Amnesty International, would be to weight the corruption scores with a development indicator, like the UNDP's *Human Development Index* (HDI). The logic, according to the authors of this new index, was that 'it would be unfair to compare the impoverished Rwanda with oil-rich Algeria without placing the human rights records of both countries in their economic contexts' (Sweeney, Beaumont and Doyle, 1998). While the approach has a moral appeal, multiplying a corruption score with the HDI produces nonsensical rankings, where countries like Senegal and Gabon become far better placed than advanced industrialised countries. A more practical solution is to produce separate league tables, breaking down the world by geographical regions on the one hand and by levels of development on the other (the HDI divides the world into countries with high, medium and low levels of development).[22] Comparisons within these categories and intra-regionally are meaningful and they have been used in presentations of the CPI findings.

CPI Failing Nr 2: Irregular and Uncontrolled Country Coverage

The CPI requires a minimum of three sources for a country to be included. This is one of the CPI's undoubted strengths. With the exception of data generated in the context of the Bribe Payers Index survey, TI does not commission its own data sources for the CPI. It relies entirely on independently conducted surveys and expert polls. As a result, a significant number of countries cannot be included in the CPI. In 2003, some 133 countries were scored in the CPI. Based on UN membership alone, this meant that 58 countries were missing from the Index.

The failing of irregularity cuts three ways. The first is that countries may be unfairly saddled with the tag as 'world's most corrupt country' or 'the most corrupt country in the Middle East', when numerous other countries, perhaps even more corrupt, are missing from the ranking.

Second, the reliance on secondary sources means that TI cannot control countries dropping out of the Index if the minimum number of sources is missing. Government tend to respond to this with satisfaction. This occurred in the case of Kenya in 1997. Officials were understood to have briefed foreign diplomatic staff and journalists that year that Kenya's absence from the Index meant that corruption was under control and no longer needed to be monitored.

Third, in countries missing from the CPI, civil society activists, and some foreign aid donors, have found their reform efforts frustrated by governments unencumbered by the pressure and spotlight the CPI generates.[23] Because of the undoubted significance of the CPI as a catalyst for reforms (witness Pakistan, Bolivia, Cameroon and Nigeria in the examples above), it is worth asking whether TI has a responsibility to ensure that the overwhelming majority of countries in the world are included in the CPI.[24] Short of altering its methodology or lowering the entry barrier, the only way of ensuring more extensive and reliable country coverage is for TI to commission regular independent surveys, with an emphasis on those regions that are most poorly covered (significant parts of Africa and the Middle East in particular).

CPI Failing Nr 3: Biased Sample: More Than 90 per cent of the World is Missing

The CPI has frequently been criticised for being culturally biased. None too surprisingly, the argument is most commonly made by countries that are the victim of a poor score. This criticism is largely unfounded. According to Saudi Arabia's *Arab News*, for example:

> [Corruption] is a hopelessly subjective concept. What might be considered corruption in Denmark and Sweden or indeed Berlin, might be standard practice in some other countries ... [The Western press] talk about bribes and backhanders, when often all that is happening is that commission is being paid for having helped oil a deal [...] What is wrong about this particular report is that is [sic] it adopts its own, culturally subjective definition of corruption and then effectively condemns those who do not conform to it. It is an ugly and patronizing attempt to impose moral viewpoints that are the West's alone. (*Arab News* (Suadi Arabia), 2 August 1997)

If the CPI only contained data from national samples, scores could be significantly affected by the level of tolerance for corruption – as well as its visibility, the investigative zeal and integrity of the media. If the CPI only contained the assessments of foreigners, one would be left wondering whether nationals would assess their countries differently and whether nationals of country 'x' can be trusted to provide a fair assessment of country 'y'. Furthermore, since such a foreign sample would more than likely be over-represented by people from the traditional OECD countries, the sample could also be criticised for its 'Western' bias as Mahathir did. Mahathir even characterised Malaysians who believe 'such groups [as TI] as people who still have a 'strong' colonial mentality' (*The Straits Times* (Malaysia), 5 June 1996).

Since the CPI contains both sources based entirely on the assessments by foreigners or expatriates (EIU, FH, PERC, PRS), and sources that are based on samples of nationals (ICVS, IMD, WB/EBRD, WEF) there is no bias in the sample in favour of one or the other view.[25] This is one of its strengths. Furthermore, the divergence of opinion appears to be minimal since the average correlation between the two groups over several years was 0.86. This indicates that on the whole, what counts as corruption in one part of the world, is understood similarly elsewhere. The degree of tolerance and acceptance of corruption may well vary significantly (and the Global Corruption Barometer tends to support this notion), but the characterisation of a country as corrupt is remarkably consistent.

The skewed sample of the CPI is both its strength and its most significant bias. Of the 17 different institutions providing data for the CPI since 1998, only two did not have a private sector bias: Freedom House and Columbia University's State Capacity Survey (CU).[26] Freedom House uses the assessments of in-house experts as well as academics and their findings are not primarily aimed at a business audience. The CU index draws on US-resident policy analysts, academics and journalists. The remaining 15 institutions either use a sampling frame consisting of business people and/or explicitly target their findings to benefit corporations and institutional investors.

For the robustness of the CPI, the advantages of a homogenous sample are evident. Intuition dictates that business people are far more likely than a random population sample to have first-hand experience and reliable second-hand knowledge of corrupt practices. Their experience, particularly if they have some international experience, will also have the advantage of being comparative. A general respondent with little or no international experience would not be able to compare the level of corruption with any other country and, *a priori*, be more liable to influence by the media and the political and economic climate in the country.

This homogeneity, while undoubtedly advantageous, also generates a serious sample bias, which is a genuine failing of the CPI. The sample is not only private sector oriented, it is also overwhelmingly male and economically well off. Effectively, this means that this most influential of indices ignores the experiences and perspectives of most women, and of the poor and disenfranchised. It also means that the interests of 'unofficial businesses', which employ the overwhelming majority of the population in poor countries, are ignored.

TI fights corruption in the interest of a five-pronged agenda. At the centre of this agenda is the aim of bringing 'transparency to international trade and commerce' (TI, 2004).[27] TI also aims to 'reduce poverty and diminish social injustice' and to 'build democratic and open government'. This analysis suggests that only in a limited sense does this biased sample and questioning advance the interest of bringing transparency to international trade and commerce. It does nothing to deepen an understanding of corruption that might advance the other agendas set for itself by TI.

CPI Failing Nr 4: Imprecise and Sometimes Ignorant Sources

The high level of variance – the lack of consensus – between the sources has been criticised. According to Kaufmann, 'many experts suggest using caution when interpreting TI data and point out that composite corruption ratings are inherently imprecise' (Kaufmann, Kraay and Zoido-Lobatón, 1999). *The Economist* wrote that 'a combination of few sources and high variance between them makes it hard to read much into simple averages, and hence into the rankings' (*The Economist*, 30 October 1999). Kaufmann et al. (1999) contend that the data on corruption is only good enough to divide countries into three groups: the 20 or so least corrupt, the 20 or so most corrupt and the vast majority in between. This criticism of the CPI is only partially valid.

Grouping countries into broad categories would not avoid arbitrariness. Whereas 0 and 100 degrees Celsius are measures with a certain utility related to boiling and freezing points for water, a ten-point scale of corruption has little intrinsic value. The placement of a country in the highly corrupt category because it scores 2.5, while placing another country in the less corrupt grouping because of its score of 4, does not demonstrate meaningful categorisations *per se*. They are merely relative scores. Moreover, a minor change in a country score could mean that a country leapt from one category to the next, generating a media reaction that something highly significant had taken place. The underlying social and economic reality of the country is unlikely to have changed to any significant degree. One could, in theory, use confidence ranges to indicate, for example, with an 80 or 90 per cent confidence range whether a country should be characterised as 'honest', 'relatively honest', 'relatively corrupt', or 'corrupt', or by signalling the range using a traffic light as an illustration.[28] Figure 5.2 of Lambsdorff's chapter illustrates these confidence intervals for the CPI.

The criticism contained in the pages of *The Economist* would have more validity were it not an argument one could make with equal validity about a great number of other, considerably more influential aggregate statistics, such as national accounting figures. In India, where around a third of the world's poor live, there has, in the course of a number of years, emerged a growing discrepancy between the national accounts and household survey data (Deaton, 2000). Such accounting discrepancies are also to be found in advanced industrialised countries. Canadian estimates of the unrecorded (but not necessarily illegal) economy range from 0.6 to close to 22 per cent of GDP (Mirus and Smith, 2002). Studies for the US put the figures at between 4 and 33 per cent, Germany's between 3 to 28 per cent and the UK's at 2 to 15 per cent. Among industrialised countries, Italy is widely viewed as having the largest unrecorded economy, perhaps as much as one third of its recorded GDP. Among industrialised countries, Italy is followed by Spain, Belgium and Sweden, whereas Japan and Switzerland (with approximately 4 per cent) are viewed as among the economies with the smallest unrecorded economies.

Italy and the US are the only industrialised countries to officially adjust their GDP figures to allow for the shadow economy.[29] When Italy did so in the late 1980s, it was characterised as '*il sorpasso*'[30] since the country overtook the UK in the size of its GDP.

The measurement of GDP statistics for poor countries, which are presented without qualifications for variance, shadow or unrecorded economies, e.g. in International Monetary Fund or World Bank annual reports, are all the more unreliable (Bloem and Shrestha, 2000). What is true for GDP statistics is all the more so for trade and investment data.[31]

The CPI is not particularly precise. The CPI has the advantage, however, of being transparent and honest about this failing.[32] When it comes to measuring a phenomenon as contested as corruption, especially on an aggregate level, rather than undermining the index, such openness may even bolster its credibility. The CPI does not claim to be more precise than it actually is. In the context of the measurement of corruption, a degree of variance is evidently acceptable. Furthermore, the variance within and between sources contains valuable information. A change in the level of consensus in a country estimate can be a useful barometer for an evolution in the public understanding of corruption for a given country. Rather than being viewed as a vice, this openness is one that other accounting measures, especially at the aggregate level, could perhaps employ with more forthrightness as well.

Moreover, the relative ranking of Singapore, Chile and Botswana, for example, as the least corrupt countries in their respective regions, come as little surprise to most analysts knowledgeable with these regions. Findings that rank Italy as worse than Estonia, Greece worse as than Jordan and Bangladesh as considerably worse than Russia do call into question some widely held assumptions about the relative degree of corruption in different countries. It is these perspectives, based on the perceptions of thousands of business people around the world that contribute to the impact the CPI generates on a public awareness and policy level. The lack of precision goes with the territory. It is a characteristic shared with many other social and economic indicators.

Far more problematic is a basic question of source validity. Symptomatically, there is genuine puzzlement about the CPI scores in a growing number of countries. Knowledgeable people, who travel widely, frequently find it difficult to reconcile the scores in the CPI with their own experiences. A letter to a business publication in Ethiopia raises these issues.

Dear Sir,

I read with some puzzlement your recent article titled 'Combating corruption in Ethiopia'. I would like to believe your sweeping statement that institutional corruption is virtually non existent in Ethiopia, but what perplexes me is why in this case the position of Ethiopia in 'The 2003 Transparency International Corruption Perceptions Index' stands at 92 […] It's not only that Ethiopia according to this survey is far below the median which on its own should be a source of great concern but it's a fact too that its current standing is considerably worse than it was some few years back, a development that is very alarming. […] Anyway assuming your (sic.) are sincere in your recent claim, I wonder, do the foreigners behind this international survey have access to particulars that you for some reason do not have, or is it just that they were too lazy to do their homework and instead they relied on partial, erroneous data or maybe just conjured up unfounded statistics? […]

If you firmly stand by your claim and find the position of Ethiopia in the above mentioned list far off the mark, the one inescapable question will be what as Ethiopians do we need to do to rectify this misrepresentation that is probably causing us the loss of substantial amount of potential foreign investments?

Kind regards, Yonathan Berhane[33]

Berhane's letter raises the serious issue of source validity. This issue is exemplified by a dataset that was used in the CPI until 2001. Political Risk Services' (PRS) *International Country Risk Guide* has also been widely used as the primary dependent variable for a number of empirical corruption studies. It is also used in Kaufman et al's governance indicators. The PRS guide has two main attractions: it covers a wide range of approximately 140 countries and it allows for a time series analysis as the monthly updates of the dataset have been published regularly since 1980. The PRS customer base is essentially corporate, including 80 per cent of the Fortune 500 US corporations. Their proprietary data is also made available to researchers at discounted rates (www.prsgroup.com). The ICRG composite ratings and forecasts are based on the following formula:

CRR (country x) = 0.5 (PR+FR+ER), where
CRR = composite risk rating
PR = political risk rating
FR = financial risk rating
ER = economic risk rating

The political risk rating, in turn, is divided into twelve sub-components, one of which is corruption. This, however, is only one of several political risk components that contain a question about corruption. The others are 'Military in Politics', 'Law and Order', 'Democratic Accountability' and 'Bureaucratic Quality'. These components correlate well with each other but they are not exclusively concerned with corruption. They cannot, therefore, be used in an analysis of corruption. It is the corruption component alone that is of interest here. Although the CRR and the ICRG are particularly concerned with those risks that 'can make it difficult to conduct business effectively', the corruption measure is more concerned with 'actual or potential' political and administrative corruption in the form of nepotism, patronage, secret party funding, etc. (www.prsgroup.com). According to the ICRG *Brief Guide to the Ratings System*, the risk posed by such forms of corruption is that it may provoke a popular backlash or result in the fall or overthrow of a government, which in turn would have wider repercussions on the investment climate in a country. The corruption risk is first determined by calculating how long a government has been in power continuously. In the case of a one-party state or non-elected government, corruption, in the form of patronage and nepotism, is an essential prerequisite and it is therefore corrupt, to a greater or lesser degree, from its inception. In the case of democratic government, it has been our experience, almost without exception, that things begin to go wrong after an elected government has been in office for more than two consecutive terms, that is, eight to ten years […]. The lowest ratings are usually given to one-party states and autarchies (Sealy, 2001).

As a working hypothesis for determining actual corruption levels, this is at best indicative and tentative, and in many instances it is likely to be flawed. There is robust evidence, for example, that the scale of both bureaucratic and top-level corruption in most post-Communist countries in Eastern Europe and the former Soviet Union increased markedly in the first years after 1989.

The risk points per country range from 1 to 6, where the low score represents a very high risk, whereas a high score means the risk posed by corruption is minimal. On this scale, Canada, Denmark, Iceland, the Netherlands, and Sweden are among the handful of countries to obtain a score of 6. In 2002, the Democratic Republic of Congo, Indonesia, Gabon, Somalia, Yugoslavia and Zimbabwe are among the countries at the other end of the scale. So far, these ratings are not particularly controversial. What is more disconcerting is, for example, that Botswana, widely considered to be the least corrupt country in Sub-Saharan Africa, obtains a 3, when Congo-Brazzaville gets a 4; Liberia, which barely has a functioning state, even scores 5. A single party has ruled Botswana since independence, but corruption levels there are trivial compared to Congo-Brazzaville or Liberia.[34] Norway, in turn, obtains a 5, putting it on par with Liberia, Germany gets 4 and France even scores 3, level with Malawi and Yemen.[35] The editor of the ICRG explains these apparent anomalies:

> It frequently happens under our system that a country with a very low level of 'institutionalised' corruption presents a higher risk in our Corruption component than a country where corruption is institutionalised, the reason being that the political risk posed is greater in a democratically accountable system than in one where democratic accountability is severely curtailed or non-existent. (Sealy, 2001)[36]

On the one hand, there is the doubtful validity of using one-party rule, autarchy or indeed the length of a government in office as a proxy for corruption levels. On the other hand, the ICRG corruption component measures the risk posed by corruption to the private sector, not the incidence or scale of corruption *per se*. Whether or not the researchers using the ICRG in their regression analyses have been aware of these characteristics, they must cast doubt upon the validity of the ensuing research findings. A number of researchers have used a risk indicator that is at wide variance with numerous other measures of the scale or incidence of corruption.

PRS is not the only source that raises questions of reliability. The potential problem of circularity emerges with the Economist Intelligence Unit – a source that has been a staple of the CPI since its early days. The EIU obtains a 'cleansed' version of the CPI from TI that does not contain the EIU's original data. The EIU thereupon uses this as a benchmark for their ratings. The uneven level of expertise within the EIU compounds the problem. For some countries it is excellent. In other cases, 'some editors don't speak or read the language of the countries they work on and they may have little or no in-country experience'.[37] For the EIU, the corruption score is only one of several factors that contribute to a country risk rating. For the CPI, the corruption score is the only one that matters.

CPI Failing Nr 5: Far Too Narrow and Imprecise a Definition of Corruption

The sources used in the CPI only make weak distinctions distinguish between different branches of the civil service. If they were limited to any one aspect, for example, the judiciary or to corruption in political party financing, it would be difficult to justify their inclusion. IMD inquires about the 'public sphere', for EIU it is the 'public office' and PRS uses 'government'.

As was described in failing nr 3, the bias of the sources favours corruption as it affects the private sector. The private sector is likely to be particularly concerned about the forms of corruption that affect it most. The World Economic Forum's survey on global competitiveness is particularly detailed, covering 'export permits, business licences, exchange controls, tax assessments, police protection or loan applications'. In other words, any form of corruption that would be likely to be encountered by business people and investors. The surveys may also be concerned about high-level government corruption if it poses a risk to their business interests or if it is a factor in political volatility. They are likely to be less concerned by these factors, e.g. in Indonesia during the heyday of the Suharto years or in China during the early 2000s, when the political environment appears stable and favourable to foreign investors.

Table 6.1   Illustrative questions from CPI sources[38]

Information International	How common are bribes, how costly are they for doing business, how frequently are public contracts awarded to friends and relatives?
World Business Environment Survey	Frequency of bribing and corruption as constraint to business.
World Markets Research Centre	Red tape and the likelihood of encountering corrupt officials. Distinguishes between small-scale bribes, larger kickbacks and corporate fraud.
Gallup International for TI	How significant of an obstacle are the costs associated with [bribes] for doing business?

This standardisation has advantages for the CPI. Yet the understanding of corruption, particularly in the context of poorer countries, is inadequately advanced. In order to maximise response rates and in order to serve the interests of their primary clients, the questions on corruption place the respondent in the position of being an unwitting victim of the state (see Table 6.1 for illustrations). Collusion or agency by the respondent is never explored. Corruption is thereby couched entirely in terms of public extortion. The Bribe Payers Index shares this slanted approach. It asks respondents to rate the behaviour of competitors in areas of business with which the respondent is most familiar. Prosecutors and journalists (indeed, business people as well) know that this only captures one slice of the phenomenology of corruption. China, Panama, Sri Lanka and Syria all shared the same CPI score in 2003 of 3.4. Only one of these countries is a major recipient of Foreign Direct Investment. What is it that makes corruption more than tolerable in one context and yet intolerable in others? The CPI blurs the differences between corruption as an annoyance and corruption from which the private sector genuinely recoils.[39]

Cross-country comparisons of corruption levels in the different spheres of government would be particularly important in the context of reform. They may help address the question of why some venal business environments are more attractive or risky than others. From the standpoint of reformers working to promote a broader public interest, it would contribute significantly towards understanding the real pressure points and sequencing for sustained reform. The CPI in its present form, masking the trees for the forest, does not help to answer these questions.

The CPI would more accurately be called the 'bribe takers perception index' or, even more accurately, the 'extortion perceptions index'. The nomenclature of corruption is much broader than bribery or extortion. Some of the sources used in the CPI make allowances for distinctions between large and petty bribes. None of them distinguish between a wider catalogue of corrupt acts, including nepotism, extortion, patronage, facilitation payments, collusive networks, administrative and political corruption, etc.

The CPI benefits from its homogeneity. The range of activities it describes is narrower in scope and more internally consistent than it would be if it were required to subsume the entire catalogue of corrupt acts in one index. The unintended consequence has been a definition of anti-corruption globally almost entirely in terms of anti-bribery. More specifically, much anti-corruption work has been identified with the reduction of bribes that victimise private investors, investors who are frequently foreign.

Failing nr 1 described the one-sided nature of the CPI. It depicted the way in which this instrument has focused attention on bribe takers while letting bribe givers and abetters have an easy ride. Failing nr 3 expanded on the private sector bias of the CPI, particularly in terms of sampling. Failing nr 5 makes it clear that when the analysis is also limited to bribery (and more accurately to extortion by public officials) the analysis and the ensuing onus for reform have been severely constrained. Other systems of corruption, such as political patronage networks, nepotism or state capture by major private interests have only been analysed in isolation or on a regional basis by other organisations, including some national chapters of TI. Reducing corruption that victimises foreign investors is a significant agenda for reform. The CPI has contributed to making this the dominant paradigm for reform to the exclusion of other agendas.

CPI Failing Nr 6: Does not Measure Trends: Cannot Reward Genuine Reformers

The CPI's principal flaw is that it is a defective and misleading benchmark of trends. Initially set up to encourage reform, the CPI cannot answer the basic question: 'After four years, are these reforms making any difference?'

Because of the failing of irregularity (nr 2) TI is unable to control the countries that drop in and out of the CPI. If five countries drop out one year and six new countries come in, this will affect the rank order of some countries. To be fair, in its press releases, TI warns against misinterpreting such arbitrary changes in the rank order of countries. Despite these warnings, media headlines frequently refer to changes in a country's rank order and the various caveats on TI's website remain largely unreported and widely misunderstood.

Another concern voiced both by reformers in governments and civil society, is that anti-corruption drives may bring corruption into the open and thereby tarnish a country's image, precisely during a period when genuine efforts at reform are introduced. There is no evidence to support this perspective in the history of the CPI. Moreover, the judicious choice of averaging survey data from three years reduces the blips that might be caused by major one-off scandals and investigations. The working hypothesis has also been that significant structural reforms that go beyond targeted and punctual reforms in specific public procurement do take at least a few years to bear fruit.

More troubling, is the fact that changes in country scores cannot necessarily be attributed to independently verifiable changes in the corruption environment. In TI's own words:

> Year-to-year changes in a country's score result not only from a changing perception of a country's performance but also from a changing sample and methodology. Some sources are not updated and must be dropped, while new, reliable sources are added. With differing respondents and slightly differing methodologies, a change in a country's score may also relate to the fact that different viewpoints have been collected and different questions been asked. The index primarily provides an annual snapshot of the views of business people and country analysts, with less of a focus on year-to-year trends. (Transparency International, 2003)[40]

Trends cannot be assessed in terms of changes in the rank ordering. Nor, however, can they be identified in terms of changes in a particular country's scores. There are two principal reasons why country scores do not provide a cogent benchmark for trends. The first, as outlined above, is that the composition of the sources and methodologies employed frequently change from year to year. There have been numerous changes over the decade since the CPI was first introduced, both in the sources selection and the standardisation techniques used to aggregate the data. There have been three significant changes over this period. The second reason the scores do not provide a useful benchmark for trends is inextricably linked to the standardisation technique. The passage describing the current standardisation technique, matching percentiles, is worth citing in full:

Each of the sources uses its own scaling system, requiring that the data be standardized before each country's mean value can be determined. This standardization is carried out in two steps. For step 1 each source is standardized using matching percentiles. The ranks (and not the scores) of countries is the only information processed from our sources. For this technique the common sub-samples of a new source and the previous year's CPI are determined. Then, the largest value in the CPI is taken as the standardized value for the country ranked best by the new source. The second largest value is given to the country ranked second best, etc. 2 Imagine that a new source ranks only four countries: UK is best, followed by Singapore, Venezuela and Argentina respectively. In the 2002 CPI these countries obtained the scores 8.7, 9.3, 2.5 and 2.8. Matching percentiles would now assign UK the best score of 9.3, Singapore 8.7, Venezuela 2.8 and Argentina 2.5.

Matching percentiles is superior in combining indices that have different distributions. But, as it makes use of the ranks, and not the scores of sources, this method loses some of the information inherent in the sources. What tips the balance in favour of this techniques is its capacity to keep all reported values within the bounds from 0 to 10: All countries in the CPI obtain scores between 0 (very corrupt) and 10 (highly clean). This characteristic is not obtained by an alternative technique that standardizes the mean and standard deviation of the subsamples. Matching percentiles, on the other hand, guarantees that all standardized values are within these bounds. This results because any standardized value is taken from the previous year's CPI, which by definition is restricted to the aforementioned range. (Lambsdorff 2003, p. 7)

Matching percentiles is advantageous in terms of data presentation. The scores will always fall in a range between 0 and 10. With an earlier standardisation technique based on country scores – not ranks – some countries, like Finland, obtained standardised scores of more than 10.[41] At the other end of the scale, Bangladesh emerged with a score of less than zero. While this was statistically sound, in presentational terms it was incomprehensible. However, matching percentiles suffers from another defect.

When countries are ranked (or indeed scored) by respondents and even expert panels, the natural reflection is to compare a country with its major regional neighbours to have a baseline of comparison. Even if a country implements significant reforms to curb corruption and is assessed as being on a positive trend by some of the CPI's sources, its rank order *vis-à-vis* neighbouring countries may take years to change, particularly if other countries in a given region are undergoing reforms as well. In the short term, small improvements in a country's rank order might even be 'punished' by the second phase of the standardisation technique:

Without a second adjustment there would be a trend towards a continuously smaller diversity of scores. If, for example, Finland was to repeat its score from the previous year, it would have to score best in all sources listing this country. If it scores second to best in any source, the standardized value it obtains after using matching percentiles and aggregation would be lower than its current score. Thus, given some heterogeneity among sources, it seems inevitable that Finland's score would deteriorate. The opposite would be true of Bangladesh, which would obtain a better score if it is not consistently rated worst by all its sources. A second standardization is required in order to avoid a continuous trend to less diversity among scores. However, applying a simple mean and standard deviation technique might again bring about values that are beyond our range from 0 to 10. A more complicated standardization is required for the second step: A beta-transformation. The idea behind this monotonous [*should say* 'monotonic'] transformation is to increase the standard deviation to its desired value, but to keep all values within the range from 0 to 10. (Lambsdorff, 2003, p. 7)

Bangladesh currently has the reputation of being one of the most corrupt countries in Asia. Indeed, it is ranked last in the CPI. This position may be justified. Because of the failing of irregularity, one cannot know whether the inclusion of other countries from the region and beyond would moderate the country's standing. Bangladesh is also one of the poorest countries in Asia. With its sizeable population, an active aid community, and all-too-frequent natural disasters it is often in the regional media spotlight, Bangladesh is frequently associated with bad news. Moreover, most other countries in the sub-region are undertaking anti-corruption reforms; and Nepal is not included in the CPI because it only has two sources. In theory, even if Bangladesh were to make significant improvements in curbing corruption, its score (not only its relative rank), may remain constant for years. Bangladesh would need to improve its image and credibly report to the international business community and financial press that it was making strides against corruption. Institutional reforms alone (new anti-corruption commissions, higher rates of conviction, civil service reform, etc.) would not be sufficient.

For Bangladesh's CPI score to improve, something else would be needed: other countries in the region and beyond would actually need to deteriorate or experience significant setbacks. This bad news, also independently verified, would in turn need to be widely disseminated and sustained over a long period (more than 3 years). In other words, for Bangladesh's CPI score to improve, the country would not primarily be competing to improve its own standing, it would also be in a negative race against its neighbours where an overall improvement in the region would be to Bangladesh's disadvantage. (By contrast, if the other countries deteriorate and Bangladesh remain as it is, the score for Bangladesh would rise without Bangladesh having done anything more than stand still.)

By publishing the CPI on an annual basis, TI wittingly sustains this negative race to the bottom. TI accurately acknowledges that the CPI is no more than an 'annual snapshot'. However, publishing the CPI every year it invites erroneous comparisons based on both rankings and scores. The CPI cannot reward reformers because the standardisation technique emphasises rank ordering over internal reforms. It thereby reinforces negative perceptions about certain countries (and the positive images of other, already well-to-do countries). The CPI, in other words, has become a stick without a carrot. It is all but impossible for countries to improve their scores in the CPI through government reforms and sustained anti-corruption efforts.

Short of ceasing to publish the CPI altogether, a possible way forward for TI, would be for the CPI to be released at most every four to five years. The Bribe Payers Index and a new 'Index of Corruption Safe Havens', both more robust indices over which TI would have control over data collection and analysis, should be published annually. A variety of other instruments, such as the Global Corruption Barometer, could address the other lacunae of the CPI. When publishing the CPI, TI should make every effort to maximise the country coverage by commissioning its own independent surveys. A modest effort could increase the coverage by at least 35 countries.

In order to put an end to erroneous and misleading comparisons based on country scores, the CPI should simply cease to publish them. Countries should be listed only in rank order. Some misrepresentation would still occur, especially as and when a number of new countries were added to the Index. But these misunderstandings would be far less severe than the current misinterpretations of country scores.[42]

CPI Failing Nr 7: Guilty by Association – Aid Conditionality

The failing of guilt by association distinguishes between a relatively minor failing and a major problem. The minor one is the CPI's association with numerous correlation and regression analyses produced by economists and political scientists since the mid-1990s. In fairness, a majority of these studies, especially the ones published by economists, the World Bank and IMF, do not use the CPI. World Bank researchers have been able to use their own data sources generated in recent years. A number of studies relying on secondary sources use PRS's ICRG because the wide country coverage and long-standing data set appears to lend itself particularly well to time series analysis.

A reduction in corruption levels by a single point on a ten-point scale is estimated to increase annual GDP growth per capita from 0.6 to 1.8 percentage points;[43] a similar reduction would bring the Gini coefficient for income inequality from 0.9 to 2.1 Gini points (Gupta, Davoodi and Alonso-Terme, 1998). It would reduce the child mortality rate by 1.1 to 2.7 deaths per thousand live births (Gupta, Davoodi and Tiongson, 2000). On a lighter note, a study by the US Federal Reserve Bank St Louis, finds that a belief in hell is negatively correlated with levels of corruption (*Reuters*, 27 July 2004). Numerous studies are based on simple correlations that leave the question of causality open. Others, using more sophisticated techniques, seek to isolate and understand the causalities that lower corruption levels would produce.

The heuristic and political function of these studies has been considerable. These studies provided the *prima facie* case required, for example, by the Bretton Woods Institutions to legitimise their commitment to anti-corruption. This was a topic they had hitherto explicitly avoided as being 'political' and beyond their remit for 50 years of their existence. A number of these studies share one or more of four flaws. First, if the CPI is the corruption variable, then it cannot be used for time series analyses. Second, if the corruption variable is PRS's ICRG, then the study does not address changes in corruption levels; the PRS guide measures risk to investors. Third, the CPI and other aggregate indices, like Kaufmann's governance indicators, are subject to significant variance and standard deviation. They do not lend themselves well to making minute inferences, particularly when the independent variable (e.g. GDP per capita growth) is so inaccurate for many countries – see failing nr 4 above.

Fourth, a large number of countries have remained poor over the last four decades. They tend to share a basket of 'bads' that include weak public institutions, low levels of literacy, poor health statistics, weak judiciaries etc. Many of these countries are also rated as highly corrupt. Only a handful of countries have made the transition to higher standards of living in the past four decades. Some of these countries have also been rated as highly corrupt. A larger number of countries have enjoyed higher standards of living for more than 40 years. These countries tend to share basket of 'goods' that is much the inverse of the first category of countries. They are also perceived as largely 'clean'.[44] By the sheer weight of numbers, therefore, regressions, causalities and correlations reveal little that is new.

The CPI's guilt, in this case, is admittedly a minor one. Where the CPI or PRS's data have been used as the dependent variable, the research is faulty. Many of the conclusions are facile and at best heuristic. Much of the research tells policy makers little that they do not already know. As a general rule (and there are some significant exceptions), high levels of corruption are associated with much that is bad. Low levels of corruption tend to be associated with much that is good. The CPI, and the myriad studies it has inspired, provides no actionable outcomes. It can legitimise the case for reform but it cannot genuinely point reformers in any meaningful direction.

The CPI's more serious associative failing is with donor conditionality. In recent years, a number of aid donors have used the CPI in the context of bilateral negotiations. Until recently, such conditionalities were largely informal or politically expedient (as in the case of Kenya during the last years of the Moi regime). With the Bush administration's Millennium Challenge Account (MCA), the use of the CPI in the context of donor conditionality has become a matter of public record. The MCA foresees a 50 per cent increase in US core development assistance. While targeted at countries in need, the MCA rewards 'good policy' by rating countries along 16 'objective' criteria.[45] One of these criteria is 'control of corruption'. The World Bank Institute generates the data source for the corruption scores. The MCA recommends, however, that '… as additional information, the Board may also consider how the country scores on Transparency International's Corruption Perceptions Index'.[46]

The implications of this association may seem benign on the surface. After all, the beneficiaries of the MCA will receive additional US assistance. The candidates who fail, however, are likely to be penalised. Kenya, for example, is one of the countries in 2004 that 'fails to meet the 'control of corruption' standard required for inclusion in the aid programme. Kenya is one of seven countries likely to be disqualified solely on that basis' (*Financial Times*, 30 April 2004).

Leaving aside the other weaknesses of the CPI, failing nr 6 (its inability to reward genuine reform), should disqualify it from playing any role in such decisions. The CPI is a publicly available document and TI cannot, therefore, control the many ways in which the findings may be applied. TI could, however, distance itself publicly from the use of its Index in the context of aid conditionality, an application to which it is wholly unsuited. As was suggested in nr 6 above, TI would do even better by ceasing to publish the country scores.

Conclusion

Clearly, corruption can be measured. The questions remain as to how accurately, and to what effect? The CPI contributed to a shift whereby corruption measurements came to be seen as a primarily descriptive exercise, not a predominantly moral and value-laden notion.[47] Drawing on historical antecedents, there are indications that the use of comparative country rankings was seminal in this shift. One of the major innovations in the public health movement of the 1850s in the United Kingdom was the introduction of the notion of the 'Healthy Districts'. These were 63 registration districts, one tenth of the national total, where the crude death rate was one tenth of the national total. In the ensuing decades, periodic reminders were published of the tens of thousands of preventable deaths in various cities around the country that would have been avoided if the sanitary conditions approximated those of the Healthy Districts (Szreter, 1991).

Although a more sophisticated and objective ranking than the CPI, the two indices share a use of comparative measurements across units of analysis (districts in the one case and countries in the other) previously held to have been futile. In both instances, a change in awareness and concrete policy reforms followed.

The CPI played a central role in influencing the global agenda for anti-corruption reform, raising awareness by shattering the taboo and catapulting the issue of corruption to the forefront of national and international discourse. With the advent of the UN Anti-Corruption Convention in 2003, which marked the culmination of many years' efforts to produce an armoury of international and regional anti-corruption norms, anti-corruption has firmly entered a very different phase of enforcement and implementation. The immediate goal is no longer simply to raise awareness about the importance of curbing corruption. Nor is it to establish even more comprehensive and stringent international norms. In this latest phase, one to which many newly elected governments are resolutely committed, the CPI in its present form has become counterproductive.

Collectively, the seven failings of the CPI call for a complete reassessment and an overhaul of this influential social indicator. In particular, the CPI needs to be complemented by other indicators to address vital aspects of the subject that a single index can never hope to capture.

The sixth failing reveals that the CPI is unsuitable to measure trends or even to capture genuine reforms. It should no longer be published in its present form as it actually undermines the efforts of reformers. Short of abandoning it altogether, the CPI should be published at most every four to five years. The country coverage would need to be global. And the country scores should be removed. Transparency International, independently of its views on the utility of corruption-related conditionality in aid or debt relief to poor countries, should publicly distance itself from, and warn aid agencies against, any use of the CPI in such negotiations. The organisation should similarly brief recipient governments that the CPI is unsuitable in this regard.

The challenge ahead is evident: after ten years it is time to find new measurements!

Notes

1   The United Nations Office for Drug Control and Crime Prevention (ODCCP), for example, collects cross-country data on criminal justice systems. The legal and administrative definitions of corruption, bribery, embezzlement and fraud sometimes overlap and vary from country to country. A *sui generis* legal definition is not problematic in itself. Since Singapore and Hong Kong, widely known to have low levels of corruption, have among the highest *per capita* conviction rates for bribery, successful prosecutions cannot be used as a measure of incidence or degree of corruption. On the contrary, they underpin the success of these countries' anti-corruption efforts.

2   Moreover, a single high-profile international or national case, such as the bribery of public and international officials during the bidding for the 2000 Olympic Games, would significantly increase the level of press coverage without being an indicator of changes in corruption levels.

3   The only major country to have a military coup since the mid-1990s was Pakistan, where rampant corruption under Benazir Bhutto and Nawaz Sharif were used to justify General Pervez Musharraf's takover in 1999. In an opinion survey conducted in 2002 in Peru, widespread corruption was mentioned as one of the two most frequently cited reasons besides civil unrest that would justify a military coup (cited in 'Workshop on Governance and Corruption Measures', CIDE, Mexico City, 17 April 2002).

4   In the late 1990s and early 2000s, this was the case in Bolivia (Hugo Banzer), Venezuela (Hugo Chavez), Benin (Mathieu Kérékou), and Nigeria (Olusegun Obasanjo) to mention but four examples.

5   This is particularly, although by no means exclusively, true for social phenomena in the private sphere (rates of incest, extramarital affairs, or even household consumption, etc.). Global measures of poverty, with important implications for policy, also raise a host of problematic notions of comparability and changes in relative standards of living over time (see, e.g. Deaton, Angus (2000), *Counting the World's Poor: Problems and Possible Solutions'*, Research Program in Development Studies, Unpublished Monograph, Princeton University).

6   This chapter is concerned with reviewing methodological tools at the disposal of academic researchers. There are other possible sources of evidence as well. The CIA, and in all likelihood the other major intelligence gathering agencies, claimed in the 1990s to be systematically monitoring international investment and procurement transactions for evidence of bribery. R. James Woolsey, the former Director of Central Intelligence, insists that '95 per cent of U.S. economic intelligence comes from open sources' (Woolsey, R.J. (2000), 'Why we spy on our Allies?', *The Wall Street Journal*, 17 March). The data available to the CIA may therefore, on an aggregate level, be no better or worse than the information contained in these pages.

7   Transparency International is a Berlin-based anti-corruption NGO with sections in more than 90 countries. The author was a founding staff member of the organisation. As TI's head of research he had responsibility for the CPI, which was developed by Johann Graf Lambsdorff. The author developed two further international corruption measurements, the Bribe Payers Index and the Global Corruption Barometer. He is now co-director of Tiri, an NGO formed in 2003 to address the challenges of implementation, enforcement and capacity building for sustainable corruption control and public integrity reform.

8   See www.opacity-index.com [10.10.04].

9   At the time of writing, the final report on the WBES was still forthcoming (June 2001). Information can be obtained at www1.worldbank.org/beext/resources/assess-wbessurvey-alt.htm. The following comments derive from the 22-transition country conducted in the first phase of this project. See Hellman, Joel, Jones, Geraint, Kaufmann, Daniel and Shankerman, Mark (2000), 'Measuring Governance, Corruption, and State Capture: How Firms and Bureaucrats Shape the Business Environment in Transition Countries', *World Bank Policy Research Working Paper*, p. 2312.

10   See www.unicri.it/icvs [10.10.04].

11   The most recent CPI data is available at http://www.transparency.org/cpi/index.html#cpi [10.10.04].

12   A Harvard Kennedy School of Government case study has been built around this forced decision.

13   REF. missing.

14   REF: Miami Herald article.

15   'It is completely irresponsible. It's unjust, absurd and arbitrary to talk about Argentina in those terms'. Iglesias, Graciela (1996), 'Creció la corrupción en la Argentina desde 1993', *La Nación* (Argentina), 5 June.

16   'It's a mystery, even those those involved, how the classifications are done'. 'Según Transparency la Argentina ocupa el 61 puesto en corrupción', *La Nación* (Argentina), 24 September 1998.

17   'Whoever comes and says that this is a corrupt government, is not only an imbecile – and please write this down – that person is also a scoundrel'. 'Presidente critica informe', *Prensa Libre* (Guatemala), 25 September 1998.

18   In an interesting turn of events, a Paris-based NGO named Paul Biya the year's most distinguished statesman 'in a move widely considered as intended to attenuate the humiliation suffered by the Biya regime after [TI] declared Cameroon the most corrupt nation'. From 'French NGO Confers Distinguished Statesman Award on President Biya', *The Herald* (Cameroon), 5 June 1998.

19   *Interview* with Mr. Choi Byung-Rok in Ottawa, Canada, 14 September 2000.

20   In 2002, TI was given an Award for Agenda Setting by Media Tenor, an Institute for Media Analysis in large measure reflecting the impact the CPI has had in the world media.

21   From TI's mission statement: http://www.transparency.org/about_ti/mission.html [11.10.04].

22   I am grateful to Amartya Sen for his comments on this point.

23   In the first effort of its kind, the USAID office in Beirut in 2003 commissioned the Middle East survey in the hope of including not only Lebanon but also several other countries from the region. The World Bank, which has also commissioned several international corruption surveys, does not appear to have adopted the same motivation.

24   See, also, Report on Workshop of 29–30 April 2004, *Good Governance and Behavioural Change*, Phnom Penh, Cambodia: 'The CPI is of considerable interest to private corporations – especially when considering whether to invest in a country. Unfortunately, since there is little foreign investment as yet in Cambodia, there have been few corporate donors to pay for such surveys. Nevertheless, it is anticipated that sufficient survey work will have been undertaken to allow Cambodia to be ranked on the CPI within the next 2–3 years'.

25   See Johann Lambsdorff's chapter and the Transparency International website for a glossary of the acronyms for the sources. The sampling frames of ICVS, IMD, WB/EBRD and WEF consist exclusively of residents living within the countries beings surveyed. Some

respondents are likely to be foreigners, however, and in the case of IMD, WB/EBRD and WEF, which consist of samples of high to mid-level business people.

26 In previous years, the CPI has included the findings of an international survey by Gallup International, using representative samples of the general population.

27 See http://www.transparency.org/about_ti/mission.html#values [10.10.04]. The other two aims are to contribute to sustainable development and clean environment; and to strengthen global security.

28 Suggestion made by Daniel Kaufmann in a seminar on 20 February 1999, Washington, DC.

29 See, e.g. http://countrydata.bvdep.com/EIU/Help/measuringeconomicactivity.htm [10.10.04].

30 'The takeover', as in a car bypassing another one.

31 A man's shirt, for example, is recorded as having been manufactured in a given country for trade purposes according to the location where the collar and cuffs were sewn. If the Chinese export quota is filled, an almost finished shirt can be exported to Hong Kong, where a few stitches to the cuffs and collar will be added and then returned to China, where it will be finished, packaged and transported.

32 The relative degree of precision of country scores is captured in the CPI press release league table through two additional columns. The first, on the standard deviation, indicates the difference in the values of the sources. The second, the high-low range, provides the highest and the lowest value of the different sources on a standardised basis.

33 Letter to the Editor of *Capital Ethiopia* of 31 August 2004 (http://www.capitalethiopia. com/letter%20 to%20the%20editorial.htm [11.10.04]). Thanks to Rupert Bladon for pointing out this letter.

34 Botswana is a democracy whose government has not changed since regaining Independence in 1966 and it scores very favourably both on the CPI and in the opinions of those familiar with the region.

35 In TI's 2003 CPI press release (http://www.transparency.org/pressreleases_archive/2003/ 2003.10.07.cpi.en.html), Norway, France and Germany are among the countries cited as having improved their scores in recent years. A significant percentage of the upward trend of the scores for these and other countries would be accounted for by the exclusion of PRS from the data sources.

36 Thomas Sealy, editor of the ICRG, *email* to the author of 18 May 2001.

37 *Interview* an EIU country editor, London, 8 June 1998.

38 See http://www.transparency.org/pressreleases_archive/2003/2003.10.07.cpi.en.html [12.10.04] for a complete list of the questions.

39 Illustrative of the fact that leading rankings is an insufficient pre-condition for foreign investments, Haiti topped the International Monetary Fund's 'Index for Trade Openness' in the early 1990s for being the 'best student of the rules of globalization [...] Yet over the 1990s, Haiti's economy contracted [...] No surprise – if you are a corrupt and misgoverned nation with a closed economy, becoming a corrupt and misgoverned nation with an open economy is not going to solve your problems'. (Rosenberg, Tina (2002), 'The Free-Trade Fix', *The New York Times Magazine*, 18 August).

40 See http://www.transparency.org/pressreleases_archive/2003/2003.10.07.cpi.en.html [12.10.04].

41 In the final press release, the score was capped at 10.0. (See http://www.transparency. org/cpi/2000 /cpi2000.html#cpi [10.10.04]).

42   Since the late 1990s, more detailed in-country diagnostic surveys have been used as one way of measuring improvements and providing more detailed information of use to policy makers. Close to one hundred such surveys have been supported by a range of institutions, in particular the World Bank, but also numerous NGOs around the world. The heterogeneity of approaches and samples means that there is little common basis for comparison between them. And only a few surveys have been repeated with any regularity. Moreover, the CPI continues to dominate the headlines and to be the international media's benchmark by default. The incorporation of the World Bank's 'control of corruption index', in the context of the US Millennium Challenge Account (see next section) may change this balance slightly in the coming years.

43   Estimates in different studies vary quite considerably, but the relation between reducing corruption and increasing GDP *per capita* growth is generally seen to be positive (see Abed, George and Davoodi, Hamid (2000), 'Corruption, Structural Reforms, and Economic Performance in the Transition Economies', *IMF Working Paper*, 00/132; Leite, C. and Weidmann, J. (1999), 'Does Mother Nature Corrupt? Natural Resources, Corruption and Economic Growth', *International Monetary Fund Working Paper* 99/85; Mauro, Paulo (1996), 'Corruption and the Composition of Government Expenditure', *Journal of Public Economics*, vol. 69, pp. 263–79; Tanzi, Vito and Davoodi, Hamid (1998), 'Corruption, Public Investment and Growth', in T. Shibata and T. Ihori (eds), *The Welfare State, Public Investment and Growth*, Springer Verlag, Tokyo.

44   Mushtaq Khan makes a similar argument. Some of his research is on the small group of countries where 'growth has been high despite the presence of substantial corruption' (Khan, Mushtaq and Jomo, K.S. (eds) (2000), *Rents, Rent-Seeking and Economic Development: Theory and Evidence in Asia*, Cambridge University Press, Cambridge, p. 10).

45   See http://www.mca.gov/ [12.10.04].

46   Millennium Challenge Corporation, Report on Countries that are Candidates for Millennium Challenge Account Eligibility in FY 2004 and Countries that are not Candidates Because of Legal Prohibitions: Annex A: Indicator Definitions, Washington, DC, 2004.

47   Amartya Sen has described a similar trajectory in the measurement of poverty (1973), 'Issues in the Measurement of Poverty', *Scandinavian Journal of Economics*, vol. 81, pp. 285–307).

References

– (1996), 'Don't Tell us how to run our Country', *The Straits Times (Malaysia)*, 5 June.

– (1996), *La Nación (Argentina)*, 5 June.

– (1997), 'Survey Mania', *Arab News (Saudi Arabia)*, 2 August.

– (1998), *La Nación (Argentina)*, 24 September.

– (1998), 'Angry Reaction from Cameroon's Government', *Reuters*, 25 September.

– (1998), 'French NGO Confers Distinguished Statesman Award on President Biya', *The Herald (Cameroon)*, 5 June.

– (1998), *Prensa Libre (Guatemala)*, 25 September.

– (1999), 'A Guide to Graft', *The Economist*, 30 October.

– (1999), 'Honduras Surprised at Most Corrupt LatAm Nation Tag', *Reuters*, 26 October.

– (1999), 'Nigeria Backs Transparency International Report on Corruption', *Agence France-Presse*, 27 October.

– (1999), *The Independent*, 27 March.

– (2002), *Frankfurter Allgemeine Zeitung*, 16 May.

– (2004), 'Belief in Hell Boosts Economic Growth, Fed Says', *Reuters*, 27 July.

– (2004), 'Kenya Likely to be Disqualified for Share in new US Development Aid', *Financial Times*, 30 April.

Abdullah, A. and Ang, P. (1996), 'PM: Set up Malaysia Watchdog on Europeans', *New Straits Times (Malaysia)*, 5 June.

Abed, George and Davoodi, Hamid (2000), 'Corruption, Structural Reforms, and Economic Performance in the Transition Economies', *IMF Working Paper, no. 00/132*.

Bloem, Adriaan M. and Shrestha, Manik L. (2000), 'Exhaustive Measures of GDP and the Unrecorded Economy', *IMF Working Paper*.

Deaton, Angus (2000), 'Counting the World's Poor: Problems and Possible Solutions', *Unpublished Monograph*, Research Program in Development Studies, Princeton University.

Dogan, Mattei and Kazancigil, Ali (1994), *Comparing Nations: Concepts*, Strategies, Substance, Blackwell, Oxford.

Florini, Ann (1998), 'The End of Secrecy', *Foreign Policy*, vol. 111.

Galtung, Fredrik (2001), 'A Survey of Surveys in 2001', in Robin Hodess (ed.), *Global Corruption Report*, Transparency International (TI), Berlin.

Gupta, Sanjeev, Davoodi, Hamid and Alonso-Terme, Rosa (1998), 'Does Corruption Affect Income Inequality and Poverty?', *IMF Working Paper*, no. 98/76.

Gupta, Sanjeev, Davoodi, Hamid and Tiongson, Erwin (2000), 'Corruption and the Provision of Health Care and Educational Services', in A.K. Jain (ed.), *The Economics of Corruption*, Kluwer Academics, Dordrecht.

Heidenheimer, Arnold J., Johnston, Michael and LeVine, Victor T. (eds) (1989), *Political Corruption: A Handbook*, Transaction Press, New Brunswick, NJ.

Hellman, Joel, Jones, Geraint and Kaufmann, Daniel (2000), 'Seize the State, Seize the Day: State Capture, Corruption and Influence in Transition Economies', *World Bank Policy Research Working Paper*, September.

Hellman, Joel, Jones, Geraint, Kaufmann, Daniel and Shankerman, Mark (2000), 'Measuring Governance, Corruption, and State Capture: How Firms and Bureaucrats Shape the Business Environment in Transition Countries', *World Bank Policy Research Working Paper*.

Hoddess, R. (ed.) (2001), *Global Corruption Report*, Transparency International, Berlin.

Huntington, S.P. (1968), *Political Order in Changing Societies*, New Haven: Yale University Press.

Kaufmann, Daniel, Kraay, Aart and Zoido-Lobatón, Pablo (1999), 'Aggregating Governance Indicators', *World Bank Policy Research Working Paper* (paper updated and revised in 2002).

Khan, Mushtaq and Jomo, K.S. (eds) (2000), *Rents, Rent-Seeking and Economic Development: Theory and Evidence in Asia*, Cambridge University Press, Cambridge.

Lambsdorff, Johann (2003), *Framework Document 2003: Background Paper to the 2003 Corruption Perceptions Index*, Transparency International, Berlin, p. 7.

Leite, C. and Weidmann, J. (1999), 'Does Mother Nature Corrupt? Natural Resources, Corruption and Economic Growth', *International Monetary Fund Working Paper*, no. 99/85.

Leys, C. (1965), 'What is the Problem About Corruption?', *Journal of Modern African Studies*, vol. 3, p. 215.

Mauro, Paulo (1996), 'Corruption and the Composition of Government Expenditure', *Journal of Public Economics*, vol. 69, pp. 263–79.

Millennium Challenge Corporation (2004), 'Report on Countries that are Candidates for MCA Eligibility in FY 2004 and Countries that are not Candidates Because of Legal Prohibition Annex A: Indicator Definitions', Washington DC.

Miller, William L., Grødeland, Åse B. and Koshechkina, Tatyana Y. (2001), *A Culture of Corruption: Coping with Government in Post-communist Europe*, Central European University Press, Budapest:

Mirus, Rolf and Smith, Roger S. (2002), *Canada's Underground Economy: Measurement and Implications*, The Fraser Institute.

Musa, Tansa (1999), 'Cameroon Surprised at Ranking', *Reuters (Yaoundé)*, 8 October, p. 2

O'Brien, Timothy (1999), 'Trackers of Global Thievery Release Top 10 List', *The San Diego Union-Tribune* (USA), 7 November.

Rosenberg, Tina (2002), 'The Free-Trade Fix', *The New York Times Magazine*, 18 August.

Scott, James C. (1969), 'The Analysis of Corruption in Developing Nations', *Comparative Studies in Society and History*, vol. 11, p. 317.

Sealy, Thomas (2001), 'International Country Risk Guide (February)', *Political Risk Services*, p. 21.

Sen, Amartya (1973), 'Issues in the Measurement of Poverty', *Scandinavian Journal of Economics*, vol. 81, pp. 285–307.

Stein, Jeff (1997), 'In Pakistan, the Corruption is Lethal', *International Herald Tribune*, 12 September, p. 15.

Sweeney, John, Beaumont, Peter and Doyle, Leonard (1998), 'This is the World Cup that No Country Wants to Win', *The Observer*, 28 June.

Szreter, Simon (1991), 'The GRO and the Public Health Movement in Britain, 1837–1914', *The Society for the Social History of Medicine*, pp. 435–63.

Tanzi, Vito and Davoodi, Hamid (1998), 'Corruption, Public Investment and Growth', in T. Shibata and T. Ihori (eds), *The Welfare State, Public Investment and Growth*, Springer Verlag, Tokyo.

Webb, Jason (1998*), Reuters*, 23 September.

Woolsey, R.J. (2000), 'Why we spy on our Allies?', *The Wall Street Journal*, 17 March.

Wraith, R. and Simpkins, E. (1963*), Corruption in Developing Countries*, Allen and Unwin, London.

Zvekic, Ugljesa (1998), 'Corruption in Public Administration: Results of the International Crime Victims Survey', *UNICRI Working Paper*, Rome.

Chapter 7

The Non-Perception Based Measurement of Corruption: A Review of Issues and Methods from a Policy Perspective

Nick Duncan

Introduction

Although fascinating in its own right, the question of what corruption 'is' has not been settled since the topic first became distinct in the mid 1970s. Nor does it appear that there will be any consensus on what corruption is in the immediate future. As a result, each research project has adopted a definition (or, as in some cases, denied the legitimacy of definition at all) and used it as it suited the study that they intended to carry out. The fact that there is no consensus on what constitutes corruption provides a challenge to policy makers especially when one wants to ask comparative question such as: 'are we more or less corrupt than we were?' It also raises challenges when one asks absolute questions such as: 'how corrupt is the supply of pharmaceuticals?' Answers to these sorts of questions are essential if policy makers are to allocate scarce resources to priorities and to have some insight into whether the problem is responding to policy. Indeed, unless corruption can be measured in some sense, it is hard to claim convincingly that there is a problem.

When conveying information about an issue as highly politicised as corruption, having some sort of uniform index or measure is of great value. It provides a basis for communicating knowledge about an issue in a very succinct way. 'Corruption costs Country X £2 billion per year' is a powerful statement that focuses the mind: one that a qualitative description would be hard pressed to match. Quantitative data provides a basis for the employment of, perhaps, the most beloved tools of the social scientist, econometrics. With an econometric study, links between measured phenomena can often be claimed with substantial credibility. The incentive to measure is then clear. But does the evasiveness of the concept itself suggest that all such measurements are 'built on sandy ground'?

I will argue that practice has shown that aspects of corruption have been captured in a policy useful way by so called 'direct' measures and that perception and aggregated methods have a distinct, albeit partial role, in providing knowledge about the level of corruption. The quantitative measurement of corruption is, or at least should be, based on clearly identified qualitative choices, which involve policy makers in the local community, and aim to provide knowledge about phenomena, context and solutions that are of concern to them directly.

The methods briefly surveyed here address some of the policy shortcomings of perception studies which, even in refined studies, have proved to be subject to a lot of 'noise' from other held views (Abramo[1] and Seligson, forthcoming 2006).[2] The methods used here derive much of their strength when being used as part of a strategy informed by qualitative choices (that is, what aspects of the phenomena in question are important to us). These approaches can offer a far more practical knowledge for policy makers than aggregated perception measures. In many cases, they translate into immediate policy prescriptions.

Measures attempting to measure actual corruption have evolved innovative ways of trying to capture, as closely as possible, the consequences of corruption. That such measures do not contain all that might be considered corrupt is not controversial, (although, quite often, the narrowness of the corrupt activity needs clarification).

This chapter seeks to review some of the main challenges of interpretation and definition, and how different techniques, often ingenious, have been developed to provide high quality knowledge about corruption as a basis for policy.

In the first part of this chapter, I will review some of the technical challenges of context (that is, how to look in the right place for the problem *you* have) in designing and interpreting corruption measurement. In the second part, I will look at the methods that have been developed and used and how they have begun to provide policy makers with more targeted and useful knowledge about corruption.

Context Sensitivity in Measurement

One of the few areas in which there is consensus is that corruption occurs in transactions. How transactions are identified and what is measured is, in practice, highly dependent on the researcher's response to the environment and phenomena to be measured. Which transactions are identified and which of their aspects are selected for measurement provides not only the link to policy but also, in reverse, a guide to the interpretation of measures and indices. In this section, the selection and identification of what to measure in order to capture policy relevant characteristics are discussed, as are the ways in which links between actors are established in the identification of networks.

Deciding What Phenomena to Measure

Whichever definition of corruption one adopts, it still remains highly unlikely that it will be possible to measure the actual amount of corruption *directly*. In most cases, the closest one can get is first hand reports, or discrepancy checks. In many other cases, corruption is measured by proxies that are taken to be substantive evidence of corruption; for example, if the wife of a politician becomes very rich with no satisfactory explanation, despite it being impossible to identify the source of the funds, it might be considered, at least, as circumstantial evidence of corruption: a proxy. Proxies are also used to capture the consequence of corruption, as the content of a transaction may carry only part of the sense of the type and degree of corruption that has taken place. The use of proxies is common in the measurement of corruption for practical reasons. However, they need to be used and interpreted with considerable care as they are often subject to a number of influences which may be misleading especially when comparing cases.

Accounting for the Effect of Local Context on Proxies

Corrupt transactions always occur in an organisational and institutional setting. Scoping the measure of a corruption question will require identification of, for example, the degree of coordination and organisation in the phenomena in question in order to measure the appropriate transactions. If proxies are to be used and an inference of levels of corruption drawn from, for example, unexplained levels of efficiency or 'leakage', account must be taken of the impact that the political economy may have on the proxies being used. Efficiency is especially prone to contextual variation between countries (and even within countries). In Mushtaq Khan's typology of political context, the 'political settlement' and rights allocations will have a significant impact on observed consequences of corruption. Corruption, in this case, differs significantly if there is a predatory private sector or a predatory state.[3]

Table 7.1   Corruption types

Type of Corruption	Patrimonial[4]	Clientalist[5]
Efficient	Initial Rights Inefficient and corruption allows for intervention/correction	Rare: Only if Efficient Rights can be created which do not hurt existing clients
Inefficient	Initial Rights Efficient and/or large rent-seeking costs and or coordination failure between agencies	Norm: efficient rights cannot be created Inefficient rights cannot be destroyed.

Source: Khan 1995.

The relative power and behaviour of the state provides the conditions in which corruption occurs (Khan, 1995; Aidt, 2003) and affects the impact it has. If the measurement of corruption is sensitive to the political settlement, then, it must be accounted for in the measure or index used – especially if attempting cross country comparisons.

Finally, the political settlement may have significant impact on the ability to use a source of data in one context over another. For example, if the state is weak, or is subject to political corruption, the use of official statistics will require great care, especially on key indicators of governance.

Incomplete Knowledge of the Transaction Bargaining Conditions

Just as the relative power and inclination of the state affects the reliability of proxies at a macro level, so too does the relative dominance of one actor in a corrupt transaction (Reinikka and Svensson, 2001). The incidence of corruption and consequences will be located differently according to whether the actor is dominant or subservient. In petty corruption, it is often the state or local authority figures that hold that power and dominance in transactions; in clientalist cases, the situation is often reversed.

For obvious reasons, it is often much easier to obtain information from the subservient actor in the transaction than the dominant or complicit party. An example of this would be a corruption victimisation survey in which the subservient party and its experience are measured. This method tends to be more often used for petty corruption and would not, for example, give much insight into organised corruption. The balance between gathering data on both parties will depend on the degree of complicity between actors, as they will both have reason to hide the details of the transaction. This preparatory knowledge would require some quantitative research in order to identify the suitable methods of data collection.

Resolving Problems of Heterogeneous Units and the Value of Money

The quantitative measurement of corruption must specify acceptable forms of transaction and from that what constitutes abuse. From this, one can infer acceptable and unacceptable outputs from a given input. An unacceptable output or 'corruption rent' may take a number of possible forms including:

1. Monetary Rent: 'Bribery', 'Extortion', 'Fraud' etc.;
2. Product or service gain: for example, 'the transaction is for one tonne of cement: so, deliver 100 KG to my truck';
3. Investing in Social Capital: for example, the market of social obligations (Ledeneva, 1998);
4. Value/supply chain distortion: for example, enforcing selection of specific resources ('you will buy cement from the following supplier');
5. Acquisition of non-monetary personal trappings of power: social dominance in various guises: for example, 'Fear/Security', 'Prestige', 'Sexual Behaviour' etc.

As corruption often has a number of incommensurable outcomes, it is often considered prudent to balance quantitative measures with additional qualitative data. For reasons of simplicity, however, money is often used as a proxy for corruption as it is numeric and is convenient and cardinal for the purposes of ranking, and thus determining degree – the inability to determine degree being a perennial weakness of the perception based measures. The practical attractions of using money as a measure or a proxy of corruption have tended to lead to a focus on very narrow definitions of corruption – one for which money is a suitable unit. This approach can lead to failure to account for degree or externalities.

The Measurement of 'Degree' of Corruption and the Selection of Particular Characteristics of a Transaction for Measurement

Some care, as already suggested, needs to be exercised when attaching monetary values to corrupt transactions, and particularly to claims of authority in any given measure of this type. At a very basic level comparability between monetary measurements of corruption may be very misleading. In one country, a one dollar bribe may be viewed almost humorously, while in many others it represents a day's wages.

At a more complex level, the characteristic of a transaction that is important to measure can be particular to the transaction itself for example, if a corrupt land transaction results in an indigenous people loosing access to traditional lands, the measurement of the corruption involved would seem to be inadequate if the value of the corruption were measured in terms of the value before appropriation, as opposed to after. If the bribes required to grab such land were small, would this capture the corruption either? Such a transaction many have very serious consequences to local people or may have been managed with relatively little money and persuasion of other more direct forms. This suggests that analysis of the transaction and its consequences are crucial in identifying the range of phenomena that need to be quantified. Important questions indicating measurement priorities would include those in Table 7.2.

Table 7.2 Some key stages in designing and interpreting non-perception based measures

WHAT is the objective?	WHO is involved?	WHICH units are applicable?	WHERE: context and comparability
Is the objective 'disciplinary' or phenomenon driven?	Who is dominant? Petty or grand? Coordinated network or individual?	Is there a standard unit (or units) that serve as an acceptable proxy?	If consequences are to be measured are the contexts comparable?

If the impact of a corrupt transaction is viewed as the phenomenon that is to be addressed by policy, then the network of consequences as well as the transaction itself is the legitimate sphere for quantitative measurement. Locating a number of points of measurement and the selection of suitable proxies is an almost unavoidable aspect of corruption measurement.

Locating Transactions in Formal and Informal Networks

In considering where to locate corruption for the purposes of analysis and measurement, irrespective of definitions, there is some consensus that corruption occurs in transactions and the networks through which they are coordinated. It is in the characteristics and context of the transaction that the causes and consequences of corruption should be sought.

The corruption literature (Andvig, 1991; Bardhan, 1997; Goudie and Stasavage, 1998) devotes significant attention to the principal agent conditions in which corruption is suppressed or incentives provided. Empirical approaches to measurement may, thus, be identified in relation to the transaction structure and the contextual influences that play a role in the phenomenon.

Corrupt transactions occur in networks that are highly organised as well as opportunistically. Such examples may occur in the same sector without any direct link between them. Identifying the various informal and formal networks within the area that you wish to measure provides a structure around which to organise measurement.

Informal Networks

The measurement of informal networks has been achieved using a combination of survey and interview techniques (Miller et al., 2001 and Miller, 2006 for more details on these techniques):

1. In depth interviews;
2. Round table discussions;
3. National quota based studies.

Although it is beyond the scope of this chapter to review in detail these methods, they have been extensively used and refined to provide indications of contacts and networks which indicate transaction points appropriate for further analysis and measurement.

Identification of Key Measurement Points in Formal Networks

The measurement of a particular sector and its proneness to corruption has been recently undertaken for the pharmaceuticals supply in Costa Rica (Clare Cohen, 2002). In the Clare Cohen approach, the pharmaceuticals system is analysed according to decision points (that is, transactions) – these being potential nodes of corruption. The Clare Cohen approach uses the heuristic devised by Robert Klitgaard for the identification of corruption prone 'nodes' between the public and private sector. This is set out as M+D-A=C[6] 'Monopoly' plus 'Discretion' minus 'Accountability' equals 'Corruption'. This is then applied to key transactions in the supply chain that is being investigated to identify the most vulnerable points in the supply chain.

This approach provides a useful example of systematically approaching the formal networks as each of the processes involved can be scrutinised according to the ease with which the actor may engage in corruption from a procedural position. This done, proneness to corruption can be systematically traced within the incentives and structures in any formal organisational form. Locating the key transactions may not

Table 7.3 Clare Cohen Approach

Registration	Selection	Procurement	Distribution	Service Delivery
Efficacy	Determine budget	Determine the model of supply and distribution	Receive and check drugs with order	Consultation with health professionals
Labelling	Assess morbidity profile	Reconcile needs and resources	Ensure appropriate transportation and delivery of drugs to health centres	In-patient care
Marketing	Determine drugs to fit morbidity profile	Develop criteria for tender	Appropriate storage	Dispensing of pharmaceuticals
Use	Cost/benefit analysis of drugs	Issue tender	Good inventory control of drugs	Adverse drug reaction monitoring
Warnings	Consistency with WHO criteria	Evaluate bids	Demand monitoring	Patient compliance with prescription.
Full registration Re- evaluation of older drugs		Award supplier Determine contract terms Monitor order Make payment Quality assurance		

Source: adapted from Clare Cohen, 2002.

yield the networks that influence the transaction, which are unsurprisingly discrete. Methods that identify patterns that deviate from expected forms sound a policy alarm bell. An interesting example of this has recently been conducted on the US health insurance system, Medicaid.

Adaptive Corruption and Inductive Measurement Approaches: The Example of Medicaid

One of the qualities of corruption that is often overlooked when the gamut of anti-corruption best practices are invoked is the flaw of adopting a best practice approach. Corrupt actors seek niches in the systems of transactions and the characteristics that they the present. Such flaws cannot be assumed to disappear as a result of systemic 'efficiency'. An innovative illustration of this is based on the analysis of transactions that provided telling evidence of corruption levels in the US Medicaid programme (Sparrow, 2000).

The underlying trigger for this corruption measure is one of discrepancy. Although, rather than looking at inputs and outputs, Sparrow developed a diagnostic tool that permitted the estimation of corruption levels in the Medicaid system that were derived from deviance in patterns of administrative characteristics of transactions: 'who was involved?' and 'how plausible were the characteristics of these transactions?'.[7]

The Medicaid system aims at efficiency thorough high levels of automation. It becomes evident, when interviewing fraud perpetrators, that these normally positive efficiency characteristics had provided a niche opportunity for massive corruption.

The system preferred by those attempting fraud (that is, more prone to corruption) would be:

- fast (that is, quick turnover);
- transparent (that is, methods can be learned);
- perfectly predictable (that is, no surprises);
- completely automated (that is, no human intuition of problems).

Rather perversely, those administrative procedures associated with low efficiency provided the least fraud friendly conditions (particularly for those outside the system).

- slow;
- mysterious;
- unpredictable;
- risk of human review and validation.

All of these characteristics would add to the transaction costs of the managing the Medicaid system but make highly automated fraud much more difficult.

Having analysed the nature of the transactions in the Medicaid claims process, Sparrow looked for patterns in claims for payment. The insight behind the analytical approach is that there should be a spread of people involved in the claiming and provision of specific claims and an appropriate (that is, plausible) combination of treatments for which claims are made up. An algorithm was used to identify the patterns in claims, patients, locations, providers etc. for Medicaid claims. The claims data was processed iteratively to identify networks of increasing density of links between actors and transactions. As the number of iterations rose, the number of links between certain networks of individuals or organisations became so dense that there was clear evidence of deviance in expected (or even technically possible) patterns of treatment.

Using a sample approach based on the analysis of claims, corruption was identified with a significant degree of uncertainty due to the relatively small amount of the diagnosis that could be examined in detail through on-the-ground fraud examinations. Despite this, the scale of corruption was indicated at being between 10 per cent and 35 per cent of the annual spending on healthcare in the United States. Such wide degrees of uncertainty may, perhaps, suggest that this is not, in fact, a measurement of great precision; however, as an indication of orders of magnitude, it has a great deal of value. Greater precision would be achieved through increased spending on examining individual cases over the spread of analysed transactions and networks.

Analysis of this sort depends, of course, on the availability of large amounts of data, ideally in a fairly convenient format. If such data exists, it does, however, provide the basis for identifying one of the most ephemeral of the artefacts of corruption; namely, the networks involved in the value chain of corruption. Many transactions, even in developing countries, may be amenable to this sort of analysis; although, it is likely that the administrative methods may favour internal corruption rather than external corruption if the methods are akin to Sparrow's fraud perpetrators nightmare listed above.

The identification of transaction and network characteristics has provided a tool for estimating micro corruption though examination of the 'paper trail'. Estimating the value of political or grand corruption is no less important, but poses very different challenges to researchers as there is likely to be no paper trail and the number of transactions will be very restricted.

Measuring of Corruption through the Value of Discrete Political Networks

The measurement of the value of corruption to a business is distinct from the value of corrupt transaction that occurs. For example, if a bribe is paid to a local official in order to win a building project, the size of the bribe may give little indication of the value of the corrupt practice and the flows of resources that occur as a consequence. The existence of networks that are inferred inductively from transaction data as in Sparrow's work is crucial to identifying the existence of corruption. In Fisman (2001), the existence and value of corruption is identified deductively based on intelligence from country experts through the deviant link between the ebb and flow of a particular politician's fortunes and the share value of a particular company.

Like many of the measures discussed in this chapter, this method provides an indication of corruption levels rather than a comprehensive statistic. The Fisman example is particularly interesting in that it seeks a novel way to measure the value of an oft cited major source of corruption: political or grand corruption. The case that is used to illustrate this is the link between the health of President Suharto of Indonesia and certain stock prices. Stock exchange prices were used as the basis for measuring share value and newspaper reports of Suharto's health as a focal point for measuring relative share values.

In the case of the companies deemed to have strong links to Suharto, there was found to be a positive correlation between news of Suharto's failing health and falls in the share value of companies with strong links to him. Based on a weighted average of connectedness (expert perception) and the variance of share value, it was estimated with normal degrees of robustness, that 16 per cent of the share value could be attributed to the patron-client link between the company and the President.

This method does rely on a degree of hypothesis: for example, proposing the whole value of the political connection, which would be lost if the person died or otherwise became powerless. It also relies on expert opinion on the extent of connectedness. This method, as with most quantitative measures, does not provide a measure of something that is unambiguously corrupt; it does, however, provide a route to link market behaviour with information that is very hard to suppress, especially in the case of quoted companies and, therefore, overcomes a significant data availability problem. Where significant parts of the value of a company is explained by the relationship to a political leader to whom links should carry no special benefit, the existence of corruption can, perhaps, be inferred if other data also point to an absence of benign explanations.[8]

Nepotism and Corruption in Bureaucratic Practices

Nepotism is a right and a duty in many cultures. It has, however, been found to be problematic in the development of efficient bureaucracies (Rauch and Evans, 2000). The deviance from 'Weberian'[9] meritocratic practices has been taken as a benchmark for analysing the degree of corruption involved in the running of the public sector. This includes recruitment and promotion. Using the result that Weberian style practices are associated with efficient bureaucracy, the degree of deviance from this is used as a test of corruption levels within the composition of the bureaux. In this example, the entry criteria and promotion criteria were tested against nepotistic indicators deviating from a Weberian ideal.

A measure, such as this, looking at the performance and allocation of resources within the public sector through the characteristics of the employment and promotion process can provide an important complement to measures of corruption concerned primarily with the giving and receiving of bribes.

An illustration of this sort of network map is to be found in the outcome of a study of the relationships between of influential individuals in Peru.

Such a network analysis is a particularly useful diagnostic tool for identifying potential players in grand corruption and, hence, suitable targets for measurement.

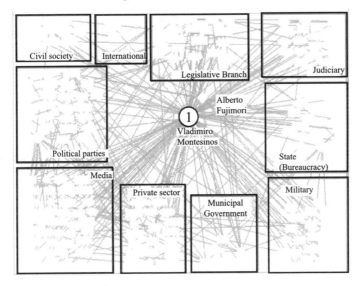

Figure 7.1   Peru: Political network 2000

Source: World Bank.

Where such networks exist and there is coordination between actors, it can be helpful to set out the linked individuals as a value chain, each member of which is contributing to the final act of corruption.

A General Framework for Locating Transactions in Networks and De-composing their Key Characteristics

The following is a diagrammatic structure for a transactions-based measurement of coordinated corruption. Each actor is a member of a value chain. Within each actor, there may be internal chains to the organisation which mirror this model.

Figure 7.2 provides a general framework on which a number of distinct transactions and outcomes, both formal and informal, can be located and related to each other. It is not intended to be prescriptive in the measurement that is taken.

The central column represents the formal value chain in any process and the various actors involved and the transactions that they carry out. The informal transactions to the left of the central column represent any additional party to the transaction that will influence its outcome. For example, if a member of a family group were hired rather than the most suitably skilled person, this would be both an investment in a kin network and a distortion in the outcome of the hiring process. Or, if a third party uses menaces or bribes to achieve the allocation of land to a certain individual, this, too, introduces an informal and distortionary element to the transaction that may be corrupt. On the left hand side, the externalities associated with a transaction are represented.

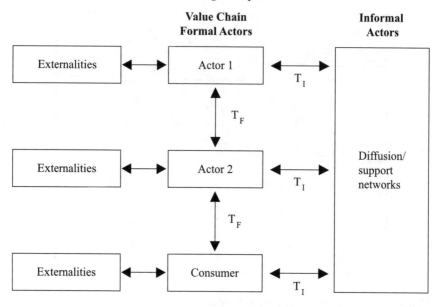

T = Transaction, subscript 'F' = Formal, subscript 'I' = Informal.

Figure 7.2   Transactions network for the location of points of measurement of corruption

Quantitative Data from Qualitative Context Sensitive Choices

In this section, we have reviewed some of the characteristics of corruption measurements that make considerable demands on both the researcher and the user of such tools.

The researcher's initial task can proceed in two directions, either of which clarifies what it is he or she is intending to measure. Either one proceeds from a 'school' or discipline, to a definition and this then suggests the phenomena that should be captured; or, the phenomena itself are identified as the subject of the measurement and this, then, indicates suitable methods, which ultimately situates the study in one or other discipline. Although most studies indicate the selected definition, the adopted definitions tend to follow familiar patterns.

The qualitative stage of the measurement process will help clarify for the user what sort of knowledge is ultimately contained in the figures that claim to summarise the problem of corruption.

The key contribution of the preparatory stage to measurement is to seek a clear statement of:

- the consequences to be ameliorated;
- the phenomena to be measured;

- the units;
- the context;
- the networks involved/the transaction points.

Measures need to provide some valid picture of what corruption is taking place and what the consequences of policy might be. In some cases, the answer to some of these questions will be straightforward; in others much more politically subtle. In all cases, however, the techniques that have proven most successful from a policy perspective are of course those that correctly identify and measure the right item in the first place.

Non Perception Measures

This section will examine some of the approaches that have been used to capture corruption and how they contribute to our understanding of corruption levels. Although measurement techniques can be used for a number of different phenomena, the maxim that the objective shapes the method tends to hold. I have, therefore, divided the methods used into the three most common types:

1. macro: for example, whole economy measures;
2. sectoral: for example, healthcare education or legislature;
3. micro: for example, individuals, organisations or facilities.

Macro Measurements

Informal sector measures have the great strength of inclusivity, even though they do not necessarily isolate corruption precisely. Where most measures of corruption are based on samples, they provide a reference point for quantifying the scale of corruption. The informal economy is generally considered to be composed of two major activities; first, production that is not a part of GNP, secondly tax evasion (Frey and Pommerehne, 1984; Johnston, Kaufman et al., 1998; Frey and Schneider, 2000). The size of the informal sector and the consequent tax evasion that occurs provides a quantified measure of the extent to which economic activity is coordinated in a very specific manner that may be illegal, inside or outside cultural norms, lacking formal regulations and without recourse to the law to protect the transfer of rights. The extent to which members of the state or the bureaucracy are complicit or have an interest in such activities will provide greater precision against which the estimated volumes and values of activity can be matched.

Theoretically, top-down measures should equate to bottom-up measures; although in the case of bottom-up methods, the corruption data gathered is likely to miss non-petty corruption. Therefore, a rough set of equivalences for corruption can be set down:

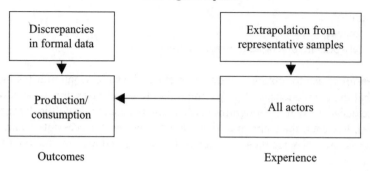

Figure 7.3 Macro methods and their basis for inferring levels of corruption

Total Corruption = a function of the informal economy
Total Corruption – Petty Corruption = Grand/Organised Corruption.

These macro measures do not require transaction detail or a link between the transactions as by its nature it captures discrepancy. While this is, perhaps, a blunt instrument, it has been used to shed light on national levels of corruption related activity and, in turn, used as a link in quantifying and understanding the bounds of corruption levels. Such methods provide a complement to corruption perception indexes in shedding light on national corruption levels. Three main sets of macro measurement approaches have evolved as follows.

Direct Approaches

Surveys   This is widely used. It has, perhaps counter-intuitively, proved to be a fairly effective method of getting data about the scale and structure of participation in informal activity.

Tax auditing   This is a selective sample based approach, generally directed at cases in which deviance is suspected.

These two measures tend to indicate a lower bound of informal activities, as it is acknowledged that they capture only a subset of transactions in an economy.

Indirect Discrepancy Approaches

Discrepancy is, perhaps, the most powerful and commonly used approach in measuring corruption: in effect, you measure what goes *in* to a process; you have an *expectation* of what should come *out* of it; and, the deviance from that expectation is measured. This overcomes the necessity of having to record the actual transactions that have taken place. Several techniques have been used to achieve this on a national level (and, in some cases, at a micro level as in the spending measure, which is effectively an income accounting measure). Each has a shortcoming but can be useful in specific cases.

1. *Spending* If spending occurs at a higher level than recorded income, it can be an indication of informal activity. This is subject to the caveats that spending over income can be achieved in a number of different ways unrelated to the informal economy (for example, savings, borrowing etc.).
2. *Comparison of labour market participation* Relatively low participation rates can indicate that activity may be taking place in the informal sector.
3. *Demand for cash* This measure considers the demand for cash that is generated by formal transactions. The remainder being a measure of the informal sector in money terms. This method also requires some care in its use as many informal transactions may not involve any money transactions (Ledeneva, 1998). A significant proportion of the demand for some currencies may be derived from outside the country. This measure is widely used in developed OECD countries to provide comparative trend data.
4. *Physical inputs* The measure of the physical inputs required for the running of the formal economy has recently been developed to try and overcome some of the shortcomings (particularly with respect to developing countries) of the cash demand method. The most used source of data for this comparison is that of electricity. Problems of non-electricity using activities, however, remain and must be taken into account when considering the use of this technique.

The Model Testing Approach

The building and testing of models using econometrics is common in cross country and time series studies. In the informal sector, these studies tend to use proxies for incentives and disincentives to engage in the informal sector. Model-based approaches consider the residual traces of activity and try to match these to a model. This is one of the theoretically most developed methods, but also one in which there is a significant problem in most developing countries as the data required is often unavailable. This tends to lead to the use of perception-based data in most model-based measures of informal activity. The model approach has been explored in its relationship to corruption and public finance (Johnston, Kaufman et al., 1998). In the Johnston, Kaufman et al. (1998) study, the incentives to exit the formal economy are modelled including 'Law and Order', 'Protection of Property Rights' and 'Bureaucratic Efficiency'.

The model testing approach has recently been used to question the reliability of perception-based data in measuring corruption. The econometric study by Abramo[10] has tested the link between experience of corruption and perceptions. The implication of the study is that measurement by means other than perception is required to give a more reliable indication of actual levels of corruption. Perceptions being more closely related to opinions on a variety of other matters than any experience or first hand knowledge of corruption.

Corruption Victimisation and Bottom-up Approaches

The corruption victimisation approach is derived from the crime victimisation approach widely used in criminology. This approach seeks to avoid problems of aggregation and data validity of perception based and 'recorded' measures.[11]

The survey approach is based on a random sample of population, and is concerned with the previous year. The reason for taking this period is that rather than obtaining general trend data, this approach attempts to quantify personal experience, which clearly decays rapidly.

These surveys address both direct and indirect experience of corruption. It was found that the indirect responses were more likely to be subject to inflation through perceptions. Prudence in using personal direct experience of corruption in the survey data has led to direct experience being used to set the lower bound of corruption among the surveyed group.

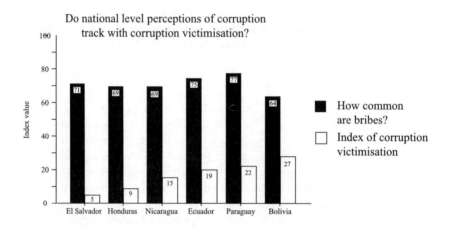

Spearman's rho = .098, sig. < .001,

Figure 7.4   National perceptions cf. corruption victimisation

Source: Seligson (forthcoming 2005).

Seligson (forthcoming 2005) re-inforces the concern over the use of perception based measures and urges caution when estimating corruption on the basis of perception rather than experience. He cites El Salvador, where those who had experienced the highest frequency of corruption had a somewhat *lower* perception of the degree of corruption than those who had been victimised only one time. (See, also, the Abramo results previously mentioned in this chapter.)

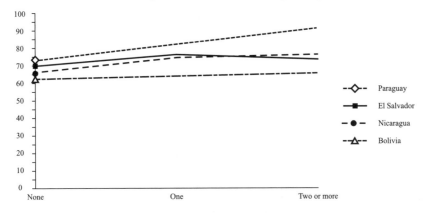

Number of direct personal experiences with corruption

All sig. < .05

Figure 7.5   Impact of corruption victimisation on perceptions of corruption

Source: Seligson (forthcoming 2005).

One of the acknowledged characteristics of such survey data is that it does not capture both sides of the transaction (especially, it is likely to miss complicit corruption). It is not possible to tell the exact extent to which the respondent is a victim or complicit in an established patron client relationship. Where the victim is subservient, it is likely that the level of corruption is accurately captured while the causality remains, to some extent, obscure.[12] This method is most widely used for measuring everyday or exploitative petty corruption, in which the power of the victim to negotiate terms is generally low. The use of victimisation surveys can provide important data on the geographic and demographic experience of (petty) corruption as illustrated in Figures 7.6 and 7.7.

Figures 7.6 and 7.7 indicate the regional unevenness of the experience of corruption regionally in Nicaragua and Bolivia. The Latin American studies are strongly suggestive that:

1. there is striking diversity of levels of corruption within countries and populations that is policy relevant;
2. perceptions are not always a good guide to forms or levels of corruption, particularly at the petty end of the spectrum.

This technique has not yet been widely used to quantify the *content* of corrupt transactions (that is, money etc.) however it has produced some of the most refined data on petty corruption experience currently available.

Corruption experience in Nicaragua:
residuals controlled for age, income, education and wealth

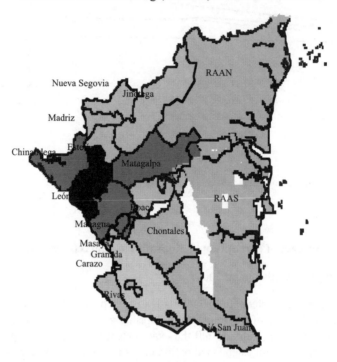

Figure 7.6   Nicaragua

Sectoral Measures

Sectoral studies are increasingly common, as donor organisations take a more holistic approach to solving governance and corruption problems. Such studies are becoming much more complex than simply recording leakage, as they look at a range of governance and performance issues. In order to measure the extent of corruption, the flows of resources and the transactions formally designated to take place are analysed and the actual inputs and outputs recorded.

A basic tool of sectoral measurement is the diagnostic survey. The diagnostic survey is designed to identify the *processes* involved in the flows of resources in the sector in question.

Generally, such studies are structured so as to draw data on corruption from a number of different sources and build a picture of both quantitative aspects of corruption and causal aspects that are related to organisational and institutional structures (as indicated in the network structure outlined above). The structure of this approach is broadly as follows:

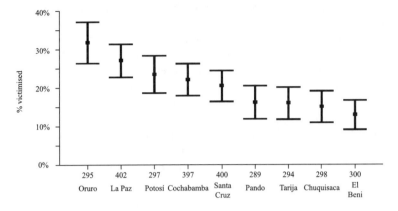

Public employee solicited bribe:
confidence intervals by department in Bolivia

Figure 7.7 Bolivia

Source: Seligson (forthcoming 2005).

1. Surveys of citizens, enterprises and public bodies. The purpose is to probe institutional and systemic weaknesses through a variety of questions drawing on general and specific experience.
2. Quantification of results.
3. Triangulation between different survey results.
4. Identification of the causes of the corruption.
5. Test with further quantitative and qualitative data.

This sequence of activities illustrates the importance of multiple data sourcing in the reliable quantification of corruption. Of the recent methods developed using this approach, Public Expenditure Tracking Surveys (PETS) and Qualitative Service Delivery Surveys (QSDS) are among the most successful.

Public Expenditure Tracking Surveys (PETS)

The PETS approach looks at the audit trail of funding, and makes discrepancy measurements at each stage. In effect, PETS verifies the extent to which paperwork matches what is actually happening in the flow of resources; this verification process explicitly recognises the strong incentive to misreport by the actors concerned. PETS also seeks to measure and explain the variation in efficiency across units in order to produce some baseline (Reinikka and Svensson, 2000) by gathering data on:

1. performance;
2. resource ultilisation rates;

3. input and output.

PETS also use the discrepancy approach to match claims for funds and the legitimacy of the resources used. One significant example of this is ghost workers, who act as a 'leakage' in the supply chain resources (Rienikka and Svensson, 2003).

In a study looking at the funding of the Ugandan primary schools (the first large scale PETS project) in 1996, the first level of measurement was that of input and output of funds. The Ugandan study was faced with gathering data over five years and verifying and cross checking data at each stage, as reliable or complete data did not exist. The study revealed that the mean funding that reached primary schools was only 13 per cent of allocated non-wage budget (see below). The impact of the PETS approach has been significant in that it has enabled analysis and modelling to be carried out which, in turn, led to successful policy initiatives.

One of the policies that resulted from these measurements was the dissemination of budget information *via* local newspapers (that is, a policy transparency of funding levels). This was found to have played a significant role in the increase in the flow of funds to primary schools. Reinikka and Svensson (2003) found that two thirds of the improvement in the flow of funds could be explained by access to these newspapers as it overcame one of the major facilitators of corruption – the asymmetry of information enjoyed by bureaucrats.

Table 7.4   **Leakage of non-wage funds in primary education in Uganda, 1991–95 and 2001**

	Mean %	Median %
1991	97	100
1992	96	100
1993	85	100
1994	84	100
1995	78	100
2001	18	18

Source: Reinikka (2001); Reinikka and Svensson (2003).

Other countries have also implemented similar PETS projects identifying high levels of leakage. This provides a valuable cross country data set at a sectoral level.

As mentioned above, PETS does not use monetary data alone in most cases, and consistent with the triangulation approach to enriching the data, other more qualitative and ethnographic methods are employed. Only after completing the testing of the data against other methods (including qualitative) can a measure of the extent of 'leakage' be ascribed to corruption.

Table 7.5   Leakage of non-wage funds in primary education: evidence from public expenditure tracking surveys

Country	Mean %
Ghana 2000	50
Peru 2002*	30
Tanzania 1999	57
Zambia 2002	**60**

*   Utilities only.

Sources: Ye and Canagarajah (2002) for Ghana; Instituto Apoyo and World Bank (2002) for Peru; Price Waterhouse Coopers (1999) for Tanzania; Das and others (2002) for Zambia.

Despite the significant successes of the PETS approach, there is evidence appearing that corrupt officials are adapting to the regimes. The PETS methodology will need to adapt accordingly if it is to respond effectively to these challenges.

Micro Measures

Case/ethnographic approaches Ethnographic approaches have been widely used to provide 'testimony' and observation data on corrupt transactions. This approach has been able to provide significant and reliable data on many specific sectors. One of the most famous studies (Wade, 1982; Wade, 1985) produced data or 'rates' and 'dues' that indicated a high degree of routineness and stability in the transactions, and thus ability to identify levels of corruption in the Indian water industry. Such precise quantitative diagnostic data would certainly have been hard to gather through other methods. More recent studies of the water industry (Davis, 2003) have used survey tools to identify how much such extra revenue derived from corruption is worth. Davis (2003, p. 60) found that members of staff '... have developed a remarkably sophisticated calculus to estimate the value of a particular post (its extra salary generating potential) and thus maximum amount they are willing to pay for such a transfer'. Such data can provide important additional data on the extent of corruption, especially in organisational and institutionally stable contexts.

The particular strength of the quantitative ethnographic approach to the measurement of corruption is that it provides a very fine level of diagnostic detail and an opportunity to understand key issues in the chain of causation and the processes involved. It also provides the opportunity to distinguish between acts that are considered corrupt and those that are not, and also simple waste through poor management skills or other legitimate reasons for leakage.

The measurement of the value of corruption at a moment in time can be derived using this bottom-up approach, as distinct from the top-down approach used in PETS.

In an ideal case, the bottom-up and top-down corruption measures should equate. The closer the two results are then the greater the likely reliability of the data. It is perhaps worth noting that case material that contain significant quantified results remain among the largest gaps in the existing literature.

The bottom-up, ethnographic approach necessarily considers individual experiences and, in that sense, is always a micro approach. Other micro measures are concerned with measuring corruption bounded by the locus of a specific organisation. It is to these measures that we will now look in more detail.

Civil empowerment and discrepancy checking   The micro-level measurement of corruption has, until relatively recently, been confined to the bottom up case approach which provides some detail on a sample of the transactions and experiences. The historical rationale, which holds in many cases today, has been lack of suitable data availability. The availability of usable data has, however, improved in many cases and in developed countries is usually quite good and often in machine-readable form. This enables the use of the most fundamental analytical tool for non-perception based corruption measurement, that of straightforward discrepancy.

A powerful low-tech example of the use of this method is given by the MKSS of Rajasthan. In this case, the key to identifying and measuring the degree of corruption in a project was to gain the legal right to compare local and district financial records. A systematic comparison of the two provided clear evidence of the scale of corruption. This approach has provided very influential data on local corruption levels, particularly relatively low level corruption. Similar to the ethnographic approach, it is a bottom-up approach in which corruption in monetary terms can be quantified through addition of the various discrepancies in the record keeping on which payment for projects is based. The practical impact of this 'low tech' approach has been significant in the case of the MKSS, with village leaders forced, in some cases, to return embezzled funds.

A top-down version of the discrepancy method has been developed and extended in the PETS and QSDS methods of measuring corruption in a supply chain and within a facility. We have looked at the basic use of PETS. Below, the QSDS method is outlined in more detail.

Quality of Service Delivery Survey (QSDS)[13]   The QSDS method aims at gathering detailed (particularly quantitative) data on the performance of a given organisation at the point of interface with its consumer. It gathers data on inputs, outputs, quality, pricing, oversight etc. The facility of frontline service is typically the main unit of observation in a QSDS in the same way as a firm is in enterprise surveys and the household in household surveys (Rienikka and Svensson, 2003).

Because of the range of data (including perceptions) QSDSs are inevitably resource hungry. Despite this, they have been used in a number of countries with some success. Primarily, targets have been the provision of health and education services in developing countries.

One of the innovations is the hybrid approach of looking at up and downstream issues in the facility – notably the cross-referencing of observable characteristics and perceptions in order to build up a reliable basis for quantifying and recording, among other things, the level of corruption over time.

The QSDS method is designed to capture a number of phenomena about the functioning of a particular unit or facility. It uses the discrepancy approach to identify 'leakage'; however, the approach is becoming increasingly developed into a form of comprehensive business analysis that integrates both quantitative and qualitative approaches. The scope of aQSDS is summarised below.

The QSDS approach measures corruption as it affects both inputs and outputs in key transactions and flows of resources. It also captures quality of service and the impact that quality of service may have on demand. An important observation made in the health sector (Reinikka and Svensson, 2003) is that demand is partially determined by supply quality – therefore, if corruption affects the quality of supply, it will, in turn, affect those who are willing to engage with the system itself. If measuring a proxy for corruption in terms of the impact it has, then, this becomes an important component. Transactions that do not take place can also be a very real consequence of corruption. Primary healthcare is a classic example.

QSDSs implicitly need to verify published data against practice. In many cases this requires surprise audits of facilities. Such audits (Reinikka and Svensson, forthcoming 2005) have revealed, for example, levels of absenteeism in hospitals and primary schools.

The corruption identified in these results, (when tested against the reasons for absenteeism in each case), provide a comparable index between countries of a non-monetary form of corruption.

Corruption, as measured in the QSDS method, is then a measure not only of leakage but also of consequence. This requires taking account of both the deviance in the transaction itself and the externalities and the supply/demand interface with the final consumer.

Firm level studies Similar, in some respects to the QSDS approach, is the firm level survey. In this approach, commercial organisations have been surveyed on their experience of graft and bribery. This approach has established some important practices in cases in which data on corruption can be obtained:

1. the organisation doing the survey should be trusted by the respondents (that is, not public sector);
2. questions about corruption should be indirect;
3. questions on corruption should be at the end of the survey;
4. Questions on corruption should be multiple and cross-referenced for reliability.

The study conducted by Reinikka in Uganda found a wide diversity of experience of corruption between firms. The quantified data indicated a significant burden on business as a consequence of bribery:

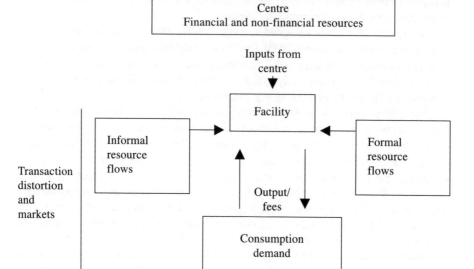

Figure 7.8   A pictorial representation of the QSDS approach

Table 7.6   Absence rates among teachers and health-care workers in the public sector

Country	Primary schools %	Primary health facilities %
Bangladesh 2002	–	35
Honduras 2000	14	27
India* 2002	23	43
Peru 2002	13	26
Uganda 2002	26	35
Zambia 2002	17	–

—   Not available.
•   Average for 14 States.

Sources: Chaudhury and Hammer (2003) for Bangladesh; Chaudhury and others (2003) for India, Peru, and Uganda; World Bank (2001) for Honduras; Habyarimana and others (2003) for Zambia.

For the firms reporting positive bribes, the average amount of corrupt payments was equivalent to US$ 8,280, with a median payment of US$ 1,820. These are large amounts, on average corresponding to US$ 88 per worker, or roughly 8 per cent of the total costs (1 per cent in the mean). Including firms reporting zero bribe payments, the average payment is US$ 6,730, with a median payment of US$ 450. (Reinikka and Svensson, forthcoming 2005)

Such surveys provide quantitative and disaggregated data on corruption that has enabled explanatory modelling of the micro-economic levels of corruption for the first time. Two features explained bribe levels: ability to pay and ability to refuse (Reinikka and Svensson, 2003). These features are consistent with the bargaining hypothesis of corruption levels that found support in the Ugandan PETS project discussed above. In the PETS and QSDS methods, data often has to be collected for the first time, especially in developing countries. In countries where data is abundantly available and systems automated, other possibilities open up for corruption and for diagnosis, location and measurement.

Conclusion

The purpose of this chapter has been to review some of the issues faced by those measuring corruption and the methods that have been developed to respond to these. Additionally, it has sought to make the case for a contextual approach focussed first and foremost on phenomena deemed to be problematic to which policy makers or interested parties wish to seek solutions. Measurement should be based on as clear and thorough understanding of the related transactions as is possible.

The value of quantitative measures is asserted on two levels. On a theoretical level, they allow the testing of hypotheses about corruption. Quantitative measures are valuable from a policy perspective as they provide succinct information about levels and, in some cases, the degree of corruption that helps policy makers decide on priorities. The attractiveness of such measure has underlined a widespread tendency to produce and use them.

The considerable number of quantitative data sources available on corruption does not obscure the fact that their meaning can be far less clear than they appear, thus undermining one of their key benefits. As there is no consensus on a general theory of corruption, the underlying qualitative judgements that underlie the measurements are crucial in adding meaning to the resulting figures. The identification of these underlying judgments should, I argue, explicitly take place within the planning stage of any measurement process and in the interpretation of their output.

From the experience reviewed here, some key dimensions that contribute to a positive policy outcome from a measurement exercise include:

- targeting specific phenomena;
- reflecting diversity of experience;
- applying an appropriate technique;

Table 7.7 A summary of techniques for non-perception based measures

Measurement	Comments	Pros	Cons
Macro			
Direct – survey	Context Setting	Inclusivity Does not require transaction details	Not always possible to extract 'corruption'
Direct – victimisation	Lower bound Experience based survey	Data generally good. Best for disaggregated petty corruption	Highly skilled process Problems with grand corruption and complicity. Light on transaction detail
Direct – tax audit	Lower bound	Good deviance data	Complex/resource hungry
Indirect – spending	Upper bounds	Provides indication of unexplained wealth	Needs to account for other sources of spending power Require reliable public recordsb
Indirect – labour market participation	Upper bounds	Participation rates are a comparable indicator between countries	
Indirect – demand for cash	Upper bounds	Provides indication of unexplained wealth	Can be unreliable if significant cash comes from abroad
Indirect – physical inputs	Upper bounds	Good deviance data	Does not capture activities that do not involve the purchase of inputs
Model resting	Statistical	Can give very powerful aggregate statistics	Risk of using poor data if nothing else available.
Sectoral			
PETS	Formal Network Analysis. Best when money is the unit	Policy indicative Pre-scoped Comparable data	Resource hungry

Micro

Case/ethnographic	Descriptive	Depth of qualitative knowledge / Can be also be quantitative	Comparability
Discrepancy	Expectation based	Policy friendly / Flexible / Can engage grass roots	Requires good access to data
QSDS	Addresses a number of non-monetary issues of service	Considers consequences and qualitative issues	Resource hungry
Firm Studies	Quantifies costs to business	Estimate of 'taxation' of corruption on companies	Less clear on benefits (see data bias in this chapter)
Identifying Networks			
Inductive transaction network analysis	infers networks from data	responds well to adaptability of forms of corruption	requires good data
Informal networks	Survey and interview based	Can provide high quality data on both sides of the transaction	Requires a highly skilled team
Network value	Tests for inappropriate correlations	Can test hypotheses where direct data is impossible to get	Suitable indirect data not always available
Process deviance	Tests deviance from standards	Can capture non-monetary corruption well	Requires uncontroversial standards

- addressing bias and data deficit;
- a balance of top-down and bottom-up approaches;
- combining sources of knowledge;
- knowledge that empowers citizens to contest abuse;
- adaptive rather than canonised studies;
- access to information.

Despite the practical difficulties that are inevitably associated with the measurement of corruption, a number of methods have been developed. It is rare that the range of tools available is set out for consideration by policy makers and integrated into a broad 'knowledge map' for policy in this area. Some of these measures have evolved because the more knotty qualitative questions of units and scope do not arise. The phenomenon that is seen as problematic is clear (for example, the leakage in school funding).

From the review of techniques that are of relevance to corruption measurement, it becomes apparent that many of the macro techniques that could provide some indicators of national context have some difficulties in developing countries, where corruption levels are often high. That having been said, national aggregates of corruption such as the CPI would be provided with additional credibility if cross-checked with such data. National disaggregated studies such as the corruption victimisation surveys also provide important data on the spread of the experience of corruption, thereby providing considerable value to policy makers particularly where petty and non-complicit corruption is concerned.

Sectoral studies pioneered by the World Bank have begun to provide real results for policy, although they do depend heavily on support within the state and considerable expert resources to carry out the measurements required, particularly in cases where record keeping is poor. Such studies have begun to yield valuable internationally comparable data that will be of help in the evaluation of policy.

Micro studies have developed into a number of forms that quantify corruption and a number of qualitative considerations. Measurement of non-monetary phenomena is increasing as is the sophistication with which data – where it is available – is used. Although it remains relatively infrequent compared to ubiquity and importance of the non-monetary component of corruption, it remains important to incorporate or target the aspects of corruption that are often excluded such as 'contempt'(Jaffre and Olivier de Sardan, 2003), which can exclude someone from a right every bit as effectively as a bribe.

Just as corruption is adaptive and responds to a set of environmental conditions, so too, does measurement. Developing a static cannon of measurement types may be quite inappropriate to obtaining a comparable set of data. A classic example would be the manner in which corruption in Meaicare in the US defrauds the community, compared to the way in which corruption in a developing country is conducted.

Flexibility of methods and a willingness to try and address relationships in which data may be hard to come by (for example, grand corruption) are evidenced by contemporary researchers. Over reliance on one, or a very narrow indicator of corruption levels, or one statistic has a very real danger of distorting anti-corruption policy. Where possible, it would be desirable to see a norm evolving in which practical and refined data on corruption levels were available to give a policy focused knowledge map at 'Macro', 'Sectoral' and 'Micro' levels of real value that could then provide the sort of feedback that policy makers really need to guide targeted action. The methods illustrated here – see Table 7.7 for summary – provide a positive, albeit patchy and dislocated progress towards this goal.

Notes

1 www.transparencia.org.br/docs/HowFar.pdf.
2 This is not to say that non-perception measures, especially those that are proxy based are free of a margin of error. The advantage of the non-perception approach lies in the close focus on expectation and discrepancy, and the general approach of seeking corroborative evidence rather than opinion.
3 See also the distinction drawn between the impact of the benign or kleptocratic state on the outcomes in Aidt, T. (2003), 'Economic Analysis of Corruption: A Survey', *The Economic Journal*, vol. 113, pp. 632–51.
4 State dominates the transaction
5 Non-state actor dominates the transaction
6 While not true equation *per se*, monopoly and discretion are co-dependent; it does provide an indication of some of the characteristics of the transaction appropriate for measurement.
7 In some cases if claimants had actually had all the symptoms for which they were making claims, they would have been dead.
8 This is subject to the caveat that such behaviour is considered outside accepted practice within the culture in question.
9 Despite the problems associated with this as an ideal, it does provide a useful benchmark.
10 www.transparencia.org.br/docs/HowFar.pdf.
11 It seeks to avoid the manipulation of incidences of corruption to suit the agenda of, for example, a police chief, a politician or a newspaper editor.
12 Seligson argues that without a lack of fairness and low efficiency in the state system, the demand for complicit corrupt transactions would be negligible
13 The World Bank Institute has pioneered this method.

References

Aidt, T. (2003), 'Economic Analysis of Corruption: A Survey', *The Economic Journal*, vol. 113, pp. 632–51.

Amundsen, I. (2000), *Corruption Definitions and Concepts*, Stockholm, Chr. Michelson Institute.

Andvig, J.C. (1991), 'The Economics of Corruption: A Survey', *Studi Economici*, vol. 43, no. 1, pp. 57–93.

Bardhan, P. (1997), 'Corruption and Development: A Review of the Issues', *Journal of Economic Literature*, vol. 35, no. 3, pp. 1320–46.

Buscaglia, E. (2001), *An Economic and Jurimetric Analysis of Official Corruption in the Courts*, United Nations, Vienna.

Clare Cohen, J. (2002), *Improving Transparency in Pharmaceuticals Systems: Strengthening Critical Points against Corruption*, Latin American and Caribbean Bank.

Davis, J. (2003), 'Corruption in Public Service Delivery: Experience from South Asia's Water and Sanitation Sector', *World Development*, vol. 32, no. 1.

del Castillo, A. (2002), *Lets Talk about Corruption*, University of Amsterdam.

Fisman, R. (2001), 'Estimating the Value of Political Connections', *American Economic Review*, vol. 91, no. 4.

Frey, B.S. and Pommerehne, W.W. (1984), 'The Hidden Economy: State and Prospects for Measurement', *Review of Income and Wealth*, vol. 30, no. 1, pp. 1–23.

Frey, B.S. and Schneider, F. (2000), 'Informal and Underground Economy', *Encyclopedia of Social and Behavioural Science*, Elsevier, Amsterdam.

Goudie, A.W. and Stasavage, D. (1998), 'A Framework for the Analysis of Corruption', *Crime Law and Social Change*, vol. 29, no. 2/3, pp. 113–59.

Jaffre, Y. and Olivier de Sardan, J.-P. (2003), *Une Medicine Inhospitaliere*, Editions Karthala, Marseilles.

Johnson, S., Kaufmann, D. and Schleifer, A. (1997), *The Unofficial Economy in Transition*, The Brookings Panel on Economic Activity, Washington.

Johnson, S., Kaufman, D. and Zoido-Lobaton, P. (1998), *Corruption, Public Finances and the Unofficial Economy*, ECLAC, Santiago.

Johnson, S., Kaufman, D. and Zoido-Lobaton, P. (1999), *Corruption, Public Finances and the Unofficial Economy*, World Bank, Washington DC.

Khan, M. (1995), 'State Failures in a Weak State', in J.H. Harriss, J. and C. Lewis (eds), *The New Institutional Economics and Third World Development*, Routledge, London.

Khan, M.H. and Sundaram, J.K. (eds) (2000), *Rents Rent Seeking and Economic Development. Theory and Evidence in Asia*, Cambridge University Press, Cambridge (UK).

Ledeneva, A. (1998), *Russia's Economy of Favours: Blat, Networking and Informal Exchange*, Cambridge University Press, Cambridge (UK).

Michael, B. (2004), *The Rise and Fall of the Anti Corruption Industry: Toward Second Generation Anti-Corruption Reforms in Central and Eastern Europe*, Open Society Institute, New York.

Miller, William L., Grødeland, Åse B. and Koshechkina, Tatyana Y. (2001), *A Culture of Corruption? Coping with Government in Postcommunist Europe*, Central European University Press, Budapest.

Miller, William L. (2006 forthcoming), 'Corruption and Corruptibility', *World Development*.

Rauch, J. and Evans, P. (2000), 'Bureaucratic Structure and Bureaucratic Performance in Less Developed Countries', *Journal of Public Economics*, vol. 75, pp. 49–71.

Reinikka, R. and Svensson, J. (2000), *Cost Efficiency in Healthcare*, World Bank, Washinton DC.

Reinikka, R. and Svensson, J. (2001), *Explaining Leakage of Public Funds*, Stockholm University, World Bank.

Rienikka, R. and Svensson, J. (2003), *Survey Techniques to Measure and Explain Corruption*, The World Bank, Washington DC.

Reinikka, R. and Svensson, J. (forthcoming 2005), 'Survey Techniques to Measure and Explain Corruption', *World Development*.

Seligson, M. (forthcoming 2005), 'Corruption and Democratization in Latin America', *World Development*.

Sparrow, M. (2000), *License to Steal*, Westview Press.

Wade, R. (1982), 'The System of Administrative and Political Corruption: Canal Irrigation in South India', *Journal of Development Studies*, vol. 18, no. 3.

Wade, R. (1985), 'The Market for Public Office: Why the Indian State is not Better at Development', *World Development*, vol. 13, no. 4, pp. 467–97.

Chapter 8

Perceptions, Experience and Lies: What Measures Corruption and What do Corruption Measures Measure?

William L. Miller

Introduction

The measurement of corruption has been plagued by vague definitions, vague questions, vague answers and credulous interpretation. That may not matter too much for a first attempt, a broad overview or even a ranking of nations (Lambsdorff, 2001). But it might. And in any case, it is profoundly unsatisfying. The problem is not only to produce an index that ranks countries in the approximate order of corruption within them – any country-level correlate of corruption would do that – but also to measure corruption itself. For that purpose, it would be better, if it were possible, to be more precise about the subject, the questions and the answers.

Vague Definitions

Michael Johnston asserts that 'no issue is more enduring in the corruption debate, and none has so frequently pre-empted promising discussions, as that of definitions' (Johnston, 1998, p. 89). Vito Tanzi claims that the question of definition used to absorb an unprofitably large proportion of the time at conferences but 'like an elephant', corruption is 'difficult to describe [but] not difficult to recognise' (Tanzi, 1998, p. 564). And, with similar impatience, András Sajó suggests that the debate over definition is a waste of time – 'Experts will never agree on any single definition' – and, worse, the definition debate can actually be pernicious: 'The problem of contemporary corruption is that its definition almost always reflects the moral opprobrium of outsiders' (Sajó, 1998, p. 38).

Clearly, a debate over '*the*' definition of corruption is best avoided. It can be avoided quite easily by focusing on less all-embracing and more concrete and specific concepts than 'corruption' itself. Perhaps that could be expressed as a focus on the components of corruption, or on specific acts of corruption. The concept of corruption functions better as an adjective than as a noun. And, even if people disagree about whether a specific act is 'corrupt', they can still proceed to measure its frequency, its causes and consequences, public attitudes towards it, and so on – separating the empirical research from the moral condemnation.

In this chapter, I focus, by way of example, on the giving and taking of bribes in dealings between ordinary citizens and junior officials in post-Communist Europe – in what are called 'bureaucratic encounters' with 'street-level officials'. Clearly, that is very different from the giving and taking of bribes at other levels such as in dealings between senior politicians, high-level bureaucrats and top businessmen. And, it is very different from other forms of corrupt activity such as using contacts, influence, nepotism, blackmail or dishonest auditing.

Rasma Karklins presents an interesting 16-element 'typology' of the 'misuse of public power for private gain' in post-Communist Europe (Karklins, 2002, pp. 22–32). But it would be impossible to 'measure' anything with so many diverse elements – although the prevalence and significance of each individual element could, and should, be measured – perhaps using different techniques, appropriate to the specific elements.

From those individual measurements, it might be possible to construct some crude overall assessment. But for what purpose? It would be far more useful to keep the measurements separate and be able to say, for example, that in a particular place bribery is not a problem while nepotism or dishonest auditing is a problem – or *vice versa*. Vague generalised measures might help to target attention on an especially corrupt country perhaps, but not on especially corrupt officials or especially corrupt practices. For that, we need a tighter more specific focus and definition as well as good data.

Alternative Techniques of Measurement

A variety of methods have been used to study bureaucratic encounters and/or corruption under Communist and post-Communist regimes, including:

- the author's personal impressions and anecdotes – some personal, some drawn non-systematically from press stories;
- direct observation – using ethnographic or investigative reporting techniques;
- systematic analysis of press-cuttings;
- official statistic;s
- cross-national correlations or similar statistical analyses of country-level statistics;
- interview surveys.

Of these, an author's use of personal impressions and anecdotes is the least systematic. It can be highly entertaining and it can convey a strong sense of insight, especially if the author has lived for many years under the regime in question (Simis, 1982, pp. 146–74). But, it is still the very personal view of a single individual and it lacks any real sense of quantity, extent or variance. Almost by definition, authors are not typical individuals and there is no reason to believe that their experience is typical. Greater reliance on the press makes the approach less personal but still not systematic (Shlapentokh, 1989). Ethnographic and investigative studies are more outward-looking, but they are still very personal accounts and often very local. They suffer from much the same restricted vision as anecdotal accounts, though not to quite the same degree.

Systematic analysis of press cuttings may be used in an attempt to broaden the vision, to depersonalise and quantify the findings (Holmes, 1993).[1] But even if the press is sampled systematically, its content is determined by the restrictions and enthusiasms of editors and censors or, in post-Communist Europe, by the post-Communist 'oligarchs' who now control much of the media. So a rash of press stories about corruption may reflect an official anti-corruption 'campaign' rather than a surge in corruption, while a dearth of press coverage may simply reflect an official cover-up.

Official statistics suffer even more directly from the fact that the authorities control them. Even some western economic statistics appear to have been manipulated for political ends (Levitas, 1996, pp. 45–65). And crime statistics in particular are notoriously unreliable. Victims under-report crime because they have little confidence in the police: the police under-record reported crime to make their record look better. Worst of all, official corruption statistics are even less reliable than other crime statistics because, as Richard Lotspeich notes, 'no party to the transaction has much incentive to report it' (1995, p. 577) and, he might have added, the police are so often involved in it themselves.

Moreover, there is a general problem of content that afflicts all studies based on anecdotal, media, or official data about bureaucratic encounters. Published anecdotes and published statistics inevitably focus on dissatisfaction rather than satisfaction and on illegal rather than legal methods of obtaining satisfaction. Anecdotes about bribing an official are more entertaining, and therefore more likely to be published, than anecdotes about arguing with an official or behaving in an ingratiating manner towards an official. Bias is therefore built-in to studies based on these types of data.

There are also particular problems when country-level data is used in a cross-national statistical analysis. The most important of these is what statisticians call the 'ecological effect' or the 'ecological fallacy' (Miller, 1995, p. 155). Briefly stated, the 'ecological fallacy theorem' proves that a correlation between two variables at one level need not exist at another level, or may even have a different sign at another level. Thus, for example, a cross-national correlation between (country level indices of) low-paid officials and corruption does *not* prove that, within countries, low pay encourages officials to take bribes. Paradoxically, it is often the highest paid officials in the poorest countries who are the most corrupt.

In principle, this 'ecological effect' can take many forms but it usually manifests itself as a 'super-additivity effect' which leads to greater differences between areas than might be predicted from the composition of their populations. In electoral studies, this super-additivity effect is familiar and powerful: the party political polarisation between richer and poorer areas can be twice as great as their class composition would predict because people tend to adopt some of the attitudes and behaviours of the social milieu in which they live (Miller, 1978, pp. 357–84).[2]

There is evidence that this super-additivity effect also operates cross-nationally with respect to bureaucratic encounters in post-Communist Europe. Unfairly treated clients are more likely to live in Ukraine than in the Czech Republic. Unfair treatment tends to affect attitudes towards reform but all clients in Ukraine tend to adopt the attitudes of an unfairly treated client even if their own treatment was not so bad. Conversely, all clients in the Czech Republic tend to adopt the attitudes of a fairly treated client even if their own treatment was unfair. When treatment seems 'exceptional' within a particular context, it can arouse strong personal feelings yet these may not translate completely into more general attitudes towards the bureaucracy. Such tendencies can never be discovered and investigated simply by correlating country-level data. For that, individual-level survey-data is essential.

A second problem with cross-national statistical studies of corruption is that they are often hybrid in nature, correlating official statistics on the economy or bureaucratic structure with survey-based indices of corruption perceptions – such as those published by *Transparency International* or the *European Bank for Reconstruction and Development*, or commercially available from *Business International* or *World Competitiveness Report*.[3] Thus, even cross-national analyses are usually based, in critical part, on limited use of survey data.

Interview surveys and associated methods such as focus-group discussions can provide much more information than that typically used in cross-national statistical studies. They can provide not only information on the country-wide level of corruption but also information on: (1) *variations* in corrupt behaviour within each country; (2) *motivations* and excuses for corrupt behaviour; (3) the evaluation and *interpretation* of corrupt practices; and (4) the *relative significance* of corruption as compared to other aspects of interactions with officials.

But interview surveys have their own peculiar faults: 'Corruption surveys may skew the results merely by asking the questions – if a person hardly thinks about corruption on a daily basis but is suddenly presented with dozens of questions on this topic' their answers may overstate the importance of corruption in their lives, or even in their dealings with officials (Gole, 1999, pp. 1–2). It probably does matter whether questions about corrupt officials are embedded in a survey about other aspects of bureaucratic encounters, or in a survey about crime-victimisation, or in an election/voting survey, or in some 'omnibus' poll that provides no context at all for a sudden question about corruption. And, survey methods are probably not the best way to study high-level corruption or what is termed 'grand corruption' at Ministerial level – although they probably are the best way to study public perceptions of grand corruption and public reactions to it.

Vague Questions

Some problems with the survey method may be insurmountable. But surveys often fail to achieve their full potential simply because they ask the wrong questions. In particular, survey questions about corruption often suffer from vagueness. This comes in two varieties: (1) they often *fail to specify the corrupt activity* sufficiently; (2) they often *fail to specify the respondent's role* – or even proximate involvement – in it.

Failure to Specify the Corrupt Activity – the Problem of Definition Revisited

In his review of the surveys used in constructing *Transparency International*'s 'Corruption Perceptions Index', Lambsdorff (2001, p. 3) notes that respondents were asked about:

- 'The level of *corruption*' (Freedom House survey);
- 'How do you rate *corruption*' in terms of its impact on 'the overall living/working environment'? (Political and Economic Risk Consultants survey);
- whether '*corruption*' is 'problematic for doing business' (World Economic Forum survey);
- 'Corruption' defined as '*the misuse of public office for personal or party political financial gain*' (Economist Intelligence Unit survey);
- whether '*bribing and corruption* prevail in the public sphere' (Institute of Management Development survey).

Most of these organisations seem to think that the meaning of 'corruption' is self-evident and precise. The *Economist* recognises the need to define the terms of its question carefully, but then defines them so widely as to make a good title for a thesis but a very bad survey question: though carefully worded it is so all-encompassing as to be functionally vague. The IMD couples 'corruption' with 'bribing', but does not equate them. In short, none of these questions is well-defined. Most suffer from vagueness about whether the question is about public officials, or private business, or both. And all suffer from vagueness of focus both as regards the *level* (for example, high or low of officials? top businessmen or small businessmen?) and the *nature of the corrupt activity* (for example, contacts, favours, bribes, nepotism, insider dealing, auditing etc).

Failure to Specify the Respondent's Role – Image versus Experience

Vito Tanzi suggests that 'questionnaire-based surveys' measure only 'perceptions of corruption rather than corruption *per se*' (Tanzi, 1998, p. 577). Indeed a recurrent criticism of survey based studies of corruption is that they focus on general perceptions of the incidence of corruption rather than personal experience – largely because the investigators fear that their respondents will be unwilling to incriminate themselves (Lancaster and Montinola 1997, pp. 193–94).

In particular, Lambsdorff notes that *all* the data used in constructing TI's CPI, as its name (Corruption Perceptions Index) suggests, consists of 'perceptions rather than to real phenomena' (Lambsdorff, 2004, p. 5). And despite its name, TI's BPI (Bribe Payers Index) is not based on bribe payers' confessions but on answers to the question:

In the business sectors with which you are most familiar, please indicate how likely companies from the following countries are to pay or offer bribes to retain business in this country – yet another question about general perceptions.

Of course the perceptions underlying the CPI and BPI might be based on actual experience. But they might just as well be based on prejudiced gossip or media sensationalism. No one knows. If you do not ask detailed questions about actually giving and receiving bribes, respondents cannot tell you even if they are willing, even eager, to do so. In themselves, perceptions are in fact a 'real phenomenon' of some importance in terms of their consequences – who wants to invest in a corrupt country? But perceptions are images that may not have a solid foundation in equivalent behaviour. Clean images may cloak corrupt behaviour, and corrupt images may not be based on corrupt behaviour so much as on something else – or falsely based on someone else's corrupt behaviour.

Lambsdorff accepts: (1) that perceptions may change rapidly without any basis for that change: 'changes might be due to high-level political scandals that affect perceptions, but do not reflect actual changing levels of corruption' (Lambsdorff, 2001, p. 2); (2) that local perceptions may be conditioned by local culturally-defined interpretations of what constitutes corruption, and (3) that some people may have no valid basis for their perceptions.

He deals with these three problems in turn by:

1. using three-year averages (to reduce the sensitivity of corruption measures to sudden media scandals or exposés);
2. excluding local people (on the grounds that their local culture may be deviant);
3. excluding the general public (on the grounds that they have insufficient expertise).

He makes a persuasive case for each of these strategies. But the first two take us further and further away from the specificity of time and place and the closeness of informants to the action. And, if our focus is on encounters between ordinary citizens and street-level bureaucrats, so does the third. So everything just gets less and less specific, more and more vague.

Suppose for a moment that diligent prosecutors and a free press expose massive corruption and in consequence nervous officials get scared of retribution. That could *increase perceptions* of corruption while at least temporarily *decreasing the practice*. Conversely, passing new but un-enforced anti-corruption laws or codes of conduct in a blaze of publicity may reduce the image of corruption without changing the practice.

Alternatively, images of corruption may be quite disconnected from events of any kind. Images may have become so ingrained and conventional that they fail to respond to actual changes, especially improvements, in behaviour (the 'criminal record' syndrome). Images may be based on uninformed speculation and gossip, or on irrelevant associations (inference from real evidence of corruption at one level to speculation about its prevalence at another; or the automatic assumption that the rich and powerful must surely use bribes simply because they are rich). And images may reflect the character of the perceiv*ers* (trustful, sceptical, suspicious, envious etc.) as much as the character of the perceiv*ed*.

All these patterns are plausible, even if they are inconsistent with each other. The only way to discover the connection between corruption perceptions and actual corrupt behaviour is to measure the corrupt behaviour directly.

One international survey quoted by Lambsdorff, though not used in the CPI index, does touch directly on experience rather than perceptions of corruption though it does not investigate it in depth: the ICVS (International Crime Victim Survey). Its question reads:

> In some areas there is a problem of corruption among government or public officials. During the last year has any government official, for instance a customs officer, police officer or inspector in your country asked you or expected you to pay a bribe for his service?

It seems that respondents were then asked about the category of official, and whether they reported the matter to the police, but not whether they actually paid. So it was not a question about the experience of bribery (though it is reported as such) but about the experience of 'attempted extortion' – which may or may not have been explicit ('asked' versus 'expected'), may have been wrongly inferred and may or may not have been successful.

More interestingly the ICCS (International Commercial Crime Survey) asked samples of businesses about perceptions and then, immediately afterwards, about experience. The questions are long, but the wording is important:

> *Perception question*: I would now like to ask you about corruption. By corruption I mean: bribing employees or companies; extorting money from a company; obtaining protection money; threats of product contamination; bribery or extortion by government officials; and it includes also attempts to act like that. Do you believe such practices are common in your line of business? Are they very common, fairly common, not very common, or not at all common?

> *Experience question*: Did anyone try to bribe you, your employees, or obtain bribes from the company, or extort money from your company in relation to its activities at these premises? This includes trying to obtain protection money or threats of product contamination. Bribery or extortion by government officials is also included.

These questions each require only one answer about a whole set of possible activities – which is not good survey practice. And in particular, both of them wrap up official corruption together with criminal extortion by private enterprise racketeers. Nonetheless, the answers show great discrepancies between perceptions and experience. Moreover, the discrepancies vary sharply across countries. Businessmen in Italy and the UK reported the same level of victimisation (under 2 per cent, and slightly lower in Italy than in the UK) but widely different perceptions about whether such things were common (only 7 per cent in the UK but 15 per cent in Italy said it was at least 'fairly common'). And while businessmen in France and the Czech Republic reported the same level of victimisation (just under 5 per cent) their perceptions about whether such things were 'fairly common' were remarkably different (34 per cent in the Czech Republic but only 1 per cent in France). Perceptions were clearly not determined by experience (van Dijk and Terlouw, 1996–1997).[4]

With all its faults, the ICCS suggests that if we wish to measure corruption rather than images based on gossip or moral panic – interesting though false images are as a real phenomenon in their own right – then we need to measure actual corrupt behaviour directly.

Forensic Questioning: Shuy's Principles of Interrogation

There are obvious problems with the direct approach however. Inevitably, most people will *not* have direct experience of many (probably most) kinds of corrupt behaviour. The respondents have to be relevant to the particular kind of corruption. The general public can be asked about their own direct experience of low-level corruption amongst street-level officials but not about high-level corruption in boardrooms or ministries. Although they rely entirely on perceptions rather than experience, both BPI and CPI do address this problem by using more or less relevant 'informants' in their attempts to measure higher-level corruption. They may ask the wrong questions (perceptions not experience) but they do attempt to use relevant sampling frames.

But, at any level, there is the problem of *lies*: the relevant informants with direct experience of giving or taking bribes may wish to 'cover-up' rather than 'expose' their own experience. Conversely, they may wish to exaggerate allegations that do not concern them directly – the old allegation: '*They* are all at it! But me? No way!'

For the future, more attention might be given to ways of uncovering direct experience. It will not be an easy task, and will require a more sceptical approach to survey design, an amalgam of 'opinion' and 'forensic' approaches to survey questionnaires and focus-group discussion schedules. To be successful, sociologists and political scientists may need to draw on the skills of investigators and journalists – to think of interviewing as interrogation.

Some who contrast 'interviewing' and 'interrogation' make the distinction on the basis that 'interrogation' has 'the distinct task of gaining an admission of confession in a real or apparent violation of law, policy, regulation or other restriction' (Yeschke, 1987, p. 25) an 'admission of guilt' (Aubry and Caputo, 1980, p. 21). But that is exactly the task in an interview designed to measure corruption! This is a distinction without a difference.

What is so very odd is that criminologists do not seem to have used the interrogative approach in their crime surveys such as the ICVS. Even the title suggests a closed mind-set in which respondents are to be treated only as victims rather than as perpetrators. That is an unambitious approach.

What advice can survey researchers get from experts in interrogation techniques?

Clearly, there is an enormous difference in the power relationships between, on the one hand a police interrogator and suspect in a police station and, on the other, a survey interviewer and interviewee. The interviewee can terminate the interview and send the interviewer away at any time; but the suspect cannot escape the interrogation. Surely that makes an enormous difference to the chances of getting a confession? The suspect can be browbeaten, threatened, or offered deals to confess while the survey interviewee cannot. But if we are interested in *truthful confessions*, rather than confessions as such, the differences between a survey interview and an interrogation are much less. Threats and deals not only infringe a citizen's civil rights, they frequently lead to false confessions. The fact that the survey researcher cannot use them is no great loss.

Certainly, many professional interrogators have their pet theories about how to detect untruthfulness[5] but these do not stand up well to scientific testing (Robinson, 1996). Surprisingly, perhaps, to the layman, the scientific advice on police interrogation is remarkably similar to the principles of really good practice in serious survey interviewing, if not to the practice of snap opinion pollsters. There is a convergence. Experts in interrogation find it useful and effective to think of interrogations as interviews! Indeed Inbau, Reid and Buckley argue that it is more effective for an interrogator to 'avoid creating the impression of an investigator seeking a confession or conviction. It is far better to fulfil the role of one who is merely seeking the truth' (Inbau, Reid and Buckley, 1986, p. 36). And Shuy reports that 'in recent years' he has 'heard many law enforcement officers testify that they do not 'interrogate', but rather 'interview', subjects (Shuy, 1998, p. 12). What they actually mean however, is that, as far as possible, they use the style of a social survey interview to conduct an interrogation aimed primarily at uncovering the truth, whether that includes a confession or a convincing denial.

So Shuy's 'basic principles of interrogation' are:

1. 'Be conversational';
2. 'Ask clear and explicit questions';
3. 'Look for inconsistencies before trying to determine deception';
4. 'Ask lots of questions'.

Without lots of questions, the interrogation cannot be conversational, and cannot uncover inconsistencies, let alone attempt to resolve them.

Surveys that ask about perceptions but then treat their findings as indicators of actual corruption rather than image, fail on the second criterion: 'clear and explicit questions'. And surveys that ask only a few, sometimes just one or two, relevant questions fail on the first and third criteria: they provide no scope for detecting 'inconsistencies' and they cannot be considered as 'conversations'.

It is worth reflecting back on the ICVS questions. Two questions, one about attempted extortion, the other about reporting it, hardly constitute much of a conversation. But, worse than that, the content of the questions is profoundly non-conversational. For example, amongst other things, the first question asked whether a 'police officer' had sought a bribe 'for his service'; and the second asked whether the respondent had 'reported the matter to the police'. If that had occurred in a conversational setting, the replies would not have been printable. All over the world policemen take bribes – but not usually for performing their service. Quite the opposite!

They take them in return for *not* performing their service! And asking whether the respondent reported the policeman's extortion to the police invites a jocular reply. It is easy to guess what information the researchers wanted, but their questions are far removed from a natural conversation. The actual verbatim replies would be interesting but were probably not recorded by the interviewers.

Although we were not familiar with Shuy's arguments when we designed the *Culture of Corruption* project, (Miller, Grødeland and Koshechkina, 2001) common sense and good survey research practice, as outlined by de Vaus (1991, pp. 80–105), pointed us in a similar direction. But it is important to emphasise that our study is only a first attempt at an interrogative approach to understanding and measuring corruption, and that it focused on only one level of corruption. It is not a universal recipe for corruption research. Nonetheless, it is worth reviewing our methodology against Shuy's four principles of interrogation: (1) 'be conversational'; (2) 'ask clear and explicit questions'; (3) 'look for inconsistencies before trying to determine deception'; and by implication (4) 'ask lots of questions'.

'Be Conversational'

We began with 26 focus-group discussions spread across Ukraine, Bulgaria, Slovakia and the Czech Republic, involving 187 participants. Associated with these focus groups were 136 semi-structured, in-depth, more private, one-to-one interviews using the same schedule as guided the focus-group discussions. One or more of the project directors attended 18 of the focus-group discussions in person (with simultaneous translation) and all were videotaped and transcribed. Although these discussions were guided by a clear schedule, they were of course far more 'conversational' than is possible in large-scale interview surveys. They generated lots of 'stories', including many specific 'confessions' as well as many specific allegations of successful or attempted extortion.

Incidentally, group-discussions impose some constraints that are similar to interrogations. Physically, participants might be free to walk away from the discussion, but psychologically they are imprisoned for the duration of the discussion. (Only one participant ran away – an ethnically Turkish/Muslim woman in Kurdjali, Bulgaria – and that was before the discussion began.) And confessions breed confessions: one participant's confession typically evoked confessions from others – somewhat as they might do at a Methodist or Salvation Army prayer meeting. In several instances, an initial denial was retracted as the discussion progressed, or a confession was expanded from one admission to a sequence of admissions. On the other hand, some denials were reinforced with very convincing detail. Participants told stories of going to some effort to insist on good service without offering money. And others told stories of offering money and having it refused by officials who had been content to give good service without 'extra' reward.

But focus-group discussions include such a small (certainly) and somewhat unrepresentative (probably) set of participants that they cannot be used for measurement. On the other hand, they do provide a good guide to what should be measured and they are an invaluable aid to designing questions – and sequences of questions – for a survey questionnaire that attempts to be as natural and 'conversational' as possible.

Basing our questionnaires on the stories, confessions, allegations and perspectives revealed in the focus-group discussions, we then commissioned 4,778 fully structured interviews with representative samples of the public, supplemented by another 1,272 interviews with additional samples of the public in ethnic minority regions and by 1,307 interviews with junior officials. Interviews with officials contained many of the same questions used in interviews with the public, plus other questions that were rephrased to cover a topic from the perspective of an official instead of a client. Our sample of junior officials consisted of nationwide quota samples of junior officials in health, education, social services, the police and legal services.

All interviews were designed to be as conversational as possible by exploring the topic in detail, *asking lots of questions*, and thus allowing respondents to qualify and nuance their responses. In addition, using lots of questions, made it possible to spend time establishing a non-judgemental, even sympathetic, atmosphere and 'set the scene' for probing without threatening and for confessions without fear of disapproval. Always – even in the interviews with junior officials – we discussed their problems in depth before seeking their confessions.

'Ask Clear and Explicit Questions'

In all our focus-group discussions, in-depth interviews and large-scale surveys, we asked explicitly and in considerable detail (a) about perceptions and gossip and later (b) about actual experience, clearly distinguishing between the two. From our focus-group discussions we expected that images of corruption would be far more widespread than experience of corruption and our findings clearly indicate a large but variable gulf between images of corruption and actual personal experience. But the reason we spent so much interview-time on general images of corruption was primarily in order to 'set the scene' for our respondent to answer explicit and specific questions about their actual experience.

It is normally good survey practice to avoid bias – either in questions' wording or in the context set by other questions. The exception to that rule is when we have reason to believe that the pressure of fear or a moral climate of disapproval is likely to constrain honest answers. By first allowing our respondents to articulate a perhaps-exaggerated view that corruption was widespread, that people 'typically' had to do it, we made it easier for them to confess later on that they had themselves behaved in that way. Our explicit questions to the public about whether they or their family had actually given a present or a bribe to an official in recent years were question numbers 141 and 142 in the interview. Even then, our question did not ask 'whether or not' they had given presents and bribes to officials, but rather 'how often – usually, sometimes, rarely or never?' Without improper pressure and without sacrificing our commitment to 'clear and explicit' questions, we nonetheless made it 'easy to confess'. Indeed, this frequency question not only made it easier to confess but also made the replies more specific rather than less.

In simple per cent age terms, our measures of corruption based on experience and confession produce much smaller numbers than those based on perceptions – as did those from the ICCS which we quoted earlier. They give a very different impression of the scale of the problem and they raise the question whether perceptions and experience are measuring different things.

We measured *perceptions or images* of corruption in several ways. First we asked:

> Now think of a person seeking something to which they are *entitled by law*. Is it *likely* or *not likely* that they would have to offer money, a present or a favour to get help from each of the following – I mean offer more than the official charge?

There followed a list of 10 kinds of junior official. On average, over two-thirds thought it 'likely' that money, a present or a favour would be necessary, ranging from 44 per cent in the Czech Republic up to 85 per cent in Ukraine.

Later on, still focusing on *perceptions and images*, we asked more specifically about eight typical ways of dealing with officials, including the use of presents and bribes:

> Suppose a person asks an official for something to which he/she is *entitled by law*. To get a successful outcome, is it *likely* or *not likely* that he/she would offer (1) a small present? (2) money or an expensive present?

On average, over two-thirds thought it 'likely' that 'money or an expensive present' would be necessary, ranging from 44 per cent in the Czech Republic up to 81 per cent in Ukraine. (The figures for the 'likely' need to offer a 'small present' were even higher.)

Later still we turned to *personal experience*, and asked:

> Thinking over these *personal experiences* of dealing with officials in the last few years, did *you or your family* usually, sometimes, rarely, or never have to (1) offer a small present? (2) offer money or an expensive present?

On average, under a quarter had offered 'money or an expensive present' even 'rarely', ranging from only 11 per cent in the Czech Republic up to 36 per cent in Ukraine. (The figures for having offered a 'small present' were higher.)

So in the Czech Republic, four times as many 'thought it likely' that citizens would have to offer 'money or an expensive present' as could recall themselves – or their family – having done so in recent years. If we believe them, their answers mean that most of those Czechs who thought it 'likely' had no direct personal experience of it. Their image of pervasive low-level bribe-giving must be based on something other than experience. The discrepancy between perceptions and experience was much less in Ukraine, but still large.

In a more recent survey, the 2001 Polish National Election survey, when we asked 'How widespread do you think corruption such as bribe taking is amongst politicians in Poland?', 94 per cent said it was at least 'quite' widespread, 56 per cent that it was 'very' widespread and 80 per cent said junior, street-level officials were more corrupt in Poland than in EU countries. But, as in the Czech Republic, only 10 per cent had offered 'money or an expensive present' even 'rarely' in recent years.

'Look for Inconsistencies before Trying to Determine Deception'

By asking lots of questions, it is possible to detect inconsistencies. That may indicate deception, but it may also indicate misunderstanding or confusion. And by itself it merely reveals a problem but does not solve it. Drawing attention to inconsistencies without giving the respondent a face-saving exit route might destroy the non-judgemental, even sympathetic, atmosphere we had spent so long establishing. Of course, we can expose such inconsistencies when we analyse the data, but during the interview we need a softer approach. One alternative is simply to ignore denials and ask the question again in a different format, allowing the respondent to correct their initial answer without losing face.

We used that technique several times, once with quite striking results. In our interviews with officials, we asked three questions, in quick succession, about officials' actual experience of gift-taking:

- 'In the last few years, say the last five years, did you *ever accept* a present from someone whose problem you dealt with as part of your official duties?'
- 'If you did accept something, was that *only after* you had solved the client's problem, or *sometimes before*?'
- 'If you did accept something, was that *only a small present* – flowers, chocolates, or a bottle for example – or was it *something more* than that?'

Despite the conditional phrasing of the second and third questions, we put each question to *all* officials, including those who had originally denied accepting anything. Of course, there was a 'silent' code on the questionnaire for those who insisted that they 'had not taken' gifts before or after, large or small, but this answer was not read out by the interviewer.

On the first question, only 30 per cent confessed to accepting a present. But on the second, 43 per cent confessed that they had accepted something either 'before' (8 per cent) or 'after' (35 per cent) solving their client's problem. And on the third, 58 per cent confessed that they had accepted either 'a small present' (53 per cent) or 'something more' (5 per cent).

The levels of 'don't knows/refusals' were low and, significantly, they *dropped* steadily across the three questions as they became less ambiguous. As the questions became more specific, the numbers unwilling or unable to reply declined.

There was an element of consistency even in the revised answers. Over a third of those who initially *denied* accepting 'a present' later admitted that they had accepted 'a small present' but none of them admitted to accepting 'something more' and very few that they had accepted even a small present 'before' solving the client's problem.

In addition, almost all of those who had given a *'depends what you mean'* response to the first question later admitted that they had taken something, but it was nearly always something small and few had accepted even a small present 'before' solving their client's problem. In sharp contrast, amongst those who had readily admitted in reply to our first question that they had *accepted* a present, 14 per cent later went on to confess that they had accepted 'something more than a small present' and 22 per cent that they had accepted something 'before' solving their client's problem.

Credible Witnesses? Sharpening Up the Analysis

In part, the initial denials and subsequent retractions merely reinforce Shuy's recommendation that questions should be 'clear and explicit'. But in part, it also reveals a tendency for many respondents to tell half-truths, to 'shade down' their replies – taking advantage of any real or supposed ambiguity in the question. We *know* that many who had (by their later confession) accepted a 'small present' were willing to shade that down into no present at all. It seems very likely that others who had accepted a 'large gift' would do something similar, shading that down to a 'small gift' – taking advantage of the ambiguity between large and small, without incurring the psychological tension of an outright lie.

For many analytic purposes, it may be better to restrict the analysis to the more credible witnesses rather than to retain every respondent in the analysis. Routinely, we tend to exclude the 'Don't Knows'. And in the surveys used for the CPI and BPI, the sampling frames are restricted to the supposedly better-informed – businessmen and experts, rather than the general public. No new principle is involved if we exclude those respondents whose witness is, for some reason, doubtful.

We have no reason to doubt that respondents who confessed to giving or receiving 'large gifts' had actually done so. And at the other end of the scale, most of those who deny giving or receiving even a small gift have probably not given or received a large one. None of the officials in our survey who later admitted accepting a large gift ever denied that they had received something. The problem lies in the intermediate category of those who admit to giving or accepting something, but not something large. The chances are that some have given or accepted something large but others really have not.

Excluding respondents who claim to have given or received only a small present may help to sharpen up any analysis of the patterns and motivations for corruption. There is then relatively little chance that any of the respondents retained in the analysis are misclassified. Those who admit involvement with large gifts should be believed. And while those who deny involvement with even 'small' gifts should not have their denials taken quite literally, it is relatively safe to assume their lack of involvement with 'large' gifts.

In an analysis of the impact of personal values and external pressures (extortion or temptation), we correlated confessed bribe giving (amongst citizens) and confessed bribe taking (amongst officials) with both internal values and external pressures

(Miller, Grødeland and Koshechkina, 2002, pp. 165–93). Bribes were defined as 'large gifts' – that is, 'money or an expensive present'.

Accepting at face value citizens' answers about whether or not they had given a 'large gift', citizens' bribe giving correlates at 0.15 with values and at 0.35 with the external pressure of extortion. Restricting the analysis, to those citizens who confessed to *giving large* gifts or *denied giving even small* presents, increases the correlations to 0.20 with values and at 0.43 with extortion. That suggests a degree of ambiguity or self-deception amongst those who claimed to have given 'only a small gift' (though either way, no matter whether we sharpen-up the analysis or not, the impact of extortion on bribe-giving appears over twice as powerful as the impact of values).

Similarly, if we accept at face value, officials' answers to whether or not they had accepted a 'large gift' then officials' bribe taking correlates at 0.15 with values and at 0.34 with the external pressure of temptation. Excluding those who admitted accepting only a small gift, and restricting the analysis to officials who either confessed to *accepting large* gifts or *denied receiving even small* presents sharpens the analysis remarkably. The correlations with bribe-taking rise even more than when we applied this restriction to our analysis of bribe-givers, to 0.25 with values and 0.51 with the temptations provided by frequent offers. That suggests an even greater degree of ambiguity or self-deception amongst officials who claimed to have accepted 'only a small gift' than amongst clients who claimed to have given them. (Again, no matter whether we sharpen-up the analysis or not, the impact of external pressure on bribe-taking appears over twice as powerful as the impact of values.)

In this example, the attempt to eliminate ambiguity only sharpens-up a pattern that was already clearly visible, but it encourages further experiment with a 'credible witness' approach.

What do Perception Measures Measure?

Finally, returning to the issue of perception-based measures, we know there are very large differences between measures of corruption based on experience and those based on images or perceptions. That answers the narrow question whether images and perceptions are accurate. Insofar as they exaggerate, they are *not* accurate. If they are systematically inflated, they may still produce acceptable country-rankings – though they may underestimate the differences between corruption levels in different countries if perceptions of corruption are more inflated in low-corruption countries than in high-corruption countries. The trouble with over-reliance on the 'anecdotes and perceptions' approach is not just that it exaggerates the extent and importance of low-level corruption, but that it fails to discriminate sufficiently. At worst that can lead to the vague and misleading over-generalisation that 'there is corruption everywhere' and consequently that nothing can be done to eliminate it. A focus on actual experience leads to the rather different conclusion that street-level corruption is very variable, that it is very low indeed in some countries and consequently that even where it is higher something can be done to reduce (if not eliminate) it.

But the broader and more interesting question about images and perceptions of corruption is: what do images of corruption reflect? Why do some people imagine they are surrounded by corruption while others do not? Are variations in images of corruption simply random? or do they reflect something? and, if so, what? Let us consider some possibilities.

First of all, images of corruption might reflect *generalised gossip* about corruption, or *media scandals/allegations* rather than anything *more personal* to the individual.

We asked respondents for their own assessment of the basis for their feelings about the behaviour of street-level officials, those that dealt with ordinary people and the ones they had just alleged (in answers to previous questions) often took presents and bribes. Only 57 per cent of our respondents said their views about even these junior officials were based primarily on personal experience, 28 per cent cited gossip ('what people generally say about officials') and 15 per cent the media ('what you have read in newspapers and heard on television or radio'). In our 2001 Polish Election Survey, only 33 per cent said their views about even these junior officials were based primarily on personal experience, 21 per cent cited gossip ('what people generally say about officials') and a massive 47 per cent the media.

Indeed, even in the case of such junior officials, many respondents did not have much actual experience on which to base their judgement. We used a sequence of 14 questions to define, implicitly, what we meant by junior officials and to remind respondents about their contacts with them. Had their own or their family's 'personal experiences of dealing with officials in the last few years' involved health problems? education? tax? official contracts? pensions or other benefits? unemployment? privatisation or restitution? customs? services such as electricity, gas or water? passports (internal or external)? housing problems? the police? court officials? other officials – which? Then we asked: 'How often have you or your family had to deal with such officials in the last few years – frequently, occasionally, rarely, or never?'. Only 14 per cent said 'frequently', 42 per cent 'occasionally', 39 per cent 'rarely' and 5 per cent 'never'. (By their own account, Ukrainians were particularly good at completely avoiding contact with officials.)

As we might expect, frequency of contact affected the basis of evaluation. The numbers who cited personal experience as the basis for their evaluation of officials' behaviour fell from 75 per cent amongst those who had *frequent* dealings to 47 per cent amongst those who *rarely or never* dealt with officials. So those who had relatively infrequent dealings with officials were self-consciously aware that their perceptions were based more on gossip and the media than on their limited experience.

Frequency of contact will affect experiences and, to a lesser degree, images and perceptions of corruption. The numbers who confessed that they had given 'money or an expensive present' to an official fell sharply from 34 per cent amongst those who had *frequent* dealings to 20 per cent amongst those who *rarely or never* dealt with officials. And the numbers who thought it 'likely' that a person would offer 'money or an expensive present' to an official declined much more modestly from 69 per cent amongst those who had *frequent* dealings to 64 per cent amongst those who *rarely or never* dealt with officials.

Table 8.1   Frequency of contact consciously affects the basis for perceptions

| | All respondents | If family have had dealings with officials … | | |
		frequently	occasionally	rarely/never
	%	%	%	%
Would you say that your feelings about the behaviour of officials are based more on …				
MEDIA: what you have read in newspapers and heard on television or radio	15	10	12	19
GOSSIP: what people generally say about officials	28	15	27	34
EXPERIENCE: your personal experiences	57	75	62	47

Table 8.2   Frequency of contact has a big effect on behaviour but little or no effect on perceptions

| | All respondents | If family have had dealings with officials … | | |
		frequently	occasionally	rarely/never
	%	%	%	%
IMAGES/PERCEPTIONS: a person would be 'likely' to offer money etc.	66	69	66	64
EXPERIENCE: have offered money etc. at least on rare occasions	24	34	24	20

Secondly, although images of corruption might reflect something more personal to the individual, the possibilities include much more than personal experience of corrupt officials. They do include (1) *experience of corrupt behaviour by officials* such as attempted extortion. But citizens' images of corruption might also reflect other experiences such as the (2) *experience of unfair treatment* leading to a sense of injustice and the easy but perhaps unjustified inference that corruption was the cause.

And citizens' images of corruption might also reflect (3) *the experience their own corrupt behaviour* such as giving bribes. Or reflect their (4) *own corruptibility* such as their willingness to engage in corrupt behaviour, even if no opportunity had yet arisen for them to indulge in corrupt behaviour. Allegations about corruption may tell us as much about the complainant as about anyone else.

Amongst all respondents, the best correlate of images of corruption (perceptions/generalised allegations) is, by a narrow margin, *corruptibility*. By a greater margin, corruptibility is the best correlate of corruption perceptions amongst those who depend primarily on the media or gossip for their views about officials. That changes amongst those whose views about officials are based primarily upon experience. Then, by a narrow margin, the respondents' experience of *their own corrupt behaviour* becomes the best correlate of allegations against officials.

Earlier, we supposed that bribe-givers might try to 'cover-up' their own corrupt behaviour with the old allegation: '*They* are all at it! But me? No way!'. Instead, it seems that they try to justify their own corrupt behaviour by transforming this into: 'Yes, I did it. But everyone has to', Allegations about the need to give presents and bribes to officials correlate better with citizens own bribe-giving, or with their willingness to give bribes, than with their reported experience of either unfair treatment or extortion.

But the pattern of allegations is a little more complex than that. It is highly interactive. Amongst those who actually *have given* money to an official even on rare occasions, perceptions of corruption are very high and remarkably uniform, averaging 84 per cent. Amongst those who have *never given* money to an official, perceptions of bribery are much lower, averaging 58 per cent.

That is still remarkably high for those with no personal or family experience of giving bribes, however, and it explains why perceptions so far exceed direct experience of bribery. Allegations of corruption grossly outrun experience.

But the level of allegations amongst non-givers is also quite sensitive to other influences on the imagination. It ranges from 38 per cent in the Czech Republic to 78 per cent in Ukraine, from 49 per cent amongst those who were 'usually' treated fairly by officials to 71 per cent amongst those who were rarely or never treated fairly and from 48 per cent amongst those who 'would refuse' to pay a bribe to 65 per cent amongst those who 'would pay if asked'. In simple terms: giving bribes is a sufficient but not a necessary cause of perceptions that bribery is widespread.

Amongst those who say their views about officials are based primarily on their own experience, their experience of giving bribes greatly affects their perceptions: it makes a 30 per cent difference (84 per cent versus 54 per cent). But amongst those who depend primarily on the media for their views about officials, their own experience

Table 8.3 Amongst those whose views are based on experience, perceptions reflect that corruption. But amongst those whose views are based on the media, perceptions reflect corruptibility

	Amongst all respondents	Amongst respondents whose views about officials' behaviour are based mainly on ...		
		media	gossip	experience
	$r \times 100$	$r \times 100$	$r \times 100$	$r \times 100$
SMALL PRESENTS: Correlation between allegations that these are 'likely' ...				
... and (i) whether official ever asked for bribe	13	7	7	16
... and (ii) frequency of unfair treatment	6	2	2	9
... and (iii) frequency of giving small presents	23	14	18	28
... and (iv) willingness to give if asked and could afford	25	19	23	26
MONEY OR EXPENSIVE PRESENTS: Correlation between allegations that these are 'likely' ...				
... and (i) whether official ever asked for bribe	17	16	15	20
... and (ii) frequency of unfair treatment	15	10	15	17
... and (iii) frequency of giving large presents	22	12	20	26
... and (iv) willingness to give if asked and could afford	22	16	21	22

only makes a 14 per cent difference. Those respondents whose personal experience *ex*cludes giving bribes are *more* inclined to allege corruption if they rely on the media. Conversely those respondents whose personal experience *in*cludes giving bribes are *less* inclined to allege corruption if they rely on the media. Relying on the media reduces the impact of personal experience, good or bad, and makes perceptions of corruption regress towards the mean.

Table 8.4   **Amongst those who have given bribes, perceptions of corruption are uniformly high. But amongst those who have not, perceptions of corruption reflect media reporting, corruptibility, unfair treatment and country of residence**

	Allegations that bribes were 'likely' to be necessary in dealings with officials	
	Amongst those who have never given money or an expensive present to an official	**Amongst those who have given money or an expensive present to an official**
	%	%
If views about officials' behaviour are based mainly on:		
experience	54	84
gossip	61	85
media	63	77
If asked directly to pay a bribe, respondent would …		
refuse	48	75
pay	65	87
If respondent received fair treatment from officials …		
… usually	49	85
… sometimes	64	85
… rarely or never	71	81
If respondent lived in …		
… Czech Republic	38	80
… Slovakia	51	85
… Bulgaria	68	83
… Ukraine	78	84

Conclusion

Images or perceptions of corruption are interesting in themselves and also because they may have consequences for compliance, for civil order and for foreign investment. But, they are not an accurate measure of corrupt behaviour. Accurate survey-based measures of corrupt behaviour itself require a clear and specific definition of the behaviour in frame, clear and explicit questions about it and a sceptical approach to the answers. However sceptical, we should not give up the attempt to measure corrupt behaviour. Instead, we should aim to put in enough effort and ingenuity to overcome our respondents' fears and inhibitions. A sceptical approach to respondents' answers means that it may be useful and effective to think of the interview as an interrogation. Experts in interrogation certainly find it useful and effective to think of interrogations as interviews!

Notes

1   Especially Chapter 3: 'Patterns of Corruption and its Reporting in the USSR and the PRC'. See also UCIPR's (Ukrainian Center for Independent Political Research, Kyiv) monthly *Corruption Watch* which trawls the Ukrainian press for corruption stories; accessible *via* kam@political.kiev ua; CSD/Coalition 2000's *Weekly Review of Bulgarian Press Coverage of Corruption*, accessible *via* www.online.bg/coalition2000; and RFE/RL's *Newsline*, accessible *via* www.rferl.org/newsline/search/.
2   Reprinted in Denver, David T. and Hands, Gordon (eds) (1992), *Issues and Controversies in British Electoral Behaviour*, Harvester Wheatsheaf, London.
3   See EBRD (1999), *Ten Years of Transition: Transition Report*, European Bank for Reconstruction and Development, p. 125; Mauro, Paolo (1995), 'Corruption and Growth', *Quarterly Journal of Economics*, vol. 110, no. 3, pp. 681–712 at p. 684; Ades, Alberto and Di Tella, Rafael (1997), 'The New Economics of Corruption', *Political Studies*, vol. 45, no. 3, pp. 496–515 at p. 499.
4   See also: van Dijk, Jan J.M. and Terlouw, Gert Jan (1995), *Fraude en criminaliteit tegen het bedrijfsleven in internationaal perspectief*, Justitiële Verkenningen, vol. 21, no. 4, pp. 119–42.
5   See for example, Zulawski, David E. and Wicklander, Douglas E. (1993), *Practical Aspects of Interview and Interrogation*, CRC Press, Boca Raton, FA.

References

Ades, Alberto and Di Tella, Rafael (1997), 'The New Economics of Corruption', *Political Studies*, vol. 45, no. 3, pp. 496–515.

Aubry, A.S. and Caputo, R.R. (1980), *Criminal Interrogation*, Charles C. Thomas, Springfield, IL.

de Vaus, David A. (1991), *Surveys in Social Research*, Allen and Unwin, London and Sydney.

EBRD (1999), *Ten Years of Transition: Transition Report*, European Bank for Reconstruction and Development, p. 125.

Gole, Juliet S. (1999), 'Public Opinion Polls as an Anti-corruption Technique', *LGI Newsletter*, vol. 1, no. 1, Local Government and Public Service Reform Initiative of the Open Society Institute, Budapest, pp. 1–2.

Holmes, Leslie (1993), *The End of Communist Power: Anti-Corruption Campaigns and Legitimation Crisis*, Polity Press, UK.

Inbau, F.E., Reid, J.E. and Buckley, J.P. (1986), *Criminal Interrogation and Confessions*, Williams and Wilkins, Baltimore.

Johnston, Michael (1998), 'Fighting Systematic Corruption: Social Foundations for Institutional Reform', *European Journal of Development Research*, vol. 10, no. 1 (Special Issue 1998).

Karklins, Rasma (2002), 'Typology of Post-Communist Corruption', *Problems of Post-Communism*, vol. 49, no. 4, pp. 22–32.

Lambsdorff, Johann Graf (2001), *Background Paper to the 2001 Corruptions Perceptions Index*, Transparency International and Göttingen University, June 2001.

Lancaster, Thomas D. and Montinola, Gabriella R. (1997), 'Towards a Methodology for the Comparative Study of Political Corruption', *Crime, Law and Social Change*, vol. 27, no. 3–4 double issue, pp. 185–206.

Levitas, Ruth (1996), 'Fiddling while Britain Burns: the Measurement of Unemployment', in Ruth Levitas and Will Guy (eds), *Interpreting Official Statistics*, Routledge, London.

Lotspeich, Richard (1995), 'Crime in the Transition Economies', *Europe-Asia Studies*, vol. 47, no. 4, pp. 555–89.

Mauro, Paolo (1995), 'Corruption and Growth', *Quarterly Journal of Economics*, vol. 110, no. 3, pp. 681–712.

Miller, William L. (1978), 'Social Class and Party Choice in England: a New Analysis', *British Journal of Political Science*, vol. 8, no. 3, pp. 257–84.

Miller, William L. (1995), 'Quantitative Methods', in David Marsh and Gerry Stoker (eds), *Theory and Methods in Political Science*, Macmillan, London, pp. 154–72.

Miller, William L., Grødeland, Åse B. and Koshechkina, Tatyana Y. (2001), *A Culture of Corruption? Coping with Government in Postcommunist Europe*, Central European University Press, Budapest.

Miller, William L., Grødeland, Åse B. and Koshechkina, Tatyana Y. (2002), 'Values and Norms versus Extortion and Temptation', in Donatella della Porta and Susan Rose-Ackerman (eds), *Corrupt Exchanges: Empirical Themes in the Politics and Political Economy of Corruption*, Nomos Verlagsgesellschaft, Baden-Baden.

Robinson, W. Peter (1996), *Deceit, Delusion and Detection*, Sage, Thousand Oaks, CA.

Sajó, András (1998), 'Corruption, Clientelism and the Future of the Constitutional State in Eastern Europe', *East European Constitutional Review*, vol. 7, no. 2, pp. 37–46.

Shlapentokh, Vladimir (1989), *The Public and Private Life of the Soviet People*, Oxford University Press, Oxford.

Shuy, Roger W. (1998), *The Language of Confession, Interrogation, and Deception*, Sage, Thousand Oaks, CA.

Simis, Konstantin M. (1982), *USSR: Secrets of a Corrupt Society*, Dent, London.

Tanzi, Vito (1998), 'Corruption Around the World: Causes, Consequences, Scope and Cures', *IMF Staff Papers*, vol. 45, no. 4, International Monetary Fund, Washington DC, pp. 559–94.

van Dijk, Jan J.M. and Terlouw, Gert Jan (1996–1997), 'An International Perspective of the Business Community as Victims of Fraud and Crime', *Security Journal*.

van Dijk, Jan J.M. and Terlouw, Gert Jan (1995), *Fraude en criminaliteit tegen het bedrijfsleven in internationaal perspectief*, Justitiële Verkenningen, vol. 21, no. 4, pp. 119–42.

Yeschke, C.L. (1987), *Interviewing: An Introduction to Interrogation*, Charles C. Thomas, Springfield, IL.

Zulawski, David E. and Wicklander, Douglas E. (1993), *Practical Aspects of Interview and Interrogation*, CRC Press, Boca Raton, FA.

PART II
THE CASE STUDIES

Chapter 9

Corruption Indices for Russian Regions

Elena A. Panifilova

Introduction

Within the field of corruption studies much attention has been paid to variations of corruption across countries and regions. In fact many can trace the global increased interest in corruption to the attention getting the Corruption Perception Index of Transparency International. However if variations in cross country comparisons across regions such as the Baltics (175,000 sq. km and combined population of approximately 8 million) or the Caucasus (190.000 sq. km with population of 16 million) can cause major controversy what about of the variations in perceived levels of corruption within large federal States? The Russian Regional Corruption Index looked at a country of 89 federal regions with 145 million population spread across 17 million sq. km and 11 time zones and provides a step towards breaking the myth of Russia as a monolithic giant mired in universal and rampant corruption.

In order to better identify the differences in perceptions and corrupt transactions between the Federal districts it was decided to conduct a series of surveys that looked at the perceptions and realities of corrupt transactions among citizens and entrepreneurs. Working with 40 of the 89 federal regions in Russia produces at least a partial view of the corruption situation across the Russian Federation during the timing of the survey.

Methodology

From January 2002 to January 2003, the Center for Anti-corruption Research and Initiative Transparency International – Russia (TI-R) carried out a public opinion survey – 'Corruption Indices for Russian Regions'. The Open Society Institute (Soros Foundation) provided funding. The main objective of this survey was to create a multi-dimensional picture of corruption in the Russian Federation and its regions. The study investigated the relative amount of bribery and characteristics of corrupt practices as well as an assessment of the degree of public confidence in government institutions. It collected and analysed sociological data of different forms and manifestations of corruption. This was the first study of such magnitude and scope in the world.

Our project was based on a sociological survey that took place in July-August 2002 and embraced 5,666 individuals and 1,838 entrepreneurs representing small and medium businesses in 40 out of 89 Russian regions. Thus, the corruption indices were created on the basis of two questionnaires – for private citizens and businessmen. Both questionnaires included a general group of questions concerning the estimations of the level of corruption and credibility of the government. Final indices were created as a composite. Aggregating other (primary) indices for the purpose of reflection complicated the phenomenon of corruption. In general, this national study was unprecedented in terms of its scale.

Questionnaires

Sociological measurements of corruption were based on two types of surveys:

1. Assessment questions
2. Questions about personal corruption practices.

Questionnaire Examples:

1. *How frequently do residents of your region encounter corruption? Please choose one of the following answers:*

   (a) Constantly
   (b) From time to time
   (c) Very seldom.

2. *When did you have to informally influence an official using a bribe, gift, service, etc. in order to solve a problem facing your business? Please choose one of the following answers:*

   (a) Less than a week ago
   (b) From a week to a month ago
   (c) From a month to six months ago
   (d) More than six months ago.

   Data collected was used for development of:

1. Perception of Corruption
2. Relative Amount of Corruption.

   The Corruption Index includes characteristics of everyday and business corruption markets. Relationships between citizens and public officials provide fertile grounds for petty corruption, but relationships between authorities and businesses – grounds for business corruption. This corruption is caused by cooperation between businesses and authorities (administrative corruption), business impact on policy (state capture) and authorities impact over the economy (economy capture). A subjective estimate of corruption levels might lead to shifts caused by an emotional attitude of respondents towards the government. Thus, we believe it was necessary to assess the degree of public trust in the state (on the Federal, Regional and Local levels) and its institutions (Executive, Judiciary, Legislative branches and Law enforcement agencies).

Results

Questionnaire for Citizens

These questions were aimed identifying the perceptions of citizens and there interaction with corrupt officials. Specifically, the levels of day-to-day corrupt acts were examined and the levels of trust in specific institutions and the various levels of Government.

Indirect Questions

1. Respondents were asked: *How can you estimate the level of corruption from the following institutions?*

Table 9.1   Estimates of the level of corruption in various institutions

Answer/ Institution	Law enforcement agencies	Security Service	Government (Cabinet of Ministry)	The State Duma	Council of Federation
Honest	2.9	8.7	3.7	1.1	1.6
Somewhat honest	15.5	34.0	22. 9	11.7	16.2
Somewhat dishonest	35.9	21.0	37.8	40.3	32.9
Dishonest	36.0	11.7	18.8	33.3	23.9
Don't know	9.1	23.9	16.3	13.0	24.0
No response	0.6	0.7	0.5	0.6	1.4

The above results produce a unique picture of the levels of trust in the various arms of Government. A particularly interesting result is the level of perceived corruption among the various bodies in law creation and enforcement. A 'dictatorship of law' for Russia as proposed by President Putin, will be difficult to enforce in Russia given the low levels of trust in the law enforcement agencies. Additionally, the high levels of perceived dishonesty among the legislature and executive branches points to a low levels of trust in those who legislate and execute the laws of the land. Given that the 'people's representatives' of the State Duma are considered to be the least trustworthy with 73.6 per cent of the respondents considering them to be dishonest and somewhat dishonest, there are serious considerations to be made on the future for the democratic system in Russia. Certainly, the culture of 'parliamentarism' is not being developed in Russia and the low levels of trust in the legislature are bad indicators for the current system.

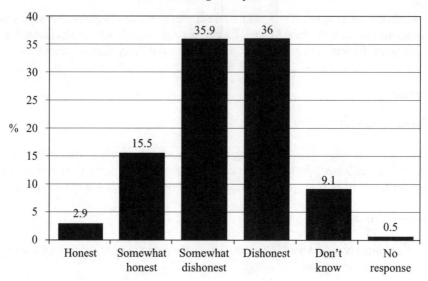

Figure 9.1 Law enforcement agencies

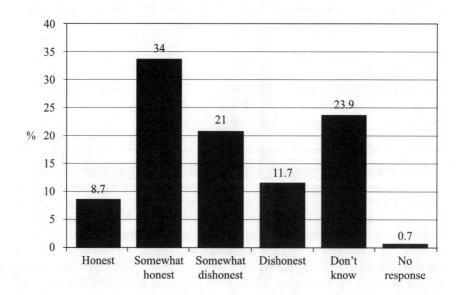

Figure 9.2 Security services

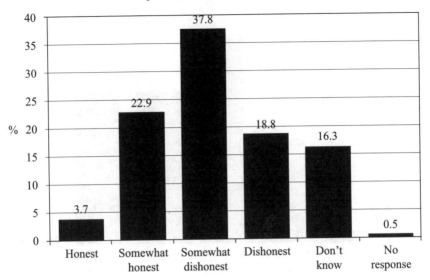

Figure 9.3   Government (Cabinet of Ministry)

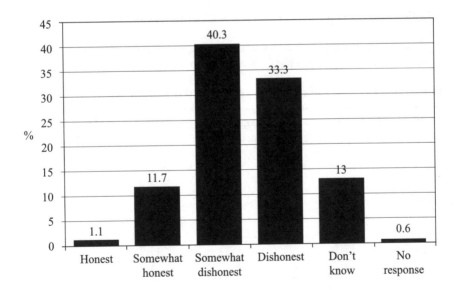

Figure 9.4   The State Duma

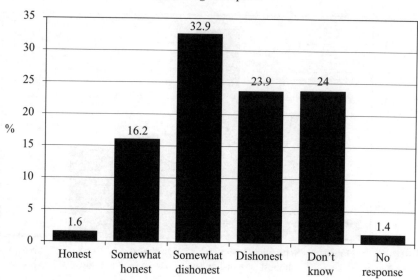

Figure 9.5   Council of Federation

Sample of Direct Questions (about personal experience)

1. Respondents were asked: *According to your opinion, how often do people as you suffer from corruption in the following day to day situations.*

Table 9.2   Estimates of corruption in day to day situations

Answer/ situation	Conscription	Legal proceedings	Police	Motor licensing and inspection department
Never	37.4	37.8	36.6	27.2
Seldom	7.9	14.3	16.3	8.9
Sometimes	13.2	17.2	18.0	16.2
Fairly often	23.2	17.2	16.2	23.3
Very often	17.1	12.1	11.7	23.3
No response	1.2	1.4	1.2	1.1

2. Respondents were asked: *Sometimes citizens of this country have to 'stimulate' officials by paying bribes, making presents etc. Have you (or members of your family) had such an experience?*

Table 9.3   Experience of bribing officials

Answer	%
Yes	56.4
No	43.3
No response	0.3

3. *In what situation with an official did you understand (feel) that you had to pay a bribe for getting the outcomes?*

Table 9.4   Situations of bribing officials

Service/situation	%
Medical service	25.3
Motor licensing and inspection department	17.4
High education	12.1
House maintenance	6.1
Getting the registration/passport	5.1
Getting the housing property	4.8
Primary school	3.9
Legal proceedings	3.8
Conscription	3.5
Kindergarten	2.4
Police	2.3
Other	11.5

* Data rounded to 1 decimal point

Context

It comes as no surprise that there is daily involvement in bribery by the citizens of Russia. The majority of respondents indicate that bribery is used to 'cope' with day-to-day Russian life. However, surprisingly enough, a full third of the population surveyed do not engage in corrupt acts on a daily basis in certain key institutions (Question 2) which suggests that it is possible to cope with daily life and achieve goals in Russia without resorting to bribery. This is a positive sign for the future development of concrete anti-corruption actions that can further reduce the need to bribe officials as well as helping to dispel the myth that Russia is an inherently corrupt country. The number of respondents who show that medical services are overwhelmingly a situation for bribe taking is indicative of the general state of the state health system. Primary care givers receive minimal salaries and services are delivered through informal payments. This form of 'direct payment' for public services is often considered by the public to not be 'bribes' as such (Miller, Grødeland and Koshechkina, 1998). The perceived extortive methods of the traffic police, which accounts for the second highest category of officials that are perceived to demand bribes in exchange for delivering services, may be a factor in distrust towards law enforcement and, in general, the state.

Questionnaire for Entrepreneurs

These questions focused on revealing the levels of corruption from the private sector perspective. In their dealings with the State, they are exposed to a great range of opportunities for confronting public malfeasance and the questionnaire reflected their experiences – particularly, perceived levels of corruption and frequency of corrupt acts.

Sample of an Indirect Question

1. Respondents were asked: *How would you rank officials in the following institutions?*

Table 9.5   Ranking of officials

Answer/ Institution	Law enforcement agencies	Security Service	Government (Cabinet of Ministry)	The State Duma	Council of Federation
Honest	1.4	5.6	2.7	0.7	1.2
Somewhat honest	12.8	34.6	24.4	11.8	18.5
Somewhat dishonest	39.6	22.1	37.8	40.1	33.8
Dishonest	34.0	10.9	15.5	30.6	20.4
Don't know	11.5	26.3	19.2	16.2	25.4
No response	0.7	0.5	0.4	0.6	0.7

Analysis

The resulting answers of the survey were used to develop maps of corruption across the Russian Federation. These maps reveal a number of interesting relationships and provide a rich field for further study by experts in the various fields concerning corruption. On the basis of what has been produced, Transparency Russia experts have put together a few of the more interesting points for this Chapter. In the near future, more analytical material will be available.

Sample of a Direct Question

2. Respondents were asked: *Could you remember the last time that you had to bribe to an official to obtain an outcome for your business?*

Table 9.6   Most recent incidence of bribery

Answer	%
During the last week	8.7
From a week to a month ago	17.3
From a month to a six months ago	18.6
From a six month to a year ago	9.5
More than a year ago	10.4
Never	35.0
No response	0.5

Leaders and Outsiders of Corruption

According to the generalised perception of respondents, the Krasnodar krai, the Saratov oblast, the Republic of Udmurtia, the Primorski Krai, the Republic of Karelia are the regions most contaminated by corruption. The Republic of Bashkortostan, Arkhangelsk, Kemerovo, Tyumen and Yaroslavl oblasts are among the regions least affected by corruption. More objective indicators, which characterise more corrupt practices than mere perception of corruption, demonstrate a somewhat different picture. In this case, the Moscow, Nizhni Novgorod and Saratov oblasts, the City of Moscow, the Chelyabinsk oblast and the City of St Petersburg are the leaders in terms of corruption, while the regions least affected by corruption are the Republic of Karelia, the Yaroslavl, Tyumen, Arkhangelsk and Omsk oblasts. If we look at the geography of corruption, we see a 'Southern belt' of regions deeply affected by corruption – stretching from the Rostov oblast to the Volga region.

Different Places – Different Life for Businesses

Statistical analysis reveals that three varieties of *business corruption – administrative corruption* (often related to ordinary extortion), *state capture* (businesses initiate the purchase of administrative decisions) and *business capture* (officials unlawfully seize control over firms) – are closely related. As a rule, where one type of business corruption is prevalent, there is also evidence that the other forms of business corruption are present and proportionally problematic. However, there are also specific regions where certain types of business corruption are disproportionately represented. For instance, Bashkortostan is a leader in terms of administrative corruption (it is ranked thirty-fifth that is, only 5 regions out of 40 are ranked *higher* in terms of administrative corruption); however, Bashkortostan is only eighth in terms of state capture. The Tula oblast is a quite different case. It clearly demonstrates the weakness of its authorities: state capture (twenty-third place) there, clearly overweighs the administrative corruption and business capture (both ranked fourth). Similar specifics are registered in the Khabarovsk krai and the Tyumen oblast, where business capture overweighs administrative corruption and state capture, while the overall level of corruption in these regions is relatively low.

Regional Methods of Extortion

Research data provides the opportunity to present *everyday corruption* (i.e. corruption encountered in everyday life) and *business corruption* (i.e. corruption involving businesses) measured in comparable units. Each type of corruption is measured in annual amounts of bribes paid respectively by both individuals and businesses in comparison with the gross regional product. As a result, it becomes possible to single out regions where everyday corruption prevails, for instance, the Pskov and Rostov oblasts. In some other regions, including the City of Moscow, the Tula and Kemerovo oblasts, business corruption prevails, which may somewhat decrease the corruption quit-rent paid by individuals. Of course, there are registered regions where officials 'fleece' both individuals and businesses with equal zeal (among such regions are the Moscow oblast, the City of St Petersburg and the Saratov oblast).

Paradoxes of Public Trust

The attitude towards different levels and branches of authority varies strikingly across regions. Figure 9.6 demonstrates that in the Novgorod oblast citizens despise federal authorities ranking them the last among all 40 regions, but have some confidence in the regional (thirteenth place) and local authorities. The Nizhni Novgorod oblast demonstrates an opposite picture. Local residents have no confidence in local (thirty-seventh place) and regional (thirty-first place) authorities, but are rather loyal to the federal authorities (twelfth place).

Similarly striking differences are observed with regard to the perception of different branches of authority. Figure 9.7 demonstrates that residents of the Krasnoyarsk krai are rather skeptical about law enforcement agencies (they are ranked twenty-sixth in the list including respective perceptions from all regions) and are rather suspicious about the judiciary (thirty-seventh place), but respect the legislative (fourth place) and executive (seventh place) branches. At the same time, residents of the Stavropol krai rate law enforcement agencies and the judiciary high, while ranking the legislative and executive branches thirty-second and thirty-third, thus expressing their lack of confidence in these authorities.

It is important to note that perceptions of public trust and the level of corruption of authorities expressed by both individuals and businesspersons are rather closely related. It is rather safe to say that in Russia the authorities win as much public trust as they are honest in the eyes of the citizens.

Map of Regional Corruption: South versus North – East versus West

The major result of this project was creating a 'Map of Corruption' of the most indicative Russian regions reflecting heterogeneous inner structure of corruption in the Russian Federation.[1]

There were several main tendencies of the geographical spreading of corruption in Russia:

1. According to the survey results, the Southern part of Russia was more corrupt, than Northern one. It was showed up the "Southern belt" of old agricultural pro-communist regions deeply affected by corruption, which stretched from the Rostov Oblast[2] to the Volga region. At the same time northern regions (such as Arkhangelsk Oblast, Karelia and Yaroslavl Oblast) tended to be seen as less corrupt.
2. In a very general connection, the eastern part of Russia (Khabarovsk Krai and Primorski Krai which have known recent corruption scandals) was estimated as more corrupt than the western regions.
3. In the west, the 'Capital Region' – Moscow City, St Petersburg City and Moscow Oblast – was assessed as one of the most corrupt regions. It is the most developed dynamic area with huge human, economic and political potential.
4. Contrary to common assumptions, the degree of corruption in the natural resource rich regions (such as Tyumen Oblast or Bashkortostan) was below average for the regions studied.

The differences demonstrated by this survey in the geographical regions of Russia open up the avenue for further research. The relations brought out by this survey have not been completely analysed but are grounds for additional speculation:

1. The North-South differential may lie in the fundamental disparity in development and cultural influences between the modern state European/Scandinavian influenced regions of northern Russia and the more traditional Caucasus influenced areas of southern Russia. The stronger family and 'clan-like' structures (similar to the traditional parts of the North and South Caucasus) have proven to be facilitators of corruption.
2. The East-West split may be accounted for by the classic differences between centre-periphery governmental structures. The further from the central authorities' local government are, the more opportunities there are for corrupt activities. As the Russian proverb goes, 'The Tsar is far away and God is up above'. On the other side, the closer towards North and Central Asia one goes the greater the incidents of corruption, which also points to cultural differences between the 'Euro' and Asian cultures of the Eurasian landmass.

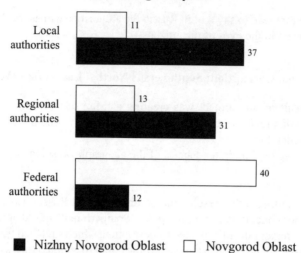

Figure 9.6 **Confidence in authorities in Novgorod oblast and Nizhni Novgorod oblast**

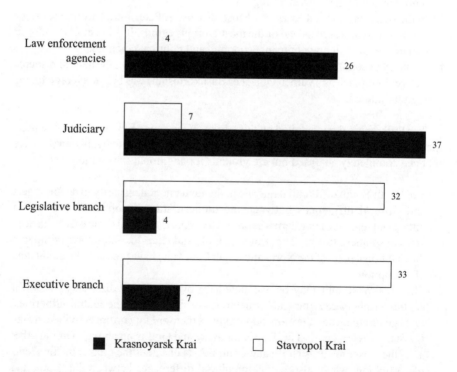

Figure 9.7 **Confidence in authorities in Krasnoyarsk krai and Stavropol krai**

a

To the different levels of authorities

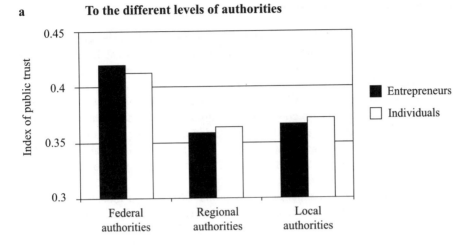

b

To the different sectors of authorities

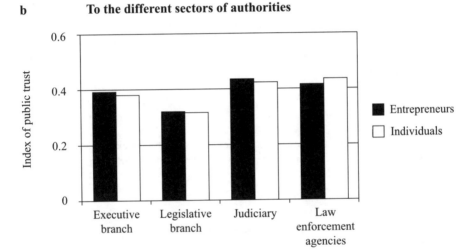

Figure 9.8 Index of public trust

3. However, the Capital regions present the dilemma of being within the European part of Russia but suffering the most corruption. This can be explained by the more opportunities to engage in corrupt acts at the centre of power.

Finally, the results of resource based regions being less corrupt opens up a very interesting field for future studies. The simple explanation of richer regions equals better paid civil servants goes against the nature of the federal public service in Russia.

Perspectives and Recommendations

It is planned to conduct such surveys on the regular basis in order to be able to monitor changes in the scope and structure of corruption in annual basis. All 89 Russian regions will be surveyed regularly in order to construct a map of regional corruption across the Russian Federation.

The results of this study will be thoroughly analysed to make recommendations to help the authorities to curb corruption. For instance, it is planned to compare the region-specific corruption data with various regional indicators reflecting respective economic, social, and political characteristics. Moreover, the study makes it possible to estimate the level and structure of corruption across different sectors of the economy and government agencies.

The dissemination of results of survey project 'Corruption Indices for Russian Regions 2002' through the media induced the different levels of government and the public to pay closer attention to the issue of corruption in Russia. Regardless of the conclusions of regional reviews, the very fact that no regions disregarded the survey is revealing in itself.

This survey was the pilot study. Although it did not reflect an overall picture of corruption in Russia and all its diverse aspects, the project was vital to corruption research and for producing information to enable the development of effective anti-corruption policy.

Notes

1   All maps are available at http://www.transparency.org.ru/proj_index_doc.asp.
2   *Oblast* and *Krai* are the administrative districts of the Russian Federation.

References

Miller, William L., Grødeland, Åse B. and Koshechkina, Tatyana Y. (1998), *Are the People Victims or Accomplices? The Use of Presents and Bribes to Influence Officials in Eastern Europe*, Discussion Papers, No. 6 Local Government and Public Service Reform Initiative, Budapest.

Chapter 10

Corruption Risk Areas and Corruption Resistance

Angela Gorta[1]

Introduction

The main theme of this chapter is that measuring corruption is not an end in its own right. Corruption measurement is simply a tool to achieve a purpose. When considering the question of how to measure corruption, one should first consider why one is seeking to measure corruption.

The chapter then provides an example of an empirical approach taken by the New South Wales Independent Commission Against Corruption to identify corruption risk areas in order to measure 'corruption resistance'. This measurement approach is a qualitative rather than a quantitative one. It takes the organisation as its unit of analysis and involves identifying corruption risks by examining the nature of the work the organisation undertakes, asking those who know the organisation the best what they consider the corruption risks to be, identifying the corruption prevention strategies in place and examining staff awareness of relevant policies and practices. This information is used to develop a corruption risk profile which, in turn, is used to identify how and where to intervene to make the organisation more corruption resistant.

Considerations When Measuring Corruption

While a number of different approaches have been taken in trying to measure corruption, it is an understatement to say that measuring corruption is not straightforward.

We usually associate measurement with assigning a numerical value to a physical attribute so that one object can be compared to another or compared against a standard. For example, consider the relatively straightforward task of measuring a box. A box is visible and its dimensions (length, breadth and depth) are known and agreed upon. To measure a box, one uses a ruler or measuring stick to calculate its length, its breadth and its depth. From these measurements, the box's surface area and its volume can be calculated. Different boxes can be compared using these measures to determine whether one box is bigger or smaller than another.

Corruption on the other hand is frequently not visible and its dimensions are not agreed upon. Unlike the task of measuring a box, to begin the task of measuring corruption, one must first determine *what* should be measured as well as *how* should it be measured.

There are many reasons why the measurement of corruption is not straightforward. Some of these are discussed below.

The Hidden Nature of Corruption

The hidden nature of some corruption is one of the factors that add to the difficulties in measuring corruption. Some types of corrupt activities (and no-one knows how many of these there are or how frequently they occur) tend to be carried out in secret with few witnesses. That which is not witnessed cannot be reported. Even corrupt conduct that is witnessed may not be reported for a wide range of reasons (e.g., the individual not considering that it is their responsibility to report, fear of reprisal, belief that nothing will be done about it if it were reported).

Corruption is not the only phenomenon where some portion is hidden. There are also difficulties in measuring the amount of crime committed because not all crime is reported. However, most crimes (such as theft, assault) have direct victims. Hence criminologists attempt to measure the unreported portion of crime by conducting 'victimisation surveys' which involve interviewing a representative sample of the population to find out what, if any, crimes they have been subject to within a given period of time. However, it is not possible to do this with corruption, as the potential victims (usually members of the community), are unlikely to know about any corrupt conduct. For example, the potential victims of a corrupt act would be unlikely to know if a public official had been bribed to award a contract to a particular company. Nor would they know if an inspector had been bribed to say that a piece of equipment met safety standards.

Lack of Consensus on Definition of what Constitutes Corruption

Another factor is that there is no universally accepted definition of corruption. There is a very large body of literature about the number and range of definitions of corruption (Gorta and Forell, 1994, pp. 22–32). This lack of a universally accepted definition provides a particular challenge for studies that seek to provide a cross-country comparative analysis.

The Multifaceted Nature of Corruption

Corruption is not a unitary phenomenon. It is common for commentators to write about corruption as if it were a single phenomenon. However, corruption is a term which can encompass many different forms of misuse of power or misuse of office. It is not a single issue, not a single problem. For example, the term 'corruption' can be applied to behaviours as varied as bribing a government official to approve a land development application, theft of office equipment for use at home, fraudulent allocation of monies, misuse of confidential information, or police planting evidence to facilitate the conviction of a suspected offender.

The multifaceted nature of corruption raises several questions: what would a measure of corruption look like?; what are the different facets of corruption?; and can these different facets (e.g., bribery, favouritism, abuse of power) be combined into a single measure?

Reasons to Measure Corruption

There are many reasons for attempting to measure corruption, for example:

1. To draw attention to the issue of corruption and promote the need to take action to reduce corruption.
2. To identify how and where best to intervene – if one knew what types of corruption were most widespread in different systems and in which types of systems corruption was most likely to occur, one could decide where to most effectively place the limited available resources to reduce corruption.
3. To evaluate the success of different corruption minimisation strategies or to measure the performance of an anti-corruption agency – to be able to assess the effectiveness of anti-corruption efforts it would be useful to compare the amount (and type) of corruption that was occurring before an intervention with the amount that occurred after the intervention and to see how any change in the amount or nature of the corruption compares to 'before' and 'after measures' with similar systems where there was no intervention.
4. Simply to learn more about corruption by making the attempt to measure it.

In order to determine how best to measure corruption, it is important to decide what decisions one wishes to be able to make based on the measurement exercise. For example, less precision would be required if one is seeking simply to draw attention to the problem than if one were seeking to evaluate the success of different corruption minimisation strategies.

Moving Forward – Developing a Corruption Risk Profile for the NSW Public Sector

Despite these difficulties, different people have tried to measure corruption, or indirect indicators of corruption, in a range of ways – from opinion polls to public sector expenditure tracking and in-depth diagnostic surveys. The Corruption Prevention Index,[2] the TI Global Corruption Barometer and a study of the 'leakage' in a non-wage school grant program in Uganda provide some examples of these approaches.

The development of a corruption risk profile, as outlined in this chapter, provides a very different type of approach to those taken so far. Corruption risk areas are of interest because they present opportunities for minimising corruption and building corruption resistance (Gorta, 1998).

The approach described in this chapter relies on the collection of a structured set of information from each individual organisation that can be used to develop a corruption risk profile of the individual organisation or can be combined to form a profile of groups of related organisations or of the entire sector.

The broad aim of this research, undertaken by the Independent Commission Against Corruption (ICAC), is to identify opportunities where future intervention, both by individual organisations and by the ICAC, is likely to be most effective.

The NSW public sector is very diverse in the functions it performs. Another of the aims of this work is to gain a better understanding of how corruption risks and issues differ among public sector organisations so that the ICAC can tailor its efforts to cater for these differences.

To place the description of the development of a corruption risk profile for the NSW public sector in context, it is important to consider the role and the nature of the work of the Independent Commission Against Corruption. The following, very brief, introduction is provided to give some background.

The NSW Independent Commission Against Corruption

The New South Wales Independent Commission Against Corruption (ICAC)[3] commenced operation in March 1989. It was established by an Act of Parliament to expose and minimise corruption in and affecting the NSW public sector.[4] It seeks to build and sustain public sector integrity. That is to say:

- it has jurisdiction in NSW (one Australian state);
- its focus is on *public sector* corruption, that is, corruption in or affecting state public sector organisations, the judiciary, universities, state politicians, local councils and local councillors;
- the private sector only comes within the ICAC's jurisdiction when someone in the private sector is seeking to influence a public sector employee.

The ICAC has three main statutory functions:

1. *Investigation of allegations of corruption* – investigating, and reporting on, matters in order to expose and deter corrupt conduct and discover deficiencies in systems and procedures which allowed the conduct to occur.
2. *Corruption prevention* – reducing opportunities for corruption by advising and working with public sector organisations on improvements to procedures, policies, work systems and ethical culture.
3. *Education* – educating the community and the public sector about the proper conduct of those in public office, the detrimental effects of corruption and the benefits that flow from action to reduce corruption.

In addition to these statutory functions, the ICAC uses empirical research as a tool to help it better understand corruption in the NSW public sector.[5]

In conducting these functions, the ICAC can focus its attention at a number of different levels. It can focus on: individuals (in the case of the investigation of individual conduct); systems (both within or across individual agencies); individual agencies; groups of agencies; and/or across the entire public sector (Gorta, 2001b).

For further information about the NSW ICAC and its work refer to the ICAC's website at http://www.icac.nsw.gov.au.

Building and Sustaining Corruption Resistance

In the past, the ICAC discussed its role in terms of 'minimising corruption' or 'preventing corruption'. More recently the ICAC has changed this terminology and now talks about 'building and sustaining corruption resistance'. This change is largely because one cannot see how much corruption one has prevented. In fact, one cannot measure how much of any type of activity (e.g., sickness, road fatalities) has been prevented. However, it *is* possible to see and document what active steps an agency takes to increase its resistance to corruption, such as, reviewing its code of conduct, training staff about the corruption-related risks they face in their jobs and how they should manage these risks.

Working with public sector organisations to build and sustain corruption resistance is a key priority for the ICAC. A critical part of this process is for NSW public sector organisations to identify the risks they face, and take the appropriate steps to manage and monitor these risks.

Identifying Corruption Risk

The approach, described in this chapter, does *not* seek to quantify the amount of corruption that occurs. Instead, it identifies opportunities for corruption (or corruption risks), which is the first step in devising effective strategies to increase corruption resistance. A greater number of risks do not necessarily result in more corruption occurring – it all depends upon how the risks are managed.

A multi-pronged approach was taken that involved examining the nature of the work the organisation undertakes, the perceived corruption risks, the corruption prevention strategies in place, and staff awareness of relevant policies and practices based on organisational and staff perspectives.

The organisation and staff perspectives were collected through two separate questionnaires. The 'Organisational Questionnaire' was distributed to approximately 400 New South Wales government organisations at the end of September 2001. The organisational questionnaires and covering letters were addressed to the Chief Executive Officer (CEO) or Chairperson for each organisation, asking them to select a suitable person to complete or coordinate the completion of the questionnaire on behalf of the organisation.

Individual public sector organisations were used as the unit of analysis in this approach because they are in the best position both to describe the issues they are facing and to implement strategies to develop and sustain their capacity to resist corruption.

The wide range of state-level public sector organisations that comprise the ICAC's jurisdiction were invited to participate. In addition to government departments and authorities, this questionnaire was also sent to government trading enterprises, state owned corporations, universities and a range of boards and committees. Local councils were excluded because corruption risks and corruption resistance strategies in local councils had been the subject of a previous ICAC research study (ICAC, 2001a).

Table 10.1 illustrates the range of different types of public sector organisations surveyed and their response rates.

Table 10.1 Organisational response rates

Type of organisation	No. sent	No. returned	Response rate (%)
Area Health Services	20	20	100
Universities	10	10	100
State-owned corporations	19	17	90
Departments	63	55	87
Declared authorities	13	12	92
Other agencies	57	37	65
Boards/committees	180	114	63
Total	**362**	**265**	73

The 'Staff Survey' was distributed to a sample of 594 public sector employees at the end of October 2001 (ICAC, 2003, pp. 3, 73).

The following sections of this chapter describe the four strategies used for identifying corruption risks:

1. examine the nature of the work the organisation undertakes, particularly high-risk functions;
2. ask those who know the organisation best what they consider the corruption risks to be;
3. examine the CEO views of the corruption prevention strategies in place;
4. identify staff awareness of relevant policies and practices and their views of the implementation – areas where staff thought that organisations did not have a policy or did not know whether or not the organisation had a policy.

The rationale approach used some key findings and the benefits of the approach are outlined for each of these four strategies. It is beyond the scope of this chapter to report findings to all survey items.[6]

Consider High-Risk Functions

Rationale Clearly the corruption risks faced by an organisation and the individuals working within it depend, amongst other things, on the functions that organisation performs. One strategy for identifying corruption risks is to consider the types of functions the organisation carries out. There is currently no developed taxonomy to use to classify organisational functions in terms of their level of risk. For this reason, a preliminary list of functions that might put employees at a greater exposure to corruption was developed. For want of a better name, these functions are referred to here as 'high-risk functions'.

The concept of a high-risk function can best be understood by considering an example. 'Inspecting, regulating or monitoring standards of premises, businesses, equipment or products' was classified as a high-risk function in this research because of the combination of the employee's discretion in this role with the potential importance of the outcome to the member of the public. When a government employee is inspecting or monitoring premises or equipment to see if they meet safety standards, the member of the community who owns the premises or who has designed the equipment wants to receive a favourable report. In order to receive a favourable report, some members of the community may attempt to corruptly influence or pressure the government employee who is responsible for that decision. An employee responsible for inspecting and certifying business premises is more likely to face corruption risks, such as being approached with a bribe, than an employee who is responsible for administrative tasks and does not have interaction with members of the community as part of their role.

This is not to suggest that a function such as inspection is more likely to be performed corruptly than other functions: recognition of the risks and well-developed control mechanisms may mitigate opportunities for such corruption to occur. Organisations that require employees to engage in these types of high-risk functions need to be aware of the increased potential for corruption and ensure that the appropriate steps to minimise this risk have been taken.

Methodology In the study 15 high-risk functions were identified. Some of these functions (such as the inspection function used as an example above) were selected because of the combination of the discretion exercised by the public official undertaking the role and the potential importance of the outcome to the member of the public. Others were selected in terms of the client group. Still others were selected because previous ICAC experience shows that they provide the opportunity and temptation for fraud. These 15 functions were identified through ICAC experience (e.g. investigations, hearings, corruption prevention work and/or complaints received) or through analysis of activities that clearly have unique and obvious corruption risks (e.g. discretion over issuing fines or other sanctions).[7]

The 15 high-risk functions are listed below:

1. inspecting, regulating or monitoring standards of premises, businesses, equipment or products;
2. providing a service to new immigrants;
3. issuing qualifications or licences to individuals to indicate their proficiency or enable them to undertake certain types of activities;
4. providing a service to the community where demand frequently exceeds supply;

5. allocating grants of public funds;
6. issuing, or reviewing the issue of, fines or other sanctions;
7. receiving cash payments;
8. providing assistance or care to the vulnerable or disabled;
9. providing subsidies, financial assistance, concessions or other relief to those in need;
10. making determinations/handing down judgments about individuals or disputes;
11. testing blood, urine or other bodily samples from people or animals;
12. having discretion concerning land rezoning or development applications;
13. selling tickets;
14. undertaking construction;
15. having regular dealings with the private sector other than for the routine purchasing of goods and services.

It should be acknowledged that this is not an exhaustive list of all functions that could be considered high-risk. For example, some potentially high-risk functions (such as tendering, recruitment, purchasing, use of public resources) are common to almost all organisations. However, this research focussed on less universal functions (such as issuing qualifications or licences; allocation grants of public funds). Also, it is important to recognise that the 15 functions would not, on every occasion, be assessed as high-risk on the criteria used in this research. However, the high-risk functions identified are those that the ICAC considers, across the range of NSW public sector organisations, will more often than not present some type of distinct corruption risk.

Findings Responses to the surveys provided information on how common these selected high-risk functions are across the NSW public sector. Most of the organisations that responded said that they perform some of these 15 high-risk functions. On average, each organisation said they perform four (of the possible 15) types of high-risk function. The largest number of these high-risk functions performed by a single organisation was 13. In contrast, some organisations (17 per cent of boards and committees and 4 per cent of other types of organisation) reported that they did not perform any of these functions.

Some types of organisation are more likely to perform more of these high-risk functions than others. The organisations that perform the most high-risk functions tend to be large (with more than 1,000 staff). This is not a surprise. The work of large organisations tends to be more diversified and therefore would be more likely to involve a greater range of high-risk functions.

The results showed that at least some of these functions are commonly performed across the public sector. Most of these functions are performed by at least one-quarter of agencies. Two of the functions ('receive cash payments' and 'have regular dealings with the private sector other than the routine purchasing of goods and services') are performed by about two-thirds of the agencies that responded to this survey.

Benefits of this Approach

The very introduction of the concept of 'high-risk functions' tends to promote discussion of corruption risks because it gives organisations another way to think about the corruption risks they may face. Defining the high-risk functions assists in alerting organisations to the unique corruption opportunities that characterise these functions and the need to address them. It also provides the starting point for a way of structuring a step-by-step process of thinking about managing the risks associated with these functions. For each high-risk function, organisations should consider:

- Whether their organisation undertakes this function.
- If so, which staff undertake this function and for what reason?
- What are the associated risks?
- Strategies and capacity to deal with identified risks.
- Staff training and supervision to inform and advise staff on how to minimise and manage the identified risks.

The responses have also provided the basis for a map of how many and which NSW public sector organisations perform each of these functions. Such a map helps the ICAC better tailor its messages. If, for example, the ICAC wants to send a particular message to organisations that allocate government grants, by having a picture of which organisations perform this function, the ICAC is better placed to do this.

Perceived Corruption Risks

Rationale A second strategy for identifying corruption risk areas is to ask those who know the organisation best what they consider the corruption risks to be. Perceived corruption risks are important because if organisations do not identify something as a risk they will be less likely to attempt to manage that risk.

When analysing what organisations identify as their perceived risks, less perceived risk is not necessarily best. The more aware organisations are of the perceived risks they face, the better placed they are to address and manage these risks. When organisations describe what they see as their corruption risks, they are identifying activities that they believe could occur and, if they did, would have a negative impact on the work of the organisation. They are not necessarily referring to events that have occurred. When considering perceived corruption risks, it should be remembered that not all risks are equal. Some risks are more likely to occur than others and some would have a greater impact if they were to occur.

Methodology In order to find out what individual organisations saw as their corruption risk areas, organisations were given a list of approximately 40 workplace activities such as 'tendering for services', 'recruitment', 'use of confidential information' and asked to rate each of these activities in terms of the extent that they thought each was a corruption risk within their organisation. Organisations could choose amongst five possible options – whether they thought each of the activities was:

1. a *major risk area* for corruption within your organisation that is *currently being well handled*;
2. a *major risk area* for corruption within your organisation that *currently requires more attention*;
3. a *minor risk area* for corruption in your organisation;
4. *not* a risk area for corruption at all in your organisation;
5. or, *not applicable* because your organisation does not carry out this function.

All organisations were also asked to write in their own words what they saw as:

1. their *most significant* corruption risks;
2. their *most potentially damaging* corruption activities;
3. *possible emerging corruption* risks for their organisation over the next three to five years.

Findings One positive finding from this research was that most of the organisations responding to the survey were able to identify risks that they were facing. The detailed responses provided by some organisations reflect the amount of consideration they have already given to the risks they need to manage.

The activities that agencies (with boards and committees excluded from the analysis) most commonly rated as being *major corruption risk* areas that are *currently being well handled* and the percentages of agencies that gave them this rating were:

- use of organisation's funds or bank accounts (33 per cent);
- how confidential information is used (29 per cent);
- purchasing and tendering for goods (29 per cent);
- tendering or contracting for services (29 per cent);
- cash handling (27 per cent).

The activities that agencies most commonly rated as being *major risk* areas *in need of further attention* and the percentage of agencies rating them this way:

- use of internet/email/ecommerce at work (17 per cent);
- use of agency resources, materials and equipment (16 per cent);
- tendering/contracting for services (15 per cent);
- record keeping (15 per cent);
- how staff are accountable for time worked (13 per cent);
- purchasing/tendering for goods (13 per cent).

As can be seen from the list above, when examining the results across the varied organisations of the entire sector, the percentage of organisations rating any one particular risk area as being 'in need of further attention' is not large. However, when the focus is narrowed to what one type of organisation considered to be a major risk area in need of further attention, there is more consensus. For example, there tends to be considerable agreement across the universities about some of their corruption risk areas. Approximately three-quarters of the ten NSW universities rated 'use of agency resources, materials and equipment' and half rated 'how staff are accountable for time worked' as 'a major corruption risk in need of further attention'.

Overall, organisations most commonly nominated corruption risks in the areas of:

- use of confidential information;
- purchasing/tendering for goods and services;
- use of agency resources, materials and equipment;
- fraud;
- use of organisation's funds.

Organisations identified the opportunities posed by new technology, information security and increased commercial activity as possible emerging corruption risks over the next three to five years.

Staff most commonly nominated corruption risks in the areas of:

- how staff are promoted;
- tendering;
- how staff are accountable for their time;
- use of confidential information.

The areas that organisations do *not* consider to be a risk are also of interest.

Benefits of approach The responses are useful, not to say whether perceived risks are right or wrong, but to promote further discussion about the major corruption risks facing organisations. Failure to recognise the potential risks faced by an organisation is a significant risk in itself.

Each organisation completed its questionnaire in isolation. By providing a summary of both the sector-wide results and the results for different types of organisations (ICAC, 2003), the reporting of this research enables organisations to compare their own risks with the risks identified by organisations of a similar size and function. This may highlight some potential risk areas that individual organisations have not previously considered.

Examining Corruption Prevention Strategies in Place

Rationale A third strategy for identifying corruption risk areas was by collecting information about the corruption prevention strategies organisations have put in place to manage the their risks.

Methodology The survey focussed on corruption prevention strategies in a number of key areas:

- risk identification and documentation strategies;
- codes of conduct;
- gifts and benefits policies;
- information management and technology;
- recruitment;
- contracting and procurement strategies;
- providing information on ethical work practices to staff;
- audit procedures;
- protected disclosures;
- internal investigation capacity.

Organisations were not only asked about the existence of individual policies: *Does your organisation have a code of conduct?* They were also asked about the review and implementation of these policies, for example: *When was your code of conduct last reviewed? How often does your organisation provide code of conduct training or refresher information for staff? What areas do your code of conduct cover?*

Findings Collation of the responses to the questionnaires provides a picture of how many organisations have begun to implement a range of different strategies to increase their capacity to resist corruption. (See Figures 10.1 and 10.2 for examples.)

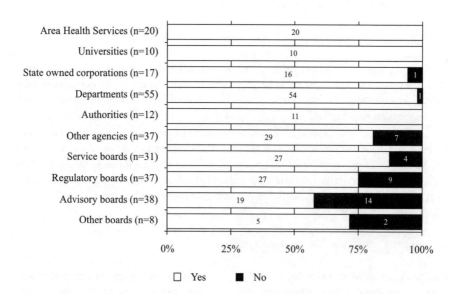

Figure 10.1 Does the organisation have a code of conduct?[8]

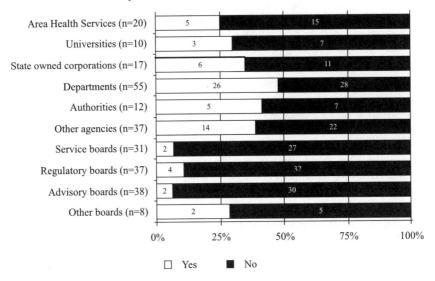

Figure 10.2 Does the organisation have a gift register?[9]

Overall, the survey responses provide an encouraging picture of the sector's capacity to resist corruption. Some examples of strengths identified include:

- most agencies have a broad range of prevention strategies in place;
- many organisations described taking a multi-pronged approach to minimising corruption in their organisation;
- there is widespread adoption of codes of conduct across the sector;
- internal audit is considered 'essential' or 'very important' by just about all of the agencies – the large number of agencies with internal audit plans and other audit procedures backs up this level of expressed importance;
- the types of organisations that tend to be exposed to more high-risk functions are also the organisations that are further advanced in implementing strategies to increase their capacity to resist corruption.

The research also provided a mechanism to identify areas for improvement. For example, while most organisations said they have a policy or procedures covering gifts and benefits, gift registers are relatively uncommon across the sector (see Figure 10.2). A gift register is a relatively straightforward tool that can bring offers of gifts and benefits into the open. In this way, it can remove any associated suspicion arising from these offers. A gift register also provides a way of tracking patterns of who are offering gifts or benefits to what types of positions and under what types of circumstances.

Benefits of approach The research has provided a tool to identify both current strengths in building corruption resistance as well as areas for improvement. By providing a picture of prevention strategies in place across the sector, the reported results enable organisations to benchmark their own efforts and in this way help them identify areas where they may be able to improve their own corruption resistance.

Staff Awareness of Relevant Policies

Rationale A fourth strategy for identifying corruption risks is to examine staff awareness of various corruption prevention policies and their recollection of participating in training.

To improve any organisation's capacity to resist corruption, it is important that staff understand the organisation's values, what is expected of them, the possible ethical dilemmas and conflicts of interest they may face and how to manage these dilemmas.

Staff who are not informed about the corruption risks associated with their work are less likely to manage these risks than staff who are aware of the risks. Similarly, staff need to be aware of the corruption prevention strategies an organisation have in place if they are to comply with them.

Methodology A sample of staff from 20 of the organisations was asked what they considered to be the major risks facing their organisation. They were also asked about their awareness of corruption prevention strategies and their memories of participation in training.

Findings While a high percentage of staff surveyed (89 per cent) were aware of their organisation's code of conduct, nearly-one third said that they had *never* received any training on their code of conduct.

Of the surveyed 65 per cent of staff reported their organisation had provided them with information on ethical work practices, 52 per cent reported they had received information on what a conflict of interest is and what to do if one arises and 43 per cent reported that they had received information on what constitutes public duty.

One-third of respondents reported that they had received information on ethical leadership (35 per cent), corruption risks associated with your work (36 per cent) and corruption prevention strategies (33 per cent).

Benefits of this approach Staff responses suggest that sizeable groups of staff may not be aware of some of the corruption prevention strategies that organisations have in place. The information obtained from staff may broaden the organisation's understanding of its risks. It also provides some measure of the messages that reach staff and are retained by them.

Organisations should provide and promote information to all those that undertake work within the organisation (including short-term staff, specialist staff, board members, consultants and private sector contractors) on:

* organisational values;

- public duty requirements;
- conflicts of interest and other corruption risks that they are likely to face in their role and how to manage these risks.

Responses to the staff survey provide a way of identifying where knowledge gaps are largest and prioritising areas for future training.

Conclusion: Limitations and Benefits of Building a Corruption Risk Profile

This chapter provides an example of how the combination of an organisational questionnaire and staff survey can be used to collect information on high-risk functions, perceived corruption risks, corruption prevention strategies in place and staff awareness in order to develop a corruption risk profile. A picture of the corruption issues facing a group of organisations or the entire sector can be built by combining the individual organisation perspectives.

While this approach does not calculate a single number to summarise the level of corruption risk within an organisation or across the sector, it does provide a framework for deciding where to intervene at an organisational level, for groups of similar organisations or on a sector-wide level.

This approach can be used to inform, and more generally promote, discussion of corruption risks and corruption prevention strategies within individual organisations and across the sector as a whole. The findings can assist public sector managers and internal audit managers who have responsibility for ensuring that risk is identified, monitored and effectively dealt with to ensure that their own corruption risk assessment is comprehensive. Public sector managers can assess their own organisation against the findings, and identify areas were further improvements can be made to improve their organisation's 'corruption resistance'.

It can also help the ICAC plan how it can use its resources to most effectively assist organisations build their corruption resistance.

Like other surveys, this methodology has its limitations. For example, the responses made to the questionnaires have been accepted at face value. While the response rate was high, with 83 per cent of the agencies, 63 per cent of the boards and committees and 60 per cent of the staff completing the survey, it is not possible to know how those who did not respond would have differed from those who did respond. Some of the questions asked in both surveys are limited to measuring respondents' perceptions relating to risks. Such perceptions are subjective and different groups, for example CEOs and staff, will have different, but equally valid, perceptions on particular issues.

Notes

1   This chapter is based on a paper 'Developing a Corruption Risk Profile for the NSW Government Sector' that was presented at the *International Institute for Public Ethics*

2002 Biennial Conference, Brisbane, 4–7 October 2002. Although the empirical research described formed part of the research programme of the Independent Commission Against Corruption, the views expressed in this chapter are those of the author and do not necessarily reflect the views of the Independent Commission Against Corruption (ICAC).

2   See Lambsdorff, J. (2001), 'Measuring Corruption: State of Art and Future Challenges', in J. Andvig, O. Fjeldstad and A. Shrivastava (eds), *Corruption: Critical Assessments of Contemporary Research – Report from a Multidisciplinary Workshop*, Chr. Michelsen Institute Development Studies and Human Rights, Working Paper 17; Lambsdorff, J. (2003), 'Measuring the Dark Side of Human Nature', *TI Q Transparency International's Quarterly Newsletter*, June 2003, p. 12; Langseth, P. (2001), 'Qualitative versus Quantitative Methods', in J. Andvig, O. Fjeldstad and A. Shrivastava (eds), *Corruption: Critical Assessments of Contemporary Research – Report from a Multidisciplinary Workshop*, Chr. Michelsen Institute Development Studies and Human Rights, Working Paper 17; Reinikka, R. and Svensson, J. (2002), 'Measuring and Understanding Corruption at the Micro Level', in Donatella Della Porta and Susan Rose-Ackerman (eds), *Corrupt Exchanges: Empirical Themes in the Politics and the Political Economy of Corruption*, Nomos Verlagsgesellschaft, Baden-Baden, pp. 134–46; Galtung, F. (2003), 'Are Anti-Corruption Efforts making a Difference? Introducing the TI Global Corruption Barometer', *TI Q Transparency International's Quarterly Newsletter*, June 2003, p. 5.

3   The ICAC is based in Sydney, New South Wales (NSW). NSW has a population of approximately six million people and an area of 801,428 square kilometres and is the most populous state in Australia.

4   The *Independent Commission Against Corruption Act (1988)* can be found on http://www. legislation.nsw.gov.au .

5   See Gorta, A. (2001a), 'Research: A Tool for Building Corruption Resistance', in P. Larmour and N. Wolanin (eds), *Corruption and Anti-Corruption*, Asia-Pacific Press, Canberra, pp. 11–29; Independent Commission Against Corruption (2001b), *Corruption trouble-shooting: Lessons learnt from ICAC research about identifying and dealing with corruption hot spots*, ICAC Report, November 2001, https://www.icac.nsw.gov.au/pub/ public/pub2_25r.pdf.

6   For a more comprehensive report of survey results see ICAC (2003).

7   A more detailed explanation of the basis for selecting each function is outlined in ICAC (2003), pp. 99–104.

8   A small number of agencies did not answer this question.

9   A small number of organisations (two agencies and ten boards) did not answer this question.

References

Galtung, F. (2003), 'Are Anti-Corruption Efforts making a Difference? Introducing the TI Global Corruption Barometer', *TI Q Transparency International's Quarterly Newsletter*, June 2003, p. 5.

Gorta, A. (1998), *Minimising Corruption: Some Lessons from the Literature*, Independent Commission Against Corruption, January 1998.

Gorta, A. (2001a), 'Research: A Tool for Building Corruption Resistance', in P. Larmour and N. Wolanin (eds), *Corruption and Anti-Corruption*, Asia-Pacific Press, Canberra, pp. 11–29.

Gorta, A. (2001b), 'Four ICAC Tools for Measuring Corruption Resistance', paper presented at *the 10th International Anti-Corruption Conference*, Prague, Czech Republic, 7–11 October 2001, http://www.10iacc.org/content.phtml?documents=101andart=173.

Gorta, A. and Forell, S. (1994), *Unravelling Corruption: A Public Sector Perspective–survey of NSW Public Sector Employees' Understanding of Corruption and Their Willingness to Take Action*, Independent Commission Against Corruption, Research Report No. 1, April 1994.

Gorta, A. and Forell, S. (1995), 'Layers of Decision: Linking Social Definitions of Corruption and Willingness to Take Action', *Crime, Law and Social Change: an International Journal*, vol. 23, pp. 315–43, https://www.icac.nsw.gov.au/pub/public/pub2_3r.pdf.

Independent Commission Against Corruption (1997), *Corruption and Related Issues: An Annotated Bibliography*, ICAC Research Unit, May 1997, https://www.icac.nsw.gov.au/pub/public/pub2_6r.pdf.

Independent Commission Against Corruption (1999), *Strategies for Preventing Corruption in Government Regulatory Functions*, ICAC Report, March 1999, https://www.icac.nsw.gov.au/pub/public/pub2_34cp.pdf.

Independent Commission Against Corruption (2001a), *Corruption Resistance Strategies: Researching Risks in Local Government Research Findings Summary*, ICAC Report, June 2001, http://www.icac.nsw.gov.au/pub/public/pub2_22r.pdf.

Independent Commission Against Corruption (2001b), *Corruption Trouble-shooting: Lessons Learnt from ICAC Research about Identifying and Dealing with Corruption Hot Spots*, ICAC Report, November 2001, https://www.icac.nsw.gov.au/pub/public/pub2_25r.pdf.

Independent Commission Against Corruption (2003), *Profiling the NSW Public Sector: Functions, Risks and Corruption Resistance Strategies*, ICAC Report, January 2003, https://www.icac.nsw.gov.au/pub/public/Report_final.pdf.

Lambsdorff, J. (2001), 'Measuring Corruption: State of Art and future Challenges', in J. Andvig, O. Fjeldstad and A. Shrivastava (eds), *Corruption: Critical Assessments of Contemporary Research – Report from a Multidisciplinary Workshop*, Chr. Michelsen Institute Development Studies and Human Rights, Working Paper 17.

Lambsdorff, J. (2003), 'Measuring the Dark Side of Human Nature', *TI Q Transparency International's Quarterly Newsletter*, June 2003, p. 12.

Langseth, P. (2001), 'Qualitative versus Quantitative Methods', in J. Andvig, O. Fjeldstad, and A. Shrivastava, *Corruption: Critical Assessments of Contemporary Research – Report from a Multidisciplinary Workshop*, Chr. Michelsen Institute Development Studies and Human Rights, Working Paper 17.

Reinikka, R. and Svensson, J. (2002), 'Measuring and Understanding Corruption at the Micro Level', in Donatella Della Porta and Susan Rose-Ackerman (eds), *Corrupt Exchanges: Empirical Themes in the Politics and the Political Economy of Corruption*, Nomos Verlagsgesellschaft, Baden-Baden, pp. 134–46.

Chapter 11

The Public as Our Partner in the Fight Against Corruption

Ambrose Lee[1]

Introduction

Corruption is a corrosive crime. It undermines quality of life, causes injustice, blunts competitive edges and inflates business costs. The world community is unanimously, and rightly so, concerned to contain corruption. Corruption has haunted Hong Kong for decades until the Independent Commission Against Corruption (Hong Kong ICAC) was established in 1974. Since its inception, the Commission has set its mind to taking forward the investigation of any alleged corruption offence. At the same time, it has also determined to tackle this pervasive social ill by changing the tolerance of the public towards the crime.

Armed with strong government commitment and support, sufficient legal powers and a holistic three-pronged strategy of detection, prevention and community education, the Hong Kong ICAC helps to transform Hong Kong from a graft stricken city to one of the world's cleanest metropolitan cities. Now, the fight against corruption story in Hong Kong is regarded in the global arena as a model of success. An example of what can be achieved through perseverance and a good strategy.

The story could not have happened without the support of an essential partner – the Hong Kong community. From tolerance to repulsion, the public's attitude towards corruption has undergone a sea of change over the years.

The Hong Kong ICAC was conceived when the patience of the public was running thin on the prevalence of corruption within the society. The escape of the chief superintendent of police while under corruption investigation triggered a demand from the public to the government to act to rectify the situation. Public confidence in the Anti Corruption Office set up within the police service had fallen to a low ebb. At the initial stage of the Hong Kong ICAC's establishment, the community was also sceptical about its effectiveness and impartiality. Many questioned whether the Hong Kong ICAC was a gesture to pacify the discontented public.

Knowing that it could not succeed without the community's support, the Hong Kong ICAC determined at the outset that a transparent and credible system in gauging public attitude should be set up. The community should have the channels and confidence to come to the Hong Kong ICAC and report any suspected corrupt practices. In the early years of the Hong Kong ICAC's establishment, with a sceptical public, it was necessary for the Hong Kong ICAC to take tough and decisive enforcement actions to gain public trust and confidence. These actions include a series of high-profile arrests and prosecutions. The indictment of many 'big tigers', as corrupt senior government officials were described by the media, impressed on the public that the government was determined in its anti-corruption drive and that the Hong Kong ICAC was resolute.

To properly gauge the sentiments of the community towards corruption, the Hong Kong ICAC conducts regular surveys and proactive focus groups. In addition, the Hong Kong ICAC also develops an ever-expanding web of community networks to reach out to the community. These networks range from civilian advisory committees, meet-the-public forums and specific trade corruption prevention groups to a Hong Kong ICAC Club comprising of citizens who volunteer to assist Hong Kong ICAC publicity activities.

Graft Stricken Days

In stark contrast to its contemporary reputation as a clean city, corruption was once tolerated and accepted by the community in Hong Kong during the 1960s and early 1970s. To ordinary citizens, bribe-paying was viewed as a necessary evil to 'get things done'. Hong Kong saw an exponential growth in its population from the late 1940s to 1950s due to a massive migration from mainland China in the wake of the Second World War and civil war. Its population soared to 2.2 million in 1950 from 600,000 people in 1945.[2] The sudden upsurge of people arriving in Hong Kong exerted tremendous pressure on the Hong Kong government in regard to its public service.

As competition for limited public resources grew keen, corruption began to rear its ugly head when some resorted to bribing through the 'backdoor'. With the collusion of some civil servants, corruption spread like wildfire and soon permeated every stratum of the society. Parties to bribery were indulged in the 'satisfied customers syndrome', rendering a mockery of the Prevention of Corruption Ordinance enacted in 1948.

At the height of the corruption epidemic in the 1960s and early 1970s, no government departments were immune to this social illness. Corruption was institutionalised in some of the most afflicted departments, including the police. It was unfortunate that essential public services including medical services and fire fighting were involved. Citizens who were sick or in need of a job placement were sometimes denied the service unless a bribe was paid. Some revealing anecdotes in those days include:

- a patient had to pay 'tips' to the ward amahs for a glass of water in hospitals;
- a candidate had to pay bribes to get a driving licence;
- a squatter could not obtain subsidised housing unless he paid an official under the table;
- a sick person would pay ambulance officers 'tea money'.

The police were badly affected at that time.[3] Syndicates of corrupt officers offered blatant protection to rackets running illegal gambling, vice activities and drug dens. People making an honest living on the streets became the subjects of extortion. Expatriate police officers were no exception. The syndicates paid many with a handsome monthly fee for turning a blind eye to what was happening around them. Ms Elsie Elliot, a social activist, summed up succinctly the ordeal then facing the common people at that time:

> Almost everybody was suffering. Every shopkeeper in a resettlement estate was having to pay; every hawker in a bazaar or marketplace was having to pay ... it was squeezing them to death. Hawkers had to pay for the licence and then they had to pay regularly to operate. (Hong Kong ICAC, 1999)[4]

Corruption, no doubt, had eaten into the fabric of the society and the government seemed powerless to do anything. As Hong Kong developed, the tide of public discontent was rising, particularly at corrupt police officers. The Anti-Corruption Branch of the police force, which was perceived to be the most corrupt at the time, did not inspire confidence at all. Senior Puisne Judge, Sir Alastair Blair-Kerr, described police corruption as a ramming bus in his 1993 report:

> Some get on the bus, others run alongside it, yet very few stand in front of it.[5]

Public frustration erupted into the open in 1973 when a chief superintendent of the police, while under corruption investigation, fled to Britain. This triggered waves of street protests spearheaded by university students who demanded decisive action from the authorities.

In response, the government appointed a Commission of Inquiry, headed by Sir Alastair Blair-Kerr, to probe into the circumstances of the escape of the chief superintendent of police and the wider corruption problem in Hong Kong. The subsequent Blair-Kerr Report pointed to the need for an independent anti-corruption agency. The governor of Hong Kong, Sir Murray MacLehose, then took the recommendation a significant step forward. He decided to set-up a dedicated corruption fighting force, making it independent of the police and the rest of the civil service. He explained to the Legislative Council of Hong Kong in October 1973:

> I think the situation calls for an organisation, led by men of high rank and status, which can devote its whole time to the eradication of this evil: a further and conclusive argument is that the public confidence is very much involved.[6]

Far-Sighted Strategy

Realising deterrence alone could not prevail, the administration should be credited for foresight in adopting a holistic strategy for the newborn anti-corruption force. A three-pronged strategy of detection (deterrence), prevention (systems controls) and education (attitudinal change) has since been mandated to the Hong Kong ICAC. This strategy proved to be central to the subsequent success in containing the problem and in rallying the community behind the anti-graft battle. Accepting no double standards in the moral code of the city, the administration also concluded that Hong Kong could never come out of its corruption doldrums with a corrupt private sector co-existing alongside a clean public sector. The Hong Kong ICAC was also charged with the statutory duty to rout out corruption in the business sector under a hardened Prevention of Bribery Ordinance. Resistance from the private sector was strong in the beginning until business leaders were convinced that illegal kickbacks, long regarded as a lubricant to business, impeded business growth and that it paid to have a high standard of business ethics. The war against corruption began with renewed vigor on 15 February 1974 when the Hong Kong ICAC was officially established.

The Elusive Foe

The Hong Kong ICAC was thrust into the battlefield in the full knowledge that corruption was omnipresent and rampant. As described by the founding Commissioner Jack Carter, who joined the Hong Kong civil service in the late 1940s and had since worked in various government departments:

> I was on the lookout for it all the time. I couldn't think of a department really which was totally honest.[7]

The symptom was crystal clear. Yet the Hong Kong ICAC had to seek out the elusive enemies before they could be tackled head-on. Corruption syndicated in the police force was one of the primary targets but where were the corrupt officers with pockets bulging with illicit cash? How serious was the problem in the rest of the civil service, businesses and trades? How to obtain solid evidence that could stand up in a court of law? All these and many others were daunting but practical questions confronting the Hong Kong ICAC. The task was made more difficult with the community generally tolerating corruption after years of ineffectual government action. Would the community as a whole, and the victims in particular, believe in the administration's determination and commitment this time after repeated disappointments? How should we prioritise our targets in our public education campaigns so that a culture of probity could be instilled in the community given the constraints in resources?

Adding to the difficulty in charting the corruption contour is the fact that many corruption cases might have gone unreported for various reasons for example, a lack of confidence in the authorities or fear of retaliation.

Corruption is both a crime and a social phenomenon. Corruption at its worst had taken many forms, ranging from the seemingly harmless gratuity for a junior civil servant to the millions of dollars that benefited corruption syndicates over a period of time. Whatever guise it may assume, corruption is a secretive and conspiratorial offence with no readily identifiable victim nor one who is willing to come forward to point a finger at the perpetrators of the crime. To the investigators:

> There is no scene of crime susceptible to forensic examination, no corpse to be identified for clues, no victim witness and rarely any untainted witness.[8]

Decoding Public Attitudes

In the face of tall barriers to a concise measurement of corruption, it was concluded earlier in the search that systematic and regular polls would be a feasible and practicable means of collecting public views and pertinent information on the problems of corruption. Information collated from the community, which embraces victims or potential victims of corruption would not only help the law enforcement side of the agency but views and perceptions expressed about the problem would also enable continuous finetuning of its anti-corruption strategy.

The Community Relations Department – the public relations arm of the Hong Kong ICAC – was thus assigned to undertake the research work in addition to its community liaison programme, another powerful toll in tapping the pulse of the community. A research unit was subsequently established under the department with the primary objectives to study:

1. motivation for corrupt behaviour;
2. areas most vulnerable to corrupt practices in Hong Kong.[9]

The first Hong Kong ICAC mass survey was conducted in 1977 after the public had seen anti-graft fighters in action for several years and public confidence in the administration's determination had been partially restored. Despite the fact that corruption as a social problem has had a long history in Hong Kong, it is worth noting that hardly any systemic study had been conducted prior to the founding of the Hong Kong ICAC in 1974.

The survey took the form of face-to-face interviews so that follow-up questions and testing scenarios cold be put to respondents to elicit a clearer picture of their attitudes towards bribery and their perception of the severity of the problem in various sectors. Following the benchmark 1977 survey, similar surveys were carried out in 1978 and 1980 and thereafter every two years.

Running into 120 questions for each interview, these surveys had provided the Hong Kong ICAC with revealing insights into people's values, perceptions and attitudes towards corruption with regard to their ages, family backgrounds, occupations, education levels and income profiles. They also provided the Hong Kong ICAC clues as to where the most corruption-infected areas were. Misconceptions and widely held beliefs about bribe taking and offering were either dispelled or confirmed, enabling the Hong Kong ICAC to map out its work priorities and foci.

Benchmark Survey Findings

The benchmark survey conducted in 1977 also proclaimed a bipolar attitude in the community towards government and private sector employees. Demanding a high level of integrity in civil servants, respondents expressed no tolerance of corruption in government departments. They believed that corruption existed either in most or some departments. However, the public appear to be less strident on unauthorised business kickbacks though almost every other respondent (45.9 per cent) thought that corruption was common in the business sector. However, one in every four respondents deemed illicit commissions as a necessity in doing business. In other words, the public had yet to appreciate the adverse effects of corruption on the business development of Hong Kong if not kept in check. The public also tended to condone 'tipping' of low ranking and relatively low paid public servants and did not regard such act as bribery and contrary to the law.

Reasons for Paying Bribes

At a time when government procedures and practices remained relatively opaque and public resources such as subsidised housing were in great demand, it was not surprising to learn the most common reasons cited for resorting to bribery.

Table 11.1　Reasons for bribery

	1977 (%)	1978 (%)
Convenience	48.9	50.2
Faster service	33.0	32.0
Concealment of offences committed or planned	20.0	26.7
Get help to solve a problem	12.4	14.7

These findings, unflattering as they might be, offered valuable insights into the attitudes of the community. The fact that a significant number of citizens had declined to be interviewed also demonstrated the fragile public confidence in the Hong Kong ICAC after five years of operation.

Applications

As expressed distrust of the authorities, discriminating tolerance of corruption in public and private sectors and reasons cited for offering bribes as disclosed in these surveys provided the Hong Kong ICAC with a roadmap in revising its three-pronged approach. For example, persuasion and education efforts were conscientiously intensified in the business sector and the message focused on the overriding significance of a level playing field for sustained and long-term growth. Investigative resources were zoning in more on departments and trades that were reckoned to be more corruption-prone. The Hong Kong ICAC's corruption prevention specialists also fanned out in force to scrutinise the procedures and practices of target government departments with a view to plugging loopholes and improving transparency. Changes in public attitude were noticeable by 1980 when compared with the two preceding surveys.

Table 11.2   Perceived prevalence of corruption in the government

	1977	1978	1980
Most departments	38.3	34.8	16.1
Number of departments/one or two departments	45.9	48.3	31.3
No corruption	1.0	1.1	7.4
No answer/don't know	14.5	15.8	21.5

Note: Comparison of responses in three mass surveys. No surveys were conducted in 1979.

Surveys do have limitations. They demonstrate a broad picture but are devoid of specifics. The rest of the corruption puzzle has to be filled in by other sources of information such as corruption reports statistics, intelligence and other channels of community contacts and liaison.

Evolution of Monitoring Mechanism

With Hong Kong entering into a new phase of economic boom and quickened development in the 1980s, a biennial survey was considered not frequent enough to closely monitor corruption. Taking into account resource constraints, the Hong Kong ICAC decided to switch to a feasible and more economical alternative – annual telephone survey – from 1992. To ensure consistent criteria in the measurement of changes in the corruption scene, it was decided that a set of core questions should be specially designed and repeatedly deployed. Only minor modifications were made at times to deal with extraordinary events including the 1997 unification with the mainland China.

Such an approach was considered desirable as it would allow the detection of even subtle changes in the populace with regard to values, degree of intolerance towards corruption and its willingness to report to the Hong Kong ICAC any suspected dealings. Most importantly, the Hong Kong ICAC could monitor and respond promptly to any abrupt shifts in public confidence and track its effectiveness.

From the beginning, face-to-face surveys and telephone polls were and continue to be entrusted to professional and independent research companies to ensure objectivity. As a further safeguard, the whole process of selecting the research company, data collection and subsequent interpretations of survey findings are put under the supervision of an independent civilian committee. This committee comprises research professionals and university academics all of whom are appointed by the Chief Executive of the Hong Kong Administrative Region.

Importance of Trends

The same set of core questions generates valuable data on the direction of public values and attitudes either in favour of the anti-corruption fight or otherwise. Plotting against a sufficiently long span, the can also be alert to any swings in public's areas of concern and make timely amendments to its strategy. When the public, for example, expresses through these surveys, a reluctance to provide their particulars when filing corruption complaints, the Hong Kong Hong Kong ICAC can correspondingly reinforce through all channels the assurance that all complaints will be treated with absolute confidentiality.[10] On the other hand, if surveys findings indicate less and less respondents, either by themselves or people they know, have encountered or become aware of corrupt dealings in their community, the Hong Kong Hong Kong ICAC knows that it on the right track.

Listening to the Community

Gauging the views of the community on corruption is one of the most important tasks for anti-corruption agencies and concerned organisations worldwide. Hong Kong is no exception. Hong Kong ICAC realised from past experience that an effective conduit to the heart of the anti-corruption course is to let members of the public become partners. The precondition is that people are willing to speak the truth. For this to happen, the Hong Kong Hong Kong ICAC must gain itself the reputation of being trustworthy, impartial and professional in seeking views and information from the people it serves.

Views and information collected from regular surveys provide the feedback necessary for strategic planning. It is comforting to note that the public has expressed:

- almost total support for the Hong Kong ICAC;[11]
- increasing intolerance towards corruption in the public as well as in the private sectors;
- growing willingness to file open complaints;[12]
- rising trust in Hong Kong ICAC's impartiality and effectiveness in tackling corruption.[13]

Lessons Learned

To reinforce the partnership with the community, the Hong Kong ICAC has engaged in a massive liaison program targeted at different segments of the community. Through a network of strategically located regional offices, officers from the community relations arm of the Hong Kong ICAC meet face-to-face with citizens at discussion and training sessions, seminars, workshops and district activities. Through these activities, the evil of corruption is explained to more than half a million citizens in an average year. In addition, various networks based on trust and a common vision of a clean society gradually take shape with district organisations, professional bodies and business and trade organisations. Members of organisations, in turn, have become the eyes and ears of the Hong Kong ICAC. The community's active involvement in the fight against corruption was most revealing when thousands of citizens applied to join the Hong Kong ICAC Club as volunteers in 1997 in a bid to help spread the probity message.

The desire for a clean culture and level playing field in Hong Kong has grown so robust that professionals from various disciplines enthusiastically co-operated with Hong Kong ICAC in forming corruption prevention networks to tackle specific concerns. A corruption prevention banking network of compliance and internal control officers form virtually every bank in Hong Kong and a task force on lifting the integrity standards of the construction industry are but two examples.

The Hong Kong ICAC has learnt that the bond with the community has to be nurtured through a just and transparent system of checks and balances. At the operational levels, all three functional areas of the Hong Kong ICAC are each supervised by an advisory committee consisting of community leaders appointed by the Chief Executive. In addition, another independent committee is established to oversee investigations into corruption complaints against Hong Kong ICAC officers. All these committees meet the press annually and publish their own annual reports for public scrutiny. They are directly accessible to the Chief Executive. In addition to their supervisory responsibility, committee members have demonstrated that they would not hesitate to take the Hong Kong ICAC to task for any deviation or convey their concerns over any corruption issues in their respective fields of speciality.

One should not overlook the importance of a vigilant press to the work of the Hong Kong ICAC. The mass media in Hong Kong is supportive of the efforts to fight crime. It also helps to spread the anti-corruption message to the general public through extensively reporting any wrongdoings. The press also acts as a watchdog on behalf of the community to criticise even the slightest straying of the Hong Kong ICAC when discharging its duties.

Conclusion

The Hong Kong ICAC harboured no illusions that the battle would be easy when it commenced tackling corruption 29 years ago. Experience gained over the years confirms that a lasting victory is attainable if the community can be mobilised to take an active role in the anti-graft battle.

Hong Kong has been justly rewarded by tapping into the community for assistance through an extensive and comprehensive community liaison programme in the fight against corruption.

A credible and elaborate checks and balance system contributes, to a large extent, to the success that Hong Kong ICAC enjoys today. Persistent education should continue in order to press home the relevance of the anti-corruption battle in the community. The Hong Kong ICAC has adopted the right anti-corruption strategy and approach from the onset. The support of the community has helped uphold Hong Kong's reputation as a clean cosmopolitan city.

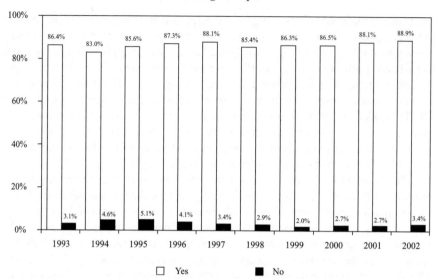

Figure 11.1 Whether ICAC would keep reports received confidential

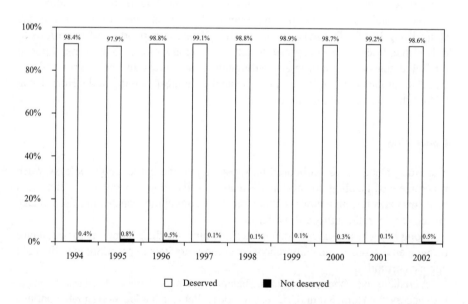

Figure 11.2 Whether ICAC deserved support

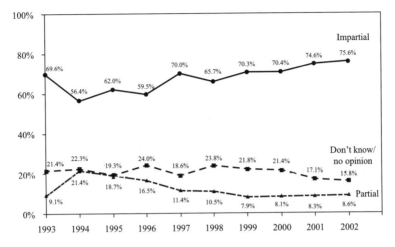

Figure 11.3 Whether ICAC was impartial in investigation

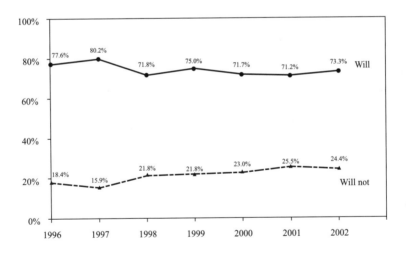

Figure 11.4 Willingness to reveal identity in reporting corruption

Notes

1 Commissioner, Independent Commission Against Corruption, Hong Kong Special Administrative Region, China.
2 See Hong Kong (2003), *Illustrated Chronicle of Hong Kong and Population Policy Paper 2003*, Hong Kong Government.
3 Almost one in two complaints received in 1975 related to the police. It represents 13 per cent of total complaints in 2003.
4 Hong Kong ICAC (1999), *25th Anniversary publication.*
5 See Hong Kong (1993), *First Report of the Commission of Inquiry, July 1993*, Hong Kong.
6 See Hong Kong (1993), *Legislative Council Hansard.*
7 See Hong Kong ICAC (1999), *25th Anniversary Publication.*
8 See Hong Kong ICAC (1994), *Report of the Hong Kong ICAC Review Committee*, December.
9 See Hong Kong ICAC (1977), *Mass Survey.*
10 See Appendix Chart 1.
11 A total of 98 per cent of the community said that they supported the work of the Hong Kong ICAC.
12 Rose from 35 per cent in 1974 to over 70 per cent in 2002.
13 See Appendix 1, Charts 2-4.

References

Hong Kong (1993), *First Report of the Commission of Inquiry, July 1993*, Hong Kong.
Hong Kong (1993), *Legislative Council Hansard.*
Hong Kong (2003), *Illustrated Chronicle of Hong Kong and Population Policy Paper 2003*, Hong Kong Government.
Hong Kong ICAC (1977), *Mass Survey.*
Hong Kong ICAC (1994), *Report of the Hong Kong ICAC Review Committee*, December.
Hong Kong ICAC (1999), *25th Anniversary publication.*

Chapter 12

Citizen Report Cards

Gopakumar K. Thampi and Sita Sekhar

Introduction

A major fault-line in governance, where corruption appears to be rampant and impinges directly on the everyday life of citizens in most developing countries, is the domain of public services. In India, although the state has made many impressive strides in expanding the access of citizens to basic public service infrastructure, the poor quality of service delivery and the high levels of rent seeking behaviour by public officials point to extremely low levels of public accountability. Before we proceed further on the issue of low levels of accountability and responsiveness in public services, it is necessary to understand the context in which they operate (Paul, 2002). First of all, the state has traditionally been dominant in this area and often the sole provider of public services in India. The downside of this 'monopoly power' is that users of most public services do not have the option to 'exit' from one supplier to another. It also creates a pronounced tendency on the part of the service providers to withhold information from the customers thus creating huge information black holes that make it difficult for the customers or users of the services to demand accountability.

Second, there is little evidence that those in authority who are charged with enforcing public accountability are always effective and committed to this task. The absence of market competition has not been compensated by any other institutional mechanism to ensure efficient service delivery. Traditional mechanisms such as public audit of government expenditure and legislative oversight focus only on a review of inputs. Expenditures are audited to see whether proper procedures and norms have been adhered to. While this is an aspect of accountability, it does not tell us anything about how well the money was spent. This is because very little attention is given to the outputs and outcomes of the inputs. The problem is exacerbated by the difficulties in measuring outputs and in monitoring field level activities. Legislative oversight has been blunted by the vastness of the scope of services and the lack of information available to the legislators. An even more disturbing problem is the collusion between service providers and those responsible for monitoring their performance. The internal working and decision making of public agencies cannot easily be monitored or even observed by those outside the system. The scope for the pursuit of parochial and self-serving interests and for corruption is considerable under these circumstances.

Third, citizens – who directly or indirectly pay for all public services – are seldom able to engage in sustained collective action to demand increased public accountability from the service providers with which they deal. There is an implicit assumption that once people elect a government, it is for the latter to enforce accountability on all service providers. Perhaps an even more important reason for this attitude of citizens is that their motivation to engage in collective action is usually weak. The fact that the severity of problems people face concerning public services generally, tend to vary from day to day and from household to household. This shows that sustaining collective action is difficult even when a group is able to initiate action at some point in time. In any case, some may not invest time and energy for collective action as they feel they could get a 'free ride' from the success of the efforts of others. This is a major reason why the incentives for collective action are weak except in certain critical situations.

Fourth, the legal framework of the country can be a barrier to improved public accountability. Administrators typically try to work within the framework of the laws and regulations of their organisations. Accounts get audited because it is a legal requirement to do so. Investments are made according to the laws and regulations governing the organisation. If the law is silent on the standards and other attributes of services, provider agencies are likely to pay less attention to them.

Given this highly disabling environment, what are the practical ways to use 'voice and participation' to change the highly disabling ambience of public service delivery? Increasing opportunities for citizens' voice and participation can create powerful incentives for change: when competition is absent, as in the case of most public goods, popular voice can reduce information asymmetries which can challenge service providers to perform better and lower transaction costs (Paul, 1998). When low incentives and weak monitoring combine to produce inefficient public services, voice mechanisms can inform public officials of the problems and act as a pressure for demanding improvements (Drez and Sen, 1999).

One promising approach is for the public to give their assessment of services to the public agencies concerned in the form of Citizen Report Cards and act as watchdogs in the process. Information is a source of power that can be used to create greater public awareness of where the problems are and what needs to be done. Campaigns and dialogues will be more purposeful and meaningful when people are armed with information that is well focused and pertinent. Civil society institutions can potentially play an active role in assembling and using such information to stimulate public agencies to improve their services. This chapter explores the potency of one such approach.

Conceptual Building Blocks

The evolution of 'Report Cards' from a leap of faith to an institutionalised mechanism is an interesting story. It all started with a pioneering individual experiment in Bangalore in 1992 when Dr Samuel Paul, a distinguished academic and internationally renowned public sector expert, organised a public feedback exercise with some friends as a concerned citizen's response to the appalling quality of civic services. The response this experiment evoked in both state and non-state arenas led to the formation of the

'Public Affairs Centre' (PAC) in 1994 in Bangalore as a national institute dedicated to improve the quality of governance in India. Over the past nine years, PAC has emerged as a major resource centre for stimulating public action through focused knowledge creation.

Citizen Report Cards (CRCs) on public utilities, pioneered by PAC is now widely recognised as a powerful voice mechanism. The concept of user feedback, 'citizen report cards' provide a simple and widely replicable tool for improving transparency and public accountability. When the citizens' voice provides an objective assessment of both qualitative and quantitative aspects of different public services, based on first-hand interactions with the agencies providing these services, it is possible to rank the agencies on the quality of performance. This *'report card'* can be used to stimulate collective action by citizens, and provide organisational leaders with an opportunity to design reforms and bring in a strategic reorientation (Gopakuimar, 1997). Experiences with report cards, both national and international, have amply demonstrated their potential for demanding more public accountability and providing a credible database to facilitate proactive civil society responses.

The CRC Methodology presents a simple but highly flexible approach for organising public feedback (Upp, 1995). The methodology supports the following objectives:

- Generates citizen feedback on the degree of satisfaction with the services provided by various public service agencies and provides reliable estimates of corruption.
- Catalyses citizens to adopt pro-active stances by demanding more accountability, accessibility and responsiveness from the service providers.
- Serves as a diagnostic tool for service providers, external consultants and analysts/ researchers to facilitate effective prognosis and solutions.
- Encourages public agencies to adopt and promote citizen friendly practices, design performance standards and facilitate transparency in operations.

In more practical terms, Citizen Report Cards give the following strategic inputs:

1. Provide benchmarks on access, adequacy and quality of public services as experienced by citizens: Citizen Report Cards go beyond the specific problems that individual citizens face and place each issue in the perspective of other elements of service design and delivery, as well as a comparison with other services, so that a strategic set of actions can be initiated.
2. Provide measures of citizen satisfaction to prioritise corrective actions: Citizen Report Cards capture citizens' feedback in clear, simple and unambiguous fashion by indicating their level of satisfaction or dissatisfaction. When this measure of citizen satisfaction or dissatisfaction is viewed from a comparative perspective, it gives very valuable information to prioritise corrective actions. For example, the most basic feedback a citizen may give about power supply is total dissatisfaction. To appreciate this feedback, it must be related to the ratings given to other services

by the same person. For example, water supply may be rated worse than power supply. When these two pieces of information are compared, one can conclude that power supply may be a cause of dissatisfaction, but the priority for corrective action may be water supply.

3. Provide indicators of problem areas in the delivery of public services: Citizen Report Cards enquire into specific aspects of interaction between the service agency and the citizen and seek to identify issues experienced by citizens in interfacing with the services. In more simple terms, Citizen Report Cards suggest that dissatisfaction has causes, which may be related to the quality of services enjoyed by citizens (such as reliability of power supply, or availability of medicines in a public hospital); difficulties encountered while dealing with the agency to solve service related issues like excess billing or complaints of power supply breakdown.

4. Provide reliable estimates on corruption and other hidden costs: Corruption, though widespread and rampant, often exists in the realm of anecdotes without any quantitative base. This 'subjectivity' of corruption has severely undermined both corrective and collective responses.

5. Provides a mechanism to explore citizens' alternatives for improving public services: Citizen Report Cards go beyond collecting feedback on existing situations from citizens. They are also a means of testing out different options that citizens wish to exercise, individually or collectively, to tackle various problems. For example, Citizen Report Cards can provide information on whether citizens are willing to pay more for better quality of services or be part of citizens' bodies made responsible for managing garbage clearance in the locality.

A typical CRC study is organised along the following lines:

- identification of issues through focus group discussions;
- designing the instruments;
- identifying the scientific sample for the survey;
- survey conducted by an independent agency;
- collection of qualitative data;
- placing the results in the public domain;
- implementing advocacy and partnership arrangements.

The increasing application of Report Cards reflects a growing awareness of the potency of empirical approaches in providing useful trigger mechanisms for mobilising effective and focused demand constituencies. Empirical approaches have also helped to quantify and give shape to many themes, which hitherto existed in the realms of the abstract – corruption being a good case in point.

Examples of Utilisation

Evaluating and Benchmarking Civic Services in Bangalore

The First Report Card Study of public services in Bangalore (1993) involved a random sample survey of city households (Paul, 1995). The residential areas of the city were stratified by the age of the locality and six areas were picked at random from among the old and established, the new and the intermediate areas. Within each area, sample households were selected using random numbers. Questionnaires were administered to the selected households, provided they had previously had an interaction with one or more public agencies in the preceding six months.

Separate samples were also selected from among general (middle and upper income) households and poor (low-income) households. These sample sizes are large enough so that error ranges are well within generally accepted statistical norms.

The exercise was guided by three questions: How satisfactory are the public services that matter the most to the citizens? What specific features of the services are satisfactory or unsatisfactory? What does it cost the user to get the services (including hidden costs) or to solve the problems associated with getting the services?

Respondents were asked to state how satisfied or dissatisfied they were with the public agencies. To make their responses comparable across agencies, the respondents were asked to choose a point on the scale of 1 to 7 that approximated their views. For example, somebody who is extremely dissatisfied would choose a score of 1 and another who is extremely satisfied will pick a score of 7.

The overall satisfaction with public agencies (general households) is shown in Table 12.1.[1] In this table 'satisfied' refers to 6 and 7 and 'dissatisfied' refers to 1 and 2. In between is a 'zone of ambivalence' which indicates that the respondent is not clear on his/her preferences. The table shows that none of the eight service providers in Bangalore received a satisfactory score from the respondents. Even the best average scores indicated (hospitals – 4.3 and banks – 4.0) do not go beyond the zone of ambivalence i.e. 3-5. Second, only one out of 100 respondents in Bangalore considers Bangalore Development Agency's (BDA) services as satisfactory. Only 4, 5 and 6 persons out of 100 think of Bangalore Water and Sewerage Services Board (BWSSB), Bangalore Metropolitan Corporation (BMC) and Karnataka Electricity Board (KEB) as performing satisfactorily.

The study also highlighted the phenomenon of corruption (see Table 12.2).[2] Taking all transactions with all eight services, 14 per cent of the respondents in Bangalore paid speed money (a euphemism for bribes) to the staff directly or through agents. There is evidence of higher concentration of speed money in some agencies than in others. Thus, every third person dealing with the BDA and Regional Transport Office (RTO) and every fourth person dealing with the BMC paid bribes. Respondents also reported that in 50 per cent of cases, officials demanded bribes thereby emphasising the extortionary nature of corruption.

The findings of the study elicited wide interest. A leading daily, *The Times of India*, started a weekly feature with a graphic depiction of one of the findings at a time; this

Table 12.1　Overall satisfaction with Public Agencies in Bangalore (General Households) – 1993

Agency/service	Average rating	Percentage of users satisfied	Percentage of users dissatisfied
Telephones	3.6	9	28
Municipal Corporation	2.9	5	49
Electricity	3.5	6	31
Water	3.0	4	46
Health	4.3	25	19
Regional Transport Office	3.5	1	36
Development Authority	2.5	1	65
Public sector banks	4.0	20	26

Table 12.2　Details of bribes paid to various agencies in Bangalore – 1993

Agency/service	Proportion in sample claiming to have paid (%)	Average payment per transaction (Indian Rupees)
Electricity Board	11	206
Water Board	12	275
City Corporation	21	656
Hospitals	17	396
Regional Transport Office	33	648
Telephones	4	110
Development Authority	33	1850
Average	14	857

feature continued for about two months, keeping the concept of Report Cards in the public domain. Though the responses from most agency heads and senior government officials were lukewarm, the Bangalore Development Authority (BDA), which was rated the worst across all qualitative and quantitative dimensions of service delivery, responded with a request for follow up actions.

This resulted in a unique collaboration wherein a public service agency requested an external research group to provide assistance in getting feedback on various dimensions of service delivery. The second study sought to address some pertinent questions like: Are the customers of BDA satisfied with the quality of service delivery? Is the phenomenon of corruption as rampant as alleged? What are the perceptible areas of weakness in the functioning of the BDA? Would the public be willing to participate in the process of improving the BDA's services? To give the effort a wider perception, the functional constraints experienced by the officials of BDA were also assessed through interactive discussions. Following the study, training programmes were organised for the staff of BDA.

The most important fallout of this intervention was the public awareness created by the report card on the need for active citizen participation in order to improve the quality of civic services. At the time the report card was undertaken, very few active residents' groups existed in Bangalore. Today, there are over 100 such groups in Bangalore. Networking and common activities among these groups are on the increase (Paul, 1998, p. 14).

The intervention in Bangalore demonstrated the potency of Report Cards to highlight a spectrum of qualitative and quantitative indicators. Apart from satisfaction and dissatisfaction with the services, the database also flagged themes such as staff behaviour, problem incidents and resolution and more importantly quantified an abstract concept such as 'corruption'. The disaggregation within the city between the urban poor and the general households also helped to exclusively focus on vulnerable sections.

PAC followed this effort by undertaking two more rounds – one in 1999 and recently, in 2004 (Paul and Sekhar, 1999; Sekhar, 2004). The main objective of these exercises was to assess whether the services have improved or worsened over the period and in what respects. The updated database showed the extent of progress made by individual service agencies over the past ten years. Table 12.3 narrates the comparative matrix of satisfaction scores and Table 12.4 discusses benchmarks on corruption indices.[3]

What is most striking is that, for the first time, there is a perceptible decline in corruption levels in routine transactions. Availability of buses and water has been enhanced and infrastructure, such as flyovers and new roads, has improved. Streamlined processes for paying property tax, getting bus passes and receiving accurate bills seem to have led to much greater public satisfaction. All these improvements have been matched with substantial increases in satisfaction with the behaviour of the staff of these agencies while interacting with citizens. This turnaround has been facilitated by a number of factors: the strategic significance of new institutional mechanisms that supported these efforts, such as the Bangalore Agenda Task Force (BATF) (Nilekani, 2003), which has worked hand in hand with these agencies on a number of initiatives. It is also evident that the application of better technology for delivering services, new investments and information technology for managing service agencies has played a critical role in enhancing the ease of access to government information and in making routine transactions with the state simpler. The media, too, has become an active stakeholder in making Bangalore's citizens more aware, and spotlighting issues that need to be addressed. The big change, however, has been the wide involvement of resident associations and civic groups in engaging with city agencies in campaigns and initiatives for improving service delivery.

Corruption in Maternity Health Centres in Bangalore[4]

The Bangalore City Corporation with 30 maternity homes, 37 urban family welfare centres (UFWCs) and 55 health centres funded by the World Bank under the India Population Project–VIII (IPP–VIII) is the major provider of family planning and

Table 12.3   Citizens' satisfaction with agency interactions in Bangalore – the benchmark figures[10]

Services	% satisfied			% dissatisfied		
	1994	1999	2003	1994	1999	2003
Water Supply and Sewerage Board	4	42	73	46	8	27
Electricity Board	6	47	94	31	17	6
Bangalore City Corporation	5	41	73	49	26	27
Telephones	9	67	92	28	11	8
Regional Transport Office	14	32	77	36	26	23
Public hospitals	25	36	73	19	6	27
City Development Authority	1	16	85	65	36	15
Public buses	NA	32	96	NA	18	4

Table 12.4 Report card on Bangalore – the bribery matrix

Agency	Proportion in sample claiming to have paid a bribe (%)			Average payment per transaction in INR		
	1994	**1999**	**2003**	**1994**	**1999**	**2003**
Bangalore Water Supply and Sewerage Board	12	35	2	275	584	108
Karnataka Electricity Board	11	18	1	206	929	5000
Municipal Corporation	21	52	1	656	3759	NA*
Telephones	4	26	1	110	245	80
Regional Transport Office	33	57	10	648	637	395
Public Hospitals	17	43	5	396	500	NA
Bangalore Development Authority	33	78	10	1850	7690	630
Overall figures	*14*	*22*	*11*			

* Since there is a multiplicity of services and multiple users for the services, average amounts are being computed.

maternal/child health care services for the urban poor in Bangalore. Independent reviews, stakeholder consultations and media reports in the past have significantly highlighted the alarming levels of corruption in maternity homes. Various groups working for the poor in the city expressed a strong demand to carry out a user feedback survey to empirically assess the quality of care, particularly that of the service delivery process at the maternity homes. As a follow-up, the Public Affairs Centre undertook a Citizen Report Card survey of maternity homes, IPP Centres and UFWCs all over the city in partnership with five city based NGOs. A total of 500 patients and 77 staff of these facilities were interviewed. The purpose of the survey was to obtain corroborative evidence on the poor quality of services provided, and the widespread corruption in maternity homes to strengthen the advocacy work of Civil Society Organisations. The Citizen Report Card highlighted the following issues:

1. The most distressing finding concerns the prevalence of corruption. While none of the facilities appear corruption free, maternity homes stand out in terms of the severity of the problem. Payments are demanded or expected by staff for most services, but predominantly, for delivery and seeing the baby (Table 12.5).[5] The proportions of people paying bribes vary from one service to another. On the whole, 90 per cent of the respondents reported paying bribes for services at maternity homes at an average of INR 700 (1 USD = 45 INR) *per* head. Nearly 70 per cent pay to see their own babies! One out of two pay for delivery.
2. If a poor woman paid for all services, it would have cost her over INR 1000 for a delivery. It is reported that a nursing home might give her 'hassle free' and a better quality service for INR 2000. A rough estimate of the bribes being paid in all these facilities is estimated at between INR 10 and 20 million annually. A similar estimate based on these findings is that if 90 per cent of the women pay an average of about INR 700 at the Maternity Homes then the total amount of bribes paid is estimated at approximately INR 16 million.
3. Most staff deny corrupt behaviour. They complain about the constraints on facilities, staff shortages and inadequate supplies.
4. While only 39 per cent of the patients were given the medicine free of cost at the maternity homes, 61 per cent and 63 per cent were supplied medicines free at the UFWCs and IPP Health Centres. Money was demanded for medicines from 11 per cent of women at maternity homes while only 4 and 3 per cent respectively, reported being asked to pay money for medicines at UFWCs and IPP Health Centres. The average amount paid for medicines was higher at INR 94 at maternity homes than INR 30 paid at UFWCs. But, the least amount was paid at IPP Health Centres (INR 15). Interestingly, *all* doctors, nurses and other staff at *all* three types of facilities say free medicines are given to *all* patients *all* the time.
5. IPP Health Centres are, on the whole, rated better than the UFWCs and maternity homes. For similar services provided by all three, the rating is the highest for IPP Health Centres and lowest for maternity homes.

Table 12.5 Details of bribes paid at government maternity homes in Bangalore

Purpose for payment	Proportion in sample claiming to have paid	Average payment per transaction in INR
Obtaining medicines	11	94
Obtaining a scan	38	176
Obtaining blood test*	13	21
Obtaining a urine test*	07	21
Delivery of baby	48	361
Seeing the new born child	69	227
Immunization of the child	13	18

* The official/legal rates for the services are fixed at INR 10.

Benchmarking Corruption in South Asia [6]

A major factor contributing to the poor impact of huge public investments in critical sectors like health, education and power across South Asia is the lack of effective monitoring systems. It is a fact that corruption is severely undermining development objectives in South Asian countries by hindering economic growth, reducing efficiency, acting as a disincentive to potential investors and, above all, diverting critical resources meant for poverty alleviation.

Transparency International (TI) has a strong presence in South Asia and TI national chapters are now active in most countries of the region. The TI chapters realised early on, in working with various stakeholders in designing anti-corruption programs, that objective databases such as citizen feedback surveys are highly effective mechanisms. When the citizens' voice consists of objective assessments of both the qualitative and quantitative aspects of different public services that are based on first-hand interaction with the agencies providing these services, it is possible to rank the agencies according to their level of performance. This 'score card' can be used to stimulate collective action by citizens and provide leaders with a basis to design reforms. This collective interest led to the design of a pioneering project in South Asia to make an objective assessment of the levels and forms of corruption in the five major countries of the region. What makes this initiative unique is that a common survey instrument was used to capture perceptions and experiences, thereby rendering it possible to study emergent trends in the region. The range of public services in South Asia is extensive. It would be difficult to include all in a single survey. Not only would it unduly add to the cost of the survey, but it would also test the attention of respondents. For the purposes of this survey, a decision was made to focus on a set of services that are essential for the majority of the population, especially the poor and disadvantaged sections of society. The selected services, which were examined through a common questionnaire in all countries, are: healthcare, education, power, land administration, taxation, police and the judiciary.

The survey conducted in Bangladesh, India, Nepal, Pakistan and Sri Lanka between November 2001 and May 2002, was carried out on households, both urban and rural, ranging from 2,278 households in Sri Lanka to 5,157 in India. In Pakistan, 3,000 households were surveyed, while 3,030 were surveyed in Bangladesh and 3,060 in Nepal. Commissioned by TI's national chapters, the surveys all used the same methodology about service delivery and corruption in all the selected seven public services. All South Asian Chapters of TI had previous exposure to the Citizen Report Card Methodology. For each sector, the following issues were covered in the questionnaire:

- interaction and process of interaction of the sectors;
- types of corruption;
- actors who may or may not have participated in corrupt practices;
- irregular costs due to corruption;
- nature of interaction;
- causal factors leading to corruption in service delivery.

Apart from highlighting interesting patterns of corrupt practices and quantifying the phenomenon, the survey also provides useful benchmarks to measure progress and track changes over time. The major findings of the survey include:

1. Education, health and power emerge as the three most commonly used public services across the region from the seven services probed. For a large percentage of the population, public institutions are the sole providers of these services.
2. The police are generally perceived to be the most corrupt sector in four out of five countries in the region. In Nepal, it is perceived to be the third most corrupt after land administration and customs.
3. However, experiences of actual users of services highlighted that the police and the judiciary were the two most corruption prone sectors, followed by land administration and education.
4. Access to public services is a major issue for vast numbers of the population in all five countries surveyed, especially in Bangladesh, Pakistan and Sri Lanka. This finding also implies that the poor in these countries face the danger of exclusion from public services due to high artificial barriers – economic and others.
5. The survey finds petty corruption to be endemic in all key public sectors in the five countries, with users reporting moderate to high levels of corruption in their regular interaction with public services.
6. Middle and lower level functionaries are identified as the key facilitators of corruption in all sectors probed.
7. An analysis of the nature of corruption finds extortion to be the most prevalent form.
8. Evidence of the economic costs incurred due to corruption suggests high levels of income erosion given the high frequency of bribery and the large sums paid.
9. A lack of accountability and monopoly power are quoted as the major factors contributing to corruption in public services.

The top three corruption prone sectors as *per* user feedback are (see Table 12.6):[7]

- *Bangladesh* – Police (1) Judiciary (2) Land Administration (3);
- *India* – Police (1) Judiciary (1) Land Administration (3);
- *Nepal* – Police (1) Judiciary (2) Education (3) and Tax (3);
- *Pakistan* – Police (1) Land Administration (1) Tax (3);
- *Sri Lanka* – Police (1), Judiciary (1) Land Administration (3).

The survey shows that bribes are a heavy financial burden on South Asian households, both due to the high frequency of bribes and to the large sums paid (see Table 12.7).[8] More than half of the users of public hospitals in Bangladesh, for example, reported that they had paid a bribe to access a service, with bribes averaging BDT 1,847 (US$33). In Pakistan, 92 per cent of households that had someexperience with public education reported having to pay bribes; the average amount paid was PKR 4,811 (US$86). These figures are disquieting in a region where 45 per cent of the total population of 1.4 billion live in poverty.

When asked about the source of corruption, most respondents answered that public servants extorted bribes (Table 12.8).[9] Middle and lower level civil servants were identified as the key facilitators of corruption in all sectors probed.

The survey has revealed the rampant nature of corruption that plagues vital public services, including police, education and healthcare. The findings disturbingly suggest a large number of the population to be victims of extortion when they attempt to access and use critical services. The survey strongly supports the case for empowering regulatory bodies, such as the office of the Ombudsman, to oversee the activities of public agencies, which across the region are the sole providers of many basic necessities. The findings also indicate that where the law is silent on standards of service, agencies simply provide poorer services.

Impact and Learnings

The concept of citizen feedback surveys to assess the performance of public services is quite new to India and the process is still developing. The responses and spin-offs from various studies show impacts at four levels as discussed below.

Creating Public Awareness

The mass media has played a major role in creating awareness and sensitising the public. The Report Card findings are generally publicised prominently by major newspapers. Agency specific findings and the novelty of the method used were, in part, responsible for this response. And, of course, news about corruption always makes good copy. For an issue like corruption, quantification of information transformed individual experiences to collective 'voices' and thereby provided a strong platform to launch strong, demand-led responses.

Table 12.6 Corruption in South Asia – the sector scores

Countries	Sectors (proportion in the sample reporting payment of bribes)						
	Ed.	Health	Power	Land admin.	Tax	Police	Judiciary
Bangladesh	40	58	32	73	19	84	75
India	34	15	30	47	15	100	100
Nepal	25	18	12	17	25	48	42
Pakistan	92	96	96	100	99	100	96
Sri Lanka	61	92	Sample too small	98	Sample too small	100	100

Table 12.7 Corruption in South Asia – The Income Erosion

Countries	Sectors (average amount paid as bribes)						
	Ed.	Health	Power	Land admin.	Tax	Police	Judiciary
Bangladesh	BDT 742	BDT 1847	BDT 950	BDT 3509	BDT 318	BDT 9675	BDT 7800
India	INR 745	INR 621	INR 669	INR 1005	INR 1937	INR 754	INR 1540
Nepal	NR 961	NR 1424	NR 531	NR 1220	NR 12323	NR 1637	NR 8169
Pakistan	PR 4811	PR 777	PR 1087	PR 6013	PR 3858	PR 2331	PR 9670
Sri Lanka	SLR 2700	SLR 955	Sample too small	SLR 2540	Sample too small	SLR 1379	SLR 889

BDT – Bangladesh Taka (1 USD = 56 BDT)
INR – Indian Rupee (1 USD = 45 INR)
NR – Nepali Rupee (1 USD = 71 NR)
PR – Pakistani Rupee (1 USD = 55 PR)
SLR – Sri Lankan Rupee (1USD = 96 SLR)

Table 12.8 Corruption in South Asia – profiles of extortion

| Countries | Proportion of those who paid bribes claiming extortion* | | | | | | |
	Educ.	Health	Power	Land admin.	Tax	Police	Judiciary
Bangladesh	87	61	79	82	56	84	73
India	66	55	67	59	63	67	66
Nepal	73	74	63	86	72	54	72
Pakistan	61	60	72	64	61	74	61
Sri Lanka	62	30	NA	32	NA	14	64

*   Extortion is defined as a case where the service provider directly demanded bribes.

Stimulating Agency Reforms

Report Card studies uncovered a wide panoply of issues, both quantitative and qualitativ, and sent strong signals to public service providers. The use of a rating scale permitted the respondents to quantify the extent of their satisfaction or dissatisfaction with the service of an agency. The scale was used not only for an overall assessment of an agency but also for different dimensions of its service. The inter-agency comparisons with respect to public satisfaction and corruption that a report card permits also created a platform to stimulate agency interest in addressing the underlying problems. Quantification and rankings demand attention in a way that anecdotes do not. They focus attention on specific agencies and services that can be embarrassing to those in charge especially because of the adverse publicity involved.

Strengthening Civil Society Initiatives

The findings and information provided by Report Cards have largely succeeded in catalysing citizens to take proactive and creative steps. Rather than existing as passive recipients of inefficient and unresponsive services, more citizens are, today, involved as active partners and participants. For Civil Society Organisations, the methodology has provided a strong, coherent and credible database highlighting areas of concern that help them to strategise their options and sharpen their advocacy skills.

Democratic Responsiveness

Report cards draw attention to a plethora of qualitative dimensions like satisfaction, expectation on quality etc. that are missing from the usual statistics on service delivery which focus exclusively on hard physical data. Report Cards may also stimulate political responsiveness: democracy is not just about elections, but what happens between them. In Bangalore, the Chief Minister's monitoring programs of public agencies (though an innovative forum called 'Bangalore Agenda Task Force') repeatedly uses report cards to assess progress of proposed reforms and activities. Findings from these exercises are presented to the city mayor and other elected functionaries and are widely disseminated through the media.

Critical Success Factors

The factors that facilitate successful use of the methodology are:

1. *Need for an Objective and Credible Database:* All effective advocacy interventions were launched from a need to have a credible database. Most partner organisations need the strength of numbers to make their shout more focused and amplified.
2. *Focus on Institutions:* Report Cards chart out feedback on services and not on individuals. The emphasis is on creating neutral and scientific institutional

databases and to pave the way for systemic reforms, not 'Band-Aid' solutions such as transfer of CEOs of poorly rated agencies. This helps to make advocacy less confrontational.

3. *Presence of Local Champions:* Perhaps the most critical input is the need for local stakeholders like NGOs and citizen groups who will own the database, contextualise the findings and strategise local advocacy actions.

4. *Emphasis on Experiential and not Perceptional Data:* Report Cards are not opinion polls. They represent codified experiences of users of services. This 'user' dimension gives the findings more weight and credibility.

5. *Conducted by Independent and Professionally Competent Group:* The credibility of the local champion has to be impeccable for effective advocacy.

Notes

1   See Appendix 1.
2   See Appendix 1.
3   See Appendix 1.
4   See Sekhar, S. (2000), *Maternity Health Care for the Urban Poor in Bangalore: A Report Card*, Public Affairs Centre, Bangalore.
5   See Appendix 1.
6   See Gopakumar, K 2002, *Corruption in South Asia: Insights and Benchmarks from Citizen Feedback Surveys in Five Countries*, Transparency International, Berlin.
7   See Appendix 1.
8   See Appendix 1.
9   See Appendix 1.
10 Since the Citizen Report Cards use scales to quantify feedback, percentages for Satisfaction referred to in the table reflects the total proportion of those saying that they are completely and partially satisfied with the particular service; similarly, 'Dissatisfied' percentages refer to those saying that they are completely and partially dissatisfied with the service. It is interesting to note that in 1994 and 1999, a significant proportion of respondents were ambivalent in quoting their satisfaction ratings.

References

Balakrishnan, S. (2003), 'Citizen Report Cards and the Basic Services for the Urban Poor', Background paper prepared for the World Development Report 2004.

Dreze, J. and Amartya Sen (1999), 'Public Action and Social Inequality', in Barbara Harriss-White and Sunil Subramanian (eds), *Illfare in India: Essays on India's Social Sector in Honour of S. Guhan*, Sage Publications, New Delhi.

Gopakumar, K. (1997), 'Public Feedback as an Aid to Public Accountability: Reflections on an Innovative Approach', *Public Administration and Development*, vol. 17, pp. 281–82.

Gopakumar, K. (2002), *Corruption in South Asia: Insights and Benchmarks from Citizen Feedback Surveys in Five Countries*, Transparency International, Berlin.

Paul, Samuel (1995), *A Report Card on Public Services in Indian Cities: A View from Below*, Public Affairs Centre, Bangalore.

Paul, Samuel (1998), 'Making Voice Work: The Report Card on Bangalore's Public Service', Policy *Research Working Paper No. 1921*, The World Bank, Washington DC, p. 14.

Paul, S. (2002), *Holding the State to Account: Citizen Feedback in Action*, Books for Change, Bangalore.

Paul, S. and Sekhar, Sita (1999), *The Second Report Card on Bangalore's Public Services*, Public Affairs Centre, Bangalore.

Sekhar, S. (2000), 'Maternity Health Care for the Urban Poor in Bangalore: A Report Card', *Working Paper*, Public Affairs Centre, Bangalore.

Sekhar, S. (2004), *The Third Report Card on Bangalore's Public Services*, Public Affairs Centre, Bangalore.

Upp, S. (1995), *Making the Grade: A Guide to Implement the Report Card Methodology*, Public Affairs Centre, Bangalore.

Chapter 13

Corruption and Patronage Politics: 'Harambee' in Kenya

Anne Waiguru

Introduction

Harambee ('pulling together') is a self-help movement indigenous to Kenya. It entails voluntary contributions in cash and kind (e.g. labour) to community amenities such as schools, water projects and health clinics. Almost everybody dealing with the Kenyan development prospects, problems, doing research or trying to explain about Kenya to outsiders will find it necessary to know about *harambee* as a development strategy. In Kenya, *harambee* is a way of filling needs as well as of working and living in Kenya.

Harambee has been an integral element of Kenyan nationalism. Before independence *harambee* was a grass-root form of social exchange of labour and other forms of mutual assistance. The concept became a national slogan, a motto on the nation crest and a rally cry on Madaraka Day in June 1963 when the President of Kenya, Mzee Jomo Kenyatta, formally made it such. After this day, *Harambee* is used to denote collective effort, community self-reliance, cooperative enterprises and all forms of collective self-reliance.

Ideally, a *harambee* commences with a community which identifies a need and then organises groups to meet it. These groups can have one target or a continuing program of related targets. The original *harambee* initiatives in the early 1970s built schools, health dispensaries, cattle dips and roads – later emphasising agricultural and water projects. During this time, the *harambee* groups were not formally registered as societies and the levels of *harambee* activities varied considerably among the provinces. *Harambees* were generally more active where suitable land resources favoured settlement and development efforts.

The main advantage of a *harambee* project was that it reflected a 'bottom up' as opposed to the usual 'top down' project initiation process thereby fostering ownership and accountability. It ensured that communities met their prioritised objective while at the same time ensuring that the free rider problem was kept to a minimum. Everyone was encouraged to voluntarily contribute either in cash or kind. However, the gradual erosion of the original self-help concept has corrupted this noble ideal. It has been replaced by a culture of political philanthropy used by politicians for bribing voters.

Harambee initiatives can be categorised into two broad groups – private and public. Private *harambees* typically raise funds for weddings, funerals, college fees and medical bills for family and friends. Public *harambee*s raise funds for development projects such as schools, health centres, water projects etc. This study focused on public *harambee*s.

Why Study Harambee?

Harambee has been said to predispose people and, particularly, politicians to corruption in two ways:

1. It provides an avenue for people who steal public funds to legitimise themselves to the public. A survey of the Kenyan Public Expenditure Management done by the Centre for Governance and Democracy for the period 1991 to 1997 indicated that the government lost through mismanagement more than Ksh 451 billion (Ksh 1170 billion/US$15 billion inflation adjusted). Wasteful expenditure was the main cause of loss of public funds. This waste included the embezzlement of money given to *harambee*s (Centre for Governance and Democracy (CGD), 2001).
2. There is no accountability for contributions, and few, if any, benefactors make the effort to see that their contributions were used for the intended purpose. As a result, there is no mechanism for exposing and sanctioning custodians who embezzle the funds and fraudsters who raise money for fictitious *harambee*s.

Literature Review

Different interpretations of the nature and scope of the *harambee* movement have been forwarded by the relatively few scholars who have conducted research on this topic. Some authors have stressed the role of *harambee* in fostering social cohesion and solidarity. Others recognise the links between *harambee* and the traditional forms of communal works; they stress the important use of traditional groups for mobilising and organising the rural population. Others suggest that the rural poor's effort in community self-help activities impoverish them for the benefit of the rural rich and cite cases of misuse of *harambee* funds. While still others, who are supporters of *harambee* grants but who acknowledge that fraudulent cases do exist, claim that self-help activity is a suitable way to create local resources for building facilities and providing services which have a far broader use and applicability than advantaging the rural elite (Thomas, 1977).

Reasons for the flourishing of the *harambee* movement in Kenya are also discussed. Mutiso (1975) argues that a centre-periphery, paralleling an urban-rural division within Kenya, broadly reflects different cultures. Self-help or *harambee* acts as a defensive strategy of the periphery to squeeze what it can from a seemingly opulent and arrogant centre (Mutiso, 1975).

Holmquist advances a number of reasons for the development of the self-help movement in Kenya. One reason was – besides Kenyatta's call – the rural petty bourgeois responded positively to *harambee*s because they found themselves in competition with each other for the scarce political roles which could be used to enhance their economic standing as well as general social and political prestige. Also, with the peasantry demanding social amenities and having some leverage over their leaders, the latter had to help the community extract resources from government and private sources to prove their worth to the population. Holmquist also suggested that the rural petty bourgeois needed self-help activities as the bureaucracy reserved most of the functions of programmatic policy making for itself. This alternative did not threaten their status as a class, although competition among them affected the political fortunes of individuals. He saw the rural petty bourgeois as having a far more immediate and long-term interest in local amenity development than their centrally recruited and transferable class counterparts in the bureaucracy (Holmquist, 1984).

Njuguna Ngethe, on the other hand, points out a peculiar irony. The independent and freewheeling character of the rural petty bourgeoisie in Kenya prompted President Kenyatta to encourage and almost mandate their role in self-help. Kenyatta, after independence, became increasingly disillusioned with parliamentary backbenchers sniping at government policy and he was frustrated with his inability to enforce party discipline and political order. This resulted in him haphazardly elaborating a notion of legitimate constituency service to assist the expanding number of self-help groups. This form of politics was conveniently non-ideological and non-programmatic. Kenyatta called it 'useful politics' rather than 'useless politics' of 'all talk and no action'. Self-help would unite politician and constituent in 'hard work' as opposed to 'idle chatter'. This important component of practical state ideology was cemented by the implied partnership between the state and society in the basic rule of the self-help game: 'government helps those who help themselves' (Holmquist, 1984).

Mutiso and Godfrey (1973) and Mbithi and Rasmusson (1975) cite two reasons for the proliferation of the self-help movement. Between 1962 and 1965, the ruling party (Kenya African National Union (KANU)) by absorbing leaders of Kenya African Democratic Union (KADU) and Akamba Peoples Party (APP) suppressed regionalism. This merger created conflict between KANU groups (who had been associated with the party at its beginning and at independence (KANU A)) and those who had just come in. This led to several national leaders moving into competition at the district level using the already mushrooming *harambee*.

The other reason was – before independence – nationalist ideology was couched in slogans that appeared to promise an easier life and increased material wellbeing soon after the departure of colonialist and imperialist exploiters. This led to a rising expectation of what independence would deliver. The 1962–65 period was, therefore, one of gradual disillusionment with the realities of post-independence self-assessment and apparent breach of promise by the leaders. Consequently, in 1965, *Sessional Paper No. 10 on African Socialism* – calling on self-reliance and hard work – was published. This document coincided with the publication of the first, post-independence Five Year Development Plan which also emphasised the harsh realities of development that is, reduced dependency on government and the need for hard work and self reliance.

Mutiso later interprets *harambee* as based on the dynamics of Kenya's changing social structure. He argues that the polarisation of western defined social values, social mobility patterns and socio-metric interaction patterns in the form of an emerging elite on the one hand should be seen against equally well-defined indigenous and neo-indigenous value-interaction patterns which represent the majority of the population. He sees this polarisation as creating a social cleavage, which makes the indigenous system the periphery and the elite the centre. To Mutiso, the fact that the backbone of the *harambee* movement is the periphery is a re-affirmation of the periphery's alienation from the economic and political centre and their desire to co-opt leadership from the centre or open mobility patterns from the periphery to the centre. This, he argues, is essential if the periphery is, in the long run, to be able to re-channel the allocation of resources and access opportunity.

In supporting this orientation, Frank Holmquist sees *harambee* as a pre-emptive strategy. In his studies of project choice patterns in Kisii Kenya, he inferred that such choices were dictated by an ever-present confrontation between government change agents and local interest groups. This strategy also exploits uniqueness of local criteria and uniqueness of locally designed projects to arrest government interest. It assumes that the government will continue with their traditional planning approach but is able, and willing, to take over locally initiated projects. Thus, the pre-emptive strategy is not a strategy to sabotage government development efforts but a deliberate attempt to attract attention and alleviate irrelevant planning and centralised decision making.

Barkan and Holmquist, in their attempt to address the social base of self-help, hypothesised that different strata and possibly different social classes would exhibit different levels of support for the self-help movement. Their primary concern in testing this hypothesis was to question 'whether the Kenyan self help motto is a vehicle of small farmers or whether it is a vehicle through which large land owners, in alliance with the state coopt and tax the rural masses'. They concluded that almost everybody in the rural areas supported self-help – the only difference being the degree with which they were involved (Barkan and Holmquist, 1989).

Although the *harambee* movement was initially encouraged and given the *imprimatur* of the Kenyan government to shift the cost of providing social services to the peasantry, the net result has been a greater transfer of resources from the centre than would have occurred had the movement never grown to its present size.

By the late 1970s, the government had become alarmed at the proliferation of the self-help movement and sought to slow the rate down, citing that development was now getting out of control. The problem for the government was to demobilise an overactive peasantry. The bureaucracy felt it was losing control and needed to gradually erode peasant initiative and reassert its control over local development. Hence, the government initiated a procedure by which projects had to be registered by the Ministry of Social Services to be eligible for aid.

Despite this effort and the fact that *harambee* has played an increasingly important role in the social life of millions of Kenyans and having always been a highly politicised activity, the *harambee* movement developed in a haphazard manner. *Harambee* was left out of the main stream of the government's development plan and its growth has been achieved with little or no coordination or regulation by the government.

Mbithi and Rasmusson estimated the magnitude of *harambee* as having contributed over 30 per cent of rural development investment. It was estimated that during the 1976/77 financial year alone, a total of 8.8 million Kenya pounds was collected during *harambee*s and the 1979–83 development plan declared *harambee* to have been a key tactic for hastening rural development since independence (Mbithi and Rasmusson, 1977).

It is important to note that few scholars have studied the subject. None have attempted to measure the actual magnitude of the *harambee* movement in Kenya. Most of the previous studies focussed on the period before 1980. Therefore, the need for an in depth analysis of the magnitude and trend of the current movement is apparent. This study seeks to expand this knowledge.

Study Objectives

The primary objective of the pilot study was to compile definitive data on *harambee* activity and to study the evolution of *harambee* over time. A secondary objective of the study was to conduct a preliminary follow-up of *harambee* projects.

Methodology

Data was compiled from newspaper archives of the two main national dailies (*The Nation* and *The Standard*) for the period 1980–99 and was collected by the following key variables:

- name and type of project (for example, school, health centre, water);
- district and constituency;
- host personalities (for example, local MP, councillor, school chairman etc.);
- reported individual contributions;
- total amount raised.

Since a preliminary survey established that over 90 per cent of *harambee* activity is concentrated in the months of March–September, data was collected only for these months due to limed time and resources. The analysis was based on a sample of 1,987 *harambee*s.

Project follow-ups were done in three districts (Nakuru, Maragwa and Kajiado). Random checks were undertaken to verify the amounts reported in the newspaper with actual amounts collected. A reasonable degree of accuracy between the two sources was found. Eyewitness interviews were later conducted to obtain a more detailed description of *harambee*s.

Scope and Limitations of the Study

Data on *harambee* gathered from press reports have certain inherent biases. For example, a *harambee* with prominent personalities involved have a higher likelihood of press coverage. Hence, the data will have a 'VIP' bias.

Another limitation of the data is double counting of funds collected in 'mini' *harambees* that are subsequently donated in 'major' *harambees*. Newspaper reports do not always provide sufficient information to allow the necessary corrections in the data.

Other inaccuracies include dishonoured pledges and cheques. Cases of prominent individuals who circulate the same money in several *harambees* are also not unknown. However, in so far as the reporting is reasonably consistent over time, the data provides a reasonably accurate reflection of broad trends and patterns.

Summary of Main Findings

Principal Finding

The principal finding of this study was that public *harambees* in the multi-party era have become a KANU dominated election campaign phenomena. KANU is, and has been, the ruling party since independence. Other findings were as follows.

Number of Reported Harambees

As shown in the Figure 13.1, the number of *harambees* reported doubled from 97 in 1991, to 203 in 1992 – the year of the first multi-party elections. Only 74 *harambees* were reported in the following year. *Harambee* activity picked up again prior to the 1997 general elections – from 87 in 1995, to 162 and 205 in 1996 and 1997 respectively.

In 1992, the total amount raised increased almost six-fold – from Ksh. 26 million (Ksh 85 million/US$1.1 million inflation adjusted to 1999 prices) in 1991, to Ksh 142 million (about Ksh 362 million/US$4.6 million inflation adjusted to 1999 prices). In 1993, the amount raised declined to Ksh. 60 million (Ksh105 million/US$1.3 million inflation adjusted to 1999 prices).

In 1997, the amount raised increased from Ksh. 227 million (Ksh 280 million/ US$3.6 million inflation adjusted to 1999 prices) in 1996, to a record Ksh 1.35 billion (Ksh 1.4 billion/US$18 million inflation adjusted to 1999 prices). The amount raised in 1997 represents half the decade's reported contributions.

Harambee Participation

Harambee participation has clearly changed over the years. Politicians are the principal donors in public *harambees* and patronage has become more concentrated. The former

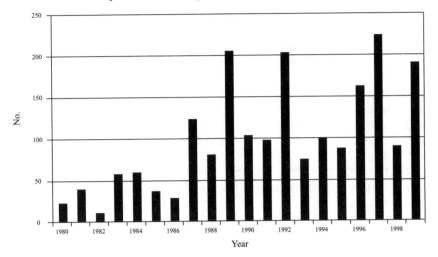

Figure 13.1 Number of reported harambees

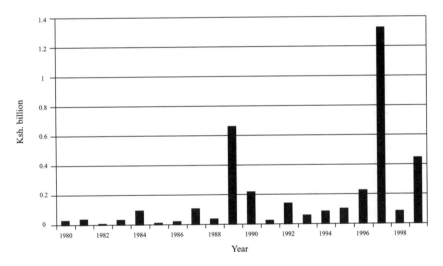

Figure 13.2 Total funds raised in reported harambees

president, Mr Moi, emerges as the principal *harambee* patron and his patronage appears to have grown over time. In the 1980s, he is reported as having contributed Ksh 24.5 million to 187 *harambee*s, in person and through emissaries, which accounted for almost 1 per cent of total contributions and 30 per cent of contributions by the principal 100 donors. In the 1990s, he is reported as having contributed over Ksh 130 million to 448 *harambee*s, constituting almost 5 per cent of the decade's total contributions and 30 per cent of principal donor contributions.

Table 13.1   Concentration of participation

| | % total contributions | | % top 100 contributors | |
	1980–89	1990–99	1980–89	1990–99
President	0.3	4.7	6.3	32.2
Top 10 donors	1.1	7.6	24.6	51.7
Top 20 donors	1.4	8.8	30.9	60.1
Top 50 donors	2.3	11.5	51.7	78.4
Top 100 donors	4.5	14.7	100.0	100.0

Source: *Harambee, Pooling Together or Tearing Apart*, Transparency International, Kenya
            2001.

It is obvious that *harambee* participation has become more concentrated, that is,
fewer and fewer individuals account for a larger share of money raised. In the 1990s,
the 100 principal donors accounted for 16 per cent of the reported contributions, up
from almost 5 per cent in the previous decade. In the single party era (1980–91),
politicians accounted for 70 per cent of the money contributed by the principal
donors. Between 1992 and 1997, KANU politicians accounted for 68 per cent of the
money contributed by the principal donors and opposition politicians accounted for
4 per cent.

Election Driven

Harambee has become an election driven activity. In the 1980s, the election years
(1983 and 1988) accounted for only 7 per cent of the decades total fund raising. In
the multiparty 1990s, the two election years (1992 and 1997) account for 60 per cent
of the decade's total. The year 1992 accounts for 26 per cent of the funds raised in
the first half of the decade (1990–94), and 1997 for 60 per cent of the funds raised in
the second half of the decade (1995–99).

It was significant that in the first half of the 1990s, 19 of the 100 principal donors
in the survey gave more than 25 per cent of their total contributions in 1992 – on
average, three and half times more than non-election years. In the second half, this
number doubled to 38, and the contributions were, on average, five times more than
in non-election years.

Case Studies

The project follow-ups revealed a critical lack of transparency and accountability.
Many of the beneficiaries could not be traced as many of the self-help group were
formed on an *ad hoc* basis during elections and disbanded after sharing the money.
The accounts below are illustrative of what occurred.

An eyewitness reports that a women's self-help group based in Maragwa district undertakes several projects financed by the women themselves through a 'merry-go-round' system. Towards the end of the year 2000, the group set-up a committee to organise a *harambee* to finance a water tank project. The committee came up with a budget and settled on whom to invite as the guests of honour. These included a local MP, prominent businessmen as well as aspiring parliamentary candidates. They targeted to raise enough money to buy all the self-help group members water tanks.

The KANU aspiring candidate talked to the group leader and told her to drop the idea of inviting guests from the opposition – a case of patronage. The MP further proposed that he would bring along more top KANU officials. The women accepted his proposal and the date of the fund raising scheduled. The event took place as planned but the amount raised was not publicly announced as is customary in a public fund raising drive. After the *harambee,* it was discovered that the money realised from the *harambee* was insufficient for the planned project and the money was shared among the women leaders and not used for the original purpose.

A politician reports that the fund drive was organised by Gathigi coffee farmers society to set up a coffee factory and milling facilities. The proposal came from the chairman of the factory committee who, at that time, was a businessman in Nairobi. Many welcomed his proposal because he was perceived to have strong links with KANU. The *harambee* was targeted to raise a large amount of money because the chairman was going to invite the KANU MPs and officials from the province.

The *harambee* was convened as scheduled and most of the guests were KANU politicians. The amount raised was not announced. The reason given was that money donated by the former president had not arrived. Later, the total amount contributed was estimated at about Kshs 3 million.

However, after the *harambee*, the project was changed from being a coffee farmers' society to a private company. The chairman sabotaged the plan and made it his own company for buying coffee from farmers and milling it. The members complained but the chairman promised to refund their registration fee. Further, he pledged to buy their coffee at a better rate than the going rate from the co-operative societies – a case of bribery.

Later, it was discovered that the person who had masterminded the plan was a prominent KANU politician. He had registered the company as a farmers' project to obtain 'funding assistance' from the government. He planned to divert these funds for his own use. The actual funds targeted were those from the presidential youth and women *harambee* initiatives.

Project Follow-ups

The District Social Development Offices (DSDOs) register self-help groups and are meant to authorise the expenditure of these groups. In the three districts visited, the DSDOs did not have any records on the finances of self-help groups. All the beneficiaries visited did not have readily available project accounts. Whereas this would not be a big problem in a small village setting where the amounts in question are not so large and everybody knows the organisers personally, in a large national *harambee* with thousands of anonymous citizens as contributors, a need for legal control arises as informal social mechanisms no longer work.

The other important finding was that although *harambee* money consisted of donations from the public, the beneficiaries did not expect members of the public to ask for accounts, in other words, they did not expect to be accountable to anyone.

The Ethics and Evolution of Harambee

The evolution of the *harambee* movement has raised various ethical questions in comparing it with similar movements around the globe such as, the Political Action Committees in the US. Though similar to the PAC movement is some aspects, the *harambee* movement is, nevertheless, uniquely different. As in the case of a Political Action Committee, the *harambee* movement is an important aspect of Kenyan politics and the Kenyan electoral system. However, it differs in that while the PACs exist legally as a means for organisations such as corporations and trade unions to make donations to candidates for federal office – something that they cannot do directly – *harambee*'s main objective is to meet an immediate common need not of politicians but of the public using locally available resources. In this aspect, the movement comes out as distinctly different.

Notably, whereas in the PAC, the money trickles up from the public to the politicians voluntarily, in *harambee*s, the money trickles down from state coffers, through politicians, to the general public. In *harambee*s, the public is usually oblivious that they are being used to further a politician's career and the use of the *harambee* movement as a campaign vehicle during election time is an evolving phenomena.

Another ethical question arose this year when members of parliament – despite Kenya's current tough economic situation – used *harambee*s to justify a 150 per cent plus increase in income (approximately US$ 6,400 per month). They argued that the increase was justified as their constituents expected them to contribute to *harambee*s. Should the same politicians who use the movement as a vehicle for bribing voters use *harambee*s to legitimise unsubstantiated salary increases?

There are some generalised characteristics that made the *harambee* self-help development effort distinct from other development activities in Kenya and the region. This included the reflection of a bottom-up rather than a top-down development project initiation. The participation of individuals in this self help movement was guided by the principle of the collective good rather than individual gain and the choice of projects was guided by the principle of satisfying the immediate need of participating members and groups. This local level ideology, which can be summarised as 'enlightened community and collective self-interest', was a very typical criterion for project choice. In most cases, it was what the group felt was necessary which determined who the group associated with, which resource mobilisation strategy would be effective, and what incentives and catch phrases would be appropriate to increase commitment.

However, as revealed by the study, these characteristics have been eroded over the years and *harambee* has evolved from its original, self-help concept into a perverse culture of political philanthropy. A 'top-down' initiative has replaced the 'bottom-up' process. Indeed, an elected leader's effectiveness is, in many places, measured almost exclusively by the number of *harambee*s conducted for constituents and the amount of money contributed. In many ways, development projects have become incidental to *harambee*; political contests are the real purpose. Participation is predominantly by politicians. The political prominence of the guests at a *harambee* and the list of those who send them with contributions has become the barometer of the host's political influence. *Harambee* has, therefore, become a tool for political patronage used by politicians to garner votes and maintain the loyalty of their electorate. Thus, it is an important arena within which political leadership at the local level is determined and sustained.

Moreover, *harambee* has played a significant role in accentuating inequalities between classes, within regions, as well as between regions – the richest districts usually being the most politically influential. This means that regions that are not politically connected to influential politicians have, in the long run, less access to development funds. It has also been suggested that the comparatively wealthy usually have a stronger interest in self-help projects than their less wealthy counterparts because they are better able to afford the user fees once the projects are operating.

Of most importance is the concern for misappropriation of funds. It is significant to note that this concern did not begin recently. In a speech made at a fund-raising meeting in the mid 1970s, Daniel Arap Moi, who was then Vice President, called for a nationwide accounting system for *harambee* money to assure the *wananchi* that their money was properly used. He also requested that the DCs form a committee of honest people to ensure that *harambee* funds were expended on the projects for which they were intended (Ngethe, 1979). This is confirmation of the existence of dishonest project leaders from a source close to the centre of government.

The succession of President Moi and the escalating world economic difficulties have translated into legitimacy and fiscal crises in Kenya. As politicians seek political positions, they tend to devote more attention to *harambee*s by bestowing considerable amounts of money on various projects especially in their constituencies. These funds are rumoured to come from several possible unacknowledged sources including businessmen 'for services rendered' and from the public treasury. When the president and members of provincial administration hold *harambee*s, chiefs and assistant chiefs often collect money from ordinary citizens to present at meeting. Such collections are not voluntary but a tax.

The Measure of Corruption

Apart form the ethical questions posed by the *harambee* movement as it is now, the activity and the amounts contributed could be used as measure of corruption in Kenya for various reasons:

1. The principal donors are politicians. However, the source of the funds donated in *harambee*s is unknown and beyond the means of many political donors.
2. *Harambee* activity and amounts donated increases significantly during election periods. Evidence that *harambee* is used by politicians as a vehicle for bribing voters.
3. The government loses significant amounts of money through wastage. This includes money donated in *harambee* particularly in election years.

Harambee activity and the amounts contributed could therefore be used as a measure of the increase or decrease of this form of corruption in Kenya relative to previous periods.

Conclusion

Following the adoption of multiparty politics, *harambee* had become a vehicle for bribing voters. If the current trend continues, bribery and patronage will become the primary function of public *harambee*s and the community objectives will disappear altogether. Bribing voters is not only a subversion of democracy but it also provides powerful motive for corruption and undermining of public ethics.

Many promote the strengthening of civil society as a safeguard against corruption or tyranny by the state. However, in the case of *harambee* – an institution that emerged from the civil society – it has been co-opted by the same politicians who control the state and has been used as an instrument for blunting accountability.

Harambee has always been political but the nature of *harambee* politics has undergone a gradual transformation from a 'bottom-up' to a 'top-down' process with resultant gradual erosion of ownership and accountability. Nevertheless, *harambee* is still an important Kenyan institution and an integral part of the nation's history, development efforts, and community life.

Recommendations

The following proposals are put forward:

1. Suspend *harambee*s during elections.
2. Prohibit contenders for elected office from contributing to *harambee*s during election campaigns.
3. Specify election-spending ceilings to include candidates' *harambee* contributions for a specific period (six, nine or 12 months) before elections.

Another proposal that could be considered is the regulation of *harambee* projects through the tax system. Introducing a withholding tax on harambee contributions that exceed a certain threshold could do this. Accountability would be promoted in at least three ways. First, *harambee* projects would be compelled to maintain financial records and reduce the scope for embezzlement of *harambee* funds. Second, it would contribute to developing a culture of financial probity and accountability among the citizens. Third, it would deter the channelling of illegitimate earnings into political patronage and revive the self-help principle and spirit of *harambee*.

In summary, the recommended regulation of *harambee*s would ensure efficiency and the protection of beneficiaries' interest while ensuring participants observed certain management and leadership ethics – putting the project's interests before personal ones.

References

Barkan, J.D. and Holmquist, F. (1989), *World Politics, Peasant State Relation and the Social Base of Self-help in Kenya*, Johns Hopkins University Press.

Centre for Governance and Democracy (CGD) (2001), *A Survey of Seven Years of Waste – Policy Brief*, Keitu Enterprises, Nairobi, Kenya.

Holmquist, F. (1984), *Politics and Public Policy in Kenya and Tanzania*, J.D. Barkan (ed.), Praeger Publishers, New York.

Mbithi, P. and Rasmusson, R. (1977), *Self Reliance in Kenya*, The Scandinavian Institute of African Studies, Uppsala, Sweden.

Mutiso, G.C.M. (1975), *Kenya: Politics, Policy and Society*, East African Literature Bureau Kampala.

Ngethe, J.N. (1979), 'Harambee and Development Participation in Kenya: The Politics of Peasants and Elites Interaction with Particular Reference to Harambee Projects in Kiambu Districts', PhD Thesis, Carleton University.

Thomas, J.W. (1977), *Creating Rural Employment; A Manual for Organising Rural Works Programs*, Harvard Institute for International Development, Harvard University.

Chapter 14

Measuring Corruption: Exploring the Iceberg

Leo Huberts, Karin Lasthuizen and Carel Peeters[1]

Introduction

Existing knowledge on corruption offers only a limited number of shared insights by researchers and practitioners. We all agree that corruption is an important and complex phenomenon and we agree that we disagree about its content. There are many different theories and conceptual frameworks, which lead to a multitude of descriptions, explanations and evaluations. As a consequence, to attempt to measure 'corruption' is, by definition, a risky and much disputed endeavour.

This is certainly true in an international context. However, it also upholds when corruption is studied within the context of one country – even when it concerns a small country with a comparatively positive corruption reputation such as, the Netherlands. In this chapter, we will present information about corruption research in this Western European country with about 16 million inhabitants.

Firstly, we will clarify the concepts that we will be using. Corruption is but one of the many integrity violations that can be distinguished. It is important to be clear about its relationship with related types of unethical behaviour – for example, fraud, theft, conflict of interest and abuse of resources. Our aim is to add to existing research and theory by the incorporation of the corruption concept into a broader theory of ethics and integrity of governance. Of course, this also has consequences for the appropriate research agenda and methodology, which we will also discuss.

There are numerous available methods that attempt to measure corruption and other integrity violations and which offer challenging possibilities for research on corruption. We have chosen to use multiple methods and through this 'triangulation' to increase our knowledge of corruption in the Netherlands. Our focus is an empirical one. By presenting the available research methodology and results concerning corruption in our country, we hope to contribute to this book's endeavour. Throughout this chapter, we will delve into questions concerning measurement and methodologies by describing different types of research that we have conducted, present some of our results, and reflect on the usefulness and limitations of the different research projects and methods.

In the third section, we will summarise the results of corruption reputation research. What has been the result of Transparency's Corruption Perception Index (CPI) research on the Netherlands and how does this relate to the expert panel research that has been done? Because Galtung and others discuss this type of research extensively in this volume, we will be brief about its contribution to our knowledge on the extent of corruption.

In the fourth section, we will present and discuss the methodology and results of research on internal corruption investigations in (local) governmental organisations. Even though it is self-evident that only a limited number of actual corruption cases will be discovered, it is worthwhile to collect information about these investigations. This is particularly true when cross-sectoral or longitudinal data become available. We researched internal investigations on corruption and fraud in municipal government in 1991 and 2002 and there is information available about these investigations within police forces for the years 1999–2000.

The third type of research focuses more directly on corruption itself. Surveys which estimate the extent of corrupt behaviour in the work environment clarify that there is much more corruption than the internal investigations detect. It also becomes clear that bribery seems to be exceptional but that corruption-related types of unethical behaviour within organisations are not. The validity of this information clearly exceeds the validity of perception and internal investigation research. However, what we discover is also limited. The knowledge of employees and managers about the presence of corruption is, by definition, deficient.

Self-reports might offer possibilities for more valid information to be collected. In the sixth section we will present an example of a survey among victims: how often are citizens confronted with (the necessity of) bribing public sector functionaries. Another promising route are self-reports of actual deviant behaviour, collected with 'Randomised Response Techniques'. We outline this research.

The last section discusses our overall attempts to measure corruption. What do we know about (the level of) corruption in the Netherlands? And how do the presented methods contribute to our knowledge? We conclude that it is necessary to triangulate on the same research object. Corruption research should involve the collection and comparison of information from different sources and methods, at different levels and in different sectors as well as in different points in time.

Concepts and Methods

In this section, we give a brief conceptual and methodological outline of our research. First, we outline our definition of corruption; discuss the merits of studying corruption from a broader perspective; and, present a typology of integrity violations. Second, we give an overview of the different types of research that we have conducted, or are planning to conduct, and explain how these projects relate to the problem of measuring corruption and other integrity violations.

Corruption and Integrity

Conceptual clarity between integrity, ethics and corruption is important, especially when it concerns public debate, policy-making and theory development on an international level. The concept of corruption is most often at the heart of that debate (Barker and Carter, 1996; Bull and Newell, 2003; Caiden, 1991; Caiden, Dwivedi and Jabbra, 2001; Crank and Caldero, 2000; Heidenheimer and Johnston, 2002; Menzel and Carson, 1999; Preston, Sampford and Connors, 2002). It is, therefore, important to be aware of at least three definitions of corruption. First, there is a more specific or narrow interpretation that is often found in definitions of corruption or bribing in legal frameworks. In the Netherlands, for example, corruption in the penal law is equated with 'bribing' (giving or accepting a bribe). This presupposes that a functionary is acting in the interest of another actor because of the advantages promised or given to him. Second, corruption is interpreted as 'behaviour which deviates from the formal duties of a public role because of private-regarding (personal, close family, private clique) pecuniary or status gains; or violates rules against the exercise of certain types of private-regarding influence' (Nye, 1967, p. 419; also see Caiden, 2001; and Gardiner, 2002). The same elements can be found in the definition used in the work of international organisations against corruption: corruption as the abuse of office for private gain (Pope, 2000). All of these definitions portray corruption as a breach of moral behavioural norms and values involving private interests. However, the presence of a third party is not seen as conditional.

The third and broadest definition views corruption as synonymous with all types of violations of moral norms and values. Almost inevitably, this brings us to a concept that has become prominent in the discussion in many countries: integrity (Fijnaut and Huberts, 2002; Huberts and Van den Heuvel, 1999; Klockars, 1997; Klockars et al., 2000; Montefiori and Vines, 1999; Uhr, 1999). We define integrity as the quality of acting in accordance with the relevant moral values, norms and rules. Integrity is a quality of individuals (Klockars, 1997; Solomon, 1999) as well as of organisations (Kaptein and Wempe, 2002). Additionally, ethics can be defined as the collection of values and norms, functioning as standards or yardsticks for assessing the integrity of one's conduct (Benjamin, 1990). The moral nature of these values and norms refers to what is judged as right, just, or good conduct. Values are principles that carry a certain weight in one's choice of action (what is good to do, or bad to refrain from doing). Norms indicate morally correct behaviour in a certain situation. Values and norms guide action and provide a moral basis to justify or evaluate what one does and who one is (Lawton, 1998; Pollock, 1998).

In our research we use a typology of categories of integrity violations as developed by Huberts et al. (1999). This typology was the outcome of an analysis of the literature on police integrity and corruption and was assessed against the results of empirical research on internal investigations in the police force. Table 14.1 gives the integrity violations or forms of public misconduct that can be distinguished (Van den Heuvel, Huberts and Verberk, 1999).

The typology clarifies that integrity or appropriate behaviour means much more than not being corrupt. Nevertheless it goes without saying that corruption, or 'behaviour on the part of officials in the public sector, whether politicians or civil servants, in which they improperly and unlawfully enrich themselves, or those associated with them, by the misuse of the public power entrusted to them', is a crucial aspect of organisational integrity.

Table 14.1 Types of integrity violations

1 *Corruption: bribing*
   Misuse of public power for private gain; asking, offering, accepting bribes.
2 *Corruption: nepotism, cronyism, patronage*
   Misuse of public authority to favour friends, family, party.
3 *Fraud and theft*
   Improper private gain acquired from the organisation (with no involvement of external actors).
4 *Conflict of (private and public) interest*
   Personal interest (through assets, jobs, gifts etc.) Interferes (or might interfere) with public interest.
5 *Improper use of authority* (for noble causes)
   To use illegal/improper methods to achieve organisational goals (within the police for example illegal methods of investigation and disproportionate violence).
6 *Misuse and manipulation of information*
   Lying, cheating, manipulating information, breaching confidentiality of information.
7 *Discrimination and sexual harassment*
   Misbehaviour towards colleagues or citizens and customers.
8 *Waste and abuse of resources*
   Failure to comply with organisational standards, improper performance, incorrect or dysfunctional internal behaviour.
9 *Private life misconduct*
   Conduct in one's private life which harms the publics trust in administration/government.

Why More Diversity and Complexity?

We have moved from corruption and fraud research towards integrity violations research. It is important to understand the reasons for this development towards more 'diversity and complexity'.

The first and most obvious reason is that it adds to our knowledge of the phenomenon under study. The description and analysis of the moral dimension of the behaviour of individuals and organisations is enriched by the availability of a more extended conceptual framework. Therefore, it seems worthwhile to distinguish more clearly the subtypes of corrupt behaviour that are included.

The second reason has to do with the implications of using an overall concept for a broad range of behaviour for our evaluation of the corruptness or integrity of individuals and organisations. We also need tools (or concepts) to distinguish morally between different types of integrity violations. When various forms of misconduct are all under one label, they are all then strapped onto the operating table for just one type of verdict; misconduct is 'corrupt' or 'it is not'. This can lead to oversimplification, over-generalisation and/or immediate condemnation ('integritism' or 'corruptism') (Huberts, 2005).

The third reason is that insight into integrity violations is supposed to be important to understand the amount and character of corruption in a more specific sense. The 'slippery slope' hypothesis suggests that serious corruption cases have started with minor offences (possibly within a culture without clear norms). As a consequence, we might learn more about the extent and character of corruption when related phenomena are also studied and measured.

The fourth aspect has to do with our research agenda which includes questions about the causes of 'corruption' and the effectiveness of 'anti-corruption' policies. A lesson we are learning is that umbrella concepts are limiting the possibilities to progress our knowledge about unacceptable and unethical behaviour. Patronage and favouritism might be caused by other factors other than bribing, or private misbehaviour, or fraud, or conflict of interest. This means that organisations or governments will have to develop specific policies against different types of integrity violations including corruption.

The last more practical reason simply has to do with the country we are working in. When serious bribery, nepotism and patronage are exceptional, other types of unethical behaviour become more decisive for the legitimacy and credibility of the political and administrative system. Examples are conflict of interest through sideline activities, fraud and private life misbehaviour.

Measurement

Of course, the shifting focus from corruption and fraud to integrity violations also has consequences on our measurement and measurement methods agenda. In the rest of this chapter, we will present a number of research projects that include corruption as well as other integrity violations.

At the same time, we are still interested in collecting information about corruption itself. We have been attempting to progress by selecting different aspects of the corruption phenomenon and by using different methodologies to measure those aspects (self-reports, reports from the working environment, internal investigations, criminal cases, reputations). Figure 14.1 clarifies the different methods we will describe in this chapter and how they relate to the iceberg-like structure of the corruption problem.

Figure 14.1 Types of research on the extent of corruption in the Netherlands

Corruption Reputation Research

One of the most common and most discussed methods to measure corruption is reputation research. The common basis is that respondents are asked to estimate the amount of corruption in their environment, their organisation, their sector of society or their country.

Most prominent is the last type of research, including the Transparency Corruption Perception Index. As part of our exploration of the iceberg, it is inevitable to pay attention to this line of research. Therefore, we will summarise the CPI for the Netherlands and we will deliberately do that for a longer time period. Over the years, the Netherlands appears to be non-corrupt in the eyes of the business people and risk analysts that estimate the country's integrity. This image is confirmed by additional research undertaken by us in 1994 among 257 experts from 49 countries, including experts from the Netherlands.

CPI for the Netherlands

The Netherlands appears to be non-corrupt in the eyes of the business people and risk analysts that estimate a country's integrity for the CPI. The much discussed Corruption Perception Index for 2004 shows that the Netherlands rank 10th with a score of 8.7

based on 10 surveys and with a confidence rate of 8.5-8.9. The positive image of the Netherlands is rather stable, as Table 14.2 shows.

Table 14.2   Corruption reputation of European countries 1980–2004

	1985 1988	1988 1992	1996	1998	2000	2002	2003	2004
The Netherlands	8.4	9.0	8.7	9.0	8.9	9.0	8.9	8.7
Finland	8.1	8.9	9.1	9.6	10.0	9.7	9.7	9.7
Sweden	8.1	8.7	9.1	9.5	9.4	9.3	9.3	9.2
United Kingdom	8.0	8.3	8.4	8.7	8.7	8.7	8.7	8.6
Germany	8.1	8.1	8.3	7.9	7.6	7.3	7.7	8.2
France	8.4	7.5	7.0	6.7	6.7	6.3	6.9	7.1
Spain	6.8	5.1	4.3	6.1	7.0	7.1	6.9	7.1
Belgium	8.3	7.4	6.8	5.4	6.1	7.1	7.6	7.5
Italy	4.9	4.3	3.4	4.6	4.6	5.2	5.3	4.8

In comparison to other countries in the European Union, the Netherlands is seen as relatively clean. Scandinavian countries enjoy an even better reputation, but the reputation of the Netherlands is consistently better than that of European Union countries like Germany, France or Belgium.

The Bribe Payers Index is slightly less positive about the involvement of Dutch citizens and companies in international corruption. The Netherlands remains among the ten countries on the list with the least perceived willingness to bribe foreign public servants but the score is 7.8 – less 'clean' than the CPI.

Expert Panel Survey

In 1994, we organised an international expert panel survey (Huberts, 1996) in which 257 respondents from 49 countries responded to a questionnaire about public corruption and fraud, about the conditions which cause these violations of public integrity and about the methods and strategies which are considered effective to combat public corruption and fraud. The survey covered all participants at three big international conferences on corruption and the members of the corruption research group in the political science association.

The resulting panel of experts represented different countries and different occupational backgrounds. From the respondents, 75 were from Western Europe, 4 from Eastern Europe, 65 from Asia, 14 from Oceania, 55 from North America, 37 from Latin America and 7 from Africa. Among them were scientists (38 per cent), representatives from the police and the judiciary (28 per cent), from the civil service and anti corruption agencies (12 per cent), auditors, controllers, accountants (10 per cent) and businessmen and consultants (8 per cent).

Such variety of expert opinion conveys information which has to be seen in the proper context. All data are the result of opinions, estimations and guesses by respondents. By selecting specific respondents, these opinions and guesses are considered to be 'expert' opinions and 'educated' guesses but it must not be forgotten that the survey is concerned with opinion research. The research is not about actual cases of corruption and fraud in a country, but about views on corruption and fraud from experts in the field. Views say something about reality but they must not be confounded with it.

We report here the experts' estimates of the amount of corruption and fraud in their own country. We defined such violations in line with the definitions discussed previously. Public functionaries are corrupt when they act (or do not act) as a result of the personal rewards offered to them by interested private actors. Public fraud is private gain at public expense without the involvement of outside actors. Public corruption and fraud both mean the misuse of public power for private gain (including gain for one's own family, group or party). The following table clarifies the estimated amount of corruption and fraud by the participating experts in their own country, aggregated for different parts of the world.

Table 14.3   Extent of public corruption and fraud (expert panel 1994)

	n	Politicians		Public servants	
		Median %	Mean %	Median %	Mean %
Western Europe	75	5.0	10.2	5.0	6.5
Eastern Europe	4	10.0	15.1	15.0	22.9
Asia	65	25.0	32.3	15.0	22.1
Oceania	14	5.0	10.5	4.5	9.3
North America	55	13.0	22.5	5.0	11.3
Latin America	37	40.0	45.2	33.0	37.3
Africa	7	60.0	48.6	50.0	47.9
Total	*257*	*10.0*	*25.2*	*10.0*	*18.0*

The 35 Dutch experts who participated in the survey estimated the extent of public corruption and fraud among politicians as 2.5 per cent and among civil servants as 4 per cent. They were pessimistic about the future. In 1994, 79 per cent thought that the extent of corruption and fraud would increase (Fleurke and Huberts, 1995, pp. 392–93).

Discussing the Reliability and Validity of Reputation Research

Over and over again, the surveys on the reputation of corruption and fraud in the Netherlands result in a similar pattern. The reliability of this type of work is not the problem. Different research firms and researchers use different types of public but the results are more or less the same. Illustrative is the relationship between our 1994 panels judgment on the corruption of countries and the Transparency CPI data of 1995. The Spearman correlation coefficient, which indicates the measure of association between these two datasets, amounts to 0.88.

Another statistic is interesting for the assessment of the usefulness of reputation data. In the expert panel, we asked every respondent to estimate the amount of corruption in their own country and we also asked everybody to rate 21 selected countries on a seven point scale concerning the level of public corruption and fraud. This enabled us to compare the two results for the countries represented by respondents (we incorporated the countries with three or more participants). The estimated corruption level of a country by the whole panel appeared to be related significantly to the experts' estimation of the amount of corruption for their own country (Spearman correlation coefficient amounts to 0.91, p = 0,00).

Nevertheless, the stability of these expert estimations is also a pitfall in terms of validity. A reputation is something that is built up over the years, because, as the term 'reputation' suggests, it is about how a country or organisation has come to be known. Therefore, reputations refer to general perceptions, not to specific (expert) experiences. In other words, the problem is that an order of reputations is based on already preconceived reputations. Known or felt reputations carry themselves into reputation research. This observation is problematic because the power of reputation research is believed to be the opportunity it gives for comparison and not its ability to make accurate estimations of the actual level of the corruption problem.

To conclude our sketch of reputation research, one extra aspect is worth mentioning. Because the discussion about reputation research centres around the failures to measure the extent of the problem, it is sometimes forgotten that the method might be more useful to collect information about other characteristics of corruption. In our expert panel research, we also tried to find out what conditions and causes are considered to be important and what strategies to combat corruption seemed to work in different countries.

Research on Criminal Cases and Internal Investigations

Corruption reputation research can provide interesting data regarding views on the extent of corruption and the mechanisms that underlie public wrongdoing. However, this type of research finds itself outside the proverbial 'iceberg' of corrupt administrative behaviour, as it is concerned with opinions, instead of data on or evidence of actual cases of corruption, fraud or other integrity violations.

The proverbial iceberg, depicting the actual structure of corruption and other integrity violations, is very complex: of all the actual cases of corruption, only a part makes itself felt or visible in the direct work environment; only a limited number of these cases are reported, leading to the occasional internal investigation; these investigations do not always lead to satisfactory evidence or a criminal investigation as a follow-up; and the criminal cases do not always lead to a conviction.

We will start at the top of the iceberg and provide an overview of empirical research on criminal cases of corruption in the Netherlands. This is followed by a view of our research into internal investigations in the Dutch municipalities and police force on which we hinge methodological problems (which will be discussed at the end of this section).

Research on Criminal Cases

Criminal cases form the top of our corruption iceberg. In these cases, the evidence of incidence is most fully crystallised. What we know about criminal cases in the Netherlands stems from various other researchers. In 1991, Hoetjes (1991) concluded that, in the period 1965 to 1989, annually 16 to 19 cases of corruption by public officials were brought under the attention of the criminal judge in the Netherlands. Approximately, two thirds of these cases did not result in a criminal conviction that is, about 6 convictions a year between 1965 and 1989.

On the basis of data released by the Central Bureau of Statistics, Bovens (1996, pp. 151–52) found that in the period 1990-1994 hardly any convictions for corruption in the public sphere were imposed. Van Hulten (2002, pp. 17–18) provided an overview of the afore mentioned cases for the years 1994 to 1998 based on data from the Dutch Ministry of Justice. In that period a total of 233 cases were brought to the attention of the criminal judge, of which 87 were followed by a conviction that is, approximately 17 convictions *per annum*.

When we compare the data over the years 1994–1998 with the available data over the preceding years, the perception is that the number of convictions has risen. This trend is also visible in the last years, due to changes in the penal code that make it easier to prove bribery (Nelen and Nieuwendijk, 2003).

The image that follows from these inquiries is that the top structure of the Netherlands corruption iceberg has been rather stable for a long time (with about 20 criminal cases and six convictions each year) but there is a tendency towards more criminal cases (50 cases with 17 convictions). For a country with 16 million inhabitants and a public sector which consists of 23 to 61 officials *per* thousand residents (dependant on which sectors are classified as 'public'), the Netherlands appears to be virtually corruption free. However, there are some difficulties with the interpretation of the available data.

First of all, it could be that the criminal cases, which by law are directed towards individual suspects, are representative of even fewer corruption cases, as it is possible to have multiple suspects for one case of corruption. There are no data available on this point. Second, the data are comparable to only a limited degree because they are provided by different organisations and it remains unclear exactly which articles in the penal code are taken into account in the various cases. Thirdly, the data over-represents officials from the municipal system and the police force. We are currently conducting systematic research on criminal cases to address these three issues.

Most importantly, there is the issue of the 'dark numbers'. With such data alone, it is impossible to assess how these convictions relate to the actual prevalence and extent of corruption (and other integrity violations). Data on criminal cases, as well as data on internal investigations, only provide circumstantial evidence regarding prevalence and incidence.

Research on Internal Investigations in Local Dutch Government

Research on internal investigations moves us towards the 'middle ground' of our iceberg. Internal investigations might follow out of reports in the work environment and can lead to the criminal cases we have just discussed. We have conducted research on internal investigations within the Dutch municipal system as well as within the Dutch police force.

To answer questions regarding the amount of internal investigations into fraud and corruption in the Dutch municipal system, we conducted a survey in 1991 with a random sample of town clerks in various Dutch cities (Huberts, 1993; 1995). In Dutch cities, the town clerk is an important public functionary. He or she assists all-important political bodies in the municipal system, functioning as secretariat and adviser to these bodies. Also, the town clerk is responsible for the administrative personnel and coordinates the different parts of the official machinery of the municipality. These characteristics mean that whenever a case of fraud or corruption is officially investigated, the town clerk is the functionary most likely to know about it. In this survey, the main question was how many investigations of corruption and fraud the town clerk was aware of during his or her career.

To look at the changes over the years in internal investigations in the municipal system, the survey was repeated in 2003 (Huberts et al., 2004). That time, all town clerks of all the Dutch municipalities received a questionnaire which contained the same questions as in the 1991 survey. The main question was how many investigations of corruption and fraud took place in the preceding 5 years. Table 14.4 provides the extrapolated mean results of the internal investigations for the 1991 and 2003 research.

Table 14.4   Yearly amount of internal corruption and fraud investigations

	1991 Mean over the preceding years	2003 Mean over the preceding years (without Amsterdam)	2003 Mean over the preceding years (with Amsterdam)
Number of investigations a year	102	103	179
Ratio			
Corruption	46%	47%	34%
Fraud	54%	53%	66%

The data provided by one municipality, the Dutch capital Amsterdam, especially proved to be problematic as well as an indication on what might be an 'integrity paradox'. When assessing the first two data columns, the keyword seems 'stability'. There was little apparent change on the extent and nature of corruption. The 1991 and 2003 surveys both indicate about 100 internal investigations a year, of which approximately half concern corruption. A remarkable result considering that in 1992 the late Minister of the Interior, Dales, gave two public speeches which put the theme of corruption on the administrative map. Since then the attention to, and awareness of, corruption and other forms of official misconduct have increased in the public arena. This apparent stability raises intriguing questions: have the concerns over administrative integrity taken gross forms as corruption is a very limited problem in the Netherlands; or is there a continuous underestimation of the problem?

The distribution of reported investigations over our respondents in the 2003 survey provides some clues to the above-mentioned questions. Over 60 per cent of the respondents, many of whom are from sizeable and populous municipalities, reported that they had not conducted any internal investigation on fraud or corruption between the years 1998–2002. It may be that they have not conducted any internal investigations, but the assumption that there would be no integrity violations regarding fraud and corruption seems – especially for the bigger more populous municipalities – improbable. The data from the city of Amsterdam makes this point clear.

When taking Amsterdam into account, the number of annual internal investigations increases by 75 per cent (from 102 in 1991 to 179 in 2003). This increase is wholly due to Amsterdam. The municipality of Amsterdam is unique in regard to its approach towards and attention to public integrity. From 1997 onwards, Amsterdam vested several bureaus, projects and initiatives especially designed to track, register and combat corruption and other integrity violations. The increase in internal investigations by the municipal administrative system of Amsterdam analogously developed with these various activities. Contrasted with other comparable cities, where there are no reasons to believe they would be corruption free, but in which no investigations were conducted, we might have evidence of an integrity paradox: those who pay more attention to certain violations will be more prone to track and investigate these violations, so that they may appear more corrupt, while that might not be the case. In other words: a large number of investigations could say more about the level of attention and openness, than about the actual levels of corruption and other integrity violations.

Thus, our research on internal investigations has raised an important interpretation problem: do more investigations into corruption and fraud indicate immaculate policy and attention or a highly corrupt institution? Although our data provide some evidence for the former explanation, more research is needed to reduce the leeway regarding the 'integrity paradox'.

Research on Internal Investigations in the Dutch Police Force

The Dutch police force consists of 25 regional forces and a National Police Agency which provides certain specialised tasks. These 26 forces employ a total of about 45,000 officers. Before 1995 most forces had no central unit for internal investigations. Since 1995, all police forces have set up a Bureau of Internal Investigations in line with the Interior Ministry's agreements regarding police integrity policy. These bureaus conduct internal investigations whenever there is 'a suspicion of an infraction of disciplinary or criminal law' (Lamboo et al., 2002, p. 9).

In 2001, all Bureaus of Internal Investigations of the Dutch police forces were requested to provide data on all the internal investigations and integrity violations (according to the earlier given typology) conducted in the years 1999–2000 (Lamboo et al., 2002). All forces submitted data on the type of investigations, the misconduct investigated, the results of the investigations and the type of sanctions imposed and measures taken. Table 14.5 gives an overview of the results.

The total police force reported 1550 internal investigations on integrity violations for the years 1999–2000, which related to 1705 suspects. This means that over the years 1999–2000 a yearly average of 1.8 per cent of the Dutch police employees were subject to an internal investigation. About 0.5 per cent of the police employees received a formal sanction.

Private life misconduct was the integrity violation most frequently investigated, followed by the use of force and waste and abuse of organisational resources. There were few investigations into corruption. While most empirical research focuses mainly on corruption and abuse of authority, the results from our study indicate that a great variety of violations are subject to internal investigations.

One must be cautious however, when one wants to make inferences from these data regarding the extent of the police integrity problem. Differences between the various integrity violations are partly due to the likelihood of discovery and the willingness to conduct an investigation into the possible violations. This partly underlies the high incidence of investigations into, for example, the use of force (because any incidence of the use of force by an officer has to be reported and investigated) and the very low incidence of investigations into corruption. Here too, we are dealing with a dark number.

Discussing the Reliability and Validity of Research on Criminal Cases and Internal Investigations

The presented research in this section can be discussed on various methodological grounds. To discuss all forms of method bias is beyond the scope of this contribution. Instead, we will focus our methodological attention on the ability of the presented research to measure or estimate the prevalence and extent of corruption (and other integrity violations).

Research into internal investigations is valid for these internal research activities, but says very little about the actual prevalence and extent of misconduct. There is a

Table 14.5   Number of internal investigations and measures in the Dutch police force 1991–2000

Total	1999–2000
Internal investigations[2]	*1550*
Suspects	1705
(of whom unknown)	138
Investigated specific	1876
Forms of misconduct	
Private life misconduct	371
Use of force	341
Abuse organisational resources	243
Abuse of information	217
Ill-treatment	195
Theft	183
Fraud	53
Investigative methods	40
Conflict of interest	32
Corruption	25
Gifts and discounts	3
Other	134
No information	39
Measures taken or sanctions	862

'dark number' of misconduct in the organisation which can be expected to remain unknown to those conducting the investigation. An additional problem here is that the dark number varies for different types of integrity violations, as it is dependent on the chance of discovery and the willingness to conduct an internal investigation.

There are additional problems, besides the issue of dark numbers, there are additional problems. First, the non-respondents could have significantly different behaviour regarding the various forms of misconduct. This non-response bias is especially relevant for our research on municipalities, in which we obtained a 77 per cent and a 46 per cent response respectively in our 1991 and 2003 surveys. We have no data on the non-respondents. Secondly, any form of misconduct is actually sensitive behaviour. Respondents could be willing to misrepresent their behaviour or the behaviour of their organisation, so as to provide a more 'positive' view of themselves or their institution. This evasive answer bias is difficult to assess.

Although we have some hints regarding the relationship, the mentioned methodological drawbacks make it very difficult to find a way out of the 'integrity paradox': do many internal investigations mean a corruption prone police force or municipality, or is it a product of superior attention to various forms of misconduct?

Further, the focus in research into internal investigations has been mainly with Dutch local government and the police force. Research into internal investigations for the whole of the Dutch public administration system is being conducted at the time of writing this chapter.

Estimations of Corruption in the Work Environment

In this section, we examine in more detail at surveys with estimations of the extent of corrupt behaviour in the work environment. This third type of research, that focuses more directly on corruption itself, clarifies that there is much more corruption than the internal investigations detect. By using the typology as described earlier, it becomes clear that bribery seems to be exceptional but that corruption-related types of unethical behaviour within organisations, according to the employees, are occurring more often.

Survey Among Dutch Police Officers

In 2003, we collected data by means of a questionnaire from a regional police organisation in the Netherlands. We have not reported on these data collections before.[3] The police force was selected because safeguarding integrity is an important issue in this sector. The sample consisted of all employees of the participating police organisation. Respondents were not required to identify themselves in any way on the questionnaire and they were given assurance that no one from their organisation would have access to individual questionnaires. Respondents sent the completed questionnaire back to the independent researchers in a sealed envelope. The anonymity of respondents and confidentiality of the information collected was therefore guaranteed. In total, 755 completed and usable questionnaires were received. The questionnaires were accumulated into one dataset.

The questionnaire included questions about 64 different manifestations of unethical police behaviour and asked for the respondents' perception on the amount of integrity violations within the last twelve months within their own team or unit (i.e. their own work environment). They are not dealing with one's own transgressions, because the validity of those answers would be questionabl. (we will return to this issue later). The scale of response for the frequency of deviant behaviour ranged from 0 = never, 1 = once, 2 = sometimes, 3 = regularly to 4 = often (on a weekly basis).

What do Dutch police officers think about the extent of integrity violations within their own work environment? Table 14.6 shows the perceived extent of 16 selected manifestations of misconduct for all nine types of integrity violations.[4] The percentages represent the proportion of respondents answering never, once or sometimes and regularly or often.

Bribery is, according to the employees themselves, not occurring on a large scale. Of the respondents, 96 per cent never observed the acceptance of money or favours in exchange for (non) action as a functionary within their work environment in the last 12 months, only 4 per cent observed this behaviour. Almost the same holds for being offered money or favours in exchange for (non) action as a functionary (93 per cent never, 6 per cent once or sometimes and about 1 per cent regularly or often). Keeping in mind that 30 police officers have reported that they noticed bribery in their team, this result is in line with our expectations that 'real' corruption is not a common practice within the Dutch police force. However, relying on perceptions as a valid indicator of the actual level of corruption is problematic as well. Employees will only have a limited view on what actually happens; corrupt colleagues will try to hide their 'dirty business' and most of the time their actions will take place outside the organisation and out of the sight of others.

When we move to corruption as nepotism, cronyism and patronage which have a higher incidence inside the organisation, we see that more employees observe these behaviours. Incidents of corruption, such as favouring of family and friends, was perceived by almost 20 per cent of the respondents and internal favouritism by the management by almost 50 per cent.

Also for the other (corruption-related) types of unethical behaviour like fraud and theft, conflict of (private and public) interest, improper use of authority, misuse and manipulation of information, discrimination and sexual harassment, waste and abuse of resources and private life misconduct, the perceived extent within the work unit in the last 12 months varies substantially.

In the last section, we will discuss how to interpret these results: what do they say about the actual amount of breaches of integrity within organisations?

Survey Among the Dutch Labour Force

The integrity violations described above and the frequency of their occurrence are not unique for the police. We also have information from a survey conducted by Kaptein (2001) among the Dutch labour force. Among this labour force, 1,000 randomly selected workers were asked their perceptions of the frequency of fifty identified integrity violations within their work department or unit. We report their perception of the occurrence of some of these behaviours in Table 14.7 (Kaptein, 2001, p. 14).

When we compare the results of the Dutch labour force against the results of the Dutch police force, we notice that although the percentages for the questioned integrity violations are higher in the labour force, a similar pattern still arises.

According to the employees themselves, real corruption such as neglecting tasks because of offered money or favours by external actors almost never occurs (93 per cent of the respondents answered never, 1 per cent answered regularly or often). Corruption like favouritism, on the contrary, seems to be a solid part of the internal organisational climate of Dutch corporations.

Table 14.6 Perceived extent of integrity violations within the Dutch police (n=755)

Integrity violations	Never	Once/sometimes	Regularly/often
1 Corruption: bribing			
Acceptance of money or favours in exchange for (non) action as a functionary	96%	3%	<1%
Being offered money or favours in exchange for (non) action as a functionary	93%	6%	<1%
2 Corruption: nepotism, cronyism, patronage			
Favouring friends or family from outside the organisation	81%	17%	2%
Internal favouritism by the management	51%	38%	11%
3 Fraud and theft			
Use of organisational resources for private purposes	39%	51%	10%
Working for private purposes during working hours	29%	60%	11%
Theft of organisational properties	82%	16%	2%
Attempts to influence a colleague to undo a ticket or fine given to a family member	71%	27%	2%
4 Conflict of (private and public) interest			
Arranging private discounts on goods and services using ones function	89%	11%	1%
Private life/ sideline activities that are in conflict with organisation interests	83%	17%	1%
5 Improper use of authority			
Improper and/or disproportionate violence	73%	25%	3%
6 Misuse and manipulation of information			
Carelessness with confidential (police) information	71%	27%	2%
7 Discrimination and sexual harassment			
Discrimination of homosexual colleagues	88%	10%	2%
Sexual intimidation	91%	9%	<1%
8 Waste and abuse of resources			
Carelessness with organisational properties	43%	46%	11%
9 Private life misconduct			
Setting a bad example in one's private life	53%	41%	6%

Table 14.7 Perceived extent of integrity violations within the Dutch labour force (n=1000)

Integrity violations	Occurs never	Occurs regularly to often
Neglect of tasks because of offered money or favours by external actors	93%	1%
The abuse of power / position	50%	14%
Internal favouritism within department	27%	33%
Favouring friends or family from outside the organisation	67%	8%
Arranging private discounts	69%	7%
Damaging sideline activities	63%	5%

Notes: regularly = once every quarter of a year, often = once a week.

Discussing the Reliability and Validity of Research on Estimations in the Work Environment

In this section, we will attempt to identify the measurement problems associated with the reliability and validity with this type of research. The question is: what do the perceptions of employees tell us about the actual level of corruption and other breaches of integrity within organisations?

It is not easy to determine how reliable this type of research is because the survey instrument is mainly used to *monitor* how employees think of integrity and integrity violations within the organisation and thereby *evaluate* the effect of integrity policies on organisational management. Surveys among employees are seldom repeated within short time periods and when repeated after a period of time results might (and should) differ as a consequence of the policies implemented by management. The surveys discussed in this paragraph, however, do show that the findings are in line with each other and result in similar patterns with regard to the different types of integrity violations.

This brings us to the validity of survey research. The question is what the perceptions of employees tell us about the actual level of corruption and other breaches of integrity within organisations.

The first problem has to do with what respondents *can* observe. Employees can only have a limited view on what actually happens. This holds for some integrity violations more than for others. Unethical behaviour that takes place outside the organisation will be harder to observe than behaviour that takes place inside the organisation. This is particularly true for private life misconduct as well as for work that takes place outside the office (for instance, police officers on patrol, or business people on the road). The fact that offenders will try to hide their actions, (e.g. bribery) and that some violations have no victims or do not need a third party, (e.g. fraud or theft), makes the validity problem of relying on perceptions as a true reflection of the actual level of unethical behaviour even more problematic.

The second problem is to do with what respondents *will* observe. When asking respondents which types of integrity violations they perceive in their work environment, they will reflect in their answers their own specific experiences. More subjective impressions will also play. Respondents need to label what they see. They need to be aware of the different aspects of the (asked) type of integrity violation and need to recognise behaviours as manifestations of the problem. Discrimination and sexual harassment are especially not always recognised as such. The attention that management gives to unethical behaviour across policies, training, codes of conduct etc. can increase awareness among employees and it might be reflected in their observations as well.

Respondents' perceptions are not neutral. Besides awareness, the acceptability of behaviour will play a role in estimating what happens. Although we do not know exactly how respondents' evaluations of the asked behaviours influence their estimations (either underestimation or overestimation), we do expect that it does make a difference if the behaviour is widely accepted or not accepted within the organisation (for instance, the private use of working hours and organisational resources such as the telephone and the internet). Also, does in-group and out-group phenomena influences what is observed? This might explain the high prevalence of perceived favouritism by management.

The third problem has to do with what respondents *report*. Respondents might be reluctant to report what is really going on in the team because of loyalty to colleagues or loyalty to the organisation. This might be especially true for improper use of authority.

The fourth problem has to do with the way unethical behaviour is *measured*. As a result most survey research omits questions dealing with personal transgressions. We assume that the validity of those answers would be questionable. But social desirability always plays a role in this type of research. What is also important, is how exactly the question is formulated. So, will it make a difference if we question integrity violations by referring to more general behaviour instead of referring to very specific behaviour? For instance, should we ask about careless use of organisational resources or careless use of stationary? For other methodological problems in survey research, we confine ourselves by referring to Podsakoff et al. (2003) who described the various problems in behavioural research and their remedies.

We conclude that, although the validity of survey research into integrity violations exceeds the validity of reputation and internal investigation research, what we really find out is also limited. The perceptions of employees are, at best, an indicator of the actual amount of integrity violations present in the organisation.

Self-Reports of Individual Behaviour

Self-reports of individual behaviour are a promising route to fill up the gap left open by other research methodologies in the measurement of corruption. In the end, what we really want to know is who and how many the perpetrators are. Individual behaviour relates directly to the 'dark numbers' regarding misconduct. However, self-reports with regard to corruption research are only promising if they are unbiased. Given misconduct is a covert activity, many researchers are wary of the leap from 'image' or 'perception' research to research on personal experience. In light of the non-sampling biases of non-response and evasive answers, we will discuss the two main foci of research on individual behaviour: self-reports of victimisation and of individual sensitive and/or deviant behaviour.

Self-Reports of Victimisation

How often do Dutch citizens in their own country experience corruption? The Netherlands Institute for the Study of Crime and Law Enforcement (NSCR) participated in a large-scale international comparative survey project called the International Crime Victims Survey (ICVS) that was conducted in 1989, 1992, 1996 and 2000. In more than 60 countries all across the globe and including the Netherlands, a representative sampling of 2,000 citizens were questioned about their experiences with diverse forms of crime (Nieuwbeerta, 2002). Since 1996, the respondents were also asked if they have experienced being a victim of corruption by type of government institution or category of civil servant. The exact question was: 'In some countries one can sometimes be confronted with corruption among civil servants. Has a civil servant, for example a customs agent, a policeman, or an inspector ever expected you to pay a bribe for his or her services?' And if so: '(The last time) what sort of civil servant was involved? Was it a governmental official, a customs agent or some sort of inspector?' (Nieuwbeerta et al., 2002, p. 169).

The findings show that corruption by civil servants occurs mostly in developing countries, followed by countries of Central Europe, Eastern Europe and the industrialised countries (Nieuwbeerta et al., 2002, p. 172). In Asia and Latin America, an average of about 20 per cent of the respondents reported to have been a victim of corruption (with Argentina and Indonesia at the top with a reported average of more than 30 per cent) and Central and Eastern Europe following with an average between 10 and 15 per cent. In industrialised countries corruption is rare: less than 1 per cent of the respondents reported to have been confronted with corruption by civil servants. The average score in the Netherlands is about 0.5 per cent.

Revealing that one has been a 'victim' of a corrupt practice is not as sensitive as revealing that one has been a perpetrator. Victimisation research can catch data on the people who stumbled unwillingly upon various forms of misconduct. However, it is not suited to uncover those who were willingly involved in the realms of misconduct. There are benefits in gathering data on self-reporting of deviant behaviour.

Self-Reports of Sensitive Deviant Behaviour

A promising route for the exploration of the base of our corruption iceberg would be to obtain unbiased self-reports of actual deviant behaviour. Corruption and other integrity violations are sensitive and covert activities. This sensitivity means many researchers shy away from conducting research on individual experiences, questioning the accuracy of these data, as respondents will not be willing to incriminate themselves. A technique which may overcome this problem is known as 'Randomised Response', to which we now turn.

'Randomised response' refers to techniques which, as a core characteristic, use the insertion of random error by an element of chance to provide the respondent optimal privacy protection when answering questions of a sensitive nature. It was the initial idea of Stanley Warner (1965) that the element of chance stemming from a randomisation device could inoculate responses to sensitive inquiries and thus reduce non-sampling bias. How does this work? Consider the following hypothetical situation. One finds oneself in a room full of academic colleagues. The speaker asks the attendants to raise their hands if they have ever twisted data so that the results became statistically significant or confirmed a hypothesis (example taken from Lensvelt-Mulders and De Leeuw, 2002). Probably nobody will raise his or her hand. But then the situation is changed. The speaker asks every attendant to flip a coin and to look if the throw is heads or tails, without revealing the outcome to others. The speaker then asks if those who have tails and/or who have ever reworked their data in an 'un-academic' way to raise their hand. Statistically half of all attendants will raise their hand due to a 'tails' score on their coin flip. If we assume 100 attendees, 50 persons should raise their hands. If 56 persons raise their hands, we can compute from the 100 attendees that 12 persons in the auditorium (12 per cent) have, at some point, unscientifically revised their data. But exactly who those people are will never be revealed. All the people with tails on their flipped coin protect the privacy of those who committed the frauds. The rationale is: if respondents are assured that their privacy is guarded then, they will be more inclined to cooperate and to respond truthfully.

This procedure can also be applied in a one-to-one setting. A respondent is redirected to a certain question or a certain response *via* a randomisation device. Part of the data obtained will then be misclassified. Due to this misclassification individual responses to sensitive questions have no definitive meaning, making it less threatening to admit to certain behaviours. But as the distribution of the misclassification is known by the use of the randomisation device (which should abide by the laws of elementary probability), an unbiased population estimate of the prevalence or extent of certain behaviour can be quite easily calculated.

Through the years, many improvements have increased the value and acceptance of this still highly unknown method (see Fox and Tracy 1986, for an overview). A meta-analysis which contained 35 years of randomised response comparison and validation data, showed that the randomised response technique gave more accurate and valid population estimates of the prevalence of sensitive behaviour than other techniques (Lensvelt-Mulders, Hox and Van Der Heijden, 2005).

The method has not been tested with regard to integrity violations in the public sphere and remains largely open with regard to quantitative data as the technique has been mostly tested towards the prevalence (which essentially is dichotomous; 'yes' or 'no') of criminal behaviour, drug use, tax evasions and abortions. We are preparing to test a special form of the randomised response technique with the use of a computer-assisted survey so as to obtain more unbiased estimations of the prevalence and extent of corruption and other integrity violations in a Dutch police force.[5] This study will be a test case to see how well this technique and our adaptations perform in exploring the regions towards the base of our iceberg. We will explore whether this technique can delve into the 'dark numbers' by comparing it to more standard data gathering techniques.

Discussing the Reliability and Validity of Research on Self-Reports

Revealing that one has been a 'victim' of a corrupt practice is not as sensitive as revealing that one has been a perpetrator. As already stated, victimisation research can catch data on the people who stumbled unwillingly upon various forms of misconduct but is not suited to uncover those who were willingly involved in the realms of misconduct. Research on individual deviant behaviour remains open terrain in the science of misconduct, mainly because researchers have to overcome a problem that is felt in all research on latent variables, but which becomes pressing regarding individual behaviour: non-response and evasive answer bias. A way to work around the silly assumption – that truthful responses can be obtained *via* direct questioning – is to use randomised response techniques, which through the use of misclassification of data *via* a randomisation device, can delve into the 'darker numbers' of certain behaviours. But these methods, too, have their drawbacks.

The first is that the randomised response technique is inefficient compared to direct questioning of any sort. The insertion of random error in the responses results in variance inflation as the use of the randomisation device leads to additional variance. The technique is thus less reliable (in terms of variance) with similar numbers of respondents when compared to direct questioning of any sort. This means that the population sample has to be larger to obtain similar levels of reliability, which also means extra costs. The benefits of lowering bias however, outweigh the extra costs. The issue of lowering bias takes us to the second remark.

The randomised response method has a stronger stance in reducing evasive answer (response) bias than in reducing non-response bias. The method will reduce item-specific non-response of respondents who feel uncomfortable with certain sensitive items. Certain subgroups of the population who are notorious non-respondents will still have to be over-sampled. But when they agree to cooperate, evasive answer bias and item-specific non-response can be expected to be lower among these non-respondents compared to methods of direct questioning. In any case, any reduction of bias gives more leverage when assessing sensitive topics.

The third remark is also related to the issue of bias. It will still be able to cheat on the randomised response method by not complying with the rules. Sensitive behaviour will always be underestimated, due to the respondents who will refuse or answer evasively under any circumstances. However, the underestimation of sensitive behaviour under the randomised response conditions can be expected – due to the level of protection it offers – to be smaller compared to other data collection methods (see Lensvelt-Mulders, 2003; Lensvelt-Mulders, Hox and Van Der Heijden, 2005; and Van Der Heijden et al., 2000). Self-reports of sensitive behaviour obtained *via* randomised response techniques yield a promising route for research on integrity violations because any reduction of bias will increase leverage when assessing sensitive topics, thus justifying the effort.

Exploring the Corruption Iceberg: Summary and Conclusions

In the previous sections, we have outlined a number of research projects on corruption in the Netherlands. In this final section, we will summarise some of the results and reflect on the usefulness of the methods. As explained in our second section, we have developed a broad typology of integrity violations of which corruption is a specific subpart, instead of using an 'umbrella' concept of corruption. This puts our findings on the prevalence and extent of corruption in perspective.

We started with corruption *reputation* research. The surveys that measure the corruption reputation of the Netherlands offer a clear and stable picture that the country is viewed as among the least corrupt in the world. The Corruption Perception Index (CPI) for 2004 showed that the Netherlands is ranked tenth with a score of 8.7. In our expert panel survey conducted in 1994, which surveyed 257 experts from 49 countries including experts from the Netherlands, the extent of public corruption and fraud among politicians and among civil servants was estimated at 2.5 per cent and 4 per cent respectively.

Secondly, we reported on research about *criminal cases and internal investigations*. The image that is formed from our research on criminal cases is that the structure of the top of the corruption iceberg in the Netherlands consists of a limited number of criminal cases and convictions each year (20–50 cases, 6–17 convictions). Research on internal investigations, from which criminal cases can follow, showed that in municipalities 179 internal investigations into corruption and fraud were conducted annually over the years 1999–2003 of which 34 per cent concerned corruption. The Dutch Police Force reported 1,550 internal investigations over the years 1999–2000 of which 25 were directly related to corruption.

Surveys with estimations by employees of the extent of *corrupt behaviour in their work environment* are the third type of research. A survey among 755 Dutch police officers from the same regional police force showed that 4 per cent of the police officers noticed bribery at least once in their team in the 12 months preceding the survey. For corruption which included nepotism, cronyism and patronage, we found much higher percentages. From the surveyed police officers, 19 per cent perceived favouritism of family and friends at least once in their work environment and 59 per cent favouritism by the management. A similar survey set of 1,000 randomly selected workers in the Dutch labour force showed similar patterns for corruption: 7 per cent bribery, 33 per cent favouritism of family and friends, and 73 per cent favouritism by the management.

The last type of research we described was *self-reports* of individual behaviour. There are two main foci in this line of research: self-reports of victimisation and individual sensitive and/or deviant behaviour. The findings from the International Crime Victims Survey showed that about 0.5 per cent of the Dutch respondents report to have been confronted with corruption by civil servants. Victimisation research can catch data on the person who stumbled unwillingly upon various forms of misconduct but is not suited to uncover those who were willingly involved in the realms of public misbehaviour. Self-reports of individual sensitive behaviour collected with randomised response techniques are a promising route to fill up the gap left open by other research methodologies regarding the measurement of corruption. We have summarised the findings of our different research projects on corruption in Table 14.8.

An important question is how to interpret these results. What do they say about the actual level of corruption in the Netherlands and how reliable and valid are the outcomes based on the different research methods?

Corruption reputation research by experts, which estimates the amount of corruption in the Netherlands, reveals a similar pattern whenever such research is undertaken. The Netherlands appears to be non-corrupt in the eyes of the business people and risk analysts that estimate the country's integrity. Experts who were questioned in a panel survey confirm this image. In other words, the reliability of this type of work is not the problem. However, the stability of these expert estimations might also contain a risk for the validity of reputation research. A reputation is about how a country or organisation has come to be known and therefore reputations refer more to general perceptions than specific experiences. Known or felt reputations carry themselves into reputation research. The outcomes are questionable when we want to view them as accurate estimations of the actual level of the corruption problem.

Research on criminal cases and convictions based on the corruption articles in the Penal Code support the image that the corruption problem in the Netherlands is very limited. However, we have to keep in mind that such data only provides information about the 'tip of the iceberg' of cases being discovered, investigated and prosecuted.

Beneath these criminal cases are the internal investigations. Our research in Dutch municipalities clearly shows that the interpretation of the number of internal investigations is difficult. A crucial aspect to take into consideration is that data about investigations appears to reflect the priority that the organisation gives to the struggle against corruption instead of being an indicator of the amount of corruption. We refer to this phenomenon as the 'integrity paradox'.

To start an internal investigation, somebody will have to report (possible) corrupt behaviour. In survey research we have conducted, employees indicated the amount of corrupt and corruption related behaviour they observed in their work environment. The findings lead to the conclusion that only a fraction of what employees perceive becomes the subject of an internal investigation.

Table 14.8 Overview of our research projects on corruption in the Netherlands

Research focus	Period	Organisational focus	Findings on corruption
1 Reputations	1985–2004	Dutch public and political sectors	The Netherlands are perceived to be relatively clean
CPI			
Expert Panel	1996	*Ibidem.*	
2 Criminal cases	1965–2000	Dutch public and political sectors	20–50 criminal cases annually from which 6–17 convictions follow
3 Internal investigations	1999–2003	Dutch municipalities	179 internal investigations into corruption and fraud annually of which 34 per cent concerned corruption
	1999–2000	Dutch police force	1550 internal investigations of which 25 were directly related to corruption
4 Estimations in the direct work environment	2003	One Dutch regional police force	4 per cent noticed bribery, for corruption like nepotism, cronyism and patronage we found much higher percentages
	2000	Randomly selected workers from the labour force	7 per cent noticed bribery, for corruption like nepotism, cronyism and patronage we found much higher percentages
5 Self reports of individual behaviour			
Victimisation research	2000	Representative sample of Dutch population	0.5 per cent of the Dutch respondents report having been confronted with corruption by civil servants
Randomised response techniques	–	One Dutch regional police force	Preparations for testing are underway

A major disadvantage of all the above sources and research methods is, of course, that the corruptor and the corrupted will try to hide their behaviour where possible. Therefore, self-report research might add valuable information. Until now, some victim research has been undertaken; it shows that the percentages of Dutch citizens confronted with (the necessity of) bribing public sector functionaries is very low. In the near future, we hope to report on data collected with 'Randomised Response Techniques'.

However, we have to keep in mind that we can never bring all corruption to the surface. Researchers on corruption will have to live with the weight of the 'dark numbers'. We are exploring different parts of the iceberg in order to find out more about its characteristics as well as its extent. All presented methods have their problems as well as possibilities. All our research contributes to our knowledge about the complex and diverse nature of the corruption phenomenon. Therefore, it is necessary to triangulate on the same research object. Corruption research should involve the collection and comparison of information from different sources and methods, at different levels and in different sectors as well as in different points in time. But also, when we want to find out more about the relationships between the findings of the different methods, it would be very helpful to use these at the same time in the same organisation(s).

For the future research agenda, it seems especially worthwhile (1) to gain more clarity and thus comparability concerning the conceptual framework on corruption; (2) to work on methods that try to measure the extent of corruption through self-reporting; (3) to add research on the willingness to report corruption; and (4) to invest in research questions on the workings of the corruption process that give insight into the variables that are crucial for measuring the extent of corruption. The future research agenda on corruption could provide an inroad to possibly the most valid question of all: just how steep are the slopes of our iceberg?

Notes

1 The authors work at the Department of Public Administration and Organization Science of the Free University of Amsterdam, The Netherlands. Leo Huberts is Professor of Public Administration and Integrity of Governance. Karin Lasthuizen and Carel Peeters both work as researchers within the research group Integrity of Governance.

2 Note that an internal investigation can have multiple suspects and forms of misconduct as its focus.

3 We did report on survey data within the Dutch police force from the so-called Integrity Thermometer: Kaptein,1998; Kaptein and Van Reenen, 2001; Kaptein and Wempe, 2002; Lasthuizen, Huberts and Kaptein, 2002; Lasthuizen, Huberts and Kaptein, 2004. The data, however, are less extensive about corruption-related behaviours.

4 We selected 16 out of the 64 integrity violations that where included in our survey. These 16 manifestations of corrupt and corruption-related behaviours give a representative overview of what kind of unethical behaviours are perceived by Dutch police officers in their work environment.

5   We will use a computer assisted qualitative (dichotomous) and quantitative 'forced' response method, which redirects the respondent to a certain forced answer *via* a randomisation device. This project is done in cooperation with the Department of Methods and Statistics, Utrecht University.

References

Barker, T. and Carter, D.L. (1996), *Police Deviance*, 3rd edition, Anderson, Cincinnati.

Benjamin, M. (1990), *Splitting the Difference: Compromising and Integrity in Ethics and Politics*, University Press of Kansas, Kansas.

Bovens, M.A.P. (1996), 'De integriteit van de bedrijfsmatige overheid (The Integrity of Businesslike Government)', in M.A.P. Bovens and A. Hemelrijck (eds), *Het verhaal van de moraal*, Boom, Amsterdam/ Meppel, pp. 150–70.

Bull, M.J. and Newell, J.L. (eds) (2003), *Corruption in Contemporary Politics*, Palgrave Macmillan, Hampshire and New York.

Caiden, G.E. (1991), 'What Really is Public Maladministration?', *Public Administration Review*, vol. 51, no. 6, pp. 486–93.

Caiden, G.E. (2001), 'Corruption and Governance', in E. Caiden, O.P. Dwivedi and J. Jabbra (eds), *Where Corruption Lives*, Kumarian Press, Bloomfield, pp. 15–37.

Caiden, G.E., Dwivedi, O.P. and Jabbra, J. (eds) (2001), *Where Corruption Lives*, Kumarian Press, Bloomfield.

Crank, J.P. and Caldero, M.A. (2000), *Police Ethics: The Corruption of Noble Cause*, Anderson, Cincinnati.

Fijnaut, C. and Huberts, L.W.J.C. (eds) (2002), *Corruption, Integrity and Law Enforcement*, Kluwer Law International, Dordrecht.

Fleurke, F. and Huberts, L.W.J.C. (1995), 'Bestuurlijke integriteit: ervaringen en perspectieven (Public Integrity: Experiences and Perspectives)', *Bestuurswetenschappen*, vol. 49, no. 5/6, pp. 385–402.

Fox, J.A. and Tracy, P.E. (1986), *Randomized Response: A Method for Sensitive Surveys*, Sage University Paper Series on Quantitative Applications in the Social Sciences, no. 58, Sage Publications, Beverly Hills.

Gardiner, J.A. (2002), 'Defining Corruption', in A.J. Heidenheimer and M. Johnston (eds), *Political Corruption: Concepts and Contexts*, Transaction Publishers, New Brunswick and London, pp. 25–40.

Heidenheimer, A.J. and Johnston, M. (eds) (2002), *Political Corruption: Concepts and Contexts*, Transaction Publishers, New Brunswick and London.

Heijden, P.G.M. Van der Gils, G., Van Bouts, J. and Hox, J.J. (2000), 'A Comparison of Randomized Response, Computer-Assisted Self-Interview, and Face-to-Face Direct Questioning: Eliciting Sensitive Information in the Context of Welfare and Unemployment Benefit', *Sociological Methods and Research*, vol. 28, no. 4, pp. 505–37.

Hoetjes, B.J.S. (1991), 'Over de schreef: Het schemergebied tussen ambtenaar en burger (Overstepping the Mark: The Twilightzone between Public Official and Citizen)', *Justitiële Verkenningen*, vol. 17, no. 4, pp. 8–32.

Huberts, L.W.J.C. (1993), 'Omvang en bestrijding van bestuurlijke criminaliteit (The Extent of and Fight against Public Wrongdoing)', *Justitiële Verkenningen*, vol. 19, no. 1, pp. 51–69.

Huberts, L.W.J.C. (1995), 'Public Corruption and Fraud in the Netherlands: Research and Results', *Crime, Law and Social Change*, vol. 22, pp. 307–21.

Huberts, L.W.J.C. (1996), *Expert Views on Public Corruption around the Globe, Research Report on the Views of an International Expert Panel*, PSPA Publicatons, Amsterdam.

Huberts, L.W.J.C. (2005, in print), 'Integriteit en integritisme in bestuur en samenleving (Integrity and Integritism in Governance and Society, Inaugural Address)', Oratie Vrije Universiteit 2005.

Huberts, L.W.J.C. and Van den Heuvel, J.H.J. (eds) (1999), *Integrity at the Public-private Interface*, Shaker, Maastricht.

Huberts, L.W.J.C., Hulschebosch, H., Lasthuizen, K. and Peeters, C.F.W. (2004), *Nederland fraude- en corruptieland? De omvang, achtergronden en afwikkeling van corruptie- en fraudeonderzoeken in Nederlandse gemeenten in 1991 en 2003 (The Netherlands, a Fraudulent and Corrupt Country? The Magnitude, Backgrounds and Measures regarding Corruption and Fraud Investigations in Dutch Municipalities in 1991 and 2003)*, Vrije Universiteit, Amsterdam.

Huberts, L.W.J.C., Pijl, D. and Steen, A. (1999), 'Integrity and Corruption', in C. Fijnaut, E. Muller and U. Rosenthal (eds), *Police: Studies on the Organization and its Functioning*, Samsom, Alphen aan den Rijn, pp. 57–79.

Kaptein, M. (1998), *Ethics Management*, Kluwer, Dordrecht.

Kaptein, M. (2001), 'De integriteitsbarometer voor organisaties, Special Organisatie-criminaliteit (The Integrity Barometer for Organizations)', *Bedrijfskunde*, vol. 73, no. 3, pp. 12–18.

Kaptein, M. and Van Reenen, P. (2001), 'Integrity Management of Police Organizations', *Policing: An International Journal of Police Strategies and Management*, vol. 24, no. 3, pp. 281–300.

Kaptein, M. and Wempe, J. (2002), *The Balanced Company: A Corporate Integrity Approach*, Oxford University Press, Oxford.

Klockars, C.B. (1997), *Conceptual and Methodological Issues in the Study of Police Integrity*, Paper presented to the Advisory Panel Meeting of the Project on Police Integrity, December 16, Washington DC.

Klockars, C.B., Kutnjak, Ivkovich S., Harver, W.E. and Haberfeld, M.R. (2000), *The measurement of Police Integrity: Research in Brief*, National Institute of Justice, May 2000.

Lamboo, M.E.D., Huberts, L.W.J.C., Van der Steeg, M. and Nieuwendijk, A. (2002), 'The Monitor Internal Investigations Police: Dimensions of Police Misconduct', paper presented at the 2002 American Society of Criminology Conference, Chicago, 12–16 November 2002.

Lasthuizen, K., Huberts, L.W.J.C. and Kaptein, M. (2002), 'Integrity Problems in the Police Organization: Police Officers' Perceptions Reviewed', in M. Pagon (ed.), *Policing in Central and Eastern Europe, Deviance, Violence, and Victimization*, Leicester: Scarman Centre University of Leicester and Ljubljana: College of Police and Security Studies, pp. 25–37.

Lasthuizen, K., Huberts, L.W.J.C. and Kaptein, M. (2004), 'Analyse van Integriteitsopvattingen (Analysis of Integrity Perceptions)', in L.W.J.C. Huberts and J. Naeyé (eds), *Integriteit van de Politie, Verslag van onderzoek naar politiële integriteit in Nederland*, Te verschijnen in 2005 als publicatie van Politie and Wetenschap, Uitgeverij Kerckebosch, Zeist.

Lawton, A. (1998), *Ethical Management for the Public Services*, Open University Press, Buckingham and Philadelphia.

Lensvelt-Mulders, G.J.L.M. (2003), 'Randomized Response Technieken voor het Onderzoek van Sociaal Gevoelige Onderwerpen (Randomized Response Techniques for Research into Socially Sensitive Topics)', in MarktOnderzoeks-Associatie, *Ontwikkelingen in het Marktonderzoek Jaarboek 2003*, Uitgeverij de Vrieseborch, Haarlem, pp. 59–74.

Lensvelt-Mulders, G.J.L.M., Hox, J. and Van der Heijden, P.G.M. (2005), 'Meta-Analysis of Randomized Response Research: 35 Years of Validation', *Sociological Methods and Research*, vol. 33, no. 3, pp. 319–48.

Lensvelt-Mulders, G.J.L.M. and Leeuw, E. de (2002), 'Vragen naar gevoelige informatie (Asking for Sensitive Information)', *Facta*, no. 34–5.

Menzel, D.C. and Carson, K.J. (1999), 'A Review and Assessment of Empirical Research on Public Administration Ethics: Implications for Scholars and Managers', *Public Integrity*, vol. 3, no. 3, pp. 239–64.

Montefiori, A. and Vines, D. (eds) (1999), *Integrity in the Public and Private Domains*, Routledge, London.

Nelen, H. and Nieuwendijk, A. (2003), *Geen ABC: Analyse van Rijksrecherche-onderzoeken naar ambtelijke en bestuurlijke corruptie* (*No ABC: Analysis of Federal Police Investigations of Official and Political Corruption*), Boom Juridische Uitgevers, Den Haag.

Nieuwbeerta, P. (ed.) (2002), *Crime Victimization in Comparative Perspective, Results from the International Crime Victims Survey, 1989–2000*, Boom Juridische uitgevers, Den Haag.

Nieuwbeerta, P., de Geest, G. and Siegers, J. (2002), 'Corruption in Industrialised and Developing Countries', in P. Nieuwbeerta (ed.), *Crime Victimization in Comparative Perspective, Results from the International Crime Victims Survey 1989–2000*, Boom Juridische, Uitgevers, pp. 163–82.

Nye, J.S. (1967), 'Corruption and Political Development: A Cost-Benefit Analysis', *The American Political Science Review*, vol. 61, no. 2, pp. 417–27.

Podsakoff, P.M., MacKenzie, S.B. and Lee, J.Y. (2003), 'Common Method Variance in Behavioral Research: A Critical Review of the Literature and Recommended Remedies', *Journal of Applied Psychology*, vol. 88, no. 5, pp. 879–903.

Pollock, J.M. (1998), *Ethics in Crime and Justice: Dilemmas and Decisions*, 3rd edition, Wadsworth, Belmont, CA.

Pope, J. (2000), *Confronting Corruption: The Elements of a National Integrity System*, Transparency International, Berlin.

Preston, N., Sampford, C. with Connors, C. (2002), *Encouraging Ethics and Challenging Corruption: Reforming Governance in Public Institutions*, The Federation Press, Sydney.

Solomon, B. (1999), *A Better Way to Think about Business: How Personal Integrity Leads to Corporate Success*, Oxford University Press, New York.

Uhr, J. (1999), 'Institutions of Integrity: Balancing Values and Verification in Democratic Government', *Public Integrity*, vol. 1, no. 1, pp. 94–106.

Van den Heuvel, J.H.J., Huberts, L.W.J.C. and Verberk, S. (1999), *Integriteit in drievoud, Een onderzoek naar gemeentelijk integriteitsbeleid* (*Triple Integrity, Research into Local Integrity Policies*), Lemma, Utrecht.

Van Hulten, M. (2002), *Corruptie, Onbekend, onbemind, alomtegenwoordig* (*Corruption. Unknown, Disliked, Omnipresent*), Boom, Amsterdam.

Warner, S.L. (1965), 'Randomized Response: A Survey Technique for Eliminating Evasive Answer Bias', *Journal of the American Statistical Association*, vol. 60, pp. 63–9.

Index